Understanding Geometry

Mathematical Reasoning™ products available in print or eBook form.

Beginning 1 • Beginning 2
Level A • Level B • Level C • Level D • Level E
Level F • Level G • Understanding Pre-Algebra
Understanding Geometry • Understanding Algebra I
Grades 2-4 Supplement • Grades 4-6 Supplement
Middle School Supplement (Grades 7-9)

Written by
Terri Husted

Graphic Design by
Karla Garrett
Annette Langenstein

Edited by
Joe Walker

THE CRITICAL THINKING CO.™
www.CriticalThinking.com
Phone: 800-458-4849 • Fax: 541-756-1758
1991 Sherman Ave., Suite 200 • North Bend • OR 97459
ISBN 978-1-60144-453-0

Printed in Malaysia by Imago (Jan. 2020)

Why Use This Book

Although the geometric concepts of perimeter, area, and volume are taught piecemeal from elementary school through middle school, too many students enter high school without the skills and knowledge to succeed in high school geometry. For example, middle school students get very little education on the properties of parallelograms and the tools needed to succeed at doing geometric proofs. The result is many students struggle with high school geometry. Poor performance in geometry usually lowers standardized test scores because geometry is a fundamental subject in high school standardized testing.

Successful completion of this middle school geometry course will virtually guarantee a student's success in high school geometry. This book teaches the properties of geometry and the reasoning behind them—instead of asking students to memorize them. It provides the tools to understand how concepts are connected, why notation is important, and introduces proofs and coordinate geometry. This book follows the National Math Standards in mathematics but it goes further. A glossary of terms that every student in high school must master is also included. Algebra is included in some of the geometry problems to show that algebra has applications to geometry as well as to other topics.

The successful completion of this colorful 272-page book will prepare middle schoolers for high school geometry. It covers more than 50% of the concepts taught in high school geometry using a step-by-step approach and teaches the reasoning behind the properties taught in geometry–instead of merely asking them to memorize them. Students are also taught the basics of geometric proofs and coordinate geometry in a way middle school students can understand. Students who struggle with high school geometry usually have lower standardized test scores because it is a fundamental subject in high school standardized testing.

A glossary of terms that every student should master is included. This book can be used as a classroom textbook in Grades 7, 8, or 9 (usually over a two-year period) or as a reference for high school students. This book covers more than the National Math Standards for middle school mathematics.

TABLE OF CONTENTS

Why Use This Book ii
Teaching Suggestions vi
About the Author vi
Student Introduction vii
Dedication viii

Chapter 1 Fundamentals of Geometry Reasoning ..... Pages 1-7
Geometry Notation 1-2
Geometry Notation Practice 3
All About Lines 4
All About Planes 5
Build It! 6
Three Planes in Space 7

Chapter 2 Uncovering All the Angles ..... Pages 8-20
Types of Angles 8
Angles Activity 9
Triangle Activity 10
Triangle Practice 11
Quadrilateral Activity 12
Complementary and Supplementary Angles 13-14
Vertical Angles 15
Angles Puzzle 1 16
Angles Puzzle 2 17
Parallel Lines and Transversals I 18
Parallel Lines and Transversals II 19
Puzzle 3 – The 20-Angle Problem 20

Chapter 3 Triangle Properties ..... Pages 21-29
Sum of Angle Measures 21
Exterior Angle Exploration 22
Sum of Two Sides 23
Triangle Properties Practice 24
Triangle Opposite Property 25
Properties of Equilateral and Isosceles Triangles 26-27
Algebra and Geometry 28-29

Cumulative Review – Chapters 1-3 30

Chapter 4 The Pythagorean Theorem ..... Pages 31-42
Exploration – What Is a Theorem? 31
Pythagorean Triples 32
Pythagorean Triples Practice 33
Using the Pythagorean Theorem 34–35
Pythagorean Theorem Applications 36-37
Solving Multi-Step Right Triangle Problems 38
Special Right Triangles – An Introduction 39-42

Review – Chapter 4 43

TABLE OF CONTENTS (Cont.)

Chapter 5 Uncovering All Polygons ... Pages 44-53

Polygons – Investigation of Angles and Sides ... 44
Polygons Angle Exploration ... 45-47
Summary of Polygon Properties ... 48
Diagonal Exploration ... 49-51
The Handshake Problem ... 52-53

Chapter 6 Quadrilateral and Parallelogram Properties ... Pages 54-80

The Quadrilateral Family ... 54-56
Venn Diagram Activity ... 57
Parallelogram Discovery ... 58-59
Parallelogram Properties ... 60-61
Working With Parallelograms ... 62-65
Experimenting With Parallelograms ... 66-68
A Look at Trapezoids ... 69-74
Kite! Kite! Kite! ... 75
Critical Thinking About Quadrilaterals ... 76
Midsegment Investigation ... 77
Using Algebra to Solve Quadrilateral Problems ... 78-79
Quadrilateral Matching ... 80

Cumulative Review – Chapters 5-6 ... 81-82

Chapter 7 Metric Geometry ... Pages 83-100

Perimeter and Circumference ... 83
Pi (π) Investigation ... 84
Perimeter and Circumference Activity ... 85
Archimedes' Idea for Approximating Pi ... 86-87
Area of Parallelograms ... 88-89
Parallelogram Area Activity ... 90
Area of Triangles and Trapezoids ... 91-93
Discovering the Area of a Trapezoid ... 94
Area of a Trapezoid ... 95-96
Area of Circles ... 97-99
The Arbelos Problem ... 100

Chapter 8 Geometric Constructions ... Pages 101-123

A Geometric Construction ... 101
How to Bisect an Angle ... 102-103
How to Copy an Angle ... 104
How to Construct a Perpendicular Bisector to a Line ... 105-107
Finding the Median in a Triangle ... 108-109
How to Construct a Line Parallel to Another Line ... 110
Geometric Construction Review ... 111
Problem-Solving With Geometric Constructions ... 112-121
Problem-Solving With Impossible Constructions ... 122-123

Chapter 9 The Geometry of Three Dimensional Shapes ... Pages 124-138

3D Shapes – Prisms ... 124-126
The Volume of Cylinders ... 127-128
Volumes of Pyramids and Cones ... 129-130

Turn Up the Volume! 131-132
Volume of a Sphere 133-134
Surface Area of Prisms 135
Surface Area of a Cylinder Activity 136
Finding Surface Area 137
Euler's Formula 138

Cumulative Review – Chapters 7-9 139-140

Chapter 10 Symmetry and Transformations .... Pages 141-173

What is Vertical, Horizontal, and Point Symmetry? 141-143
Transformations – Reflections 144-149
Transformations – Translations 150-153
Transformations – Rotations 154-159
Transformations – Dilations 160-163
Glide Reflections and Compositions 164-170
Tessellations 171-173

Review – Chapter 10 174-175

Chapter 11 Proving Triangles Congruent .... Pages 176-198

Introduction to Proofs – Congruency 176-177
SSS Activity 178
SAS Activity 179
ASA and AAS Activities 180
SSA Activity 181
The Essence of a Good Geometric Proof 182-184
Picture, Statement, and Reason 185-186
Finding Congruent Triangles 187
Two Column Proofs 188-191
Investigate Hypotenuse – Leg Theorem 191-192
Similar Figures and Introduction to Similarity Proofs 193-195
Proving Triangles Similar 196-197
Test Your Reasoning Skills 198

Review – Chapter 11 199-200

Chapter 12 Coordinate Geometry .... Pages 201-232

What is the Slope of a Line 201
Slope Formula 202-206
How to Write an Equation of a Line 207-211
The Midpoint Formula 212-215
The Distance Formula 216-220
Review Your Formulas 221-222
Introduction to Coordinate Proofs 223-232

Review – Chapter 12 233-235

Final Review .... Pages 236-241

Sample Activities .... Pages 242-246

Glossary .... Pages 247-252

Answers .... Pages 253-292

Graph Paper .... Pages 293-296

Teaching Suggestions

This book can be used as a classroom textbook in grade 7, 8, or 9 or during a two year period. In many high schools this book can also be used as a one year average high school geometry course. While some students may need more exercises per topic, the book provides the teacher with many types of exercises to review concepts and promote critical thinking.

Many activities can be tried in the classroom or at home. The more students experiment with these concepts the better they will understand and connect the concepts in this book.

The book includes a glossary of terms that every student in high school must master.

Many suggestions as to how to incorporate the history of mathematics and multicultural math are included, so teachers and parents can expand on these topics to further enrich their students.

About the Author

Terri Husted, formerly Terri Santi, has been teaching math for over 30 years. She taught middle school math for many years and is curently an algebra and geometry teacher at Ithaca High School in Ithaca, NY. Terri was the Math Coordinator for the Saturday Science and Math Academy, a program for elementary minority students, that was run by Cornell University and later Ithaca College.

In 1995, she was chosen as one of two New York State finalists for the Presidential Award for Excellence in Science and Math Teaching. Her life and work have been included in the book *Young People's Lessons in Character* (1998) Young People's Press. Besides giving many workshops to teachers in her district, Terri loves writing about math and including multicultural math in her math lessons.

Terri firmly believes that math can be made clear and simple for everyone and that critical thinking is not only necessary but also fun! Terri is also the author of *Math Ties*® and *Math Detective*® (The Critical Thinking Co.™). She holds teaching certificates in Math 7-12, Reading 7-12, Biology 7-12, Elementary Education K-12, and has a Bachelor of Science in Mathematics and a Masters of Science in Reading. Her specialty areas are reading in the content area of math, overcoming math anxiety, and multicultural math. She is a member of the National Council of Teachers of Mathematics.

Student Introduction

Mathematics is one of the few subjects you will study where rules and laws remain unchanged. Geometry is the painting canvas of mathematics. Look around and you will see right angles, curves, shapes, and symmetry. From the angle that the sun rises, to the symmetry of a butterfly, geometry is everywhere! Geometry has fascinated people of all cultures from the beginning of time. The geometry in this book is called Euclidean Geometry. It follows the rules and laws of geometry stated by a Greek mathematician named Euclid (around 300 BC). Euclid wrote 13 books called the Elements. In these books he stated definitions, postulates (statements that need no proof), and theorems (statements that can be proven). He is often called *The Father of Geometry* because he organized in book form many of the ideas that had been known for centuries. It is important to remember that many other civilizations like the Babylonians, the Egyptians, and the Mayans, made great contributions to geometry and astronomy.

Ever wonder why a circle has 360°? Why do we use 60 minutes for an hour and 60 seconds for a minute? The Babylonians used a sexagesimal system inherited from the Sumerians. They were very skilled at astronomy and commerce. They used base 60 instead of our base 10. You might wonder why they used 60 as their base. Maybe because they knew that the number 60 has many factors. The number 10 or even the number 100 does not have that many factors. Can you find the factors of 60?

Geometry is important to many cultures. Native Americans and many people of Africa still consider the circle an important shape, not only for building purposes but for its spiritual meaning.

This book was written to help you strengthen and learn geometry concepts that you will need to succeed in high school geometry. It was also written to help you read and use the correct geometry notation. More importantly, it was written to help you think critically and deeply about how geometry topics are interconnected and to help you appreciate the beauty, logic, and fun of mathematics.

Terri Husted dedicates this book to her grandson Paulo and to all her past and present geometry students.

Chapter 1 - Fundamentals of Geometry Reasoning

Geometry Notation

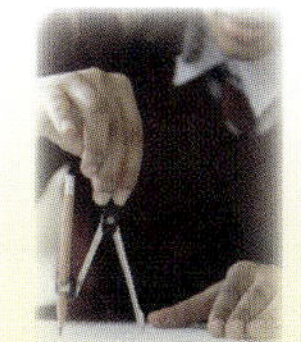

To communicate in geometry, mathematicians have agreed on important notation, **symbols** used to write. For example, capital letters are used for points.

Naming a point.

Use capital letters for points.

A means **point A**.

Naming a line.

You can use a lower case letter or two points with the line symbol on top. Two points determine a **line** (or two points is all you need to name a line).

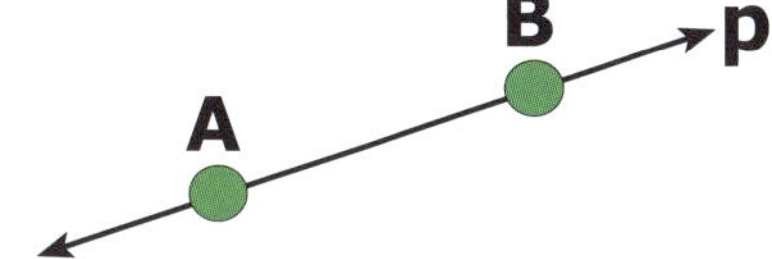

p means **line p**.

$\overleftrightarrow{AB}$ means the line passes through **points A** and **B**.

Remember
There would be no geometry without **points**!

Naming a segment or a ray.

Use capital letters for points.

$\overline{AB}$ means the **segment** has **endpoints A** and **B**.

$\overrightarrow{AB}$ means **ray AB**. The ray starts at **A** and passes through **B**.

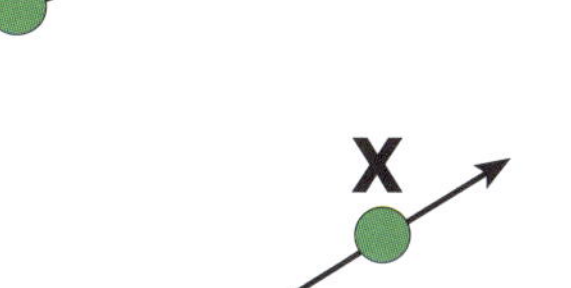

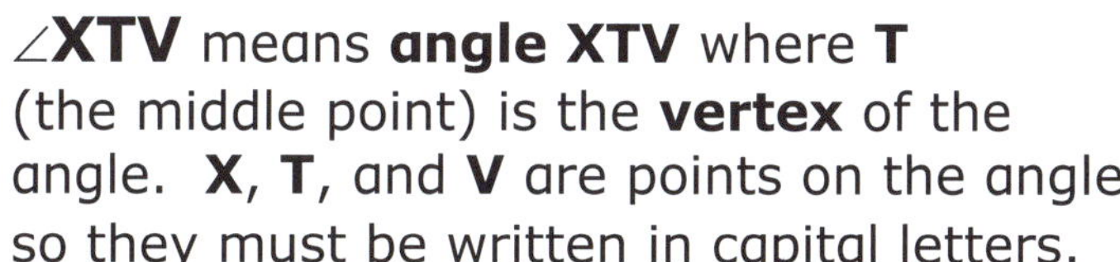

$\angle$**XTV** means **angle XTV** where **T** (the middle point) is the **vertex** of the angle. **X**, **T**, and **V** are points on the angle so they must be written in capital letters.

XTV (without an angle symbol) means **plane XTV** or the plane containing the three non-collinear points **X**, **T,** and **V**.

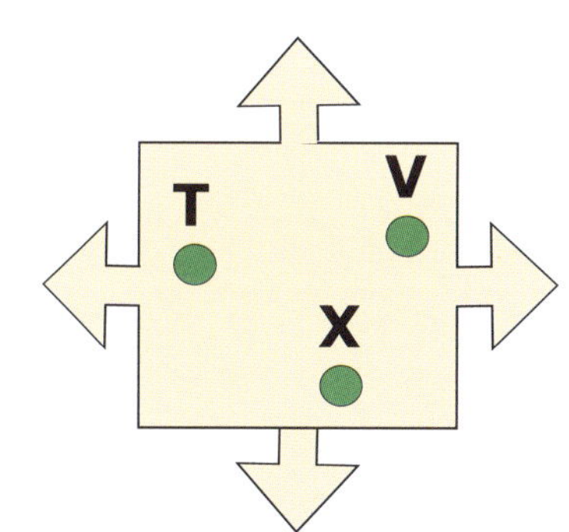

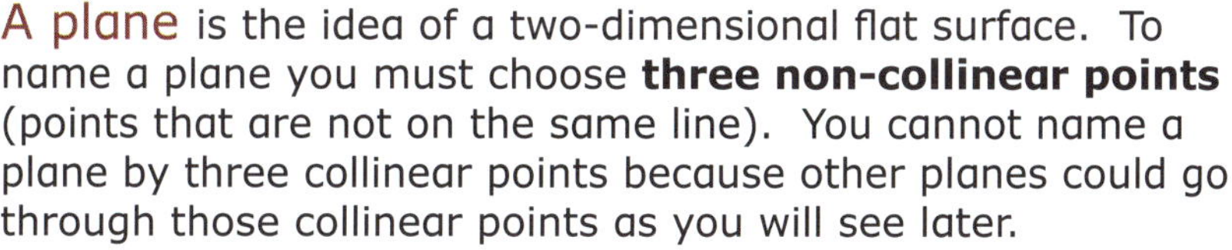

A plane is the idea of a two-dimensional flat surface. To name a plane you must choose **three non-collinear points** (points that are not on the same line). You cannot name a plane by three collinear points because other planes could go through those collinear points as you will see later.

Geometry Notation (Cont.)

The difference between = and ≅. When you compare quantities, use the **equal** symbol (=). When comparing shapes, angles, and segments, use the symbol **congruent** (≅).

Congruent means **identical** in size and shape.

m means **measure** or **quantity**. Look at the examples below.

$\angle \mathbf{A} \cong \angle \mathbf{B}$	Angle **A** is congruent to angle **B.**
$m\angle \mathbf{A} = m\angle \mathbf{B}$	The measure of angle **A** is equal to the measure of angle **B**. You are comparing degrees (quantities).

The difference between $\overline{\mathbf{AB}}$ and **AB**.

$\overline{\mathbf{AB}}$ is a segment with endpoints **A** and **B**.

AB means the **length** in units between point **A** and point **B**.

If segment **AB** is identical to segment **CD**, and you know each segment is 8 units, you can say

$\overline{\mathbf{AB}} \cong \overline{\mathbf{CD}}$	The objects are identical.
AB = **CD**	8 units = 8 units. In either case, **A**, **B**, **C**, and **D** must be in capital letters.

The symbol for parallel is ll and the symbol for perpendicular is ⊥.

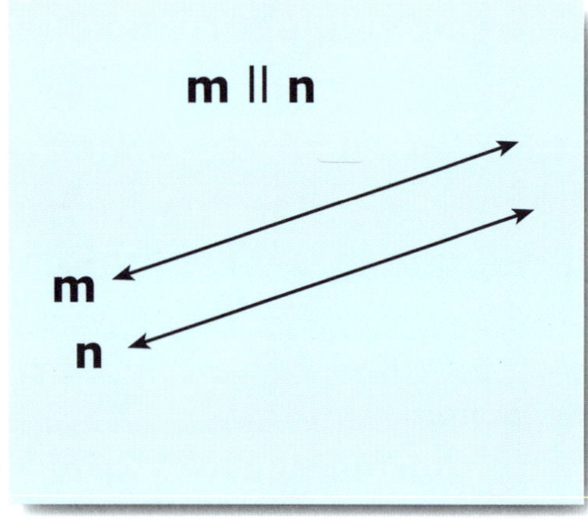

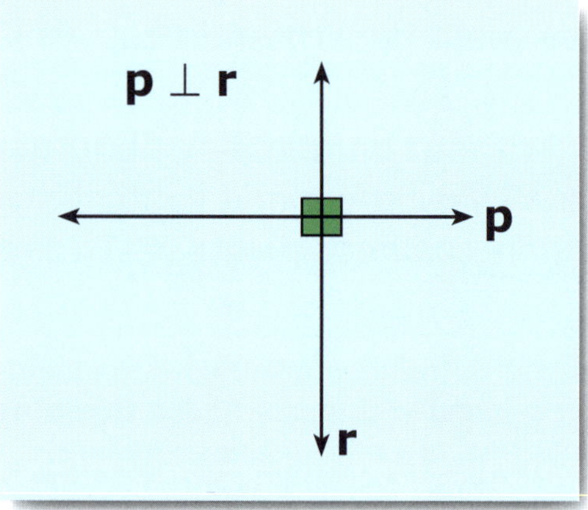

Geometry Notation Practice

Use = or ≅

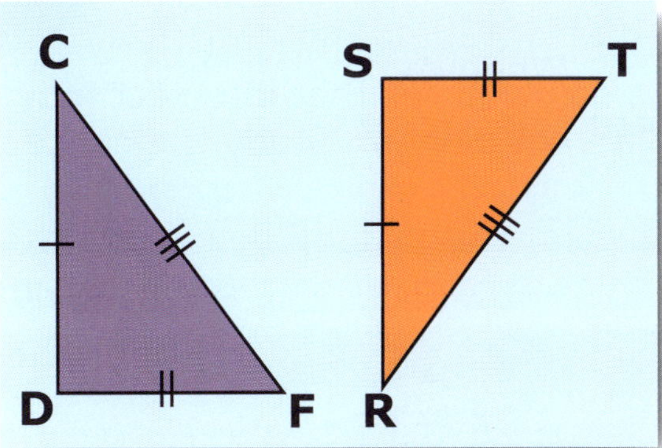

Notice the **tick** or **hatch marks**. Sides with the same number of tick marks are congruent.

1. **ΔCDF** ______ **ΔRST**
2. **DF** ______ **ST**
3. $\overline{DF}$ ______ $\overline{ST}$
4. ∠**F** ______ ∠**T**
5. m∠**DCF** ______ m∠**SRT**

Use ∥ or ⊥

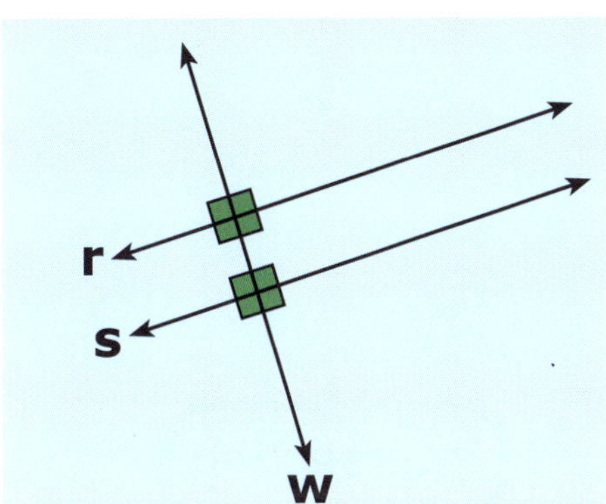

6. **r** ______ **s**
7. **w** ______ **s**
8. **w** ______ **r**
9. If ∠**D** ≅ ∠**S**, is m∠**D** = m∠**S**? Explain your thinking.

____

10. If **w** ⊥ **s** and **s** ∥ **r**, is **w** ⊥ **r**? Explain your thinking.

____

11. Why is ∠**A** the wrong notation if you wanted to name the angle in blue?

____

____

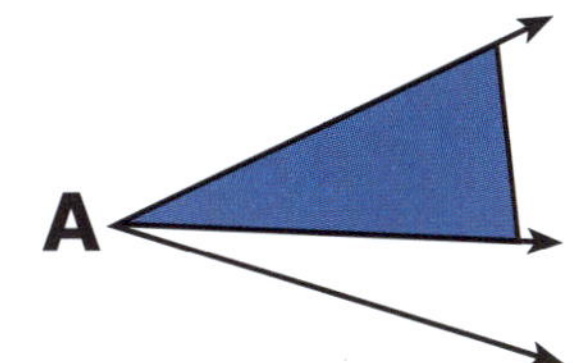

All About Lines

Lines can be parallel, intersecting, or skew. When lines intersect, they always intersect at a point. Lines that intersect may or may not be perpendicular. Skew lines are on different planes. Study the concept map below.

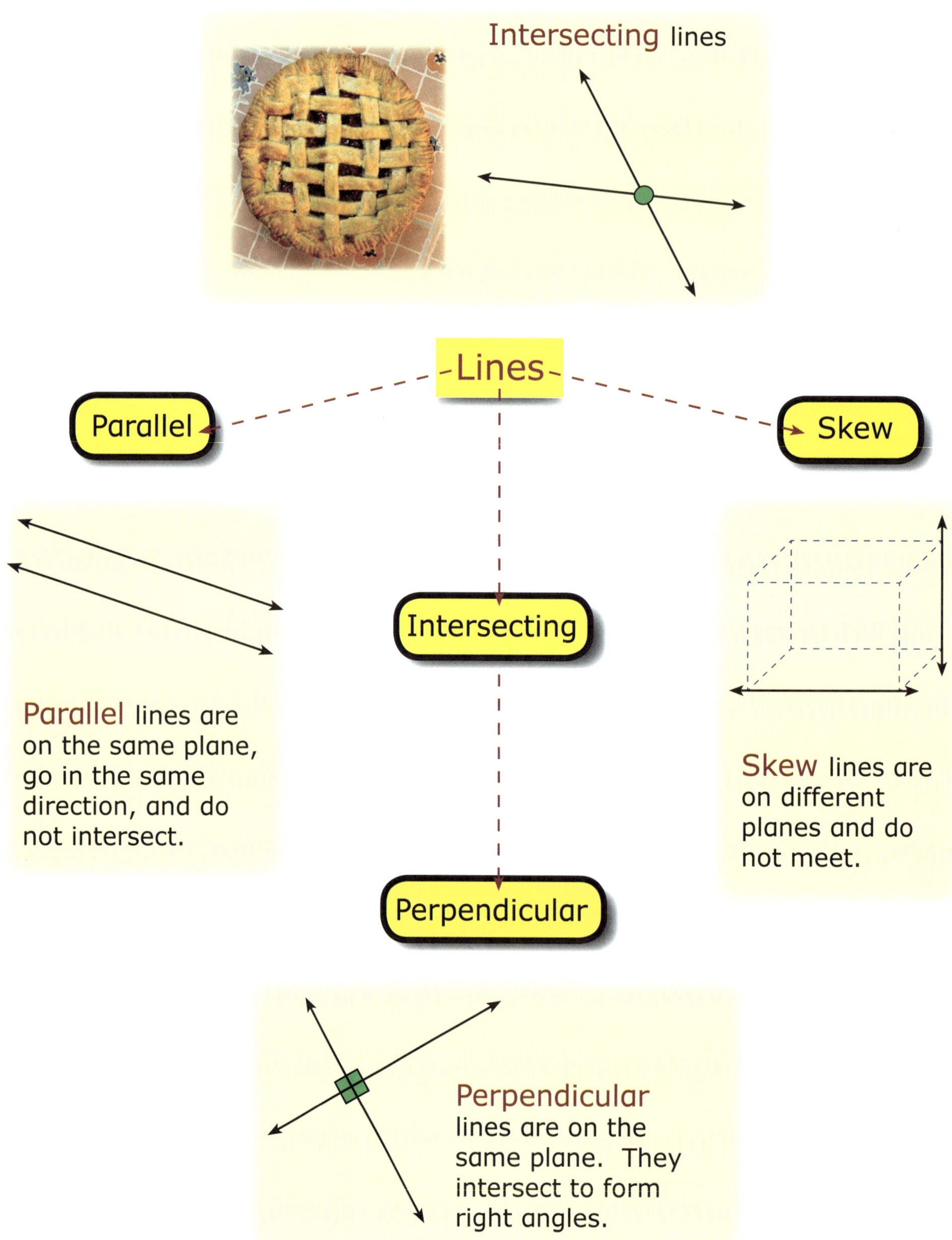

All About Planes

Planes can be parallel or intersecting. When planes intersect, their intersection is a line. Planes that intersect may or may not be perpendicular.

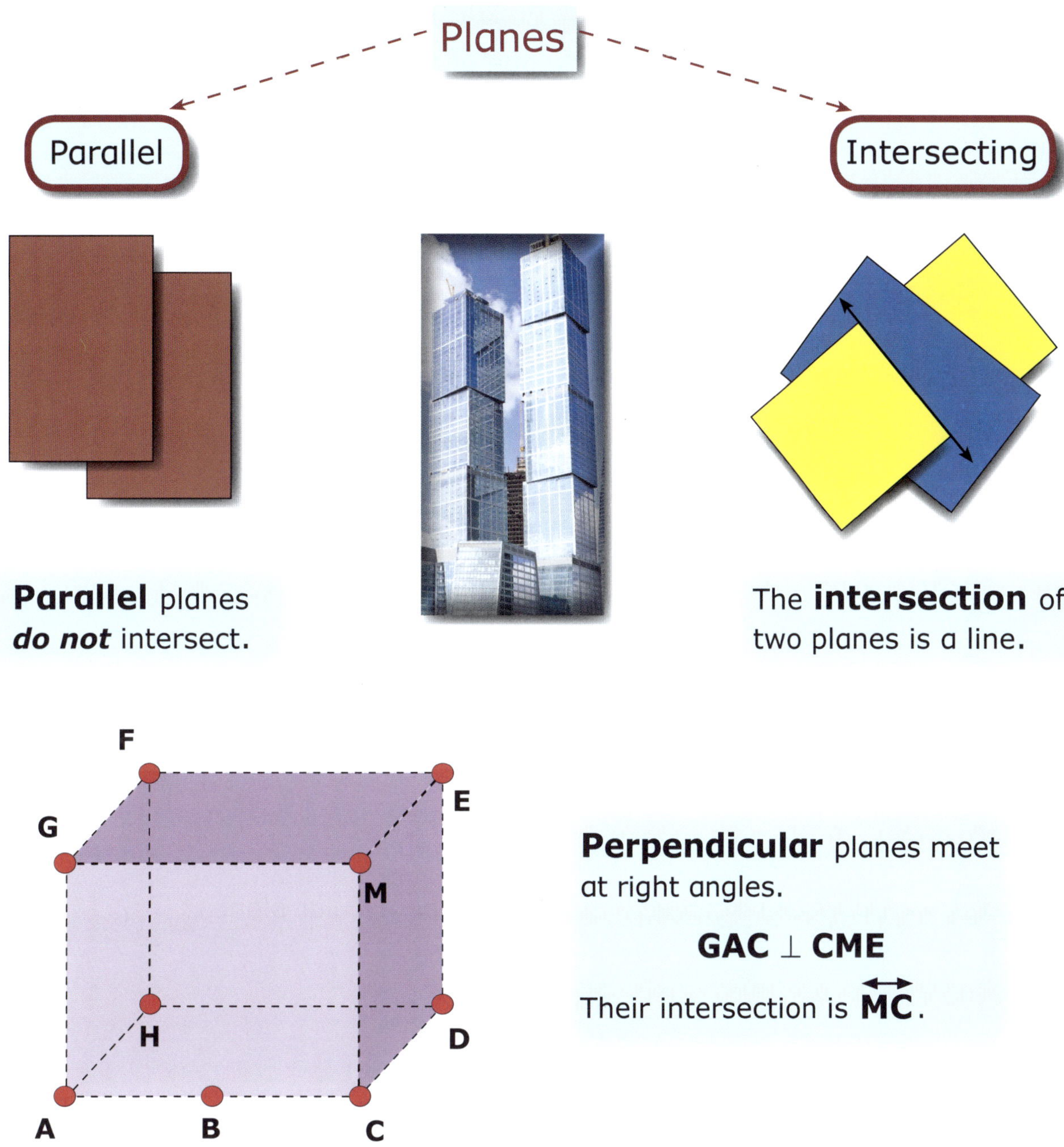

Notice: By naming three non-collinear points, you can identify the plane.

For example: **GAH** is the plane on the left side of the cube. Since **A**, **B**, and **C** are three collinear points, they are on the front and on the bottom plane and therefore **ABC** does not represent a unique plane.

Build It!

Use pipe cleaners to simulate lines and pieces of cardboard to simulate planes to build the following models. Then answer the following questions.

1. A line perpendicular to two parallel planes.
   - a. If a line is perpendicular to one of two parallel planes, is it perpendicular to the other plane?

2. Two intersecting lines lying in a plane.
   - a. If two lines intersect, do they always lie in only one plane?
   - b. If three non-collinear points determine a plane, why do two intersecting lines also determine a plane?

3. Two intersecting planes determine a line.
   - a. Is it possible for two planes to be skew? See the lines concept map to review the definition of skew.

4. Two perpendicular planes.
   - a. What is the intersection of two perpendicular planes?

5. Three planes going through one line.
   - a. What objects in real life represent this idea?

6. Three planes in 3-D space. See the next page to help you.
   - a. Describe the intersection as one point, a line, two parallel lines, or no common point.

Three Planes in Space

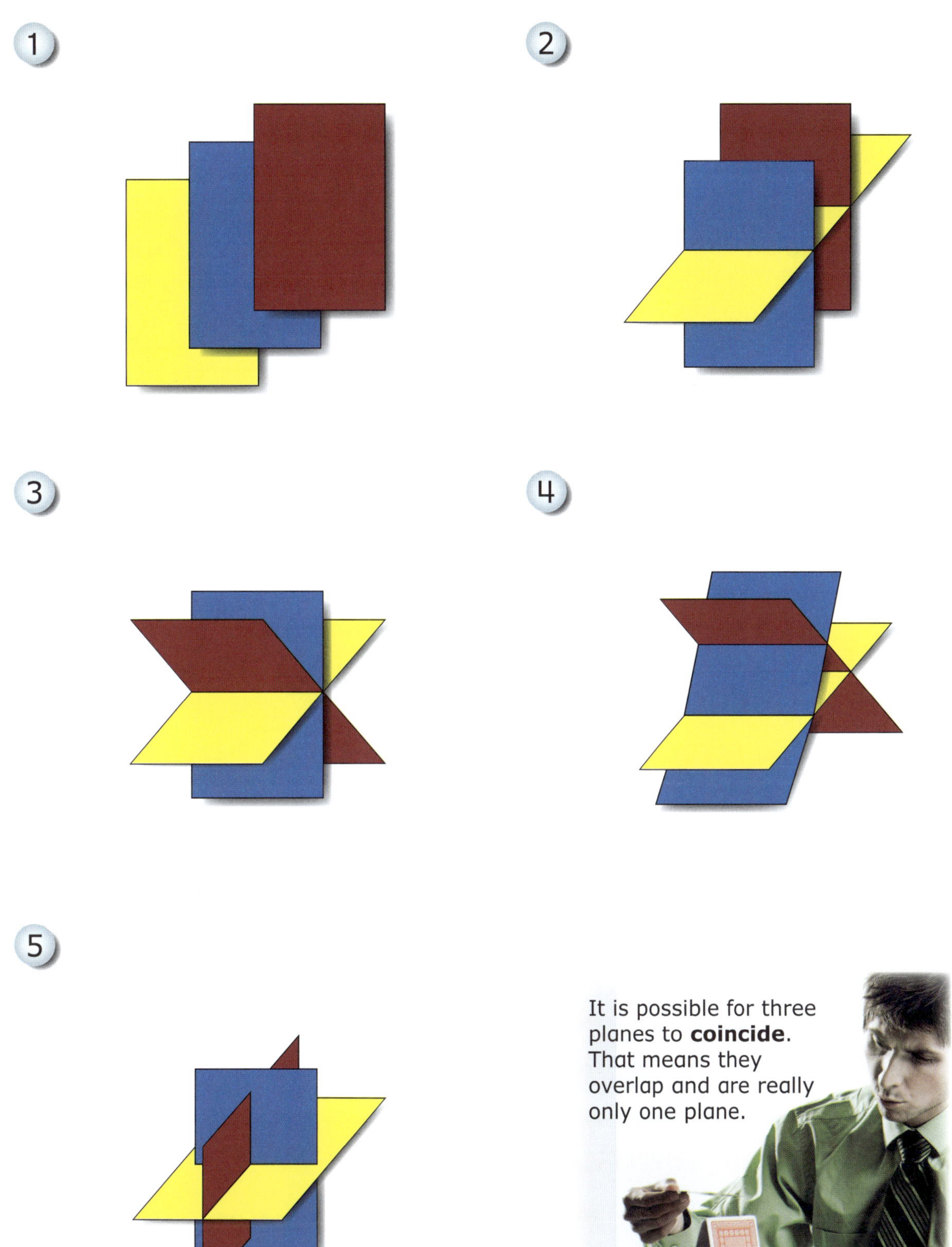

It is possible for three planes to **coincide**. That means they overlap and are really only one plane.

Chapter 2 - Uncovering All the Angles

Types of Angles

Angles can be acute (less than 90°), right (exactly 90°), obtuse (between 90° and 180°), or straight (exactly 180°).

To name an angle, you must make sure to write the **vertex point** in the middle. If there are no other angles at that vertex, you can name an angle by its vertex.

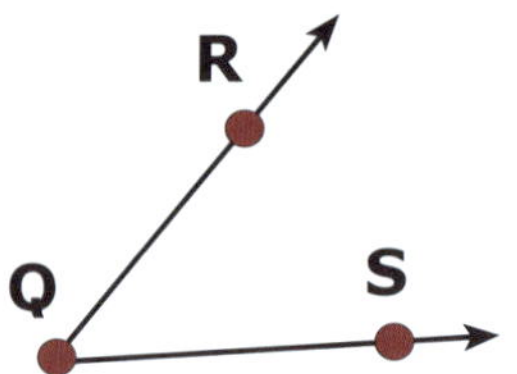

This is ∠**RQS**, or ∠**SQR**, or ∠**Q.**

Adjacent angles share a side and a vertex. Adjacent angles must be **coplanar** (on the same plane).

∠**ABD** and ∠**CBD** are adjacent.

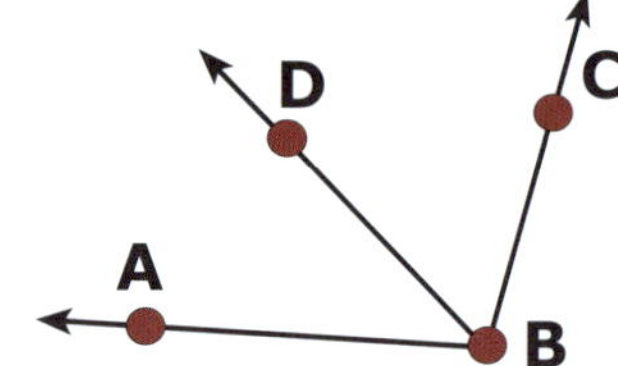

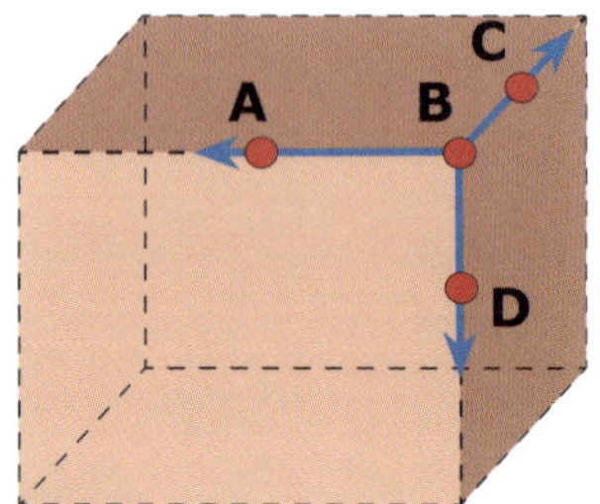

∠**ABD** and ∠**CBD** are ***not*** adjacent because the angles are not on the same plane.

A **reflex angle** is more than 180° and less than 360°.

320° is the reflex angle of a 40° acute angle. Notice they add up to 360°.

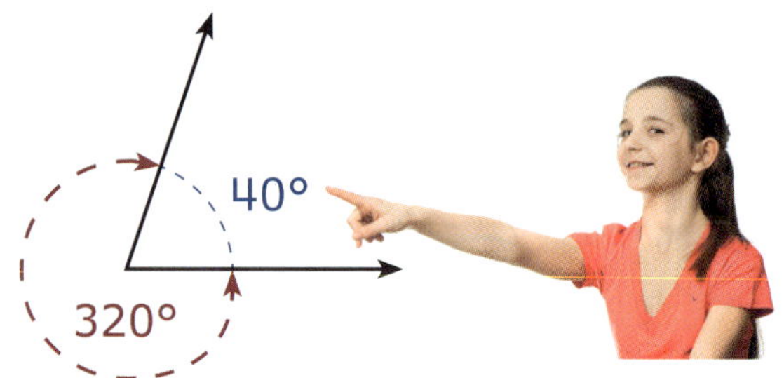

When asked the measure of this angle, say 40° unless you are asked to find the reflex angle.

Angles Activity

Look at the drawing below, then complete the chart. Use a check mark √ to identify each angle. The angles are all coplanar.

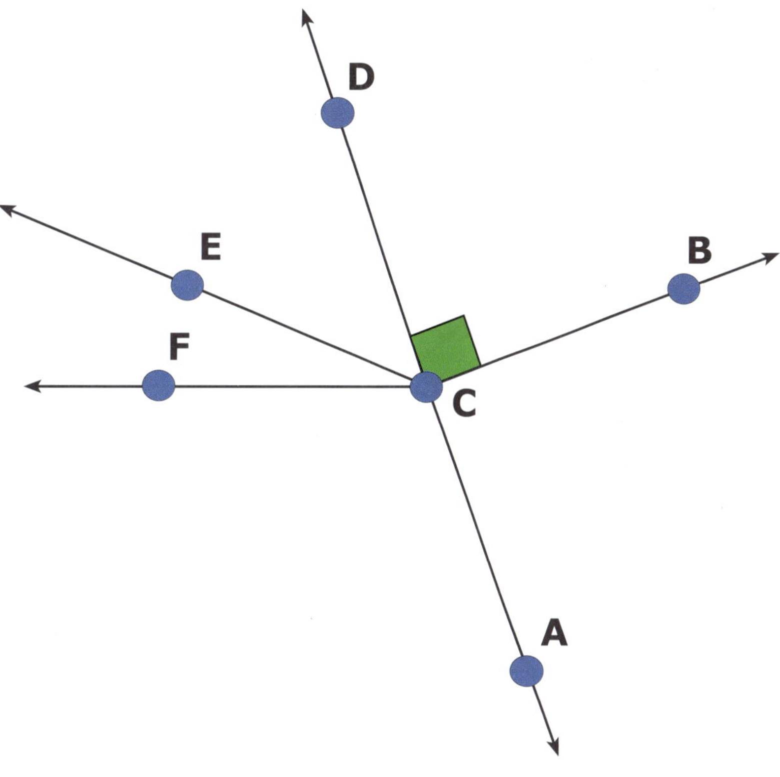

	Right	Acute	Obtuse	Straight	Adjacent to ∠ECD
∠FCE					
∠ECD					
∠DCA					
∠FCB					
∠BCD					
∠ACB					

Triangle Activity

Below is a scalene triangle.

- Trace it on a piece of white paper.
- Cut out your triangle, then cut out all the angles. See example. 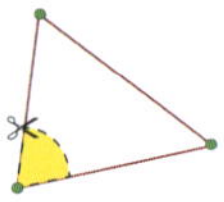
- Next place the vertices of your triangle together on the line below.

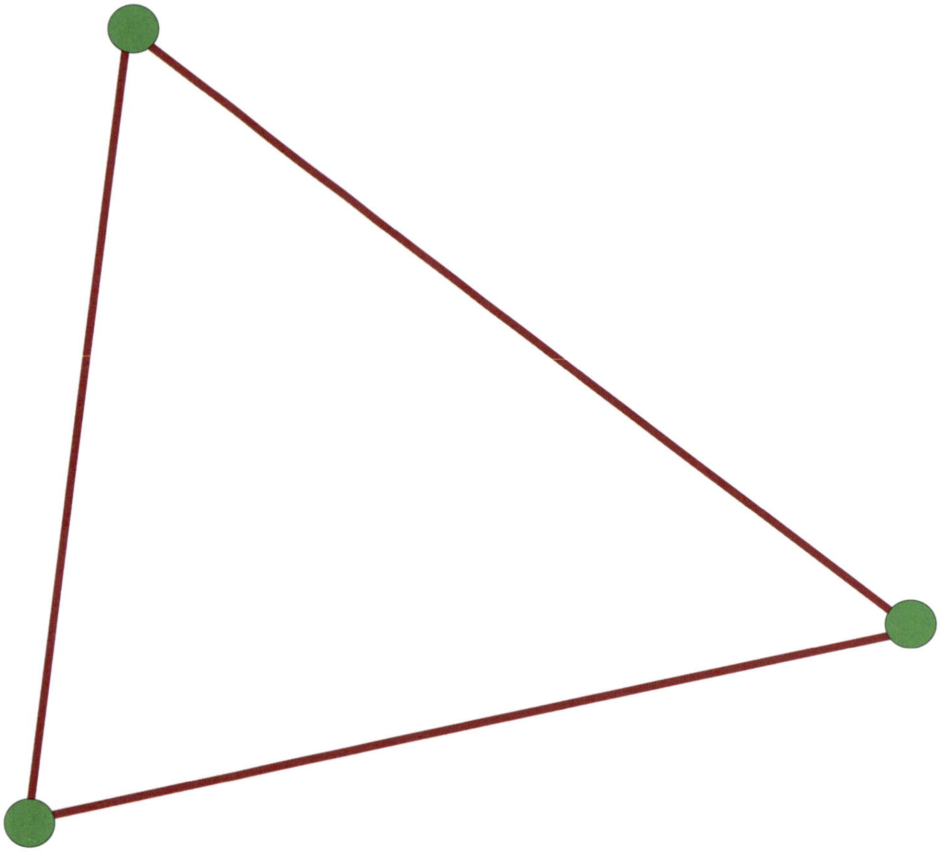

Explain what you discover.

____

____

Triangle Practice

Use your *thinking skills* to find the missing angle in each of the triangles. ***Do not*** measure.

1 ____________

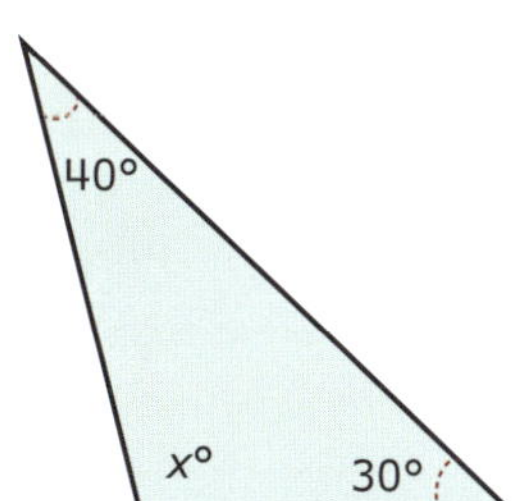

2 ____________

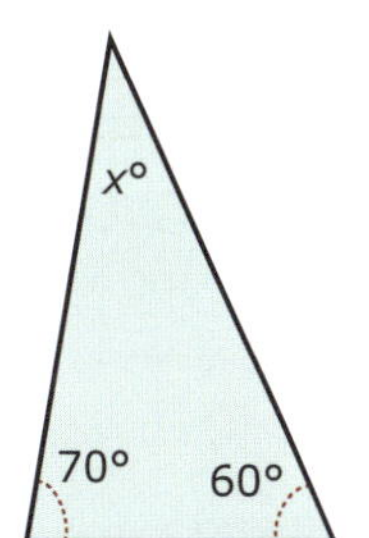

3 ____________

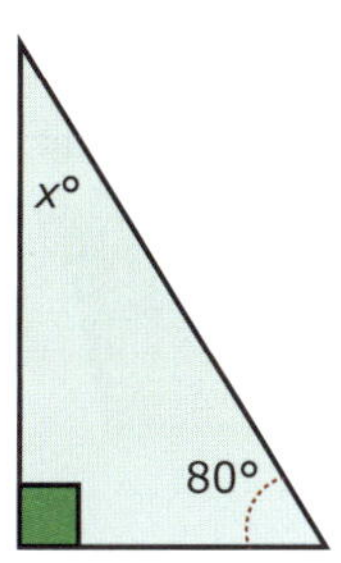

4 Can a triangle have two obtuse angles? Why or why not?

____

5 Can a right triangle have one obtuse angle? Why or why not?

____

6 Two angles of a right triangle are the same. Find each of their measures. ____________ and ____________

7 What type of triangle has three angles each with the same measure? ____________

8 For each triangle **ABC**, find the missing angle(s).

	a	b	c	d	e	f	g
A	90°	60°	100°	50°	x°	170°	(2x)°
B	45°	x°	59.5°	x°	x°	x°	x°
C	x°	60°	x°	90°	90°	x°	90°

a ____________ b ____________ c ____________ d ____________

e ____________, ____________ f ____________, ____________

g ____________, ____________

Quadrilateral Activity

Quadrilaterals are 4-sided polygons.

- Trace it on a piece of white paper.
- Cut out the angles. See example.
- Then place the vertices together so they touch on the line below.

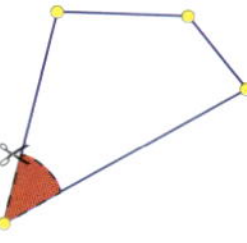

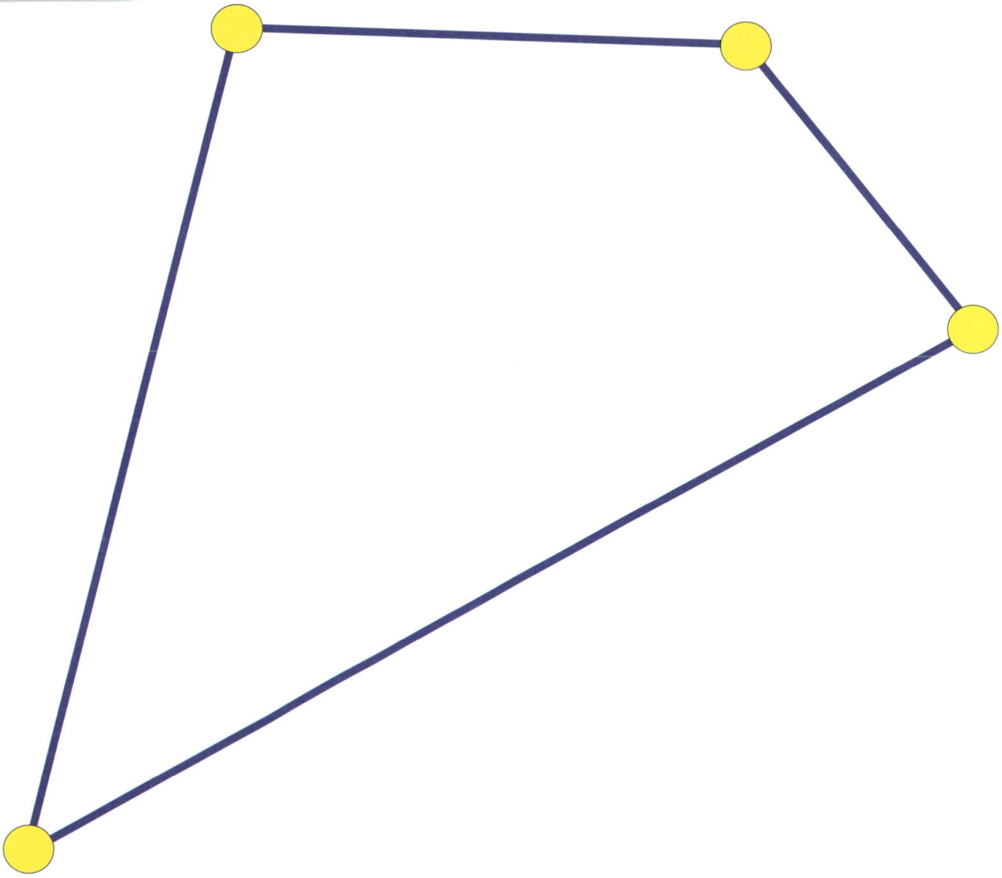

Explain what you discover.

____

____

Complementary and Supplementary Angles

Complementary angles are two angles whose measures add up to 90°.

Supplementary angles are two angles whose measures add up to 180°.

HOW TO REMEMBER

C comes before **S** in the alphabet **90** comes before **180**.

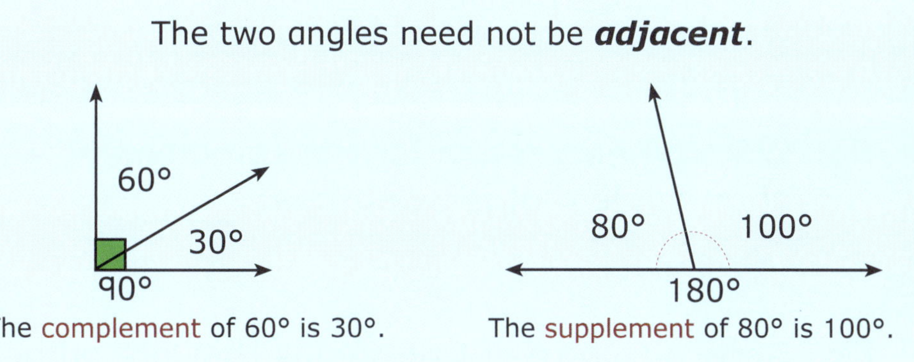

The complement of 60° is 30°.

The supplement of 80° is 100°.

1. Find the complement of 75°. ______

2. Find the supplement of 75°. ______

3. Find the supplement of (75 + 10)°. ______

4. Find the supplement of the complement of 20°. ______

5. Find the supplement of the complement of 45°. ______

6. Which is larger, the complement of an acute angle or the supplement of an acute angle? Explain your thinking.

____

____

7. Is it possible to have a complement of an obtuse angle? Explain your thinking.

____

____

Complementary and Supplementary Angles (Cont.)

8) Write an expression for the supplement of an angle that is *x* degrees. ________________

Hint: What do you have to do to find the supplement of any angle?

HOW TO REMEMBER

Adjacent means next to. Adjacent angles are on the same plane, and share a side and a vertex.

9) Write an expression for the complement of an angle that is *y* degrees. ________________

10) Draw a picture of two angles that are adjacent and complementary.

11) Draw a picture of two angles that are supplementary, but not adjacent.

12) If $\angle x$ is the complement of $\angle$**A,** and $\angle y$ is also the complement of the same $\angle$**A**. What can you say about $\angle x$ and $\angle y$?

____

Vertical Angles

When two lines intersect the angles across from each other are called vertical angles.

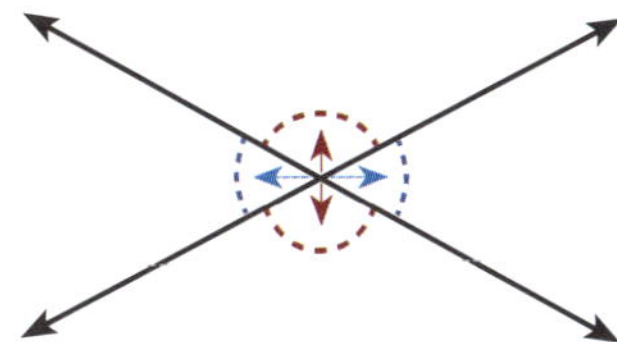

HOW TO REMEMBER

Vertical angles are opposite each other, but not necessarily up and down like their name *vertical* implies.

Vertical angles are ***always*** congruent to each other.

1. In Figure 1, find m∠x _____, m∠y _____, m∠z _____.

2. What kind of angles are ∠x and ∠y?

____

Why? _______________________________________

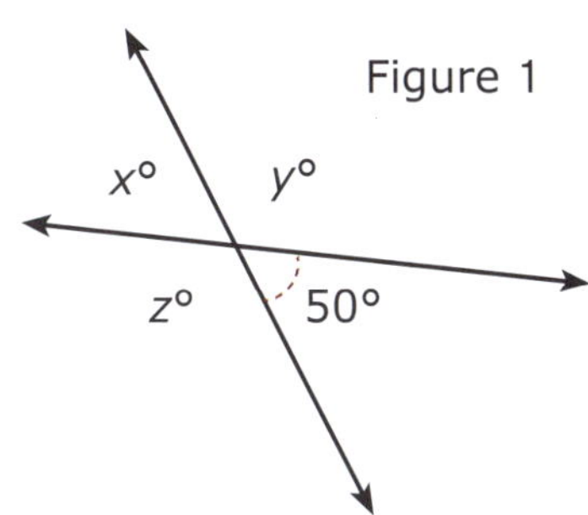

Figure 1

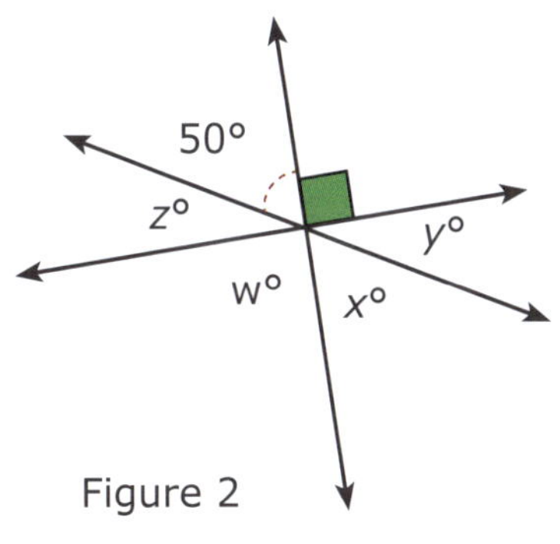

Figure 2

3. In Figure 2, find m∠x _____, m∠w _____, m∠z _____, m∠y _____.

4. What type of angles are ∠x and ∠y?

____

Why? _______________________________________

5. In Figure 3, four lines intersect at a common point. What is the least number of angles you would need to know in order to find all the angles in the figure? _______

6. Prove your answer is correct by choosing your own angle measure. ***Do not*** measure. Why must all your angles add up to 360°?

____

____

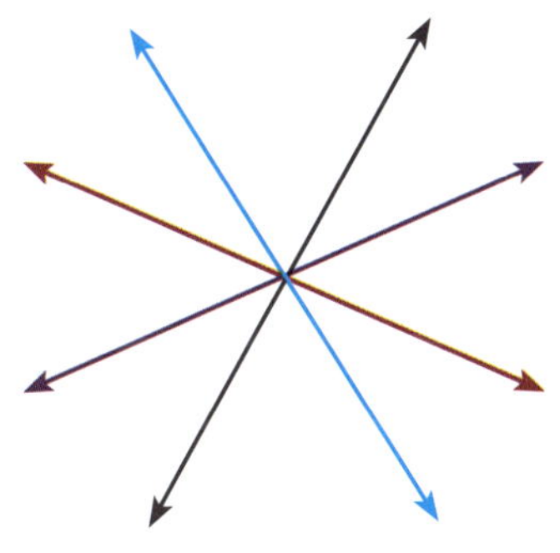
Figure 3

Angles Puzzle 1

Use your *thinking skills* to find the missing angles and record in degrees below. Figures are ***not*** to scale, so do not measure.

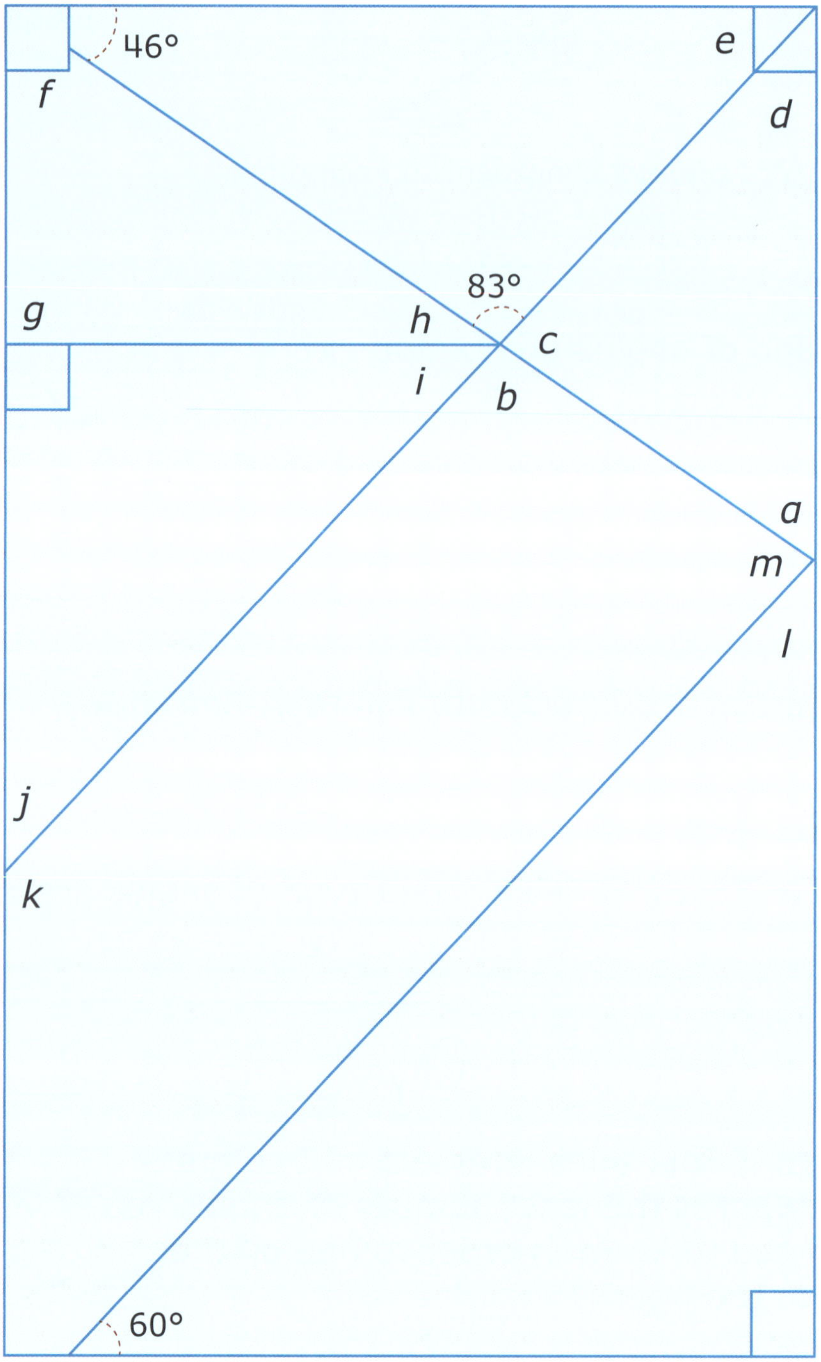

a ______ *b* ______ *c* ______ *d* ______ *e* ______ *f* ______ *g* ______

h ______ *i* ______ *j* ______ *k* ______ *l* ______ *m* ______

Angles Puzzle 2

Use your *thinking skills* to find the missing angles and record below. Figures are ***not*** to scale, so do not measure.

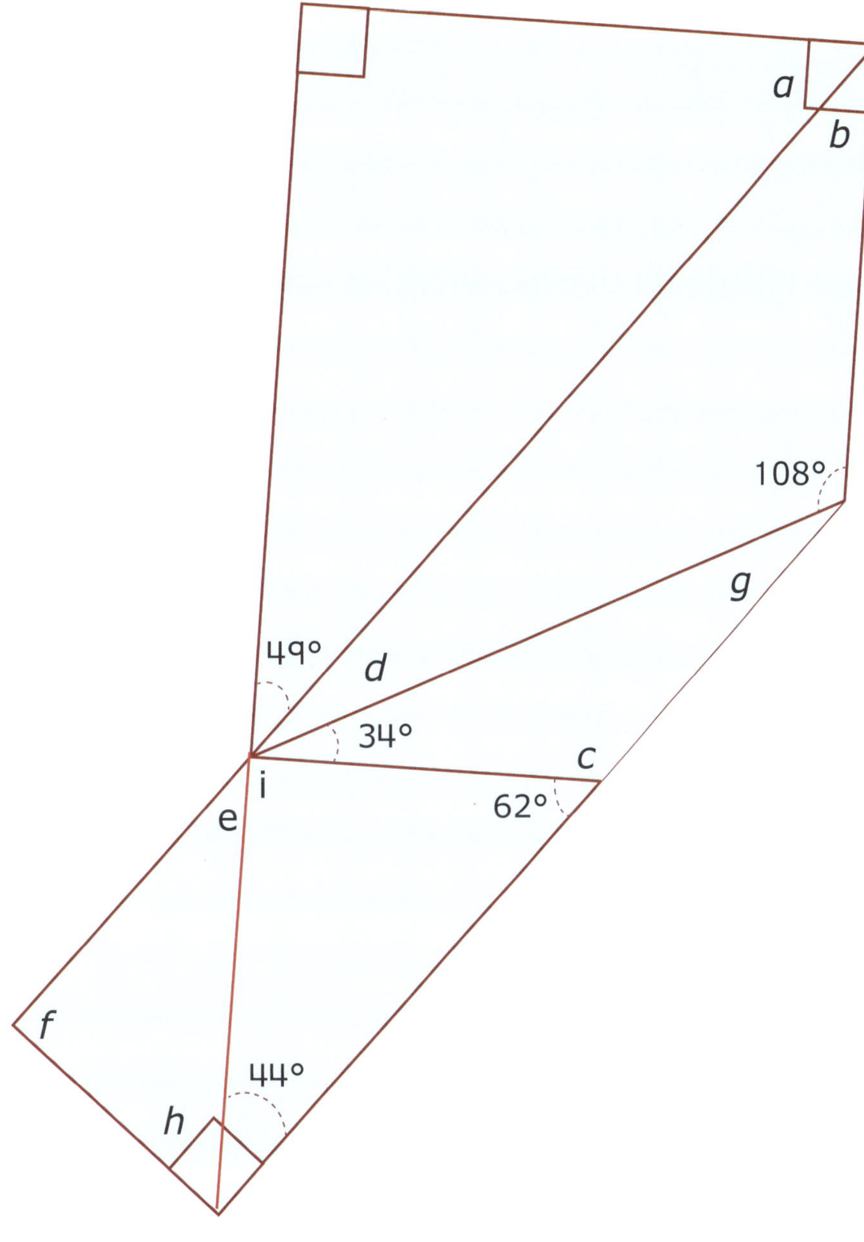

a ______ *b* ______ *c* ______ *d* ______ *e* ______ *f* ______

g ______ *h* ______ *i* ______

Parallel Lines and Transversals I

Corresponding angles are created when a **transversal** line cuts across two or more lines.

If lines are parallel, then **corresponding angles** are congruent.

The **converse** is also true. So if corresponding angles are congruent, then the lines are parallel.

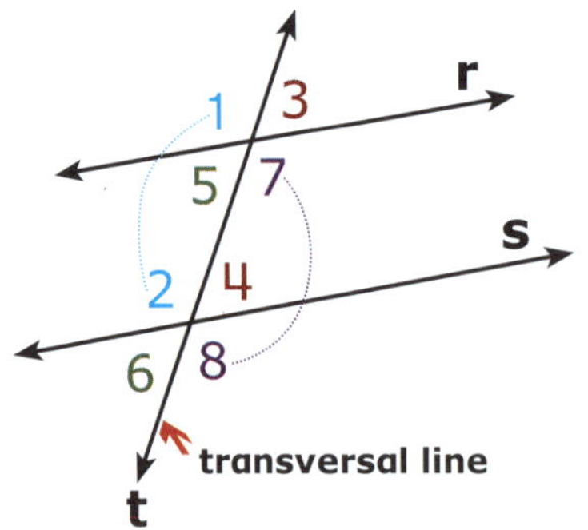

How to Remember

Corresponding means matching.

In the figure, if **r** ll **s**, then ∠1 ≅ ∠2 , and if ∠1 ≅ ∠2, then r ll s.

The symbol for **parallel** is ll.

Converse

For a statement *If p then q,* the converse is *If q then p.*

∠1 and ∠2 are corresponding angles, so are ∠7 and ∠8. Name the remaining pairs of corresponding angles. ____________, ____________

1. Find the m∠*x* if **m** ll **n**.

   m∠*x* = _______

2. Are these lines parallel? ______

   Why or why not? ___________

   ____

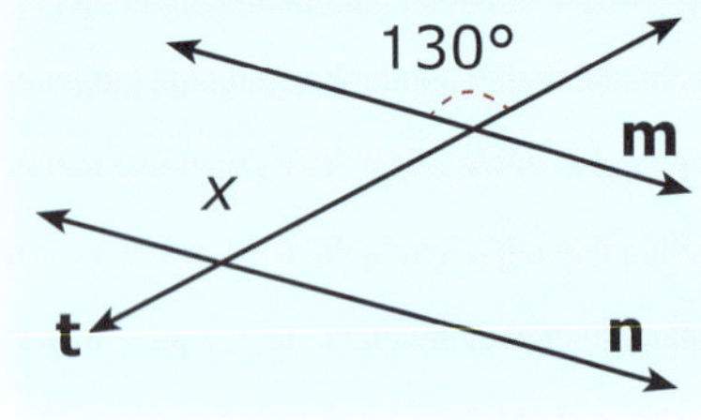

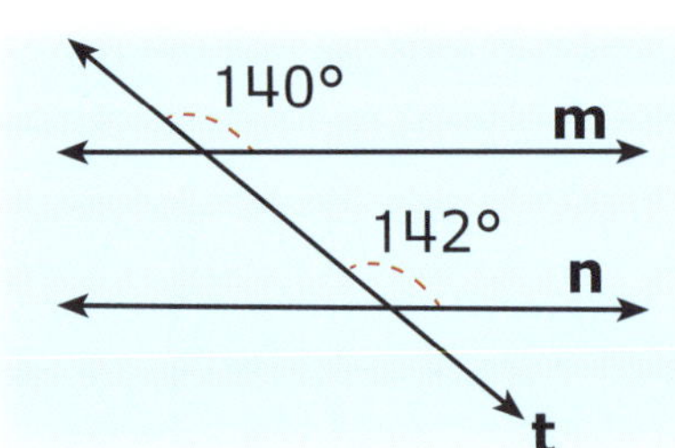

3. a. If **p** ll **q** and **q** ll **r**, why is **p** ll **r**? ___________

   ____

   b. Assume **p** ll **q** ll **r**. Find the missing angles, but ***do not*** measure.

1 ______ 2 ______ 3 ______ 4 ______

5 ______ 6 ______ 7 ______ 8 ______

9 ______ 10 ______ 11 ______

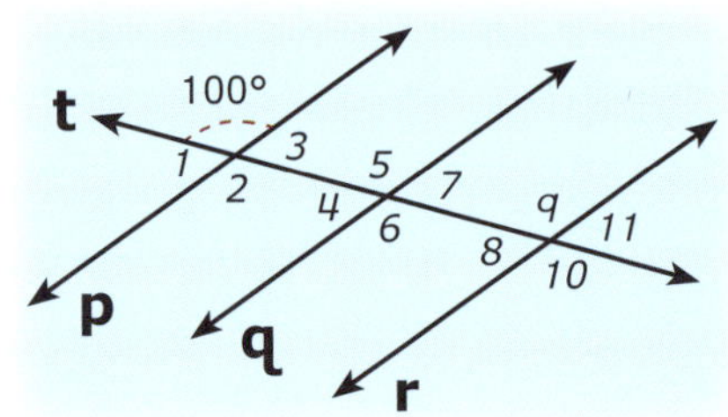

Parallel Lines and Transversals II

If lines are parallel, then alternate interior angles are congruent. And if alternate interior angles are congruent, then the lines are parallel.

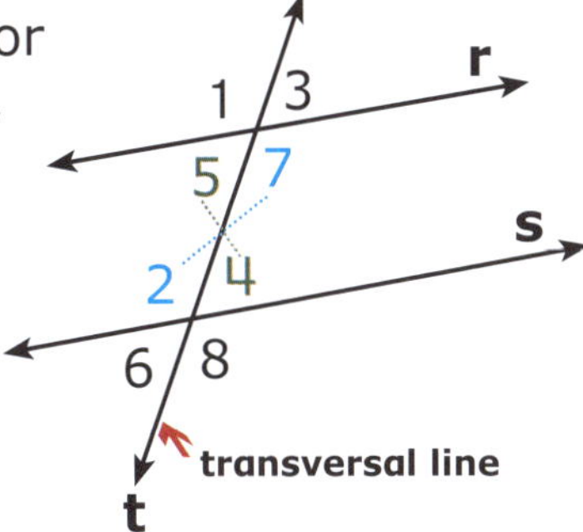

How to Remember

Interior means between the two parallel lines.

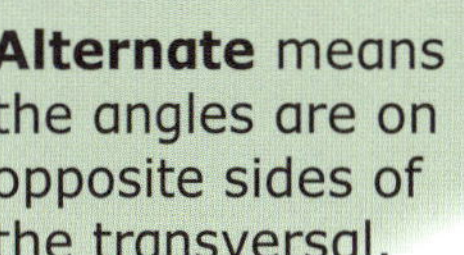

Alternate means the angles are on opposite sides of the transversal.

∠4 and ∠5 are alternate interior angles. ∠2 and ∠7 are also alternate interior angles.

1. Why is **m** ll **n**? ______________________

____

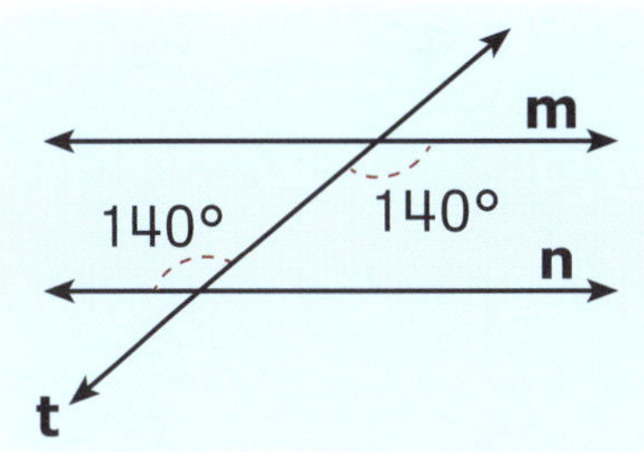

2. Find the missing angles given that **r** ll **s** and **w** ll **t**.

a. m∠1 = ______ Why? ____________

____

b. m∠2 = ______ Why? ____________

____

c. m∠3 = ______ Why? ______________________

d. m∠4 = ______ Why? ______________________

e. m∠5 = ______ Why? ______________________

Puzzle 3 - The 20-Angle Problem

Use your *thinking skills* to find the missing angles. Figures are ***not*** to scale, so do not measure.

Note: **m** ll **n** and **r** ll **s**.

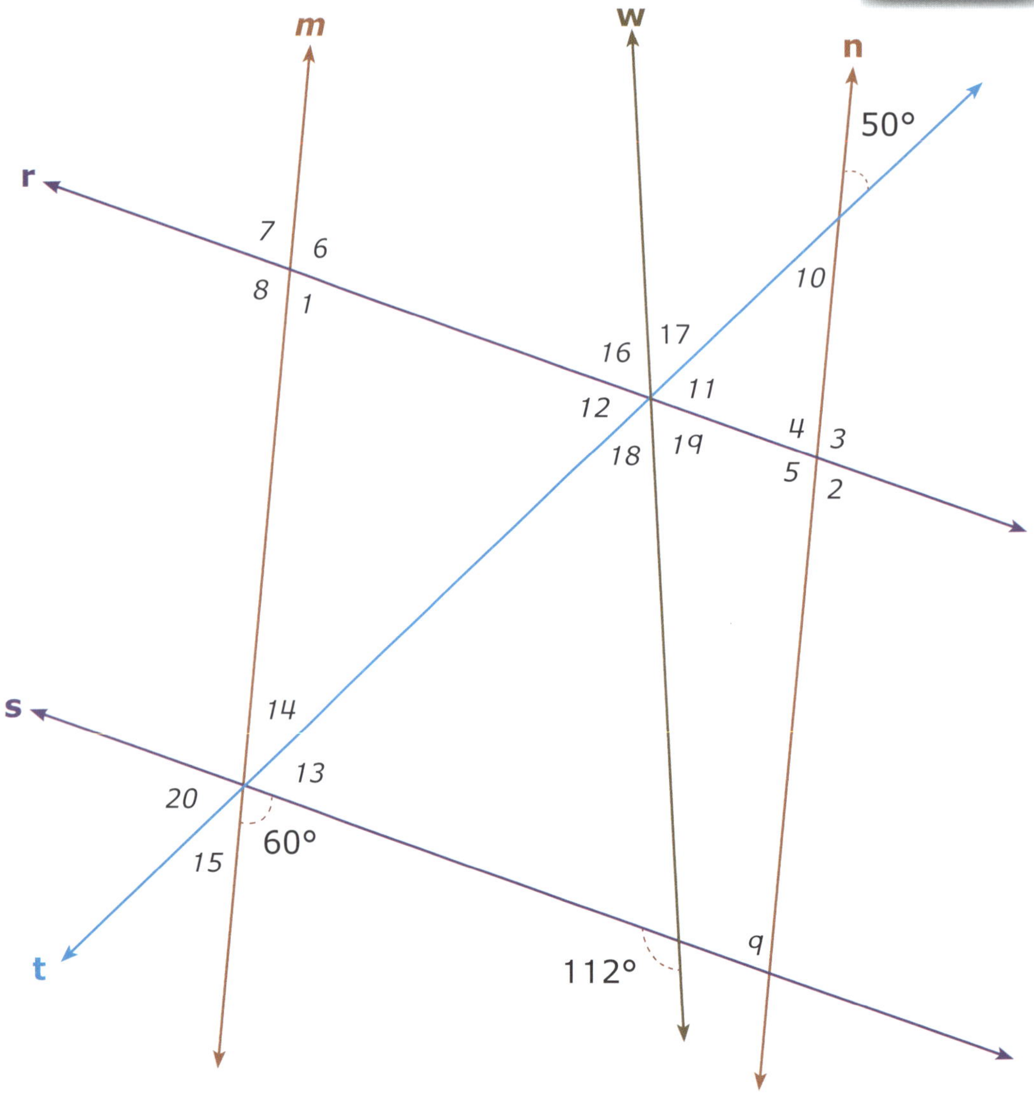

1 ______	2 ______	3 ______	4 ______	5 ______
6 ______	7 ______	8 ______	9 ______	10 ______
11 ______	12 ______	13 ______	14 ______	15 ______
16 ______	17 ______	18 ______	19 ______	20 ______

Chapter 3 - Triangle Properties

Sum of Angle Measures

In any triangle, the sum of the angle measures is 180° as you learned in the previous chapter.

Find the **measure** of the missing *x* angle in these triangles. Try to discover how the exterior *y* angle is related to two of the interior angles of the triangle. Write your answers in each drawing.

Reminder
Figures are ***not*** to scale.

1. 40° 70° $x°$ $y°$
   $m \angle x =$ ______
   $m \angle y =$ ______

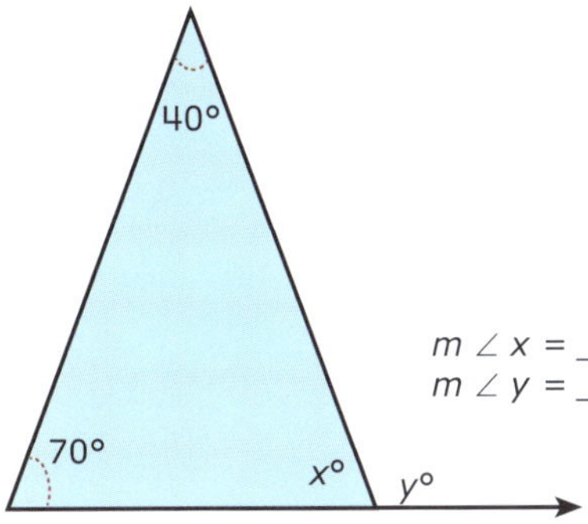

2. $y°$ $x°$ 40° 40°
   $m \angle x =$ ______
   $m \angle y =$ ______

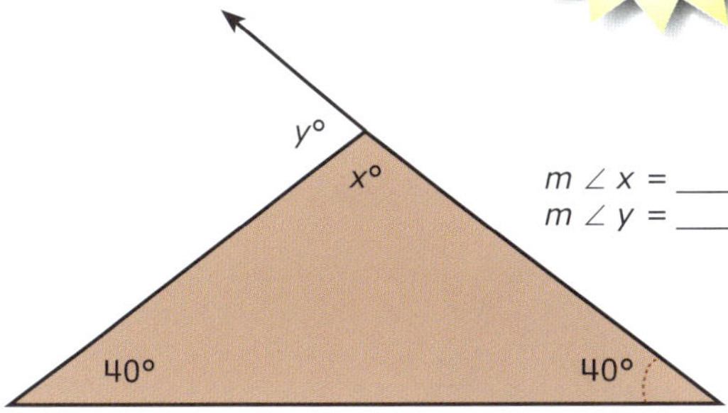

3. 60° $x°$ $y°$
   $m \angle x =$ ______
   $m \angle y =$ ______

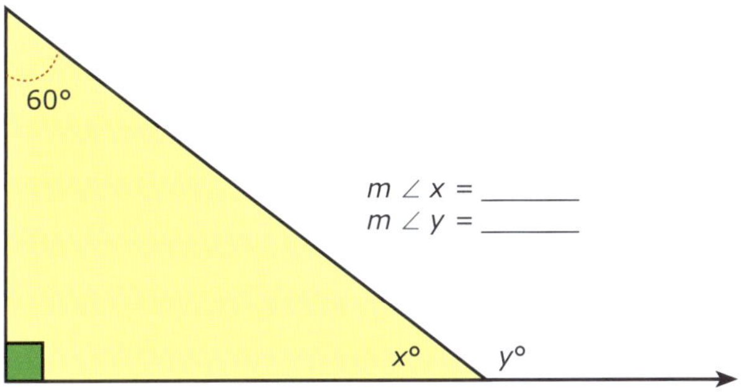

4. $y°$ $x°$ 75° 80°
   $m \angle x =$ ______
   $m \angle y =$ ______

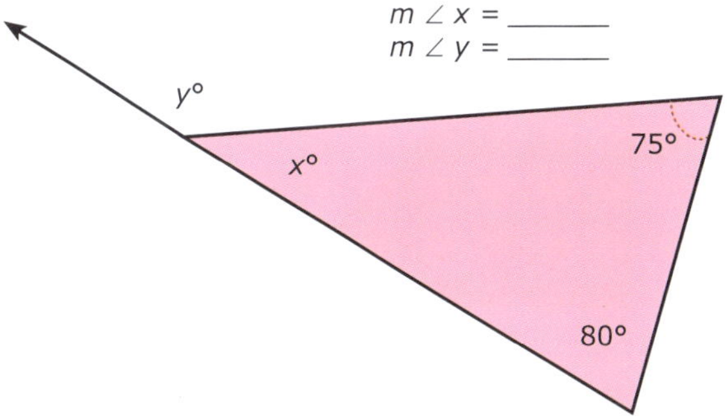

5. 115° $y°$ 70° $x°$
   $m \angle x =$ ______
   $m \angle y =$ ______

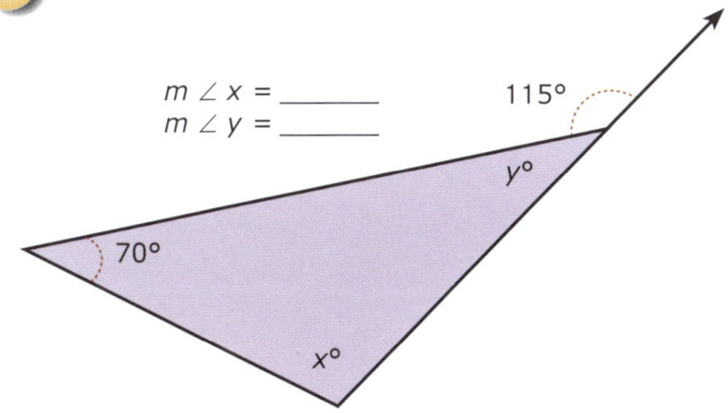

6. 20° $y°$ $x°$ 80°
   $m \angle x =$ ______
   $m \angle y =$ ______

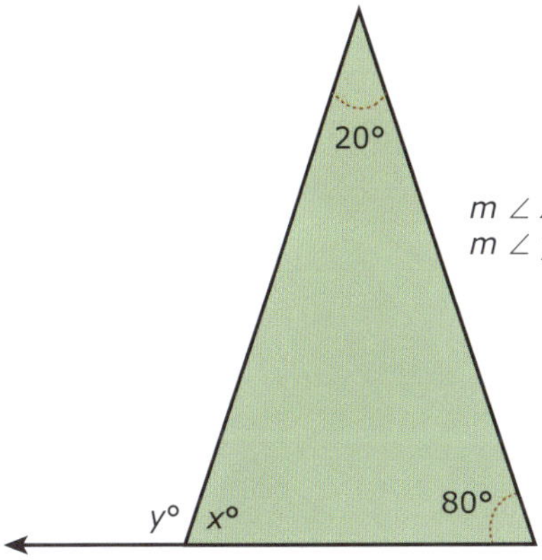

7. What do you discover? Explain your thinking.

____

Exterior Angle Exploration

Triangle Property 1: In any triangle, the sum of the angle measures is 180°.

Triangle Property 2: In any triangle, the exterior angle is equal to the sum of the two remote interior angles.

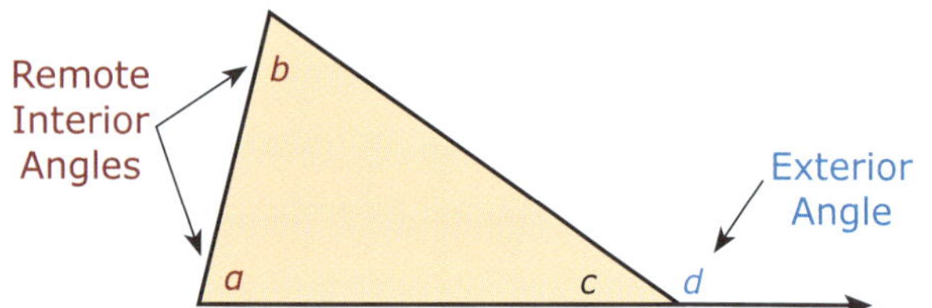

$a + b + c = 180°$

and

$a + b = d$

Use **Property 2** to write an equation for the measure of $\angle x$ in these problems.

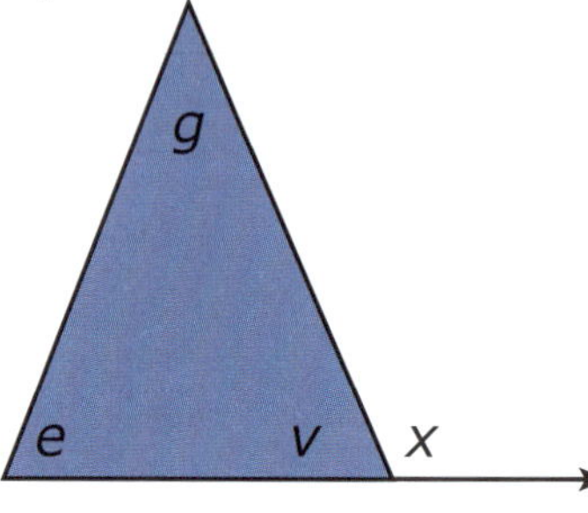

$x =$ g + e

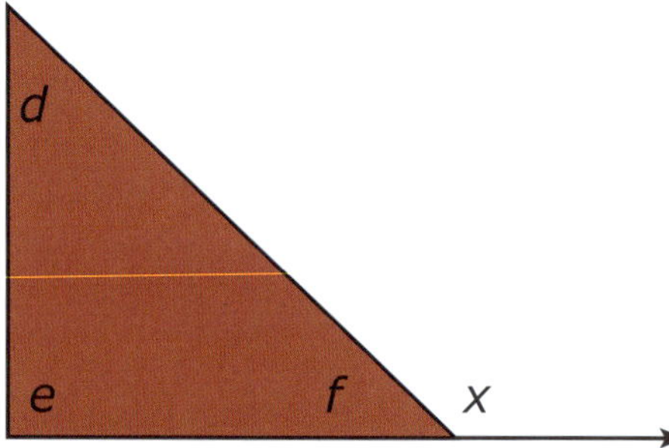

$x =$ ______

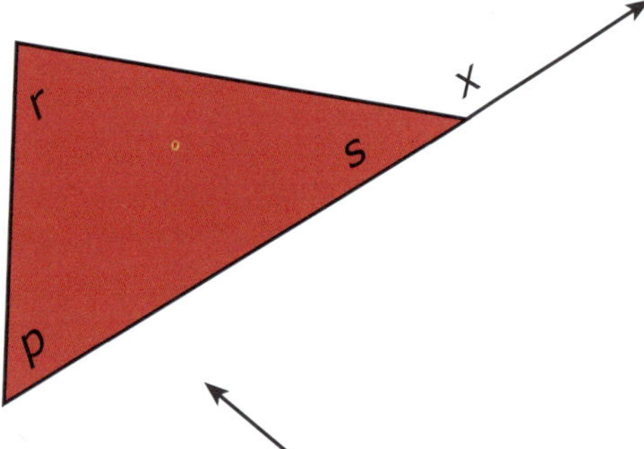

$x =$ ______

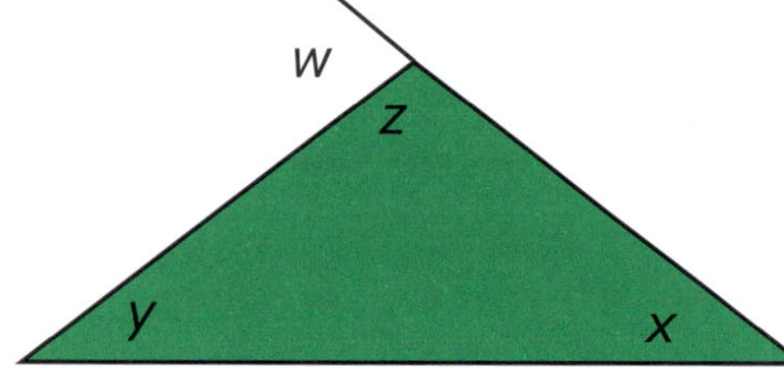

$x =$ ______

Sum of Two Sides

Triangle Property 3: (Triangle Inequality Property) In any triangle, the sum of two sides is ***always*** more than the third side.

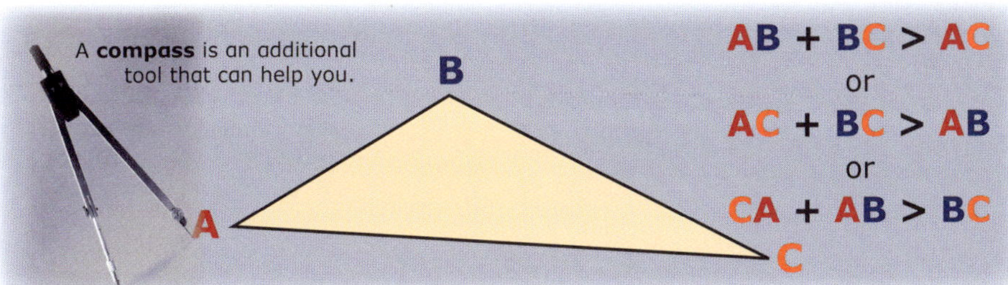

HOW TO REMEMBER

The shortest distance between two points is a **straight line**. To get from **A** to **C**, it is shorter to go straight than to go by way of **B**.

Try to draw Δ**ABC** with these measures, **AB** = 3 in., **BC** = $2\frac{1}{2}$ in., and **AC** = 6 in. Use a ruler.

1. Explain what you discover.

____

____

2. Which side would you change to make it possible to draw Δ**ABC**? Explain your thinking.

____

____

Triangle Properties Practice

Remember
In a triangle, **angles** are measured in degrees. **Sides** are measured in units. Figures are ***not*** to scale.

1. Which of the following sets of triangle measures could be the sides of a triangle?

   A = 7 cm, 6 cm, 15 cm

   B = 1 in., 1 in., 2 in.

   C = 3 in., 4 in., 5 in.

   D = 8 m, 3 m, 15 m

2. Look at Δ**DEF.** Which of the following sides could ***not*** be the measure of $\overline{\textbf{DF}}$?

   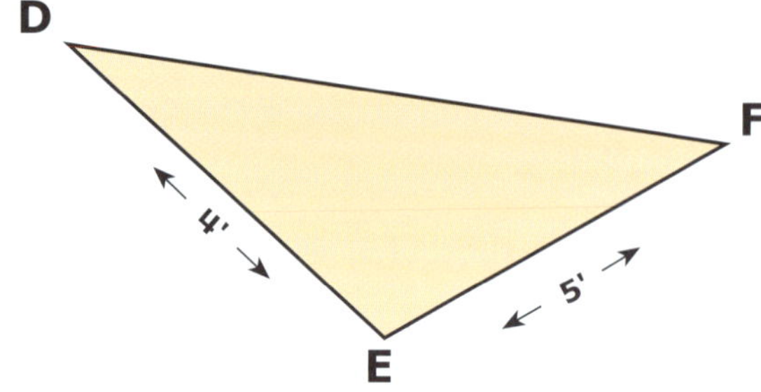

   A = 8 ft

   B = 10 ft

   C = 7 ft

   D = 6 ft

   Explain your thinking. ______________________________

   ____

3. Explain what is wrong with a triangle that has these measures 57 ft, 112 ft, and 54 ft.

   ____

   ____

4. On the triangles below, someone wrote the wrong measures for ∠**E** and for $\overline{\textbf{HT}}$. Write the correct measure for ∠**E** and a possible correct measure for $\overline{\textbf{HT}}$.

   ____

   ____

   ____

   ____

   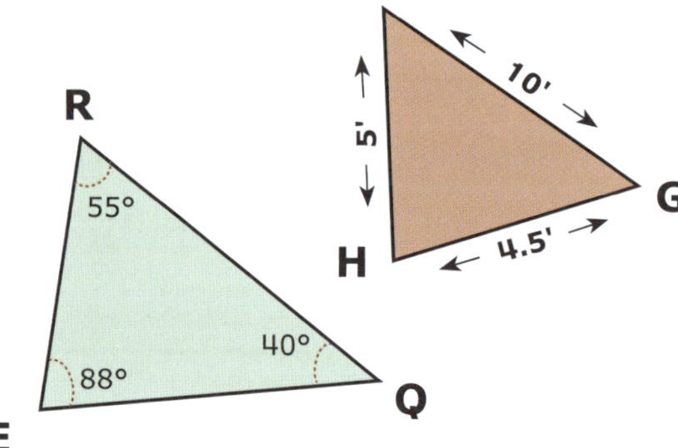

Triangle Opposite Property

Triangle Property 4: In any triangle, the largest angle is ***always*** opposite the largest side, and the smallest angle is ***always*** opposite the smallest side.

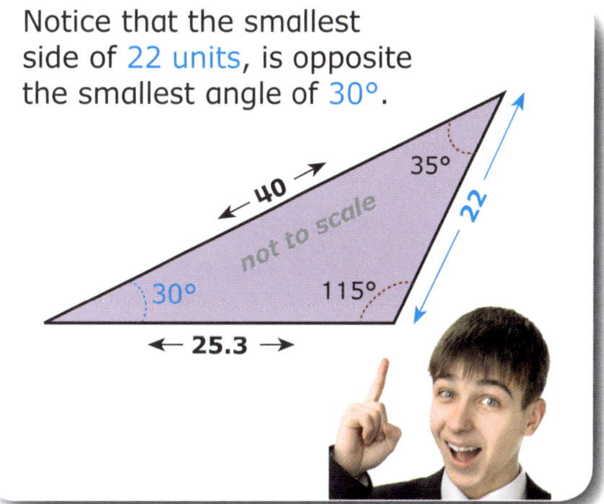

Answer the following questions.

1. The sides of the triangle measure 13.1, 35, and 40 units. Label the triangle with these measures.

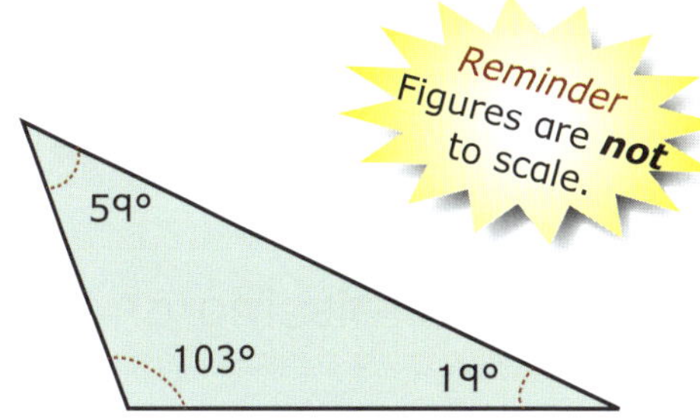

2. The angles of the triangle measure 30°, 60°, and 90°. Use **Property 4** to help you label the triangle with these measures.

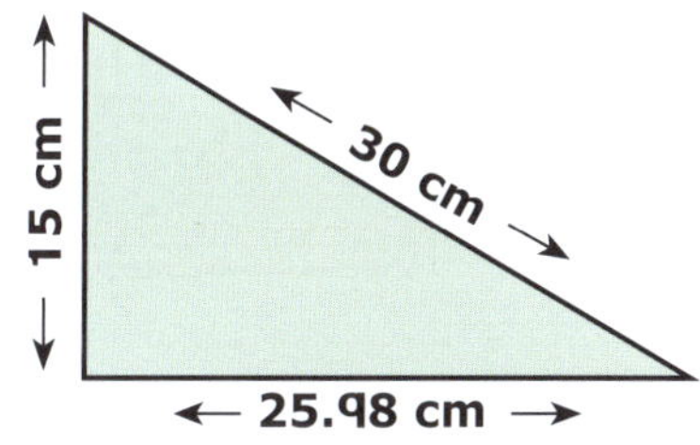

Explain how knowing the measure of the sides helps you find how to label the angles of the triangle.

____

____

3. Look at the angles.

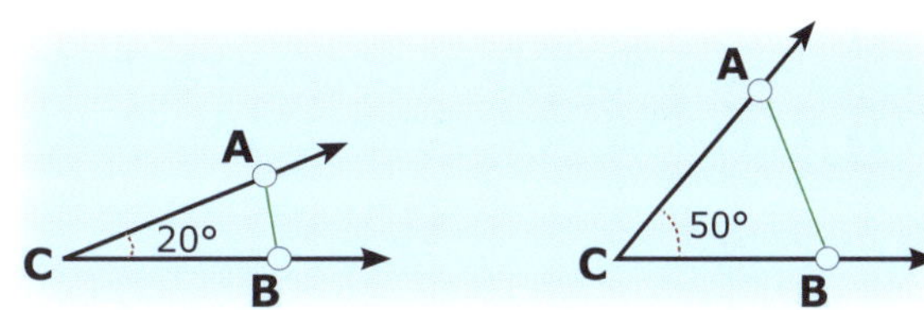

Points **A** and **B** are **equidistant** from **C**. Explain the reason why $\overline{AB}$ in the figure on the left is shorter than $\overline{AB}$ in the figure on the right.

____

____

Properties of Equilateral and Isosceles Triangles

Equilateral triangles have three congruent sides and isosceles triangles have two congruent sides.

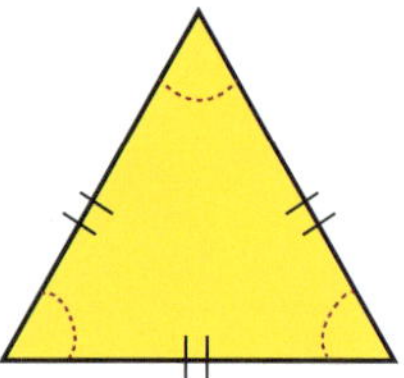

Therefore, every **equilateral** triangle is also an **isosceles** triangle.

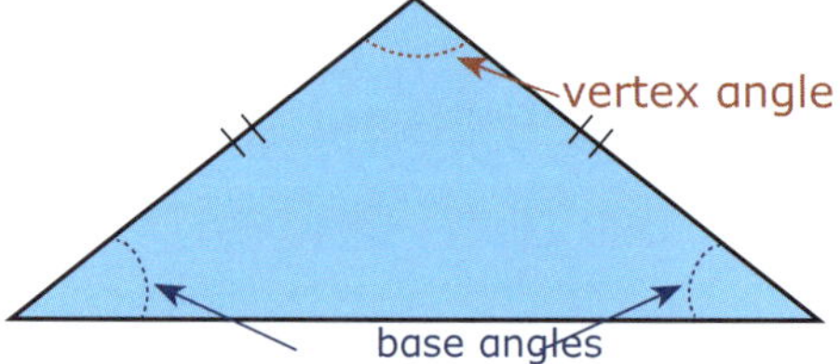

An **equilateral triangle** has three congruent sides and three congruent angles.

An **isosceles triangle** has two congruent sides and two congruent base angles. The base angles are across from the congruent sides. The third angle is called the vertex angle.

Find the missing angles of each of these triangles.

1. 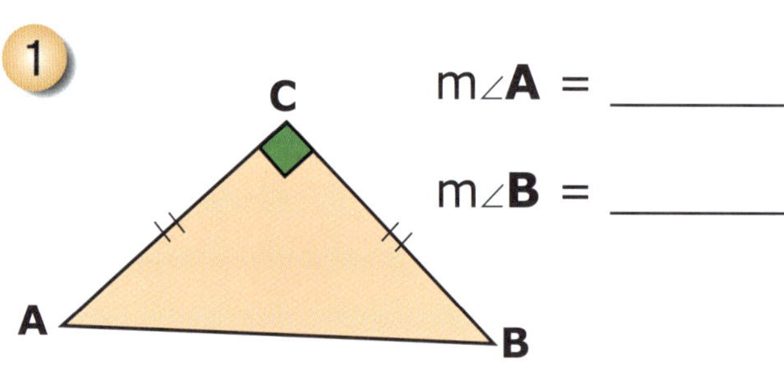

m∠**A** = ______

m∠**B** = ______

2. 

m∠**Q** = ______

m∠**R** = ______

3. 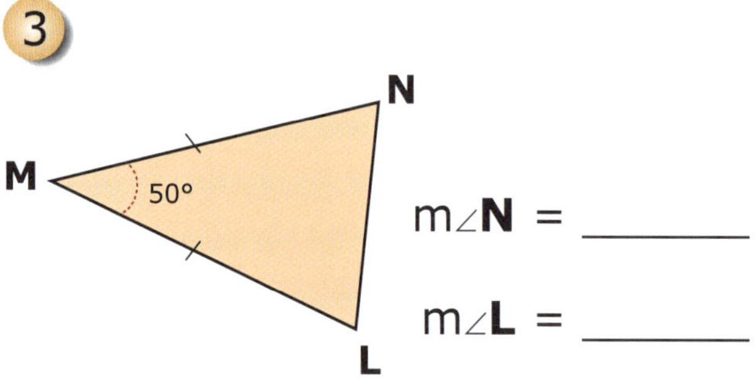

m∠**N** = ______

m∠**L** = ______

4. 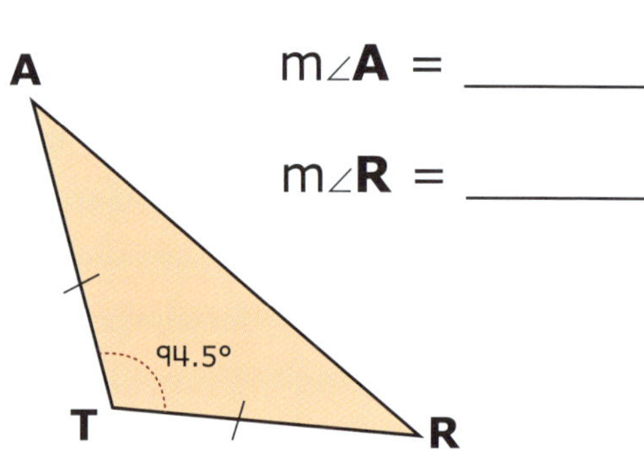

m∠**A** = ______

m∠**R** = ______

5. Label each base angle with a **B** and the vertex angle with a **V**.

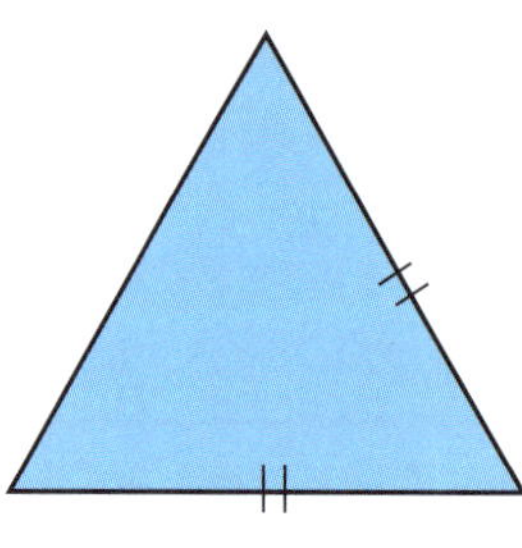

Properties of Equilateral and Isosceles Triangles (Cont.)

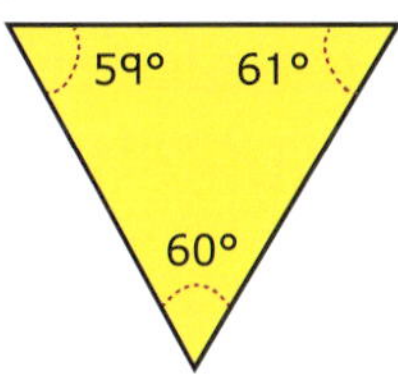

6 Explain why this triangle is not equilateral.

____

7 Can an equilateral triangle be a right triangle? Explain your thinking.

____

____

8 True or False?

_____ a Every equilateral triangle is also equiangular.

_____ b Every isosceles right triangle has 90°, 45°, and 45° for its angle measures.

_____ c If the vertex angle of an isosceles triangle is 120°, then one base angle is 40°.

_____ d Every equilateral triangle is also an acute triangle.

_____ e Every isosceles triangle can be called equilateral.

_____ f If an isosceles triangle has one base angle of 42°, then its vertex angle is 97°.

_____ g Some isosceles triangles have three acute angles.

_____ h If a triangle has two congruent angles, then the triangle is equilateral.

_____ i If a triangle has two congruent angles, then the triangle is isosceles.

_____ j The exterior angle of an equilateral triangle is always 120°.

Algebra and Geometry

Figures **not** to scale.

Use an algebra equation to solve these problems about equilateral and isosceles triangles.

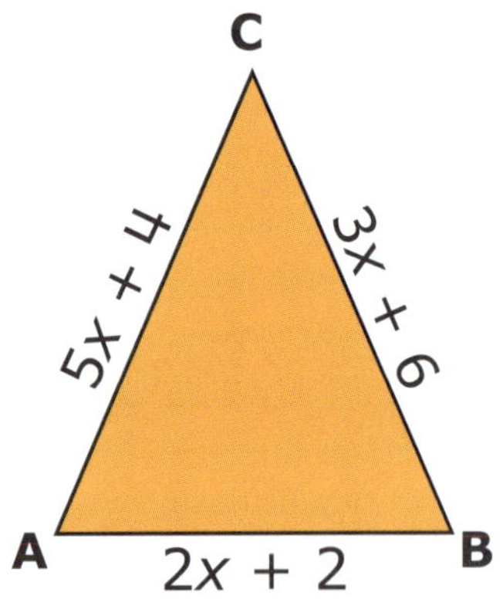

1. If $\angle$**A** $\cong$ $\angle$**B**, find x _______

Equation:

Find each side of the triangle.

AC = _______, **BC** = _______, **AB** = _______

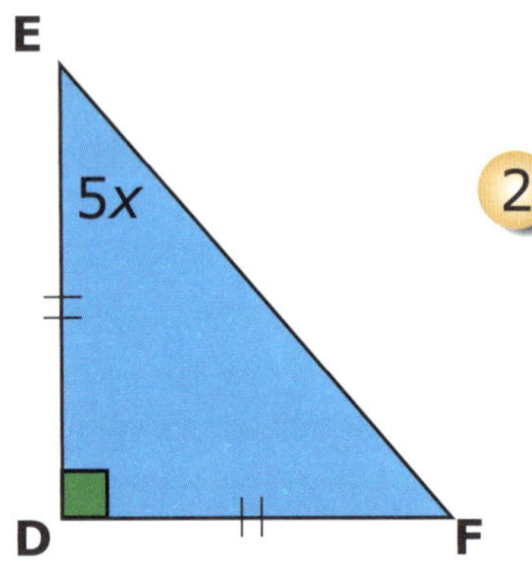

2. Find x _______, m$\angle$**E** _______, m$\angle$**F** _______

Equation:

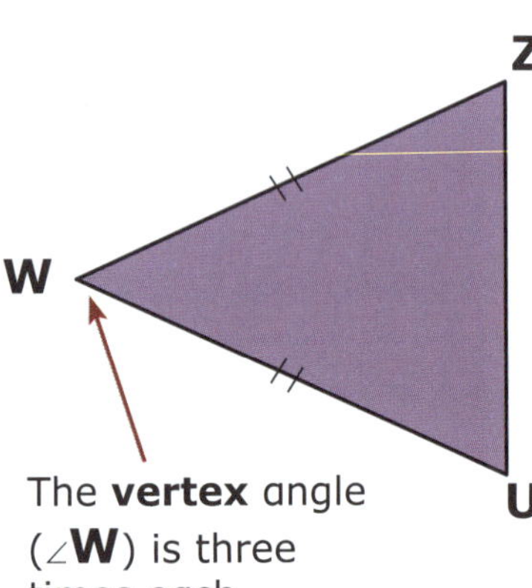

The **vertex** angle ($\angle$**W**) is three times each base angle.

3. If the vertex angle ($\angle$**W**) is three times each base angle, find x _______. Let x represent one of the base angles.

Equation:

Find the angles:

m$\angle$**W** = _______, m$\angle$**Z** = _______, m$\angle$**U** = _______

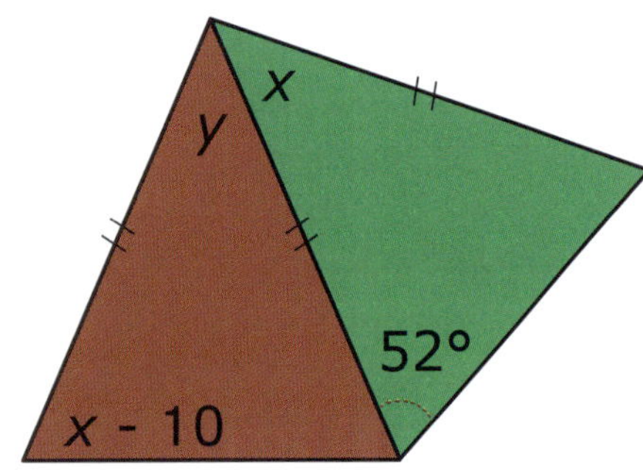

4. Find $\angle x$ and $\angle y$. m$\angle x$ = _______,

m$\angle y$ = _______

Algebra and Geometry (Cont.)

5 Equation:

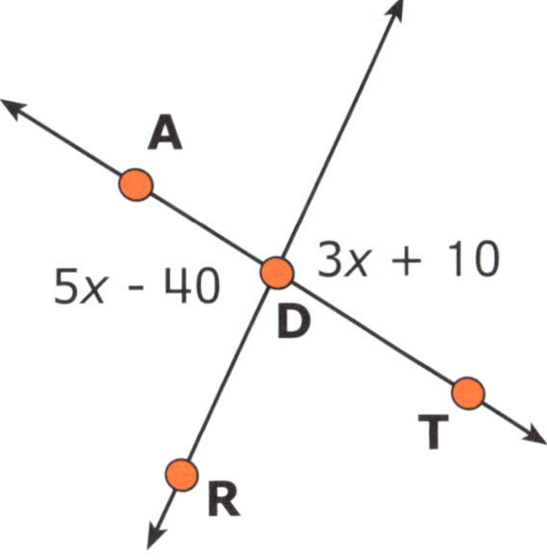

Concept Clue
Vertical angles are congruent.

$x =$ ______

m∠**ADR** = ______, m∠**RDT** = ______

6 Equation:

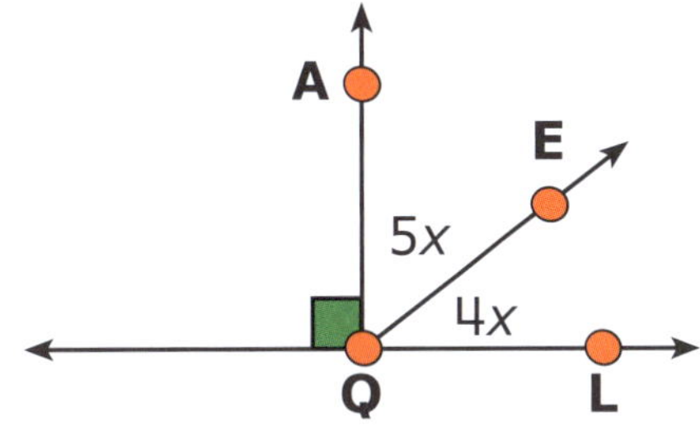

Concept Clue
Complementary angles add up to 90°.

$x =$ ______

m∠**AQE** = ______, m∠**EQL** = ______

7 Equation:

120°

$4x$

Concept Clue
Supplementary angles add up to 180°.

$x =$ ______

8 Equation:

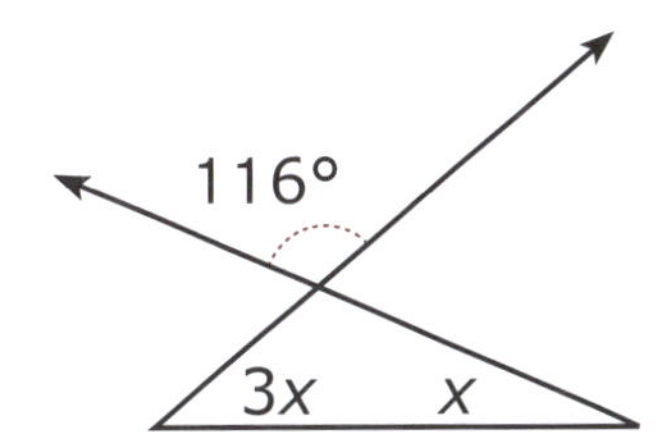

Concept Clue
Vertical angles are congruent. The **sum** of the angle measures in a triangle is 180°.

$x =$ ______

Cumulative Review – Chapters 1-3

Use a separate sheet of paper if needed.

1 What is the best description for the lines shown at right? Explain your thinking.

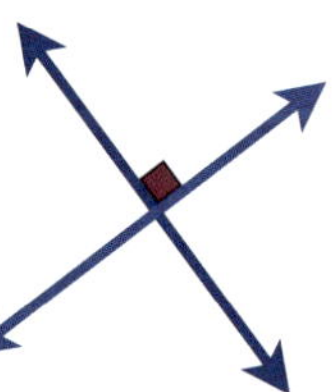

____

2 If m∠**EQR** = 50°, m∠**TCQ** = 135°, and $\overleftrightarrow{AC} \parallel \overleftrightarrow{DE}$, find

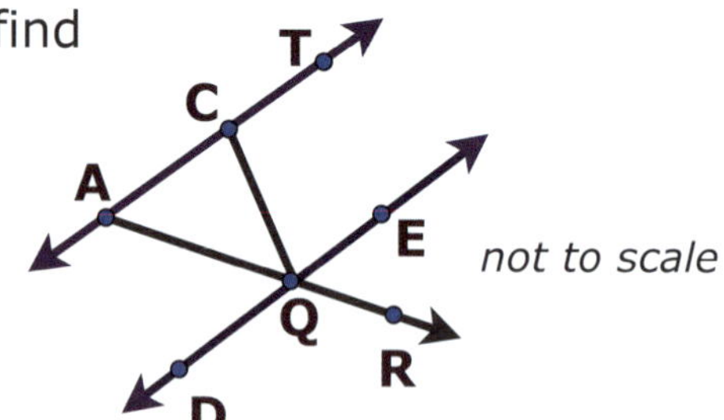

a m∠**CAQ** = _____, b m∠**ACQ** = _____,
c m∠**AQC** = _____, d m∠**DQR** = _____,
e m∠**AQD** = _____, f m∠**CQR** = _____.

3 Complete the chart below.

	Angle	Complement	Supplement
a	30°		
b		25°	
c	*n*		

4 Find *x* or an expression for *x* using your knowledge of the exterior angle property.

a 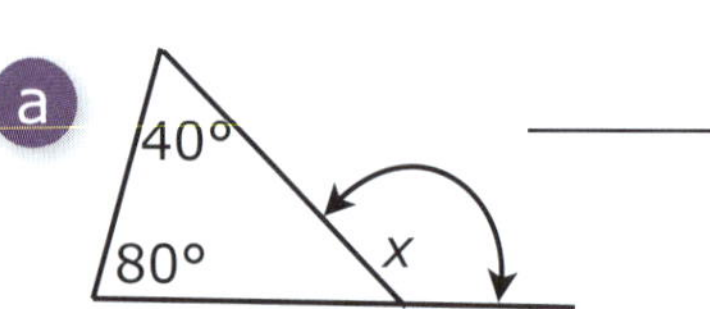

_____

b 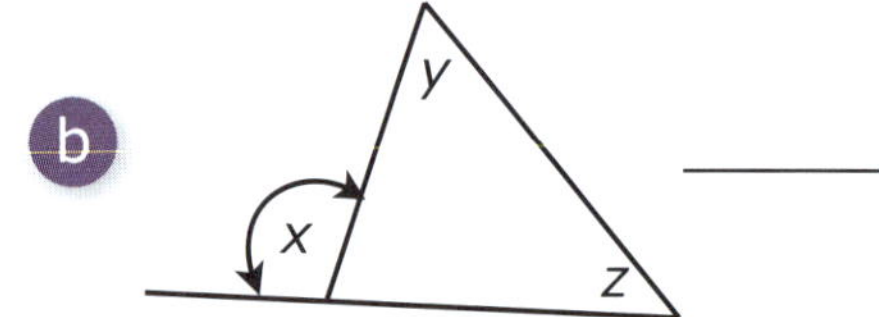

_____

5 Explain what is wrong with these triangles.

a 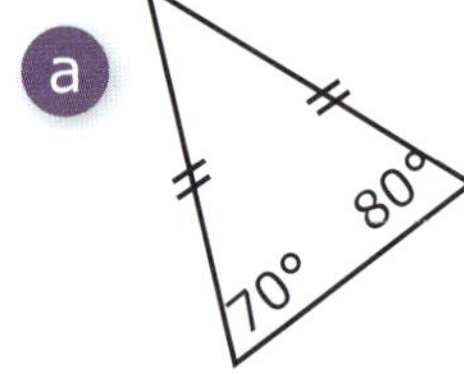

b 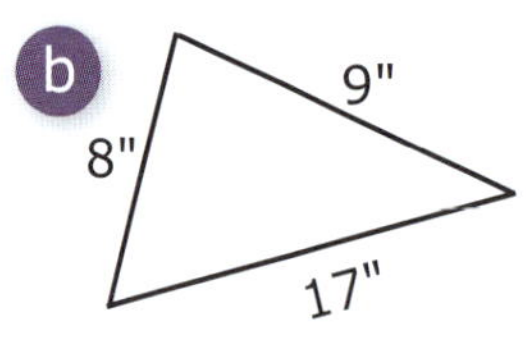

c 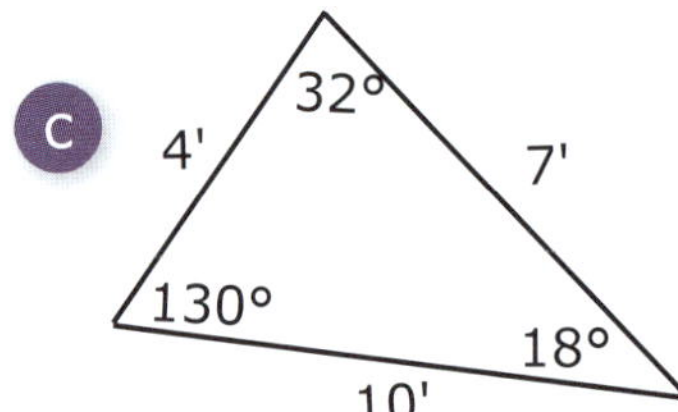

____

____

6 Use algebra to find *x*.

a 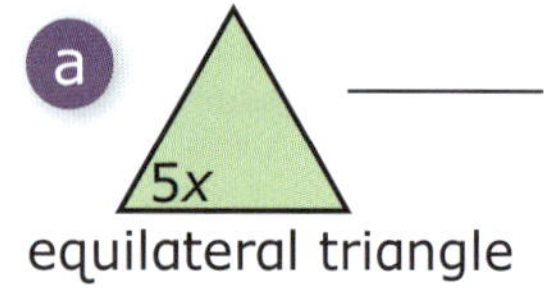

_____

b 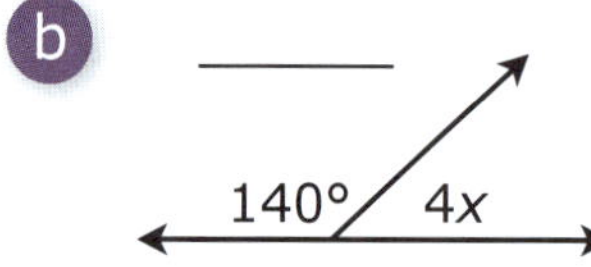

_____

c 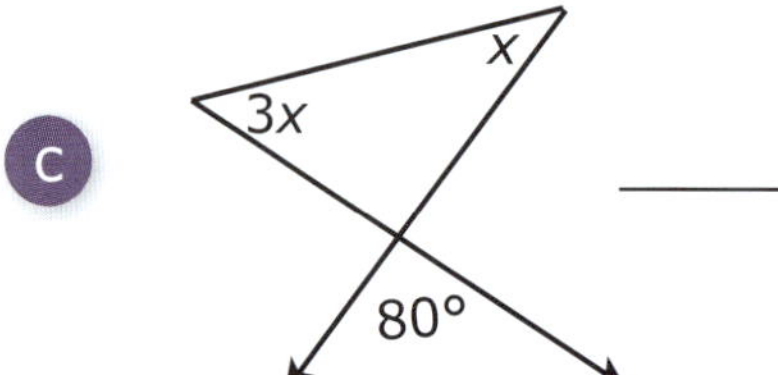

_____

Chapter 4 - The Pythagorean Theorem

Exploration - What Is a Theorem?

A theorem is any property that can be proven to be true. The name of the theorem gives credit to a Greek mathematician named **Pythagoras**, who lived from around 569 BC - 500 BC. He was one of the first to provide a proof, but it's important to know that many civilizations knew the theorem before Pythagoras.

The Pythagorean Theorem helps you find the missing side of a right triangle when you know any of the two other sides. The Pythagorean Theorem ***only*** works with (◢) right triangles.

Use a ruler and make a triangle below with the measures 3 in., 4 in., and 5 in. Then answer the questions below. A compass can also help you.

1. Look at the biggest angle. What do you discover?

____

2. Find $3^2 + 4^2$ _______.

   Does it equal 5^2 _______.

Pythagorean Triples

Any three whole numbers, a, b, c, where $a^2 + b^2 = c^2$, make up a set called a **Pythagorean Triple**. There are an infinite number of Pythagorean Triples.

For example, all the multiples of 3, 4, 5 such as 6, 8, 10 and 9, 12, 15 are Pythagorean Triples, too.

Right triangles whose sides are multiples of 3, 4, 5 are all similar because their corresponding angles are congruent, and their corresponding sides are in the same proportion.

These are the most famous **Pythagorean Triples**

3, 4, 5;

6, 8, 10;

5, 12, 13

In ***any*** right triangle,

$$a^2 + b^2 = c^2$$

a and ***b*** are the **legs** of the right triangle and ***c*** is always the **long side**. The long side opposite the 90° angle is called the **hypotenuse**.

HOW TO REMEMBER Hypotenuse

The word **hypotenuse** comes from the Greek root words ***hypo*** (*under*) and ***tenuse***, *teinein* (*to stretch*). Hypo can remind you of hippopotamus (*large*). For tenuse, think of a wire under tension stretched from the legs of the triangle across from the 90° angle.*

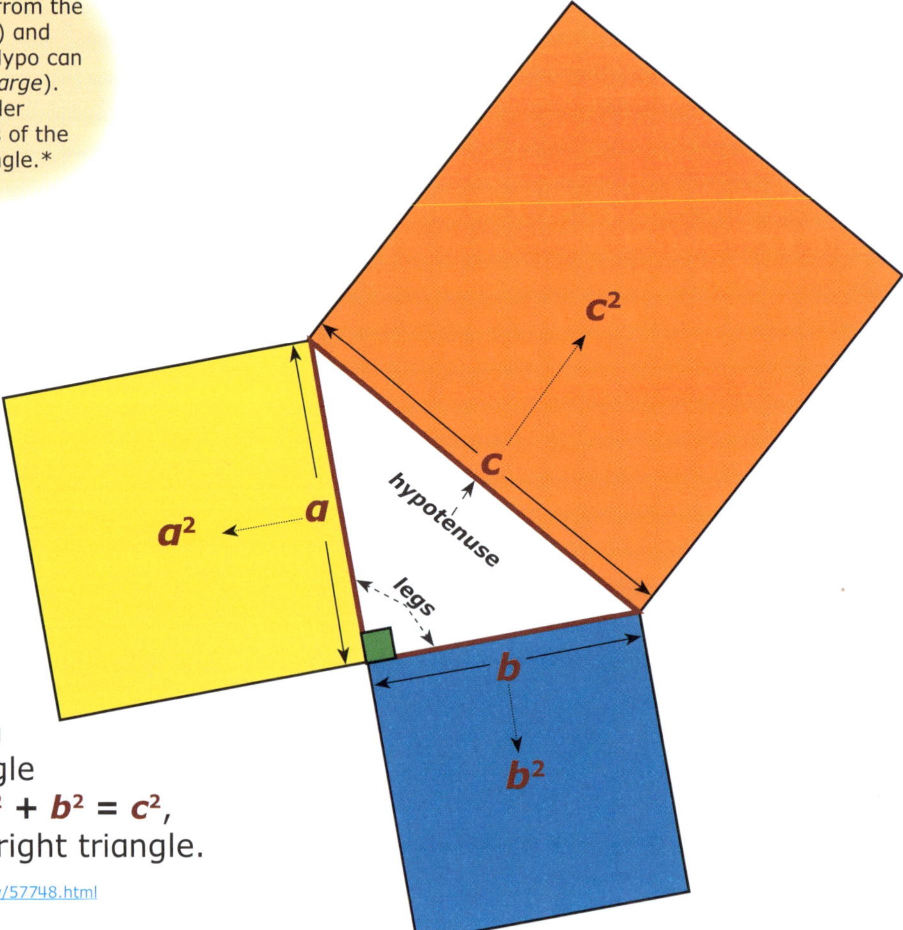

The **converse** of the Pythagorean Theorem is also true. If a triangle has sides such that $a^2 + b^2 = c^2$, then the triangle is a right triangle.

*http://mathforum.org/library/drmath/view/57748.html

Pythagorean Triples Practice

1. Show why 5, 12, 13 is a Pythagorean Triple.

2. Show why 12, 15, 9 is a Pythagorean Triple. Make sure you always let **c** be the largest number.

3. Which of the following is not a Pythagorean Triple? Why?

   a. 7, 24, 25

   b. 1, 2, 3

   c. 4, 5, 3

   d. 12, 35, 37

4. Which of the following is not really a right triangle? Explain your thinking.

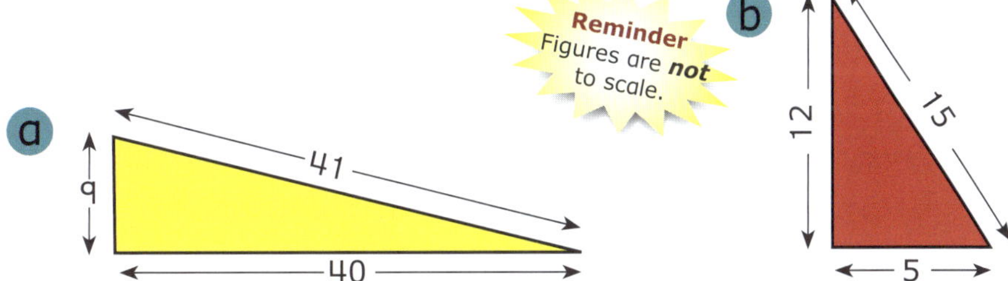

5. One way of generating a Pythagorean Triple is to pick two whole numbers where m is less than n. Then $n^2 - m^2$, $2mn$, and $n^2 + m^2$ will create a triple. Complete the table below.

	n	m	$n^2 - m^2$	$2mn$	$n^2 + m^2$	Is it a Pythagorean Triple?
	2	1	3	4	5	Yes
a	3	2				
b	8	5				

Using the Pythagorean Theorem

To use the Pythagorean Theorem, remember:

1. The theorem ***only*** works for (◢) right triangles.
2. How to find the square root of a number.

   (You may use the square root key $\sqrt{x}$ on your calculator.)
3. Taking the square root of a number is the inverse operation of squaring a number.
4. How to solve a simple algebra equation.

HOW TO REMEMBER

When you're solving an equation with a power of 2, you have two answers. It is called a **quadratic equation**.

In the case of $x^2 = 100$, the answers are -10 or 10.

Since -10 x -10 = 100 and 10 x 10 = 100, only use the positive answer. The side of the triangle cannot be negative.

(Always write the formula.) $a^2 + b^2 = c^2$

(***x*** is the hypotenuse.) $6^2 + 8^2 = x^2$

(Add down.) $36 + 64 = x^2$

(Take the square root of 100.) $100 = x^2$

$10 = x$

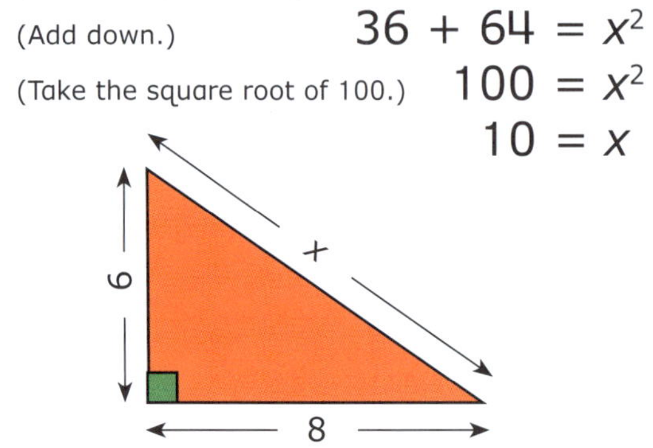

$a^2 + b^2 = c^2$

(***x*** can be ***a*** or ***b***, but 16 must be ***c***.) $4^2 + x^2 = 16^2$

(Subtract 16 from each side.) $16 + x^2 = 256$

$x^2 = 240$

(Round when needed and label.) $x = 15.5$ cm

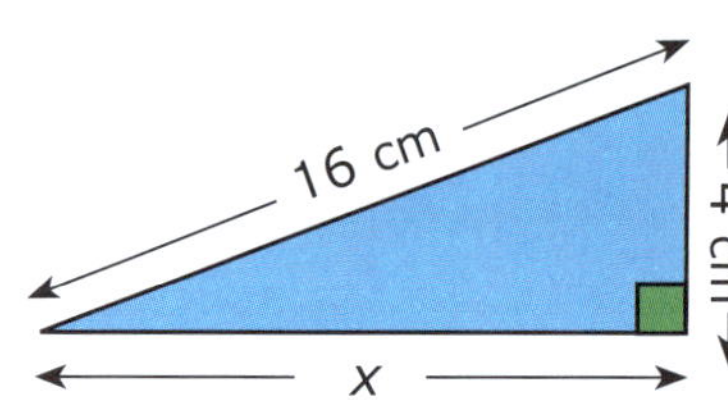

Study the examples above, then find the missing side of these right triangles. Round your answer to the nearest tenth if needed.

1. 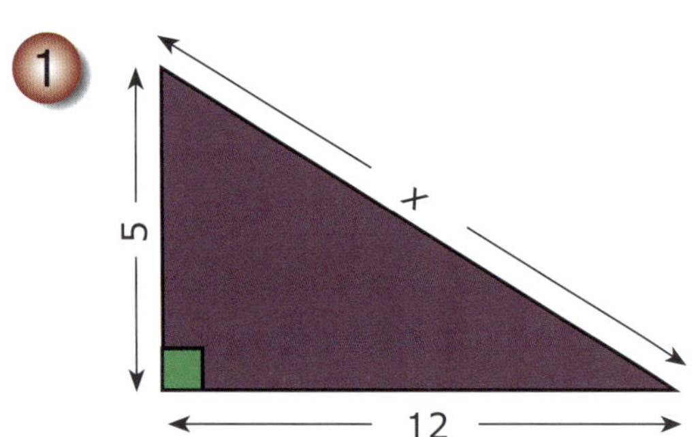

2. 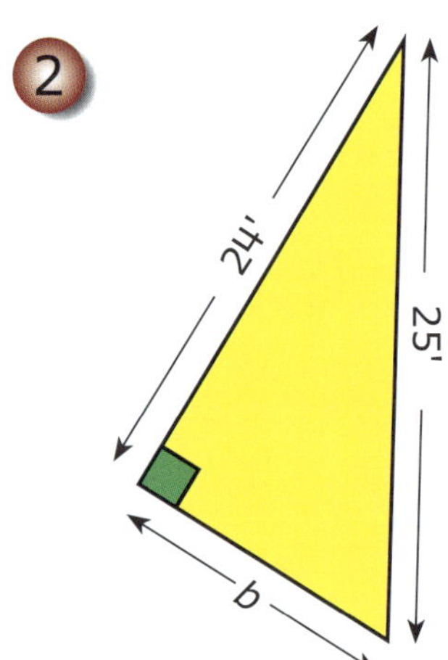

Using the Pythagorean Theorem (Cont.)

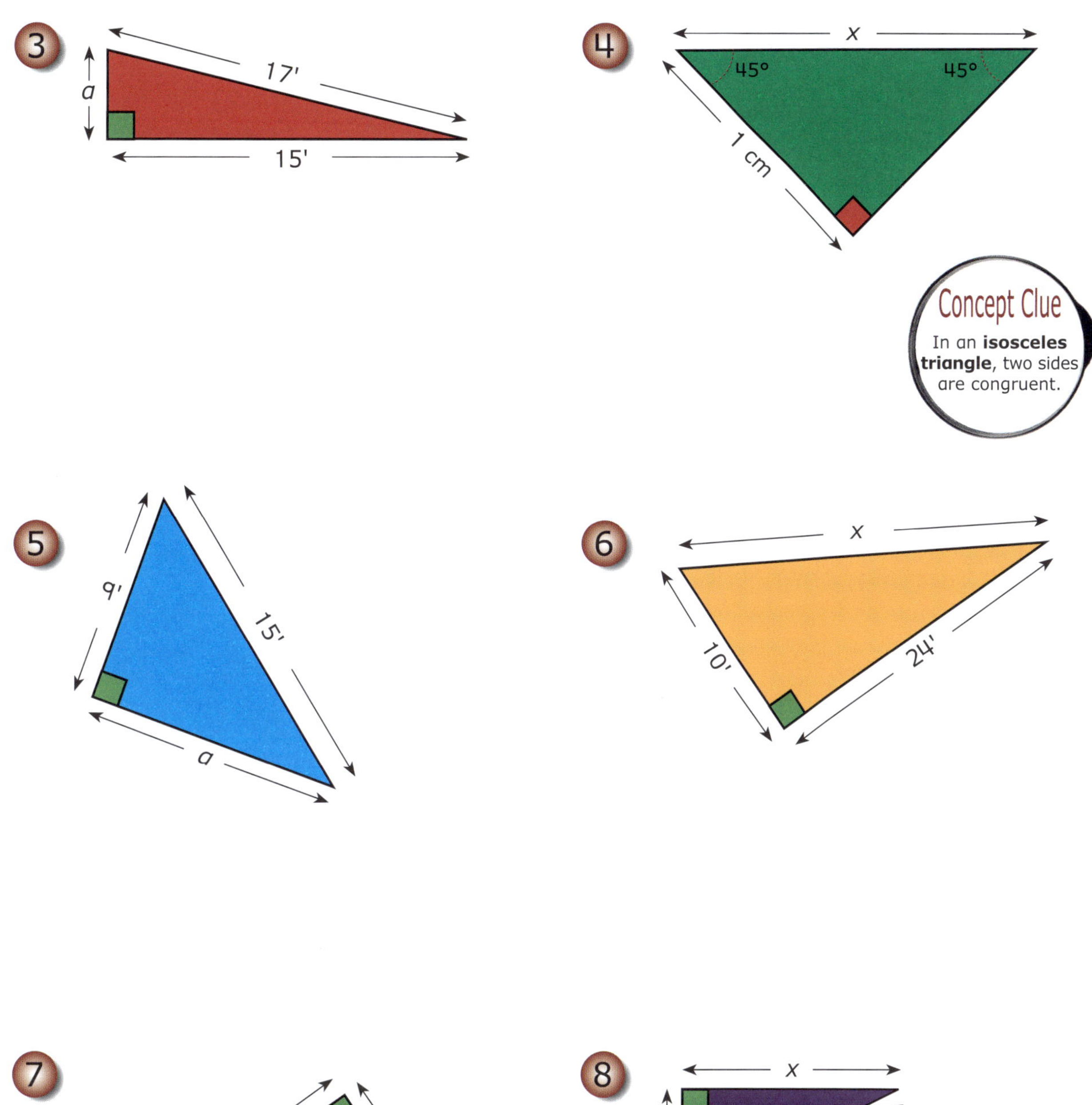

Pythagorean Theorem Applications

The Pythagorean Theorem will help you solve many real life problems. Before you start, here are some problem-solving strategies that will help you.

1. Read and re-read the problem. It helps to read it aloud.
2. Make a drawing even if you are not sure how to start.
3. Think of an easier problem similar to a problem you've solved before.
4. Make sure you know what you are trying to find.
5. When you get your answer, always make sure your answer makes sense.
6. Don't forget to label your answer.

Draw the picture, then solve the problem.

1. Televisions are measured on a diagonal. Leslie's new television is 27 inches. The width of her TV is about 16 inches, find the length of her television. Round your answer to the nearest inch.

2. A baseball diamond is not really a diamond. It is actually a 90 foot square (90 feet on each side). Find the distance from home plate to second base. Round your answer to the nearest tenth of a foot.

Pythagorean Theorem Applications (Cont.)

3. A soccer field at a high school is 100 yards by 60 yards. What is the diagonal measure of this soccer field to the nearest yard?

   a. 80 yards
   b. 160 yards
   c. 116 yards
   d. 117 yards

4. Michael went north 12 miles then east 35 miles. How far is he from his starting point?

5. 

   The front door of a house is 4 feet above the ground. Luis and Enrique have enough wood for a 12-foot ramp. What is the distance from the end of the ramp to the bottom of the door along the ground?

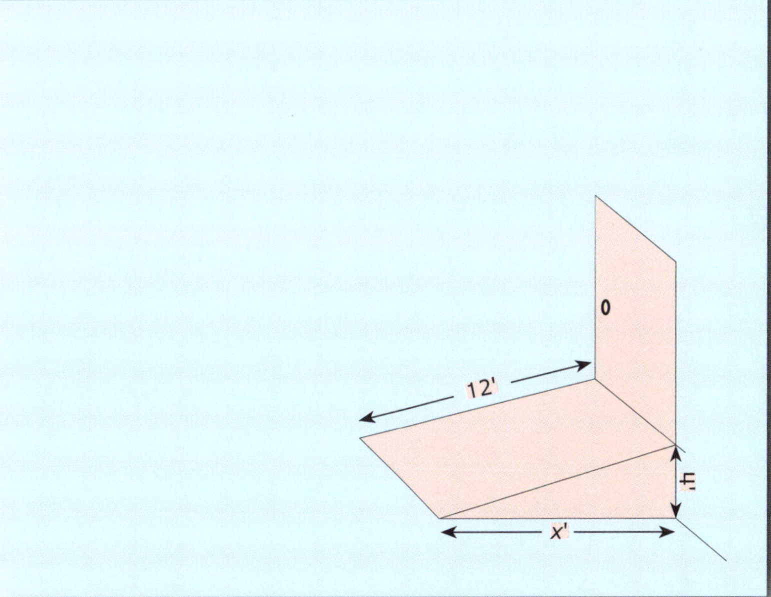

Solving Multi-Step Right Triangle Problems

Use your *thinking skills* to solve the following problems. Review the problem solving strategies from the previous section.

1. Δ**ABC** is isosceles and **CD** = 12 ft. $\overline{\textbf{CD}}$ is the **perpendicular bisector** of $\overline{\textbf{AB}}$. If **AB** = 10 ft, find the perimeter of Δ**ABC**.

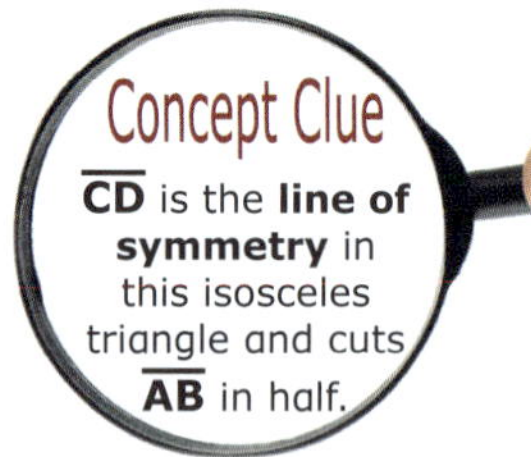

C
A
D
B

2. The diagonal of this rectangular mirror is 10 ft. Its width is 6 ft. Find the area of the mirror.

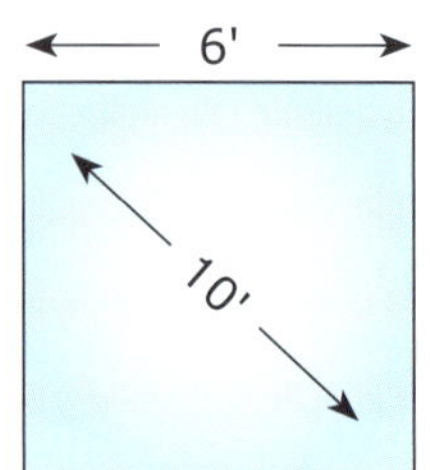

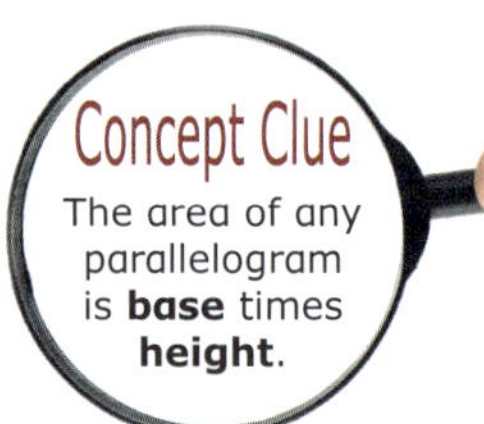

3. Paulo rode his bike 10 miles north, then 5 miles east. He stopped to rest. Then he rode another 5 miles east before turning north and going another 10 miles. About how far is Paulo from his starting point? Round to the nearest tenth of a mile.

   a. 30 miles
   b. 125 miles
   c. 22.4 miles
   d. 21 miles

4. This cube has a side of 8 in. Find the distance from **W** to Z. Round your answer to the nearest inch. Hint: Find **SZ** first.

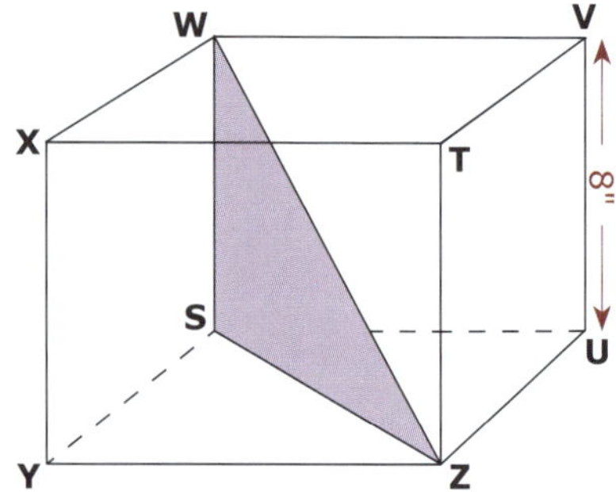

Special Right Triangles - An Introduction

The 45°-45° and 30°-60° right triangles have properties that will provide some handy shortcuts for finding their sides.

In order to understand how to solve right triangles with these measures, you will need to know how to simplify square roots.

Here is a short lesson.

- These are numbers we call **perfect squares**.

  {1, 4, 9, 16, 25, 36, 49, 64, 81,...}

- Whenever any perfect square is under the radical ($\sqrt{x}$), the **square root symbol**, the answer is a whole number.
- You can also simplify a radical by trying to find if the number has a perfect square as a **factor**. For example the factor $\sqrt{64} = 8$.
- To simplify $\sqrt{12} = \sqrt{4} \times \sqrt{3}$, write $\sqrt{12} = 2\sqrt{3}$, since $\sqrt{4} = 2$.

The 45°-45° Right Triangle

In a 45°-45° right triangle, the hypotenuse is ***always*** equal to one leg of the triangle multiplied by $\sqrt{2}$. You can see this by using the Pythagorean Theorem. Suppose one of the legs is 5 units.

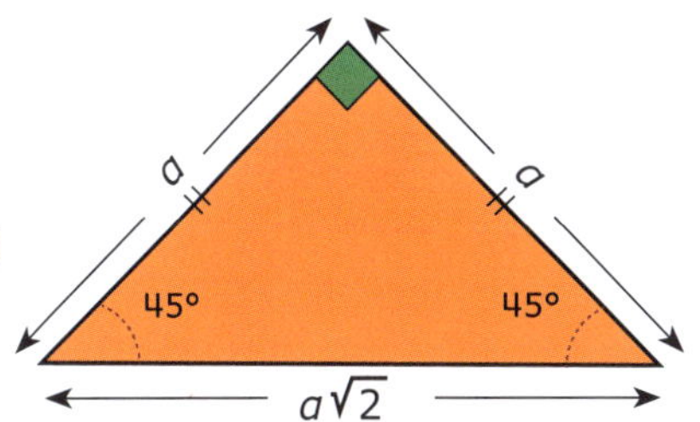

Start with the Pythagorean Theorem:

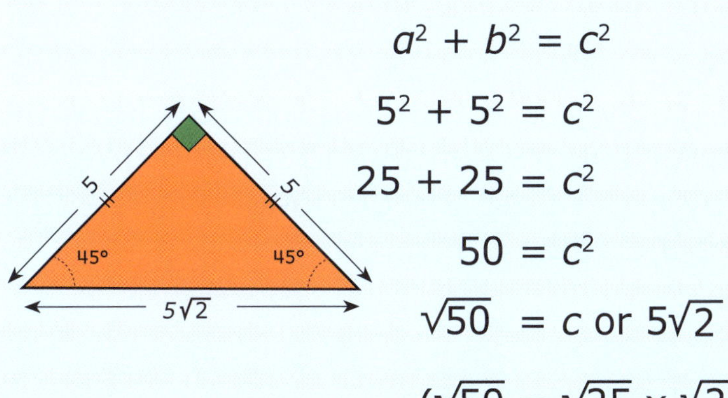

$$a^2 + b^2 = c^2$$

$$5^2 + 5^2 = c^2$$

$$25 + 25 = c^2$$

$$50 = c^2$$

$$\sqrt{50} = c \text{ or } 5\sqrt{2}$$

$$(\sqrt{50} = \sqrt{25} \times \sqrt{2})$$

HOW TO REMEMBER

If you know that one leg of an isosceles triangle is 1, then other leg is also 1, and the hypotenuse would be $1 \times \sqrt{2}$ or $\sqrt{2}$.

Since all isosceles right triangles are similar, this property ***always*** holds true.

Special Right Triangles - An Introduction (Cont.)

Solve the following problems. Use the 45°-45° right triangle shortcut. Unless asked to round, leave your answer in radical form.

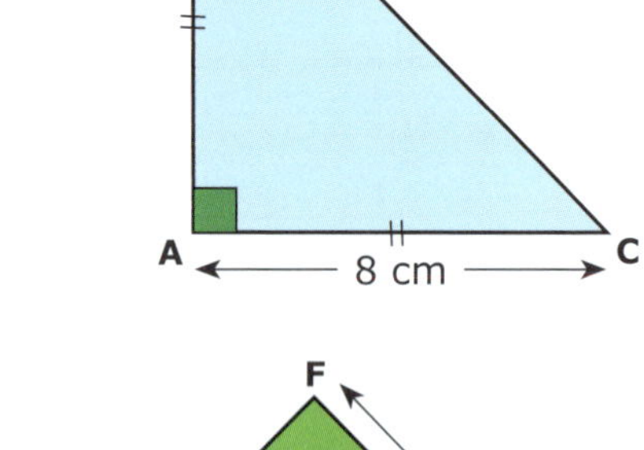

1. **AB** = _______, **BC** = _______

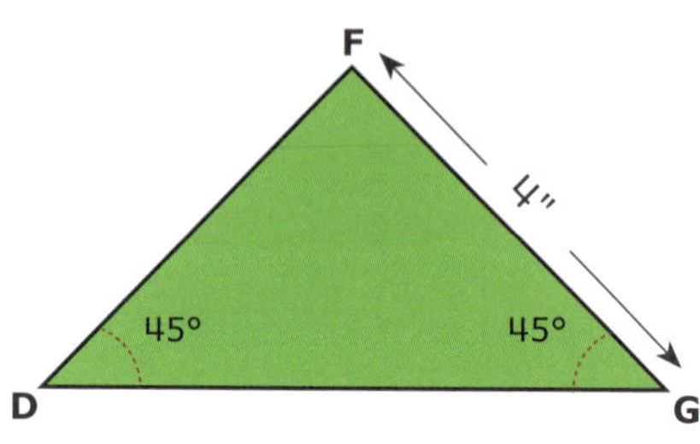

2. **DF** = _______, **DG** = _______

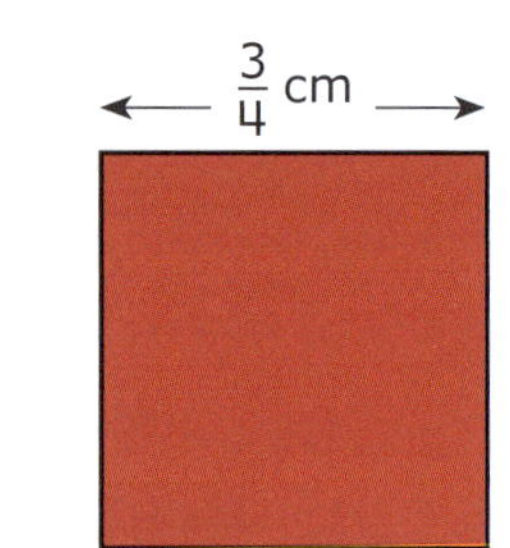

3. The square has a side of $\frac{3}{4}$ cm. Find its diagonal to the nearest tenth of a centimeter. __________

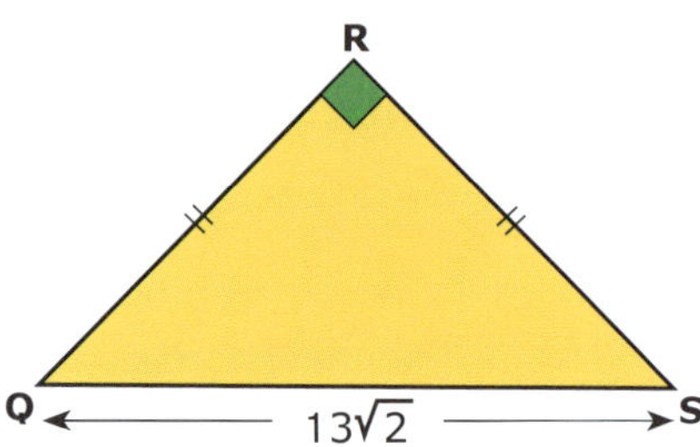

4. **QR** = _______, **RS** = _______

5. 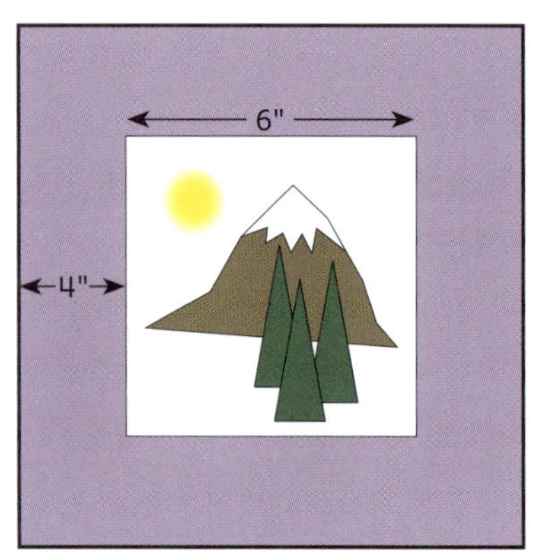

The picture on a wall has a frame 4 in. wide. The inner square containing a photograph is 6 in. by 6 in. Find the diagonal of the entire picture including its frame. __________

Special Right Triangles - An Introduction (Cont.)

It is believed that the Egyptians used their knowledge of the 30°-60° right triangle for land surveying and for building their pyramids.

In a 30°-60° right triangle (30°-60°-90°), the hypotenuse is twice or 2 times the short leg. The middle leg is equal to the short leg times $\sqrt{3}$.

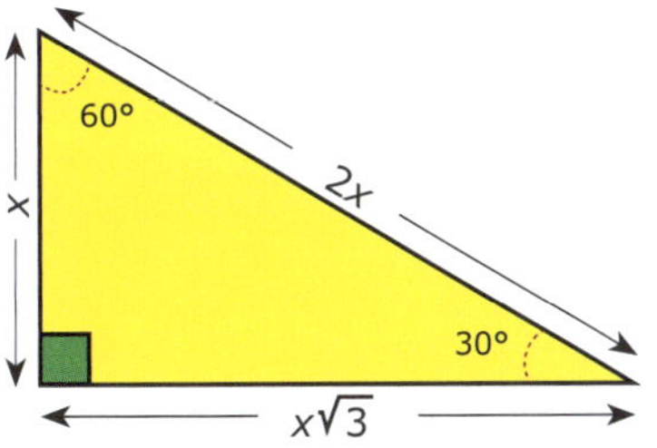

ΔABC below is equilateral because each angle is 60°. If you fold the triangle along its line of symmetry $\overline{\textbf{BD}}$, you will create a 30°-60° right triangle. **AB** is twice **AD**.

Find **BD** by using the Pythagorean Theorem.

Remember
All 30°-60° right triangles are *similar* and their corresponding sides will have this *same* proportion.

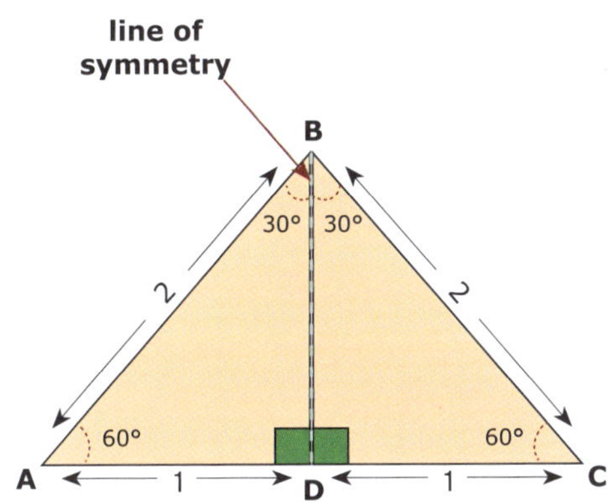

$$a^2 + b^2 = c^2$$
$$AD^2 + BD^2 = AB^2$$
$$1 + BD^2 = 4$$
$$BD^2 = 3 \quad \text{(subtracted 1 from each side)}$$
$$BD = \sqrt{3}$$

For another example, let's find the missing sides of this 30°-60° right triangle.

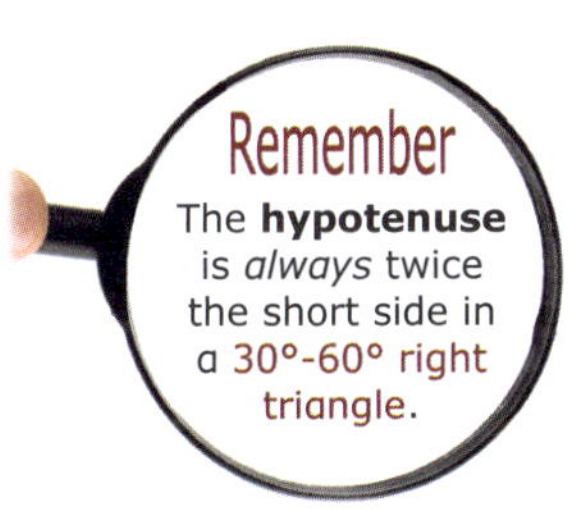

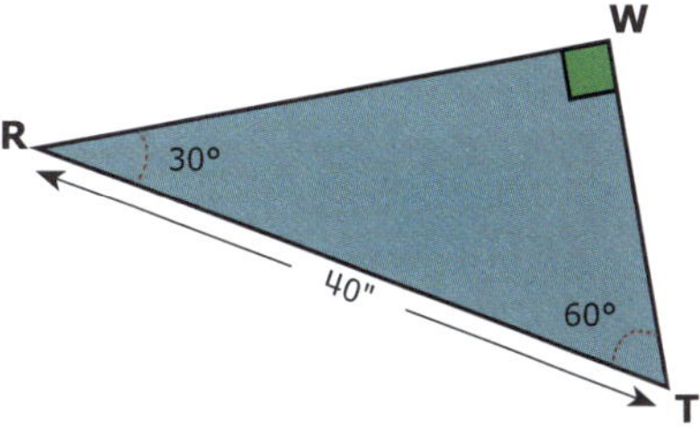

Since the hypotenuse is 40 in., then **WT** = 20 in. and **RW** = $20\sqrt{3}$ in.

Special Right Triangles - An Introduction (Cont.)

Solve the following problems. Use the 30°-60° right triangle (30°-60°-90°) shortcut. Unless asked to round, leave your answer in radical form.

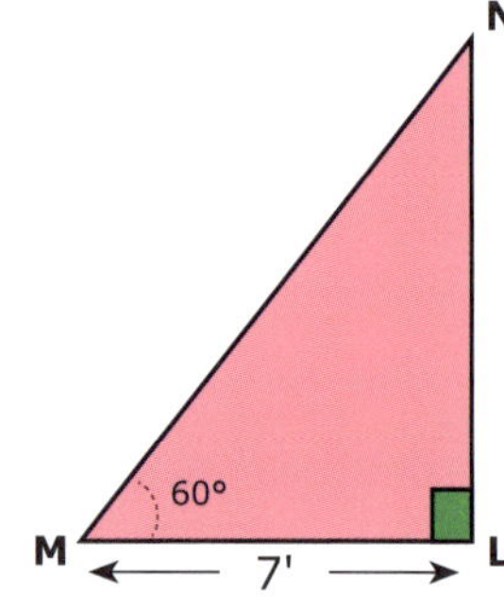

1. **MN** = ______, **LN** = ______

2. **HG** = ______, **GF** = ______
Round your answer to the nearest tenth of a centimeter.

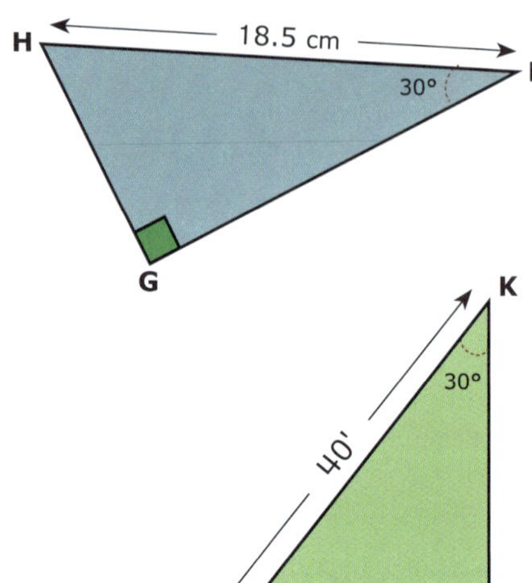

3. **AJ** = ______, **JK** = ______

4. Δ**RED** is equilateral. **DE** = 10 ft.
Find its **altitude** (**EA**).

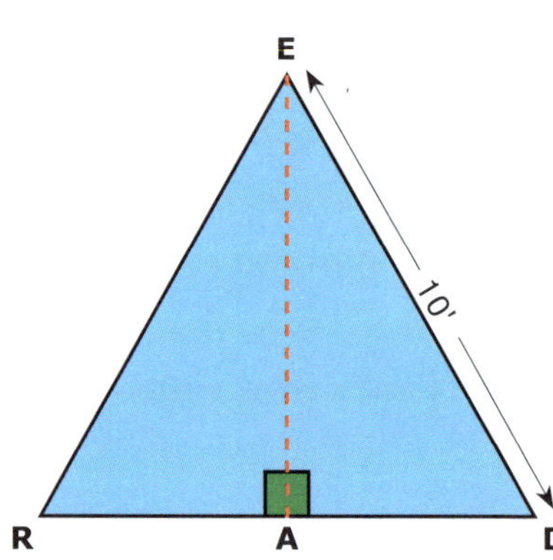

5. Is this a 30°-60° right triangle?
Explain your thinking.

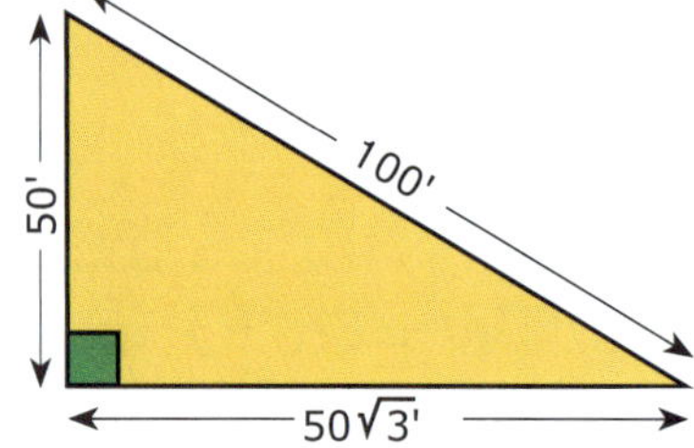

____

____

Review – Chapter 4

Use a separate sheet of paper if needed.

1. Find the missing side of these right triangles by using the Pythagorean Theorem. Round your answer to the nearest tenth.

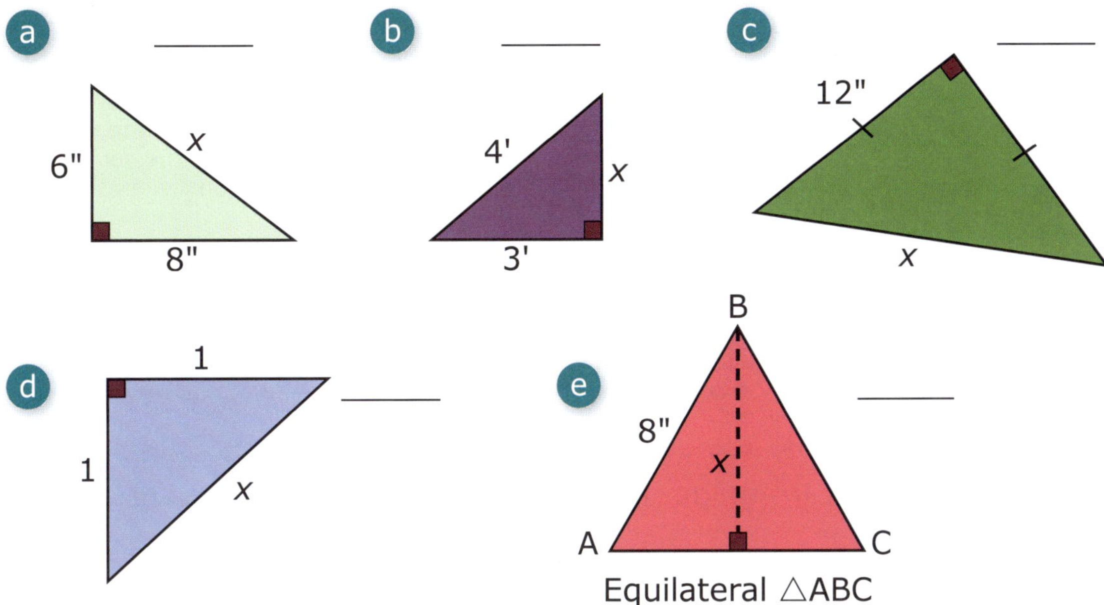

2. Use the 45° - 45° right triangle property to find the missing side x. Leave your answer in simplest radical form.

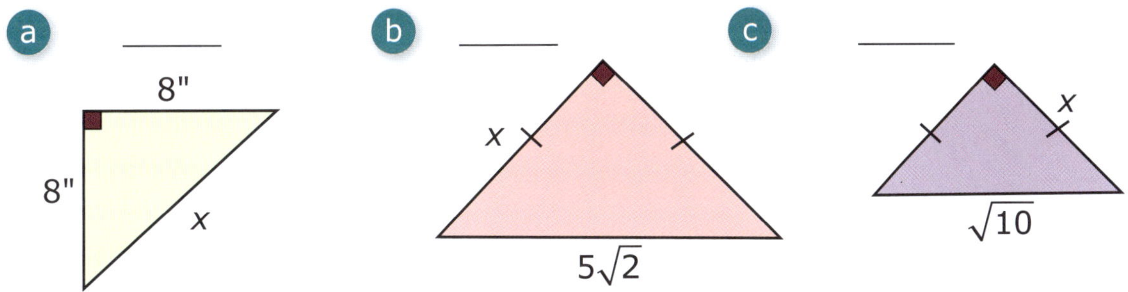

3. Use the 30° - 60° right triangle property to find the missing sides x and y. Leave your answer in simplest radical form.

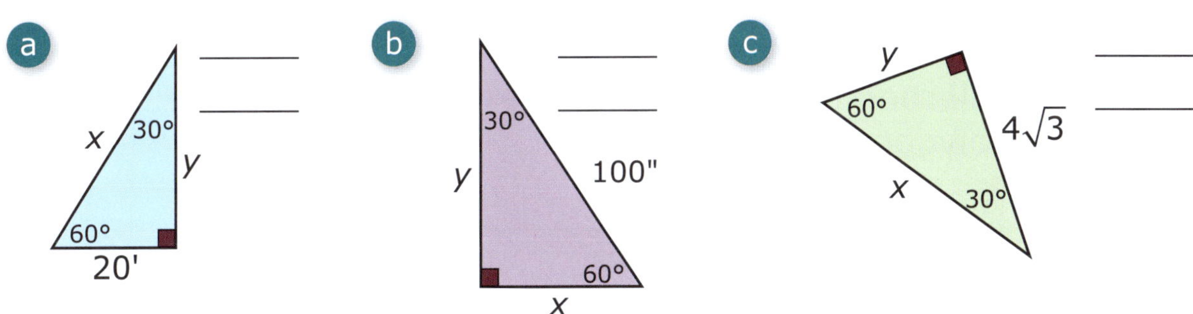

Chapter 5 - Uncovering All Polygons

Polygons - Investigation of Angles and Sides

The **Odeon of Herodes Atticus** is a stone theatre structure located on the south slope of the Acropolis of Athens, Greece.

A polygon is a two-dimensional closed shape with straight sides. Polygons can be convex or concave.

Convex Polygons

Concave Polygons

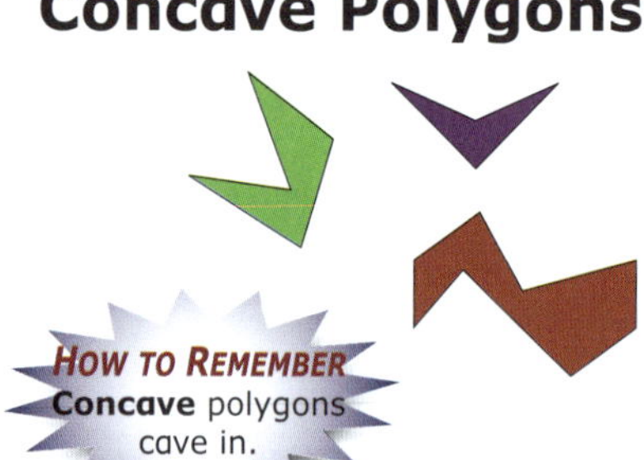

HOW TO REMEMBER
Concave polygons cave in.

The word **polygon** comes from the Greek *polys*, which means many and *gonia*, which means angle.

Polygons can be regular or irregular. Regular polygons have congruent angles and congruent sides.

The outline of the **Pentagon** building in Arlington, Virginia is a regular polygon.

Answer the following questions.

1. What is the most specific name for a regular triangle? ____________________

2. What is the most specific name for a regular quadrilateral? ____________________

3. Why are all rhombuses or rhombi (♦) ***not*** considered regular polygons?

____

____

Polygons Angle Exploration

Polygons are named according to their number of sides.

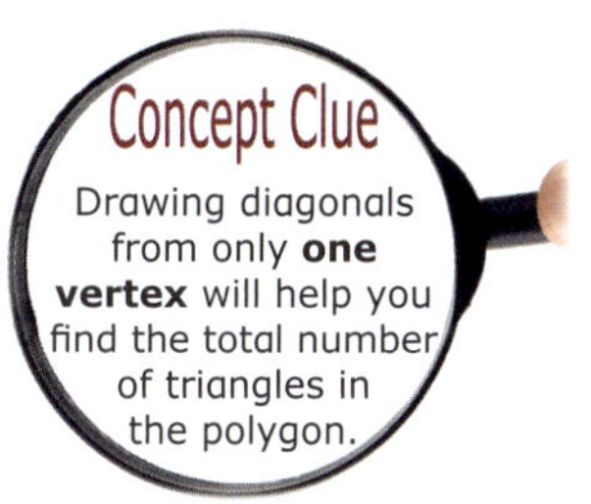

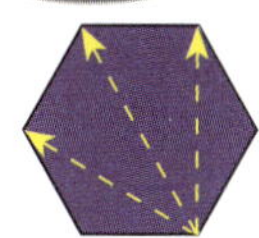

Complete the table below. Use your *thinking skills* to find a pattern for the sum of all the interior angles and the measure of one angle for each of the following regular polygons.

Polygon	Drawing	Number of Sides	Sum of All Interior Angles (Regular or Irregular)	Each Interior Angle (Regular Only)
Triangle		3	180°	60°
Quadrilateral		4	360°	90°
Pentagon		5	540°	
Hexagon				
Heptagon				
Octagon				
Nonagon				
Decagon				

Polygons Angle Exploration (Cont.)

Polygons are named according to their number of sides.

Hint: 3 sides are 1 times 180°, 4 sides are 2 times 180°, 5 sides are 3 times 180°, etc.

In the tables below are names of polygons with more sides. Can you see the naming pattern as the number of sides increase?

Polygon Names	Number of Sides
Hendecagon	11
Dodecagon	12
Triskaidecagon	13
Tetrakaidecagon	14
Pentakaidecagon	15
Hexakaidecagon	16
Heptakaidecagon	17
Octakaidecagon	18
Enneakaidecagon	19

Polygon Names	Number of Sides
Icosagon	20
Triacontagon	30
Tetracontagon	40
Pentacontagon	50
Hexacontagon	60
Heptacontagon	70
Octacontagon	80
Enneacontagon	90
Hectogon	100
Chiliagon	1000

Answer the following questions. Use your *thinking skills*.

1. Find a formula to determine the sum of all the interior angles in any polygon without having to add 180° each time.

____

2. Using the formula you discovered, what is the sum of all the interior angles of a 15-sided polygon? ____________

3. As the number of sides increases what shape is a polygon approaching? ____________

Polygons Angle Exploration (Cont.)

4. Look at the regular octagon below. An exterior angle is indicated by ∠**ABC**. Use your *thinking skills* to answer these questions.

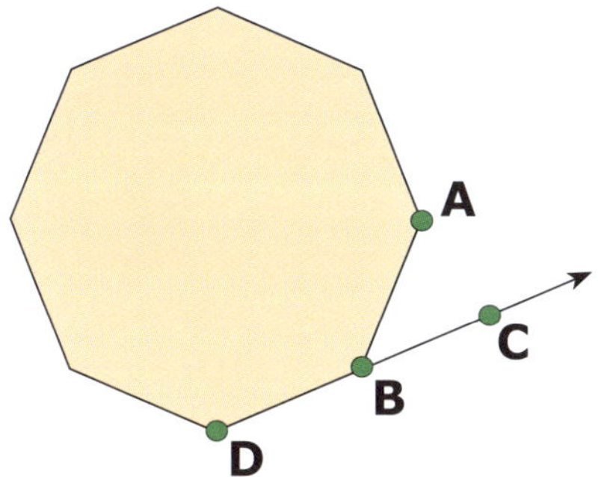

a. An interior angle plus its adjacent exterior angle always add up to ________.

b. m∠**DBA** = ________

c. m∠**ABC** = ________

5. Show that the sum of the measures of all exterior angles of the octagon above adds to 360°.

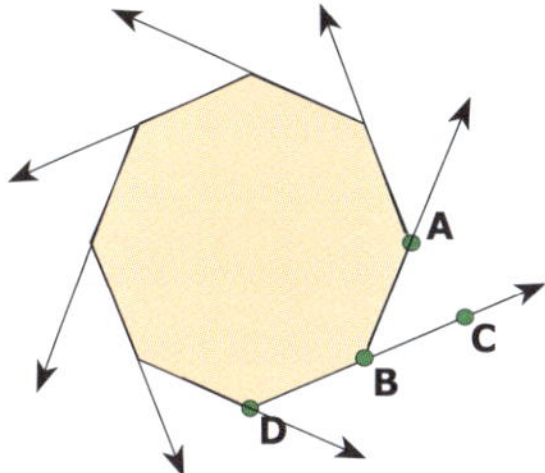

6. Choose a different polygon to show that the sum of the measures of its exterior angles is also 360°. Draw the figure first.

7. If a regular polygon has an exterior angle measure of 72°, how would you find the number of sides in the polygon?

8. Which is bigger, the exterior angle of a hexagon, or the interior angle of an equilateral triangle?

9. What is the sum of the measures of all the interior angles in a chiliagon?

10. What is the measure of one interior angle of a regular chiliagon? Is it approaching a straight line? Explain your thinking.

____

____

Summary of Polygon Properties

- In any polygon, the sum of the measures of all the interior angles is $(n - 2) \cdot 180°$ where $\boldsymbol{n}$ is the number of sides.
- To find the measure of *one* interior angle of a regular polygon use $\frac{(n - 2)180°}{n}$.
- In any polygon, the sum of the measures of all the exterior angles is always 360°.

Hint: To measure the angle in red, you will need to measure the one in blue, then subtract from 360°.

The architecture of a shopping center in Milan, Italy has many different polygons.

You are a Geometry Star!

Remember

Measuring with a tool like this protractor is ***not*** always exact.

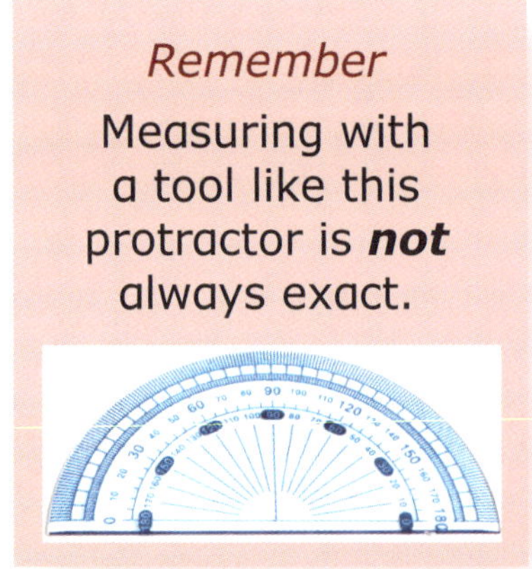

The properties above also apply to concave polygons. Using a *protractor*, measure all the inside angles of this concave decagon and show that the sum of the measures of its interior angles is also 1,440°. Explain your results.

____

____

Diagonal Exploration

A diagonal is a line drawn from one vertex of a polygon to a non-consecutive vertex of the same polygon.

In the chart below are the diagonals of some polygons. If you wish, use coloring pencils to draw your diagonal.

Diagonals form designs often seen in architecture and many forms of art. The beauty of mathematics is that we can find patterns and formulas in these designs.

Polygon	Vertices	Diagonals Drawn From First Vertex	Total Diagonals
Triangle	3	0	0
Square (diagonals drawn)	4	1	2
Pentagon (diagonals drawn)	5	2	5
Hexagon	6	3	

Any vertex of a triangle is consecutive to the next vertex.
A
B
C

Diagonal Exploration (Cont.)

Polygon	Vertices	Diagonals Drawn From First Vertex	Total Diagonals

Diagonal Exploration (Cont.)

1. Fill out the following chart based on what you discovered.

Polygon of *n*-sides	Number of Vertices	Diagonals Drawn From the First Vertex	Total Diagonals Formula
n-gon	*n*		

2. Find the total diagonals of a dodecagon. Try to prove your answer by using the formula you discovered.

3. Find the total diagonals of a 35-gon. The name of a 35-gon is a triacontakaipentagon.

4. How many diagonals in a chiliagon?

5. Let's analyze how the formula $\frac{n(n-3)}{2}$ relates to what is actually happening as you draw the diagonals.

   a. Think of n as the number of vertices or sides. What does the $n - 3$ actually represent as you are drawing the diagonals? Explain your thinking.

   ____

   ____

   b. What does multiplying by n represent as you are drawing?

   ____

   c. What does dividing by 2 represent in the drawing of diagonals?

   ____

   ____

The Handshake Problem

Suppose six people meet at a conference, and they all exchange handshakes. Each person only shakes hands once with another person.

How many handshakes are exchanged? ______________________

Use these people or make your own drawings before you start.

1. Complete the chart below.

Number of People	Number of Handshakes
1	
2	
3	
4	
5	
6	

2. Is there a formula that can represent the number of handshakes exchanged by *n* number of people?

3. How many handshakes are exchanged by 100 people? Use the formula you found to help you.

The Handshake Problem

4. Compare the formula for the number of handshakes with the formula for the diagonals of a polygon. What is the same? What is different?

Diagonals of a Polygon

$$\frac{n(n-3)}{2}$$

Number of Handshakes

$$\frac{n(n-1)}{2}$$

5. If the number of people were points or vertices in a plane, explain why the formula for the handshake problem has $n - 1$ instead of the $n - 3$ found in the diagonals of a polygon formula. Try it with 5 points representing people. Explain your thinking.

Chapter 6 - Quadrilateral and Parallelogram Properties

The Quadrilateral Family

Quadrilaterals or quadrangles are 4-sided polygons. They may be regular or irregular. Think of the quadrilaterals as a family.

Follow the arrows in this concept map and study the definitions. Each quadrilateral keeps the properties or genes of any quadrilaterals above it.

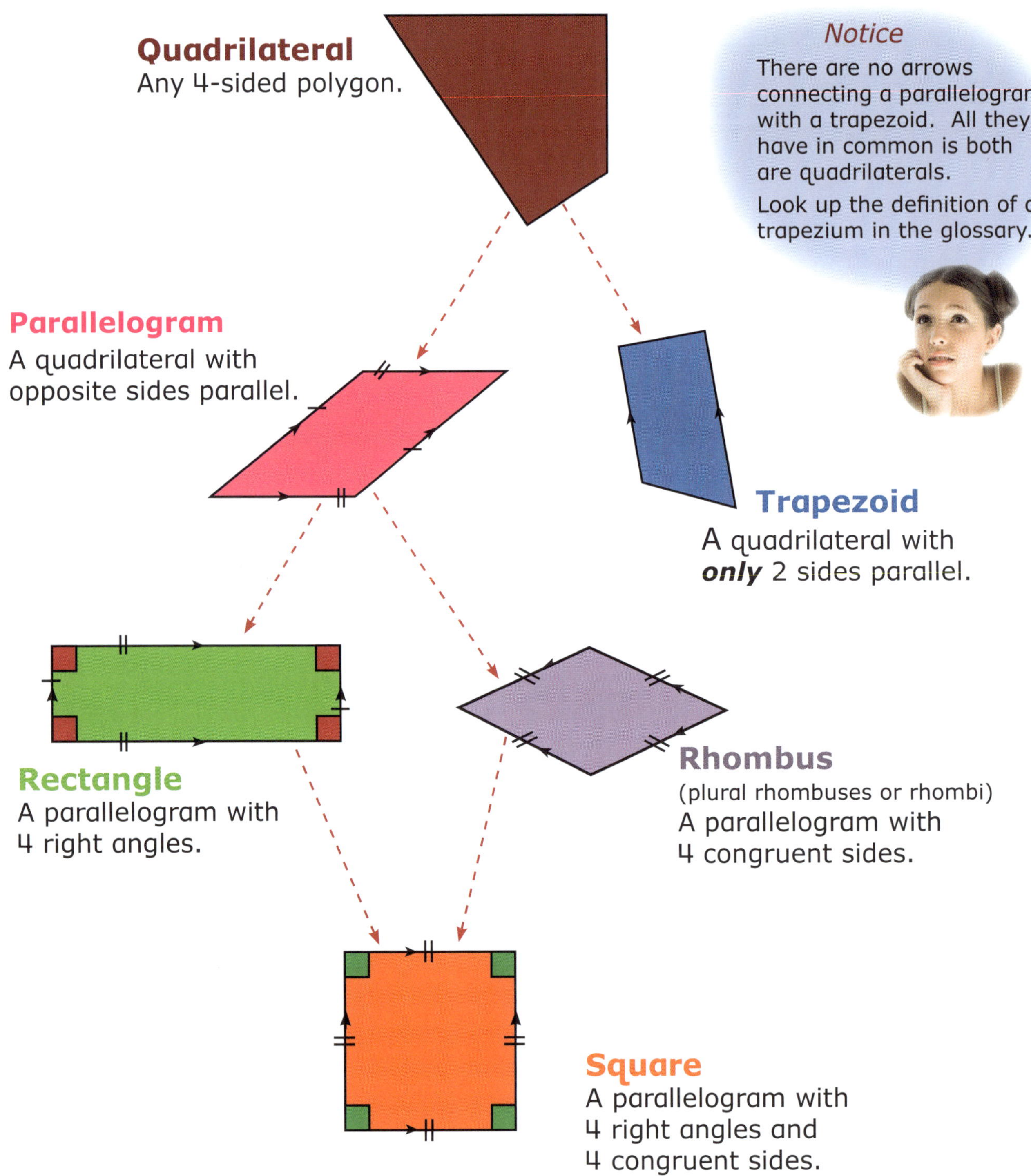

The Quadrilateral Family (Cont.)

Answer the following questions. Refer to the concept map on the previous page to help you.

1. A square can be defined in several ways. Write two more definitions for a square besides the one in the concept map.

   a. A square is a ________________ with four right angles.

   b. A square is a ________________ with four congruent sides.

2. True or False?

   a. ______ A trapezoid is a special kind of parallelogram.

   b. ______ Every square is a rhombus.

   c. ______ Every parallelogram is a rectangle.

   d. ______ Rectangles are also rhombuses.

   e. ______ Every square is a rectangle.

   f. ______ A rectangle is an equiangular quadrilateral.

   g. ______ Some rhombuses are squares.

   h. ______ Every quadrilateral is either a parallelogram or a trapezoid.

   i. ______ Some parallelograms are squares.

The Quadrilateral Family (Cont.)

j. ______ If one of the properties of a parallelogram is that its diagonals bisect each other (cut each other in halves), then the rectangle, the rhombus, and the square would have the same property.

k. ______ In any quadrilateral, the sum of all the angle measures is 360°.

3. Use Always (**A**), Sometimes (**S**), Never (**N**) next to each of the statements about quadrilaterals. Refer to the concept map on page 54 to help you.

a. ______ Quadrilaterals are polygons.

b. ______ Trapezoids are parallelograms.

c. ______ Opposite sides of a parallelogram are parallel.

d. ______ Rhombuses are squares.

e. ______ Squares are rectangles.

f. ______ Rectangles are squares.

g. ______ Squares are quadrilaterals.

h. ______ Rectangles are polygons.

i. ______ Parallelograms are squares.

j. ______ A diagonal of a parallelogram separates the parallelogram into two congruent triangles.

Venn Diagram Activity

Cut out the set of figures below and make a Venn diagram showing how they are all related.

Quadrilaterals	Polygons	Trapezoids
Squares	Parallelograms	Rectangles
Triangles	Hexagons	Rhombuses
	Pentagons	

Parallelogram Discovery

Using a ruler and a protractor, measure all the angles and all the sides of parallelogram **ABCD,** then write down what you discover. The arrows mean the opposite sides are parallel.

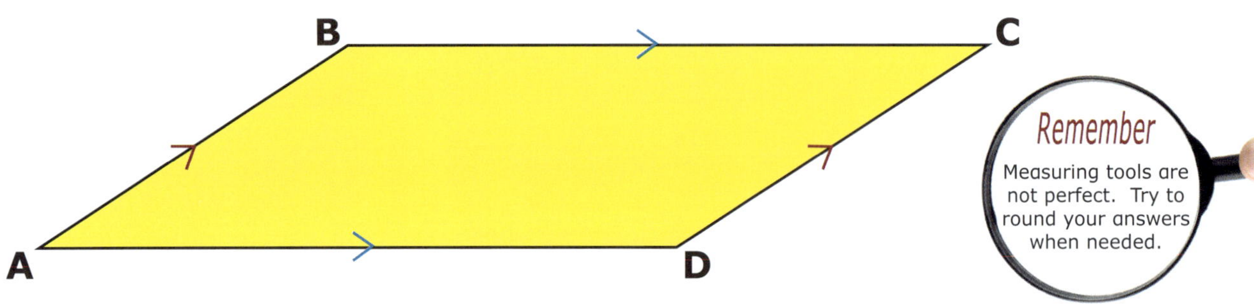

Remember
Measuring tools are not perfect. Try to round your answers when needed.

1. What did you discover about the opposite angles?

____

2. What did you discover about the consecutive angles? (∠**A** and ∠**D** are one pair of consecutive angles.)

____

3. What did you discover about the opposite sides?

____

4. Draw diagonals $\overline{\textbf{AC}}$ and $\overline{\textbf{BD}}$. Label their intersection **F**. What is true about **AF** and **CF**? What is true about **BF** and **DF**?

____

____

____

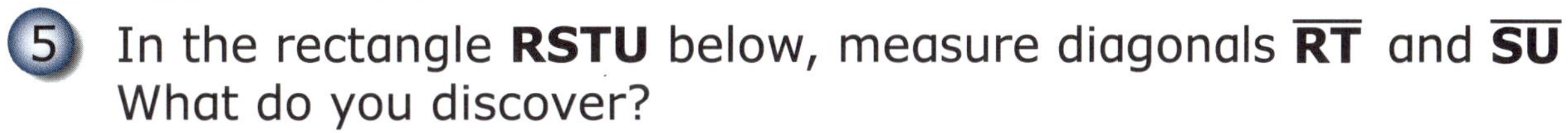

Parallelogram Discovery (Cont.)

5. In the rectangle **RSTU** below, measure diagonals $\overline{\textbf{RT}}$ and $\overline{\textbf{SU}}$. What do you discover?

____

6. In the rhombus **WZYX** and the square **ABCD**, draw and measure their diagonals. What do you discover?

____

____

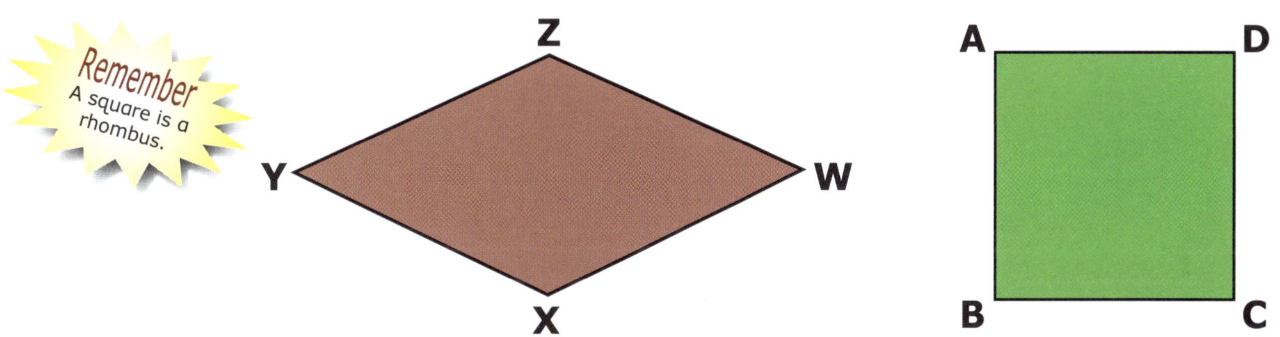

7. In the rhombus **DAHE** below, draw diagonals $\overline{\textbf{DH}}$ and $\overline{\textbf{AE}}$ and mark their intersection **P**. Measure ∠**APH** and ∠**APD**. What do you discover?

____

____

Would this be true in a square? ________

Explain your thinking.

____

____

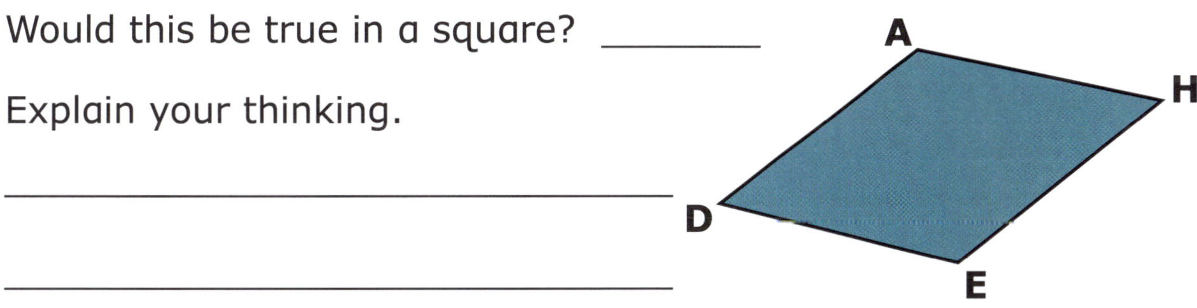

Parallelogram Properties

A parallelogram is defined as a quadrilateral with opposite sides parallel. Parallelograms have many properties. Since the rectangle, the square, and the rhombus are parallelograms, they share those same properties but they have additional ones of their own.

How to Label

To label a parallelogram or any polygon, start at any vertex but go around the outside, either clockwise or counterclockwise.

For example: Label parallelogram **RSTW**.

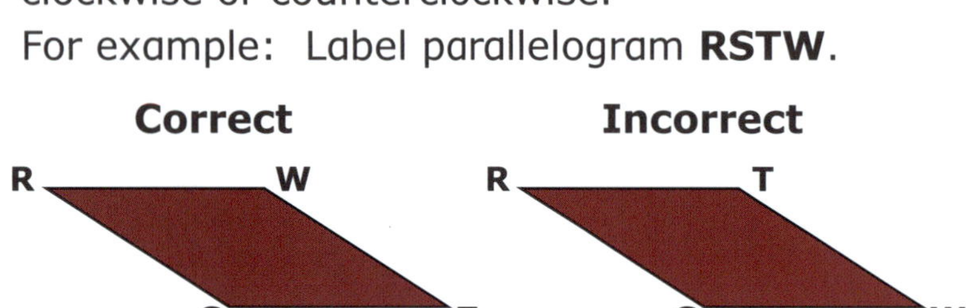

PROPERTIES

1. Opposite sides are congruent.

In parallelogram **ABCD**,
AD = **BC** and **AB** = **DC.**

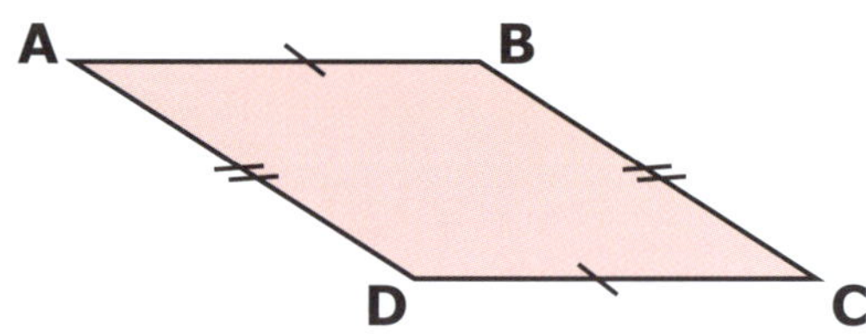

2. Opposite angles are congruent.

In parallelogram **WXYZ**,
m∠**Z** = m∠**X** and m∠**Y** = m∠**W.**

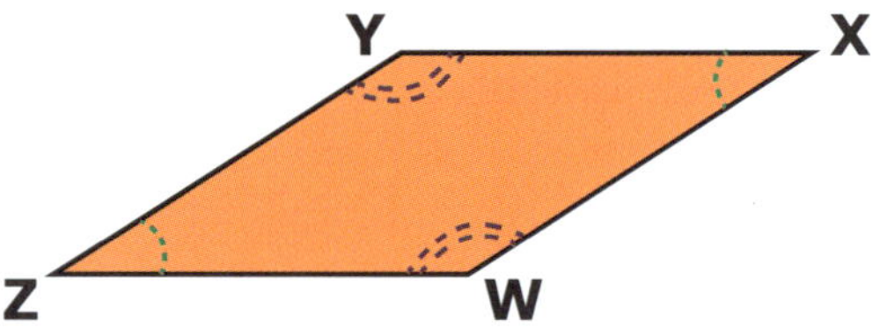

3. Consecutive angles are supplementary.

In parallelogram **MATH**,
m∠**A** + m∠**T** = 180°,
m∠**T** + m∠**H** = 180°,
m∠**H** + m∠**M** = 180°, and
m∠**M** + m∠**A** = 180°.

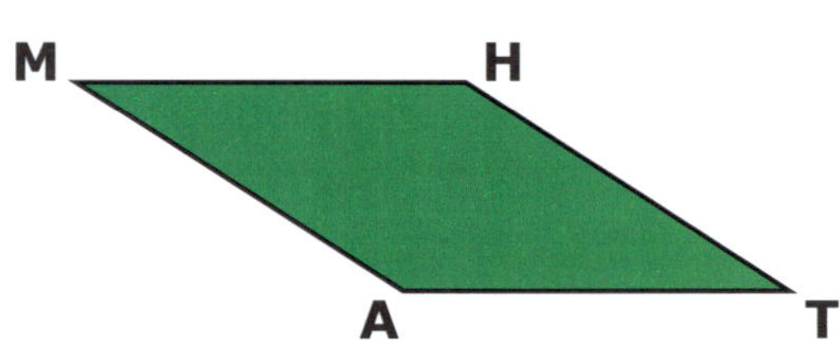

Parallelogram Properties (Cont.)

4 The diagonals always bisect each other.

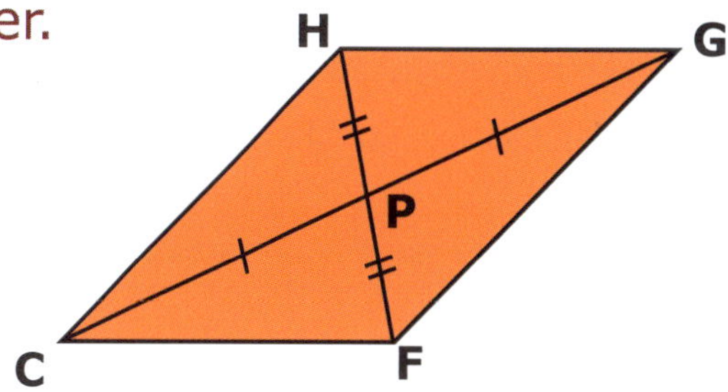

In parallelogram **GHCF**, diagonals $\overline{HF}$ and $\overline{GC}$ intersect at **P**.
HP = **FP** and **CP** = **GP**

The **converse** of these four properties holds true. Here's the converse of Property 1: If the polygon is a quadrilateral with opposite congruent sides, then the polygon is a parallelogram.

The Rhombus

In a rhombus, all the parallelogram properties hold true since a rhombus is a parallelogram. Additionally, the diagonals are ***always*** perpendicular in a rhombus. In addition, each diagonal bisects a pair of opposite angles.

$\overline{QS} \perp \overline{RT}$

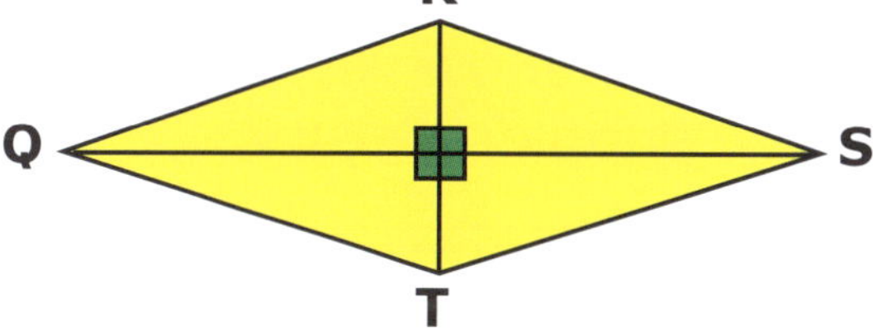

The Rectangle

In a rectangle, all the parallelogram properties hold true since a rectangle is a parallelogram. Additionally, the diagonals are ***always*** congruent in a rectangle.

SU = **TV**

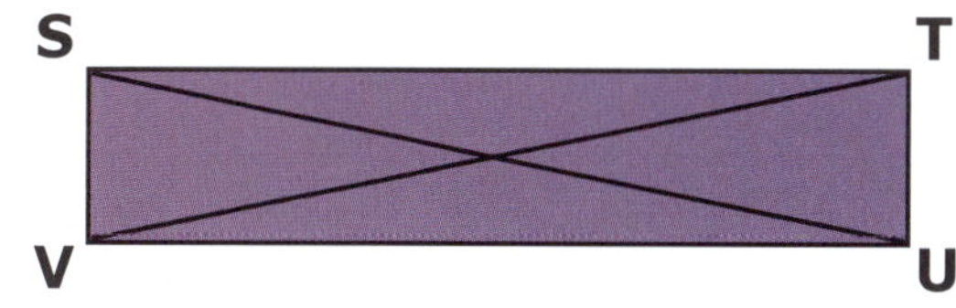

The Square

In a square, all the properties of the parallelogram, the rhombus, and the rectangle hold true since a square is ***all*** of the above.

AC ⊥ **BD** and **AC** = **BD**

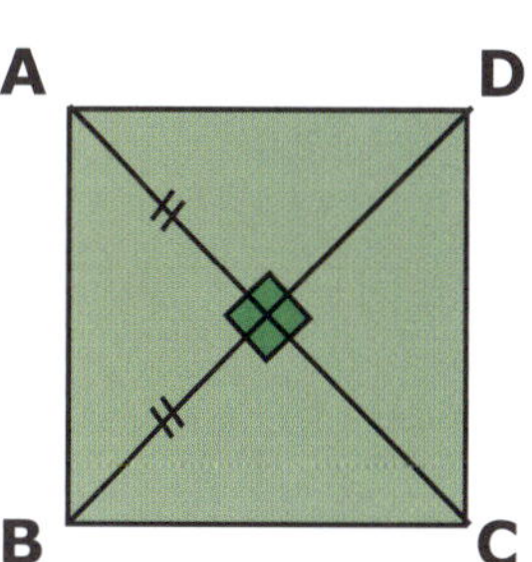

Working With Parallelograms

1. Write the converse of:
If a quadrilateral is a parallelogram, then its opposite angles are congruent.

____

____

2. Write the converse of:
If a quadrilateral is a parallelogram, then its diagonals bisect each other.

____

____

3. Look at parallelogram **ABCD** (m ll n and q ll r). By using your knowledge of alternate interior angles or corresponding angles, show why consecutive angles ∠**DAB** and ∠**ABC** are supplementary.

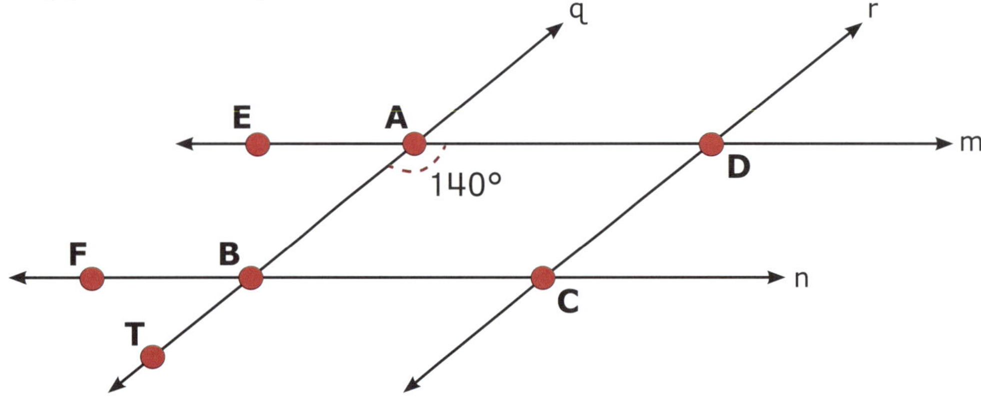

____

____

____

____

____

Working With Parallelograms (Cont.)

4 Find the missing angles of this parallelogram.

ⓐ m∠y = ______ Why? ______________

____

ⓑ m∠z = ______ Why? ______________

____

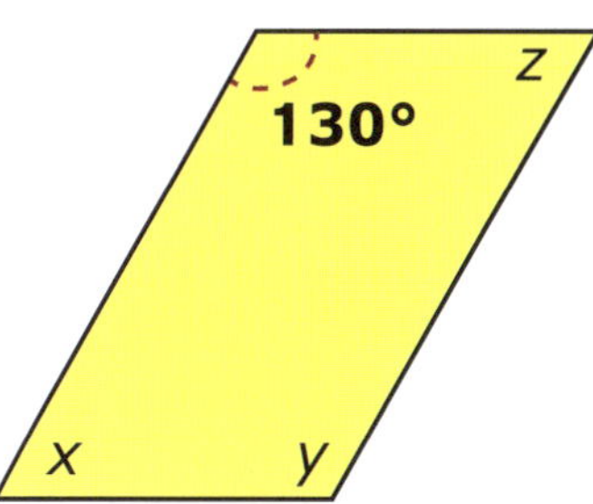

ⓒ m∠x = ______ Why? ______________

____

5 Label this rectangle **DEGB**. Draw diagonals $\overline{\textbf{DG}}$ and $\overline{\textbf{BE}}$. If **DG** = 10 units, what is **BE**? ________

Why? ______________________

____

6 Label this rhombus **ABCD**. Draw diagonals $\overline{\textbf{AC}}$ and $\overline{\textbf{BD}}$ intersecting at point **W**.

ⓐ Find the measure of ∠**BWA.** ______

Justify your answer. __________

____

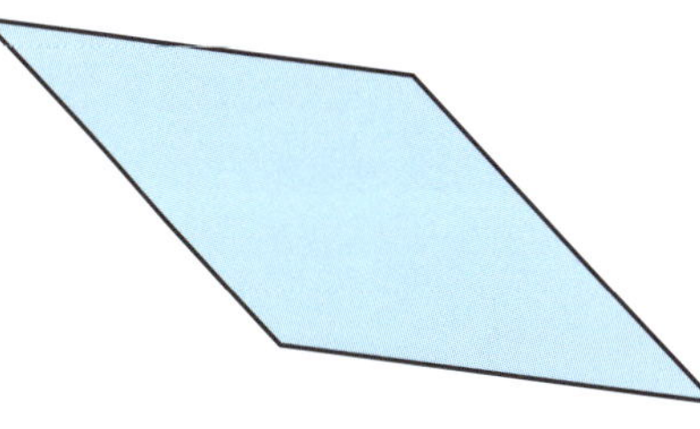

ⓑ In the same figure, if the measure of ∠**BAW** is 20°, find the measure of ∠**ABW**.

Explain your thinking. ______________________

____

Working With Parallelograms (Cont.)

Farmers create parallelograms when plowing and planting crops in fields.

7. In parallelogram **PAUL**, diagonals $\overline{AL}$ and $\overline{PU}$ intersect at **Q**. **PA** = 15 in., **PL** = 20 in., **PU** = 25 in. Find:

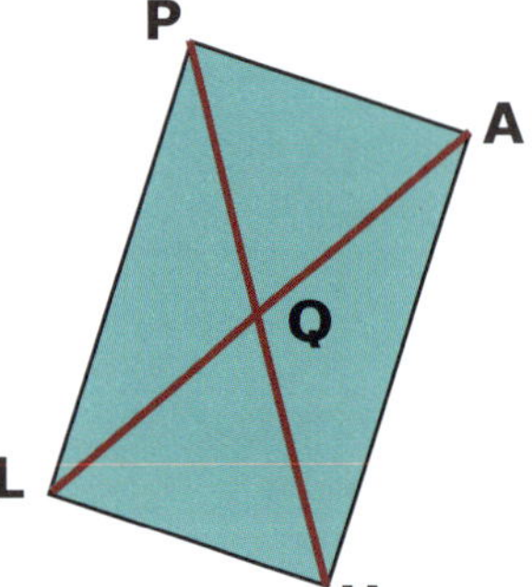

a. **AU** = ________

b. **LU** = ________

c. **PQ** = ________

d. **QU** = ________

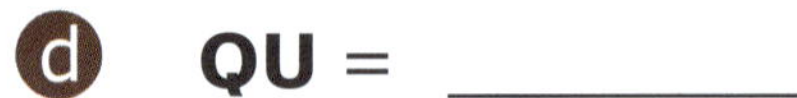

e. Based on the given measures, what type of polygon is shown and why? ____

____

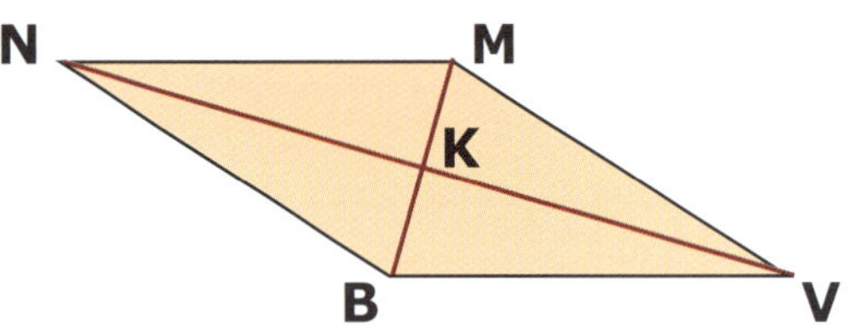

8. In rhombus **VBNM**, each side is 16 cm. Diagonals $\overline{NV}$ and $\overline{BM}$ intersect at point **K**. If **BM** = 12 cm, use your *thinking skills* to find **NK**. Show step-by-step how you determined your answer.

9. Find the missing angles of parallelogram **ABCD** if the exterior angle shown is 35°. Figure ***not*** to scale.

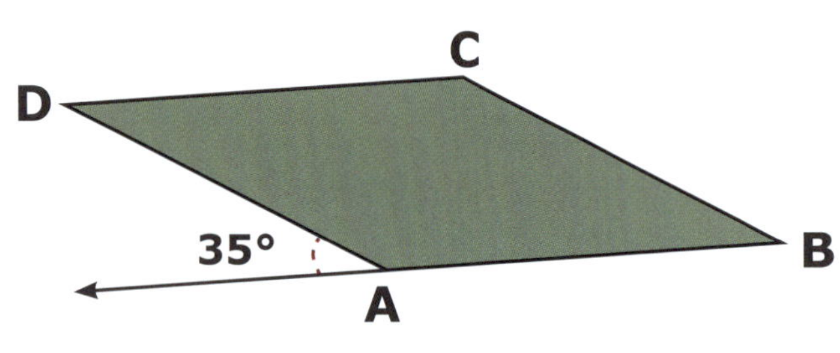

a. ∠**DAB** = ________

b. m∠**D** = ________

c. m∠**B** = ________

d. m∠**C** = ________

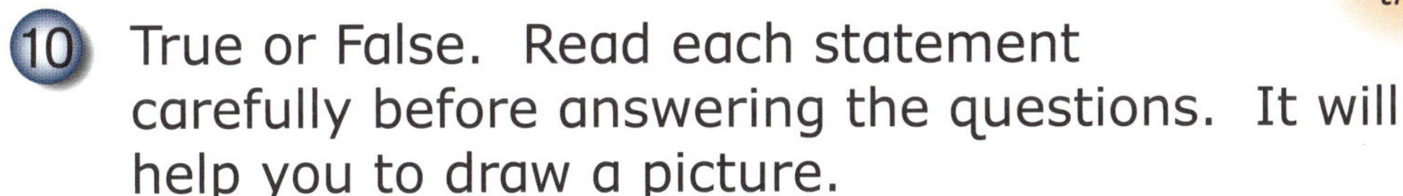

Working With Parallelograms (Cont.)

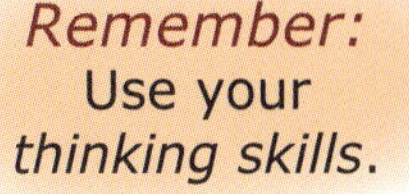

10 True or False. Read each statement carefully before answering the questions. It will help you to draw a picture.

a ________ If the consecutive angles of a quadrilateral are supplementary, then the quadrilateral is a parallelogram.

b ________ Every rhombus is a regular quadrilateral.

c ________ The diagonals of every parallelogram are congruent.

d ________ To be a rhombus, a quadrilateral only needs four congruent sides.

e ________ If the diagonals of a quadrilateral are equal, then the quadrilateral is a square.

f ________ Every polygon with congruent opposite sides is a parallelogram.

g ________ Every quadrilateral with congruent opposite sides is a parallelogram.

h ________ If a quadrilateral has one pair of opposite sides congruent and parallel, then the quadrilateral is a parallelogram.

i ________ Each diagonal in a rhombus bisects a pair of opposite angles.

j ________ If the diagonals of a parallelogram are perpendicular, then the figure is a rhombus.

k ________ In a square, the diagonals are perpendicular and congruent.

l ________ All parallelograms have diagonals that bisect each other.

m ________ Each diagonal of a parallelogram divides the parallelogram into two congruent triangles.

Experimenting With Parallelograms

1. Can you discover the center of gravity of a parallelogram?
   - Trace the following parallelogram on a piece of cardboard or oak tag paper.
   - Cut it out.
   - Try to find the point where you can balance the parallelogram on your finger (or the eraser part of a pencil).

What did you discover?

____

Experimenting With Parallelograms (Cont.)

2. Mary and Sue find two sticks of different sizes. One stick is 6 ft. and the other one is 4 ft. Mary makes an **X** with the sticks so that they meet in the middle of each stick. Mary thinks that the figure formed on the outside is always a rhombus. Sue thinks that the figure formed is definitely a parallelogram but not always a rhombus. Who is right? Try it!

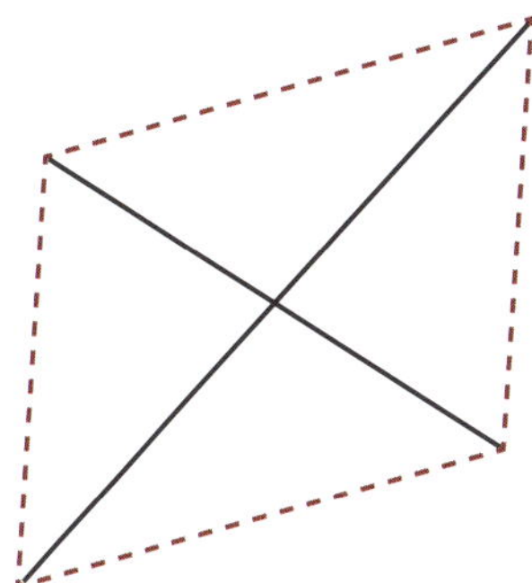

Explain your thinking. ______________________________________

____

3. Hasani believes if one pair of lines are both parallel and congruent, the figure formed on the outside is always a parallelogram. Is he right? Why? Try by drawing several pairs of lines below.

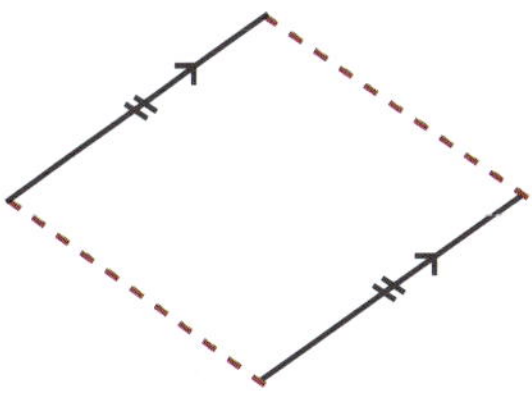

Explain your thinking. ______________________________________

____

Experimenting With Parallelograms (Cont.)

- Trace each parallelogram below on a piece of paper.
- Cut them out.
- Draw their diagonal lines.
- Then cut along one diagonal so that each parallelogram makes two triangles.
- Overlap the triangles for each figure. What do you notice?

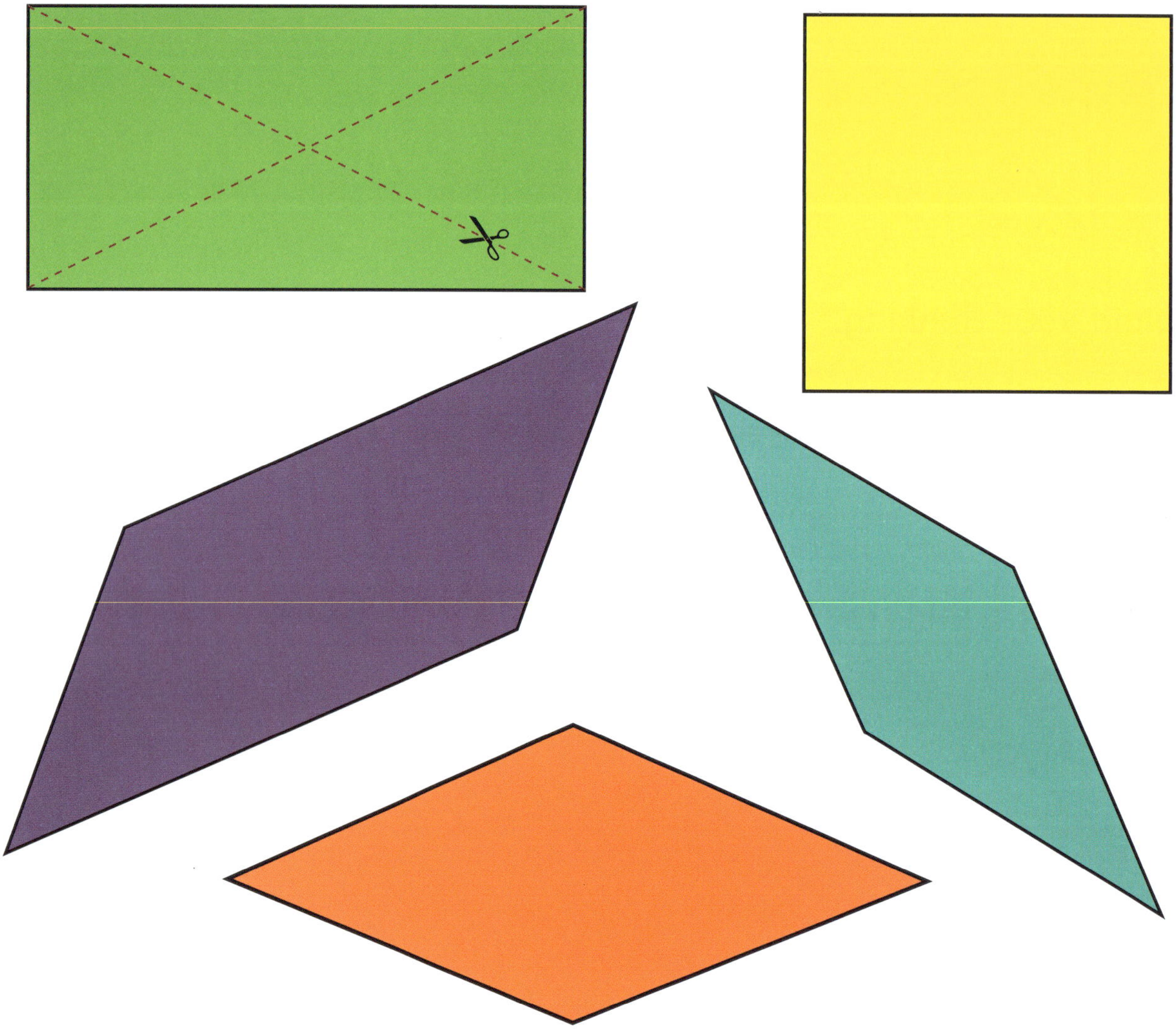

Explain your thinking. ______________________________

____

____

A Look at Trapezoids

Look at the quadrilaterals below. They are all trapezoids because they have only one pair (⇉) of parallel sides. The parallel sides are ***always*** called the bases of the trapezoid. The non-parallel sides are often called the legs of the trapezoid.

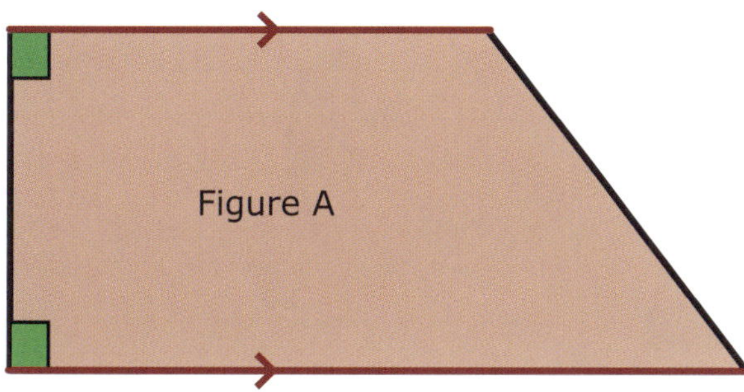

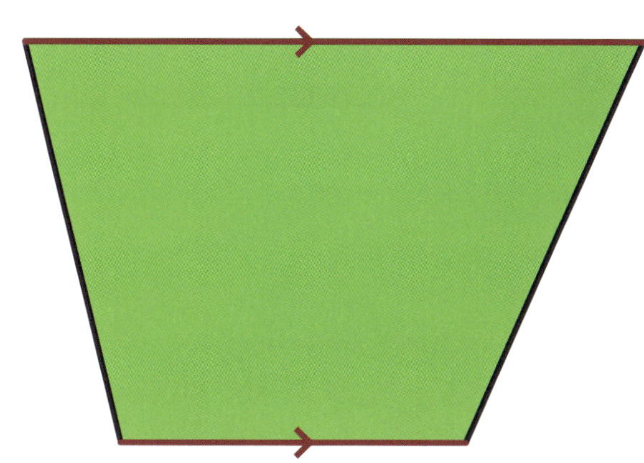

A trapezoid with two right angles is called a **right trapezoid**. (Figure A)

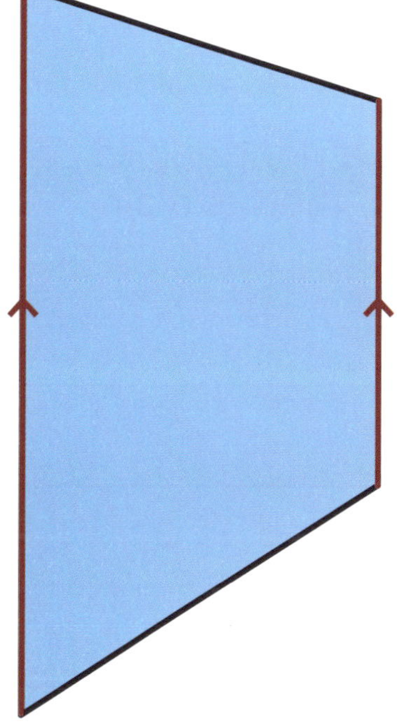

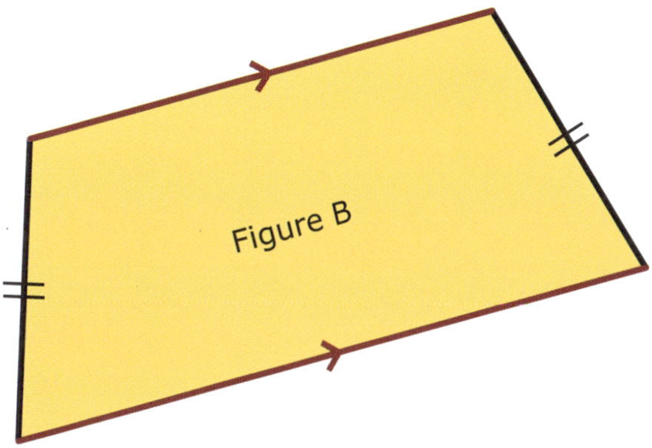

A trapezoid with two congruent opposite sides is called an **isosceles trapezoid**. (Figure B)

A Look at Trapezoids (Cont.)

A property of all trapezoids. The midsegment of a trapezoid is the segment connecting the midpoints of the two non-parallel sides. The midsegment is ***always*** parallel to the bases and **equal** to half of the sum of the bases.

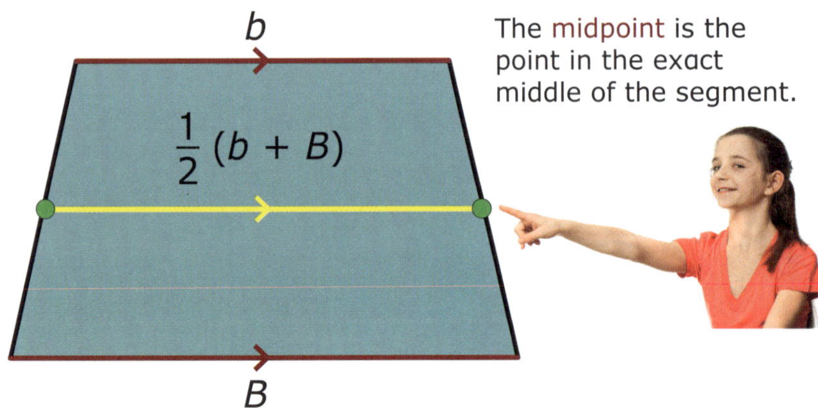

$q = \frac{1}{2}(5 + 13)$

13"

q"

5"

Answer the following questions.

1. Is it possible for a trapezoid to have only **one** right angle? Why or why not? Start by drawing some trapezoids, then explain your thinking.

A Look at Trapezoids (Cont.)

This is an isosceles trapezoid. What properties can you discover?

- Measure the sides, angles, and diagonals.
- Look at the triangles that are created by the diagonals.

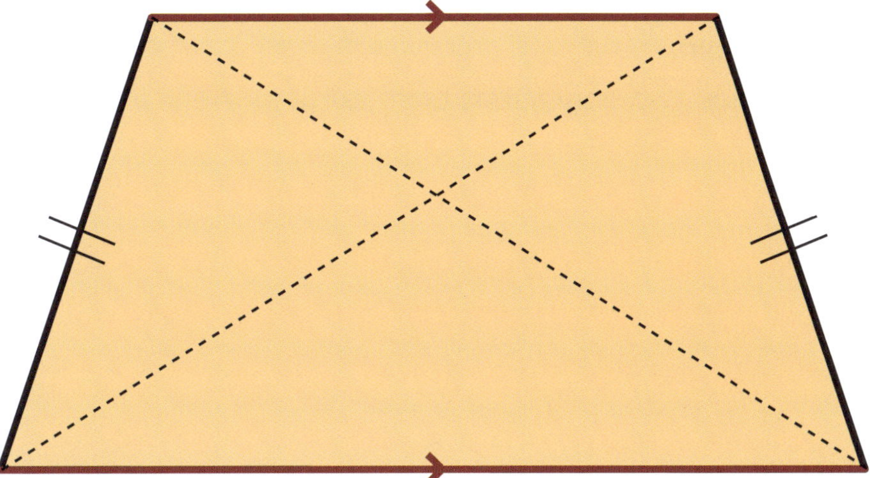

List the properties you discovered.

____

____

____

____

____

A Look at Trapezoids (Cont.)

An isosceles trapezoid is a trapezoid with two congruent sides.

These are the properties of isosceles trapezoids.

- Isosceles trapezoids have two pairs of congruent base angles.
- Isosceles trapezoids have two congruent diagonals.

The converse of each of these properties holds true.

- If a trapezoid has congruent diagonals, then it is an isosceles trapezoid.
- If a trapezoid has two congruent base angles, then the trapezoid is isosceles.

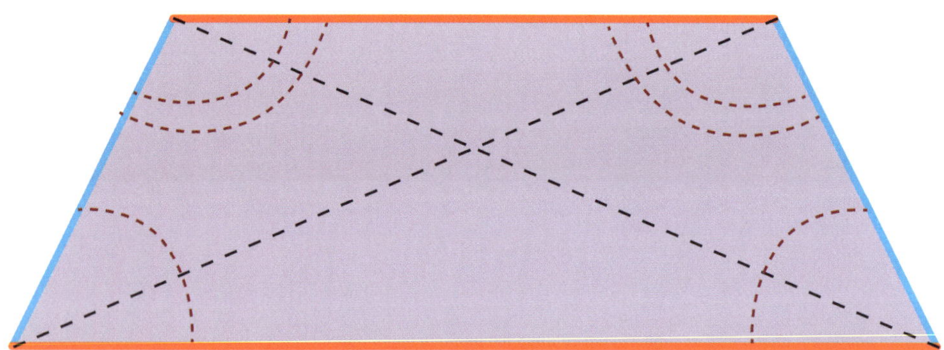

3. Can the bases of a trapezoid be congruent? Why or why not?

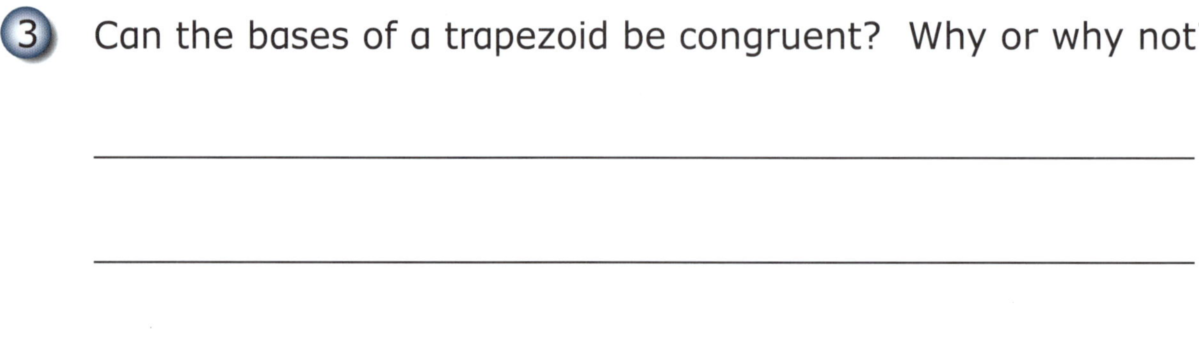

A Look at Trapezoids (Cont.)

Answer the following questions.

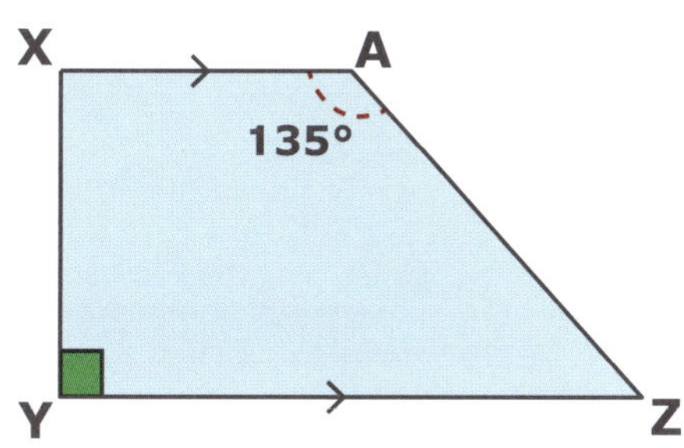

1. Trapezoid **XYZA** has a right angle at **Y**. Find the missing measure of ∠**Z**.

2. If **AC** = **BD**, what type of trapezoid is trapezoid **ABCD**?

   Why? ____________________

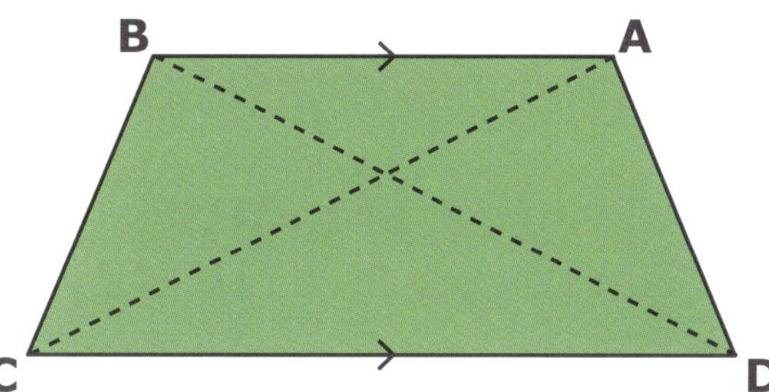

3. What type of trapezoid is trapezoid **DEFG**?

   Why? ______________________________________

   ____

   ____

   m∠**D** = ______, m∠**E** = ______

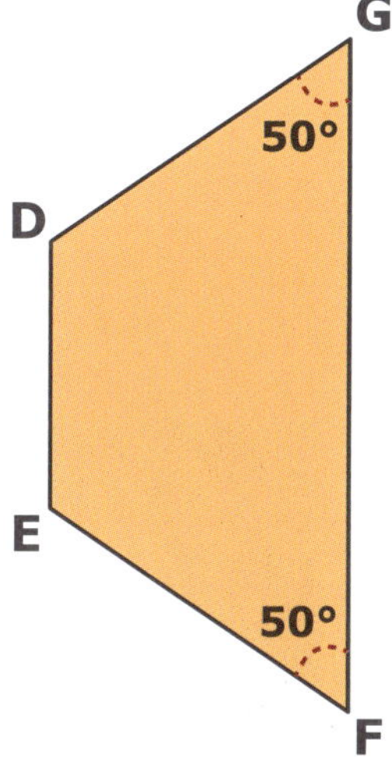

4. Find the missing information in the trapezoid below if $\overline{\mathbf{QR}}$ is the midsegment of trapezoid **ABCD**.

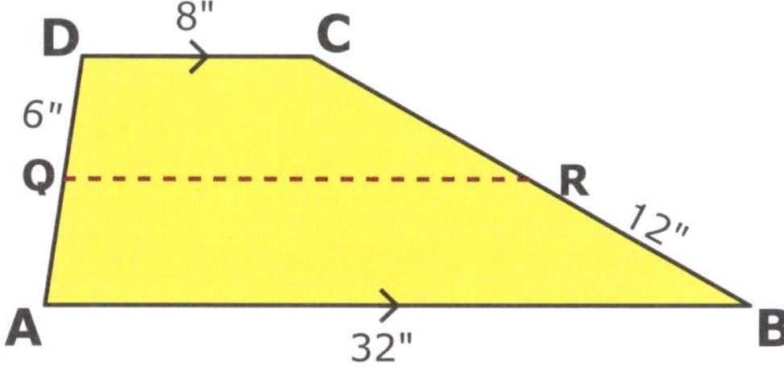

a. **QA** = __________

b. **CR** = __________

c. **QR** = __________

A Look at Trapezoids (Cont.)

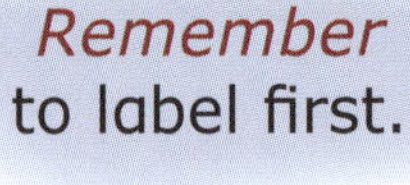

5. In trapezoid **MATH**, $\overline{\textbf{PL}}$ is the midsegment. Find **MA =** ______ if **HT** = 4 and **PL** = 7.

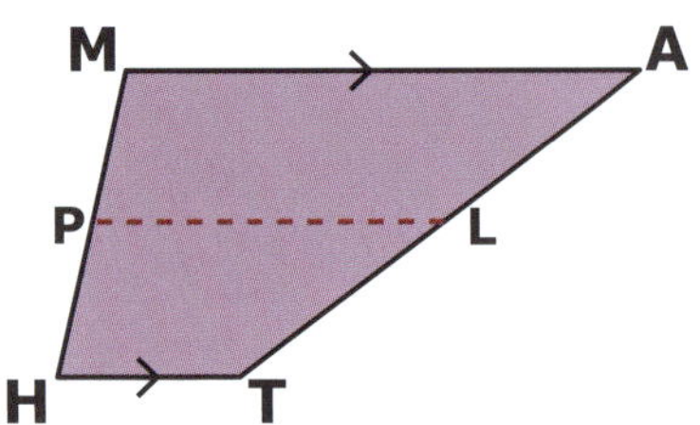

Explain your thinking. ____

____

6. Label isosceles trapezoid **QRST**, **QS** = 15 cm. $\overline{\textbf{QS}}$ and $\overline{\textbf{RT}}$ intersect at **Y**. If **RY** = 4 cm, find **YT** = ______.

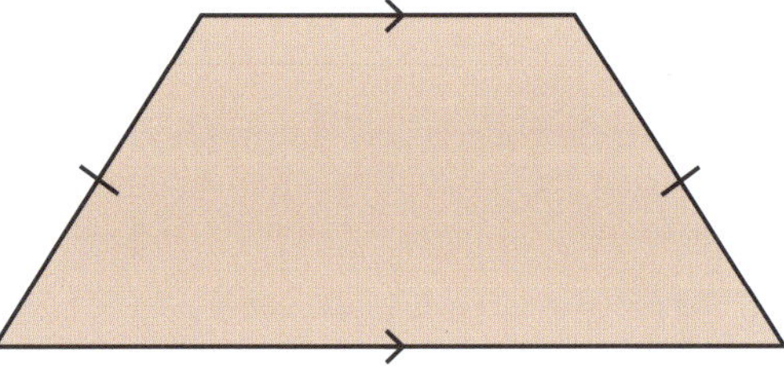

7. In trapezoid **INCA**, **AC** = 6 ft and midsegment, **PE** = 4.5 ft. Find the top base **IN** = ______.

Inca trapezoidal window

In Peru, the Incas used many trapezoids in their architecture. Scientists believe the Incas thought the trapezoid was a more stable shape to protect buildings from earthquakes.

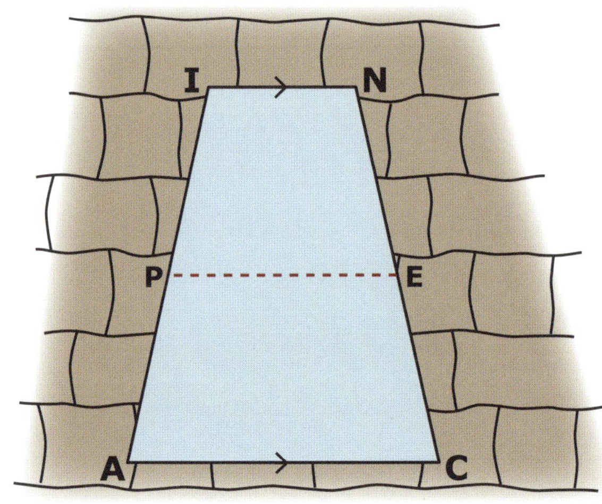

Kite! Kite! Kite!

A kite, sometimes called a deltoid, is a quadrilateral with two sets of adjacent sides congruent. Unlike a rhombus, each pair has a different measure.

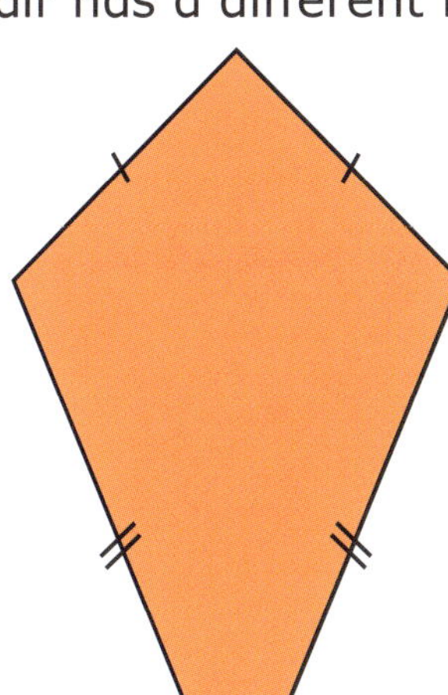

1. Draw the diagonals of the kite above and explain what you notice.

____

____

2. Draw the short diagonal in Kite 1 and the long diagonal in Kite 2.

Notice
The long diagonal is the kite's line of symmetry.

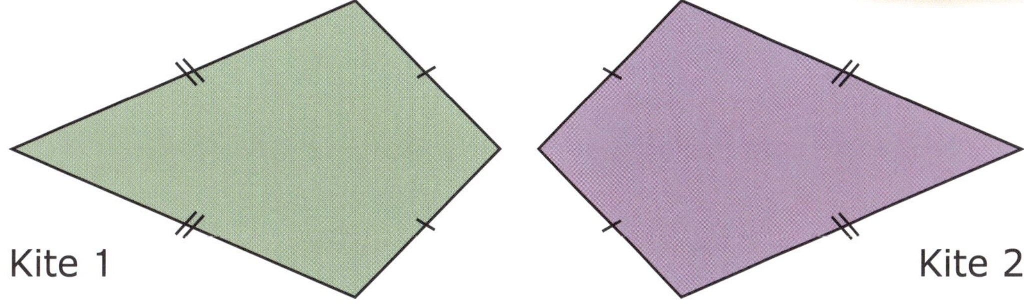

What kind of triangle(s) does each diagonal create?

____

____

____

Critical Thinking About Quadrilaterals

True or False? Before you answer the questions, make a drawing when needed. Refer back to all the quadrilateral properties.

1. _____ Any quadrilateral with perpendicular diagonals is a kite.

2. _____ Any parallelogram with perpendicular diagonals is a rhombus.

3. _____ An isosceles trapezoid is the only quadrilateral with congruent diagonals.

4. _____ The sum of the angle measures in a kite is the same as the sum of the angle measures in a rectangle.

5. _____ The bases of a trapezoid cannot be congruent.

6. _____ The midsegment of a trapezoid is parallel to the bases and half the sum of the bases.

7. _____ In a kite, the shorter diagonal bisects the longer diagonal.

8. _____ In a kite, the angles between the non-congruent sides are congruent.

9. _____ In an isosceles trapezoid, none of the angles are congruent.

10. _____ One difference between a kite and a parallelogram is the lengths of the diagonals.

11. _____ A rectangle is called a square only when all its sides are congruent.

12. _____ A kite is a special type of trapezoid.

Midsegment Investigation

We learned that in any trapezoid the midsegment (the segment that connects the midpoints of the two non-parallel sides) is parallel to the bases and equal to half of the sum of the two bases. The figures are ***not*** to scale.

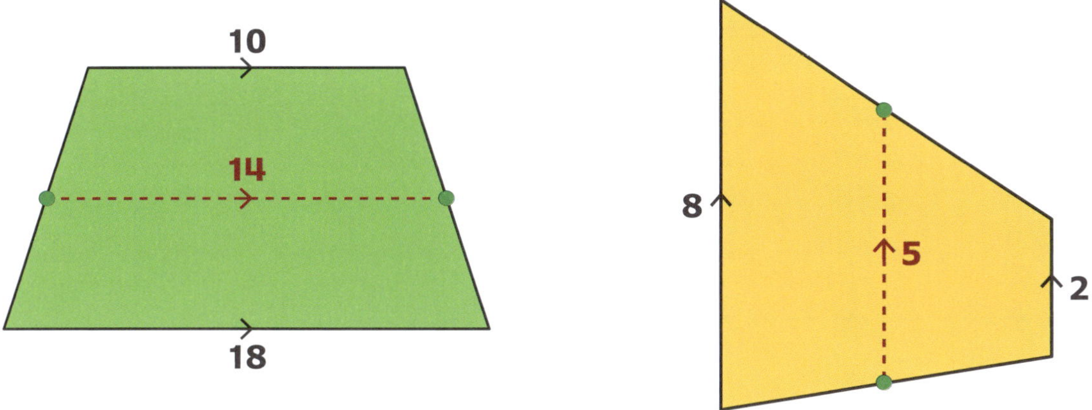

Below is parallelogram **ACQR.** Are the trapezoid midsegment properties true for parallelograms?

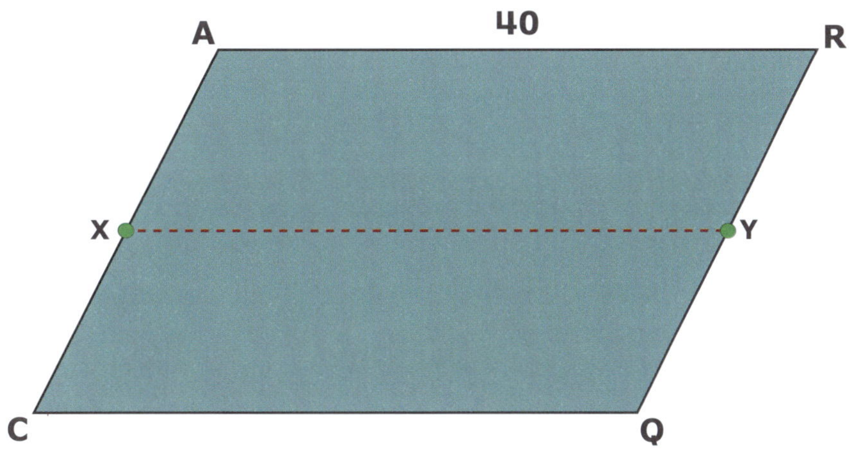

Explain your thinking.

____

____

____

____

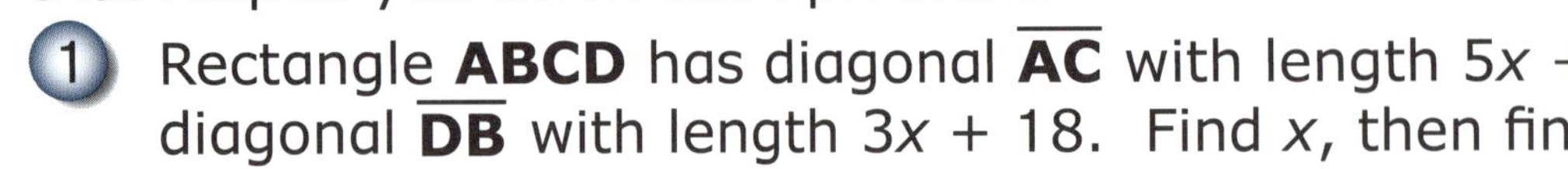

Using Algebra to Solve Quadrilateral Problems

Use your knowledge of algebra and quadrilateral properties to solve these problems. Write each equation, then state the property or properties that helped you solve each problem.

1. Rectangle **ABCD** has diagonal $\overline{\mathbf{AC}}$ with length $5x + 10$ and diagonal $\overline{\mathbf{DB}}$ with length $3x + 18$. Find x, then find **AC**.

Equation:

AC = ______

Property ____

2. In parallelogram **MATH**, m∠**A** = $(3x + 120)°$ and m∠**M** = $(2x)°$. Find x, then find m∠**T**.

Equation:

m∠**T** = ______

Property (or properties) ____

____

____

3. In rhombus **TQRS**, diagonals $\overline{\mathbf{TR}}$ and $\overline{\mathbf{SQ}}$ intersect at point **P**. If m∠**TPQ** = $(5x + 20)°$, find x.

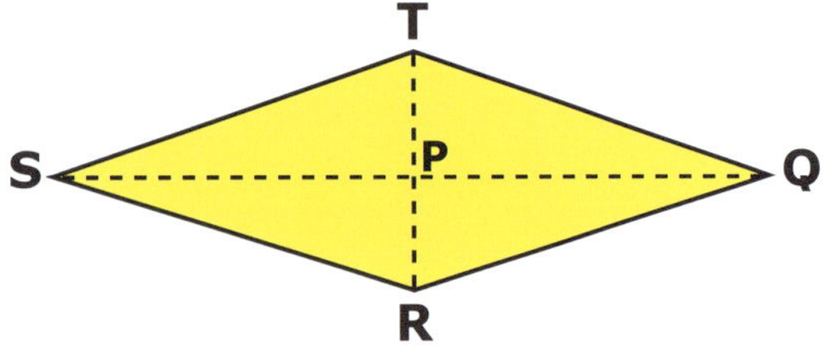

Equation:

Property ____

Using Algebra to Solve Quadrilateral Problems (Cont.)

4. In isosceles trapezoid **GHJK**, diagonal $\overline{\textbf{KH}}$ has a measure of $10y + 30$. Diagonal $\overline{\textbf{JG}}$ has a measure of $2y + 70$. Find the measure of diagonal $\overline{\textbf{JG}}$.

Equation:

JG = ______

Property ____

5. In parallelogram **QRST**, diagonal **TR** and diagonal **QS** intersect at point **K**. If **TK** = $2x + 25$ and **RK**= $x + 95$, find **TR**.

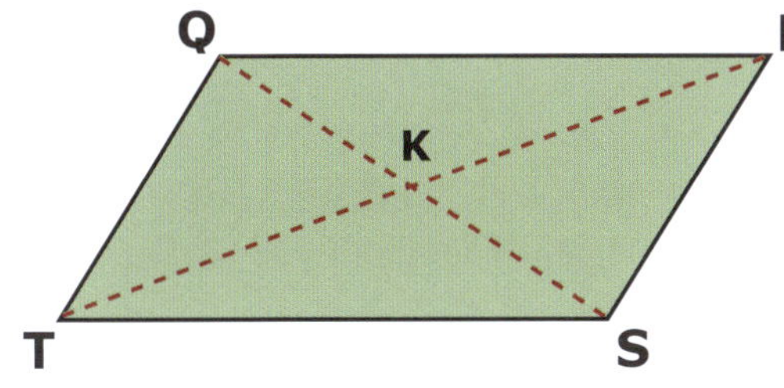

Equation:

TR = ______

Property ____

6. In kite **LARY**, m∠**A** = $x°$, m∠**Y** = $(x - 10)°$ and m∠**R** = $(5x - 55)°$. Find the measure of each angle in kite **LARY**.

Equation:

m∠**A** = ______

m∠**Y** = ______

m∠**R** = ______

m∠**L** = ______

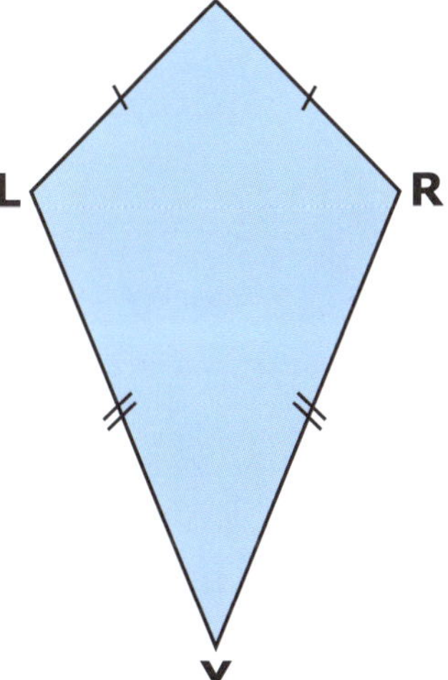

Properties ______________________________

____

Quadrilateral Matching

Match the quadrilateral with its properties. You may use an answer more than once.

1. Rectangle ____________________

2. Rhombus ____________________

3. Parallelogram ____________________

4. Kite ____________________

5. Trapezoid ____________________

6. Isosceles Trapezoid ____________________

7. Square ____________________

a. Diagonals are congruent.

b. Opposite sides are congruent.

c. Opposite angles are congruent.

d. Consecutive angles are supplementary.

e. Diagonals are perpendicular.

f. All sides are congruent.

g. All angles are congruent.

h. Sum of the angle measures equals 360°.

Cumulative Review – Chapters 5-6

Use a separate sheet of paper if needed.

1. Explain how you would find the measure of one interior angle of a regular octagon.

____

____

2. Explain how you would find the number of diagonals in a nonagon.

____

____

3. What type of regular polygon has an exterior angle of 40°? Explain your thinking.

____

____

4. Check which of the following guarantees that a quadrilateral must also be a parallelogram? Make a drawing on a separate sheet of paper to help you.

_____ a. Diagonals bisect each other.
_____ b. One angle is a right angle.
_____ c. Both pairs of sides are congruent.
_____ d. One pair of adjacent sides are congruent.
_____ e. Opposite angles are congruent.
_____ f. One pair of opposite sides are congruent and parallel.
_____ g. One angle is supplementary to both consecutive angles.

5. Draw all the possible quadrilaterals that have two congruent diagonals.

6. Draw all the possible quadrilaterals that have perpendicular diagonals.

7. Find the missing angles.

a 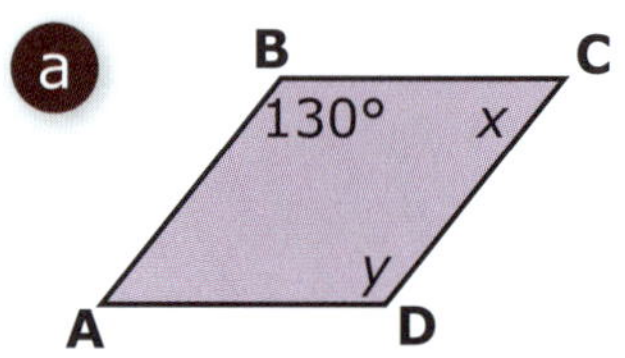

Parallelogram **ABCD**

______
______

b 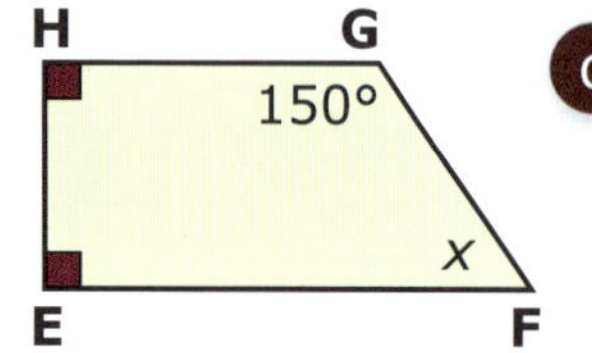

Trapezoid **EFGH**

______

c 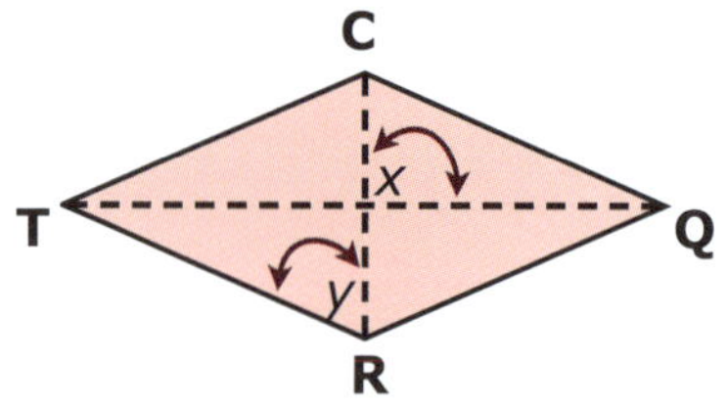

Rhombus **CQRT**
m∠**TCQ** = 150°

______
______

8. Find x and then find $\overline{\textbf{AB}}$.

a 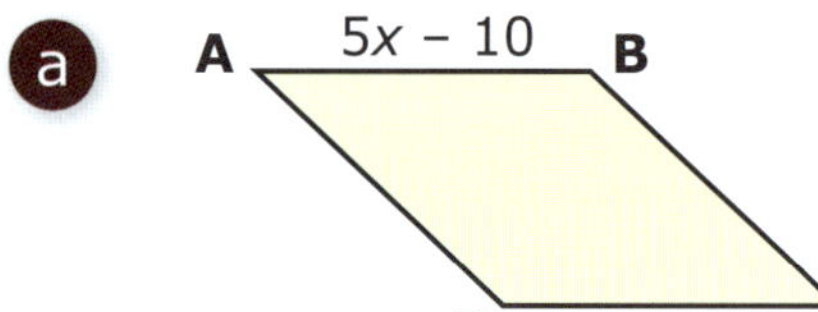

Parallelogram **ABCD**

______ ______

b 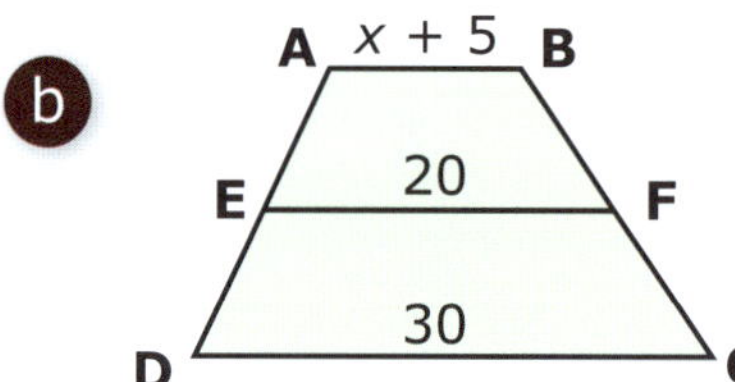

Trapezoid **ABCD** with midsegment $\overline{\textbf{EF}}$

______ ______

c 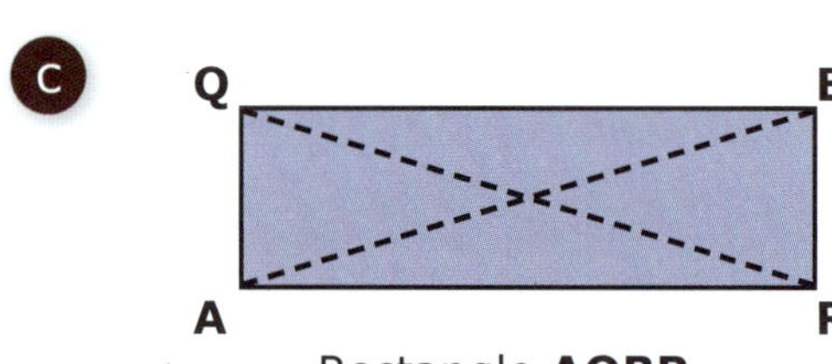

QR = $8x - 50$
AB = $5x + 16$

Rectangle **AQBR**

______ ______

Chapter 7 - Metric Geometry

Perimeter and Circumference

The perimeter of a polygon is the total distance around the outside of a polygon. Circumference is the perimeter of a circle.

To find the perimeter of any polygon, just add around the outside, but make sure that ***all*** the sides have the same dimensions.

How to Remember
perimeter
Think of the word *periscope*.
It looks *all* around.

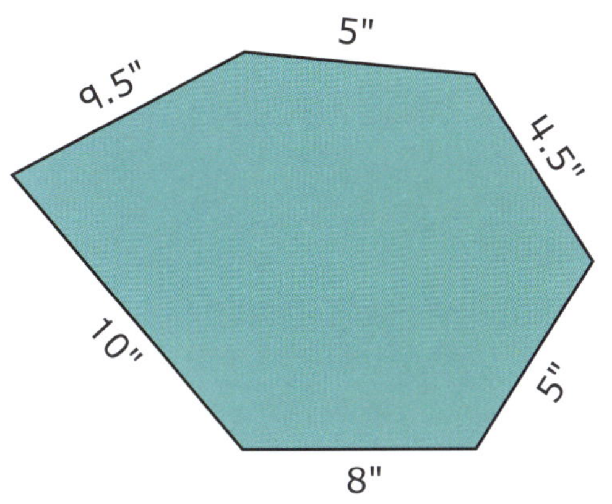

Example: To find the perimeter of this polygon, add all the numbers around the outside. The answer is 42 in.

The circumference of a circle is found by this formula, $\boldsymbol{C} = \pi\boldsymbol{d}$, where $\boldsymbol{d}$ is the diameter of the circle. Remember the diameter of a circle is twice its radius.

So the formula is also $\boldsymbol{C} = 2\pi\boldsymbol{r}$.

Example: To find the circumference of this circle, if its radius is 5 cm, use 3.14 for the symbol pi (π).

$C = 2\pi r$,

so $C = 10\pi$ or 31.4 cm

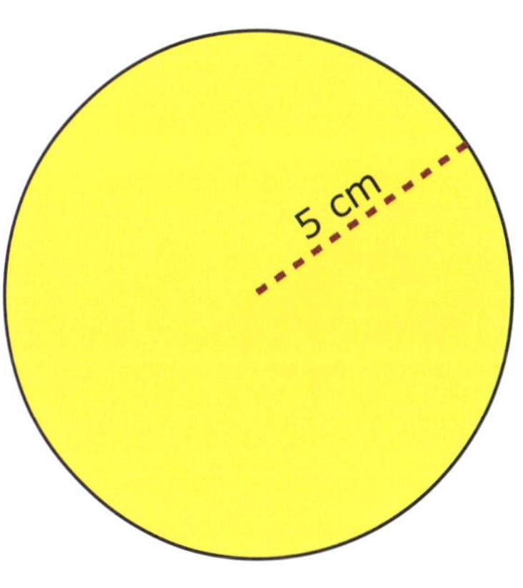

Pi (π) Investigation

What is Pi (π)? π is the symbol used to represent the ratio of the circumference of a circle to its diameter. **Pi** is approximately 3.14159265358979323846... It is an **irrational number** because it does not end and it does not repeat.

Gather some cans or any perfect circular objects in your house and fill out the following table. Use a calculator to help you.

Object Description	Circumference (Distance Around The Circle)	Diameter	Ratio (Circumference/Diameter)

Explain your results here. ______________________________

____

____

Perimeter and Circumference Activity

Solve the following problems. Make sure you read and label each figure carefully. Make a drawing when there is no drawing.

1. Find the perimeter of a rectangle that has a length is 20 in. and a width of 15 in.

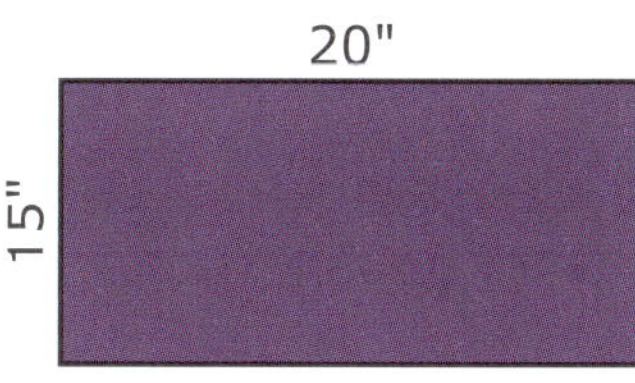

2. A rhombus has a perimeter of 196 meters. Find the length of one side.

3. Which perimeter is larger, the perimeter of a square with a side of 4 in. or the circumference of a circle with a diameter of 5 in.? Use 3.14 for π.

   Explain your thinking. ______________________________

   ____

4. If a circle has a circumference of 18.84 cm, find its radius. Use 3.14 for π.

5. The perimeter of a regular nonagon is 315 in. Find one side.

Archimedes' Idea for Approximating Pi

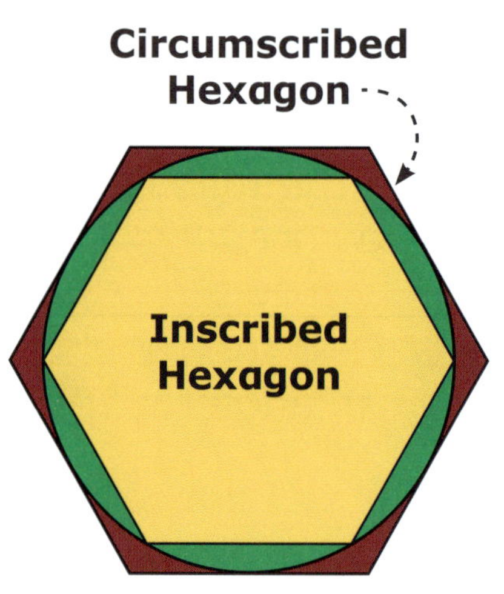

The great Greek mathematician, physicist, inventor, and astronomer **Archimedes** is credited with creating a method to approximate π (*about 287 - 212 B.C.*). Although π was known to the ancient Babylonians and the Egyptians, Archimedes came up with the idea of inscribing and circumscribing polygons to arrive at a value for π.

Thinking questions about Archimedes' method for computing π.

1. According to the picture above, what does the word inscribed imply about the vertices of the polygon in relationship to the circle?

____

____

____

2. According to the picture above, how would you define the word circumscribed?

____

____

____

3. Archimedes measured the perimeter of the inscribed polygon and compared it to the perimeter of the circumscribed polygon. How does the circumference of the same circle compare to those measures?

____

____

____

Archimedes' Idea for Approximating Pi (Cont.)

Archimedes tried using polygons of 12, 24, 48, and 96 sides.
See at: http://itech.fgcu.edu/faculty/clindsey/mhf4404/archimedes/archimedes.html

4. How does using polygons with more sides increase the approximation of the circumference?

____

____

____

5. Can the circle ever reach the same perimeter as either one of the polygons? How does this method result in approximating π?

____

____

____

Often you will be asked to find circumference or area of a circle and leave your answer in terms of π. This means that you can leave your answer with the symbol π.

For example: 24π is an answer in terms of π, instead of multiplying 24 by any fraction or decimal.

Archimedes determined that pi was between $3\frac{1}{7}$ and $3\frac{10}{71}$. Many fractions and decimals have been used as approximations for for pi (π). It's popular to use $\frac{22}{7}$ as an approximation of π, but make sure you remember that $\frac{22}{7}$ does not equal π (π is irrational and all fractions are rational).

The ancient Babylonians used 3 as their approximation while the Egyptians used 3.1605. The Chinese used $\frac{355}{113}$ for their approximation. By the way, the symbol π was not used until about the 1700s.
See at: http://www.exploratorium.edu/pi/history_of_pi/index.html

Area of Parallelograms

To find the area of any parallelogram, you ***do not*** need to memorize several formulas, just one, $A = bh$.

The area of a parallelogram equals base times height. The height is sometimes called the **altitude**.

The height or altitude is always the perpendicular segment to the opposite side or the line containing the opposite side from the vertex it originated from.

Remember

Area is the number of unit squares found in a two dimensional region. A rectangle, for example, can be measured in square inches, or square feet, or square miles, depending on its size. So the unit you are using is important and must be stated in the answer.

Find the area of the following parallelograms. Do not forget to label.

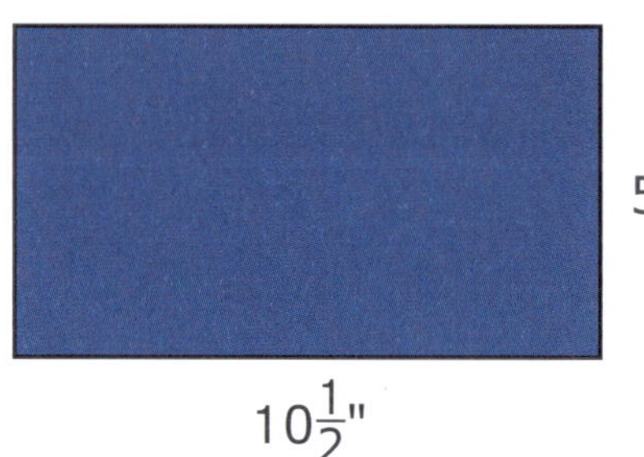

A = __________

A = __________

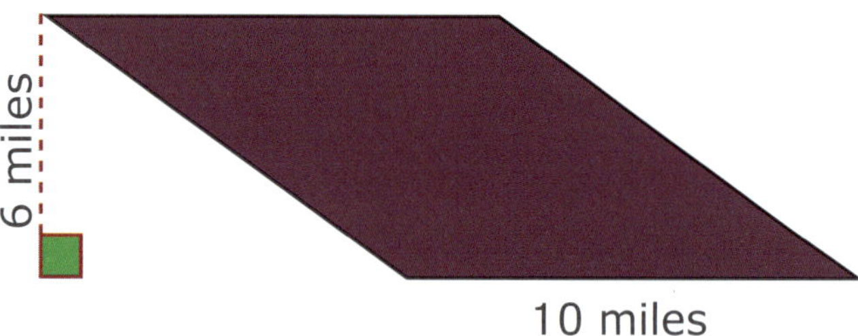

A = __________

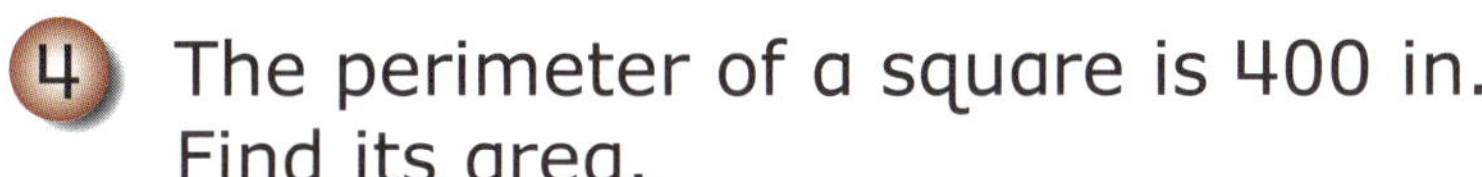

Area of Parallelograms (Cont.)

4. The perimeter of a square is 400 in. Find its area.

5. A rectangle has an area of 60 sq ft and the length is 15 ft. Find its width and perimeter.

6. Dave has a photograph of a fish he caught in Lake Ontario. The outside of the wooden frame is 14 in. by 12 in., and the picture is 10 in. by 8 in. Find the area of the wooden frame.

7. Why is the area of this parallelogram the same as the area of this rectangle?

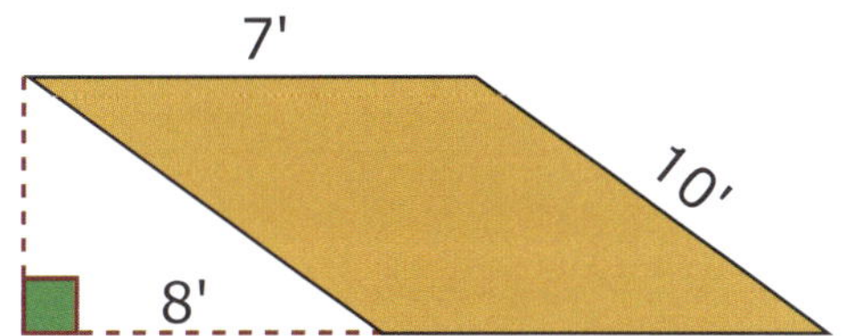

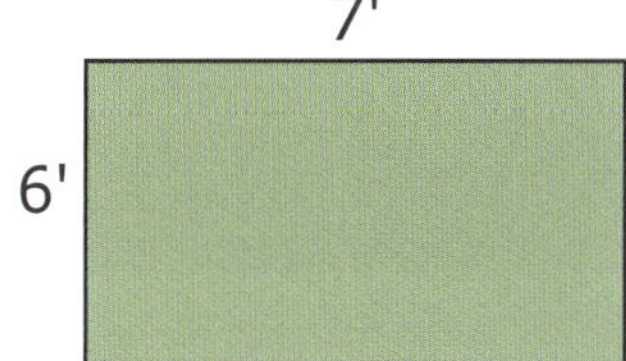

Explain your thinking. ____________________

____

____

Parallelogram Area Activity

This rectangle and the parallelogram below have the same base and the same height.

Trace and cut out the parallelogram. Then cut out section *A* and place it (you may tape it) to the right side of the parallelogram. Try to overlap the parallelogram pieces on the rectangle.

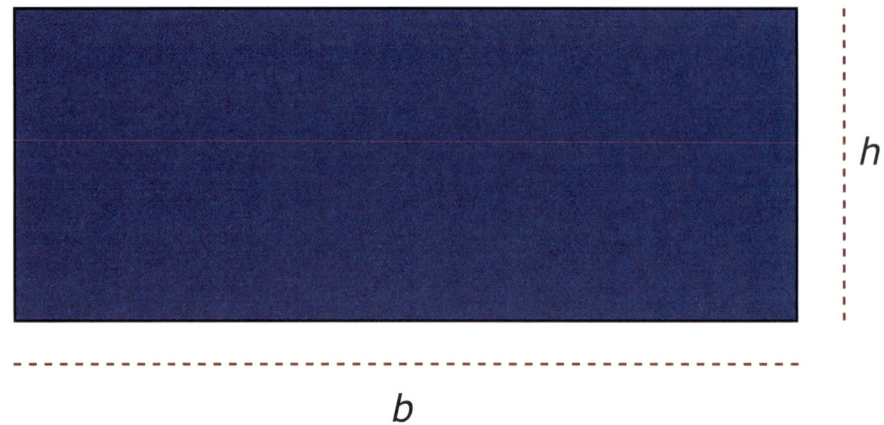

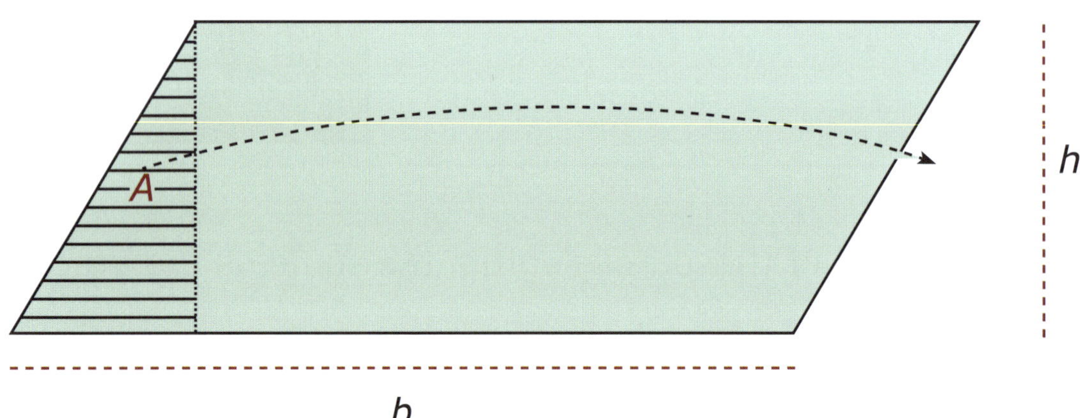

Explain what you discover.

____

____

Area of Triangles and Trapezoids

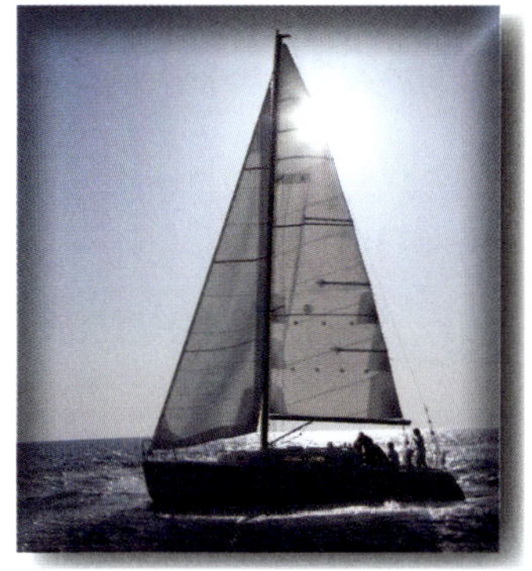

The formula for the area of a triangle is $A = \frac{1}{2}bh$ because a triangle is half of a parallelogram.

Did you know that depending on how you turn a triangle, every triangle has three bases and three altitudes? Below is a scalene triangle rotated so that each side becomes the base each time.

Base 1

Side 2
Height 1
Side 3
Side 1

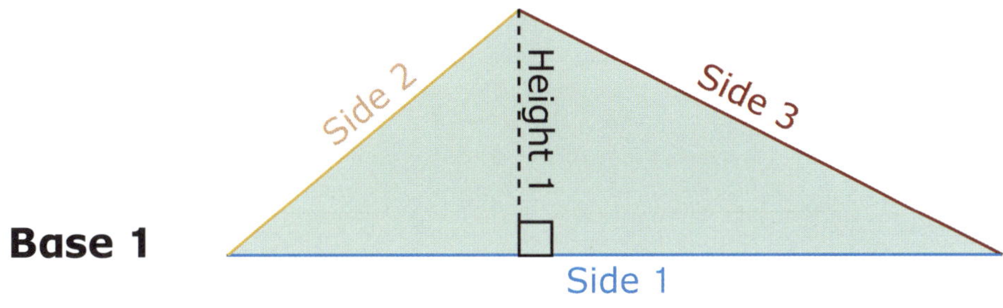

Base 2

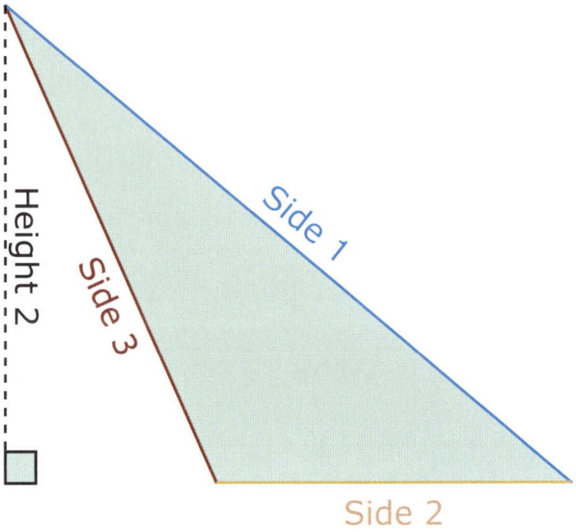

Height 2
Side 3
Side 1
Side 2

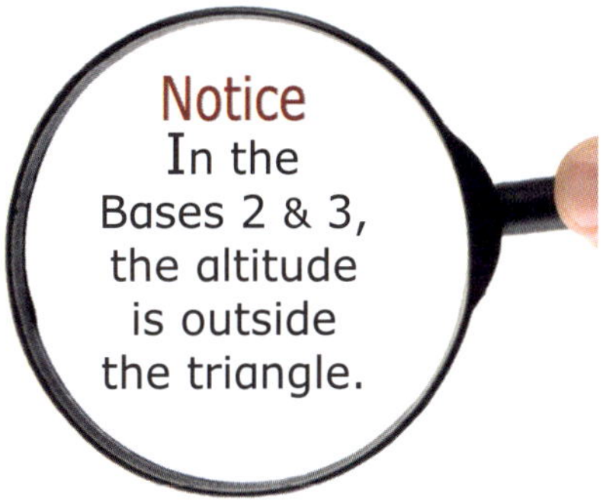

Notice
In the Bases 2 & 3, the altitude is outside the triangle.

Base 3

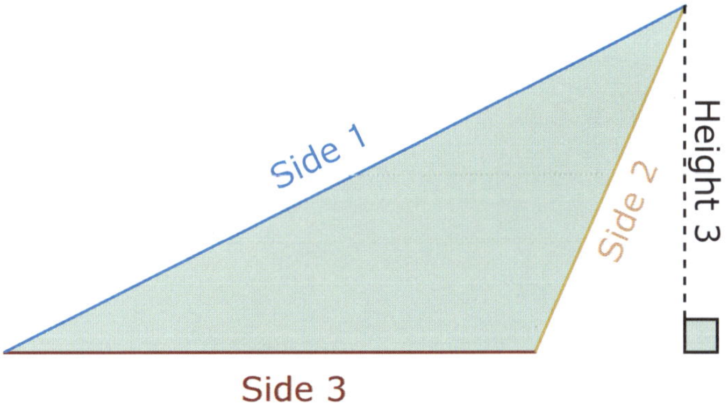

Side 1
Side 2
Height 3
Side 3

Area of Triangles and Trapezoids (Cont.)

Answer the following questions. Make a drawing when needed.

1. If you rotate the equilateral triangle below, will each base and altitude be different (like the scalene triangle on the previous page)?

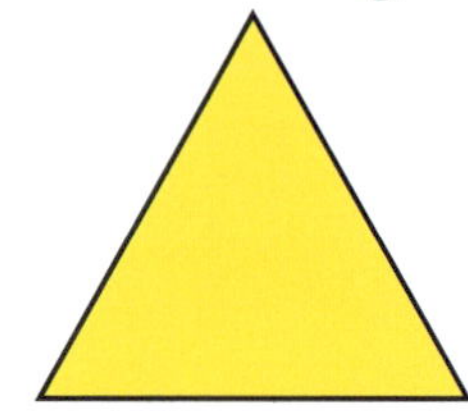

Explain your thinking. ______________________________

____

____

2. Is it possible to draw an isosceles triangle that has an altitude outside the triangle?

Explain your thinking. ______________________________

____

____

3. Which triangle has the largest area? Δ**ABC** or Δ**ADC**? Why?

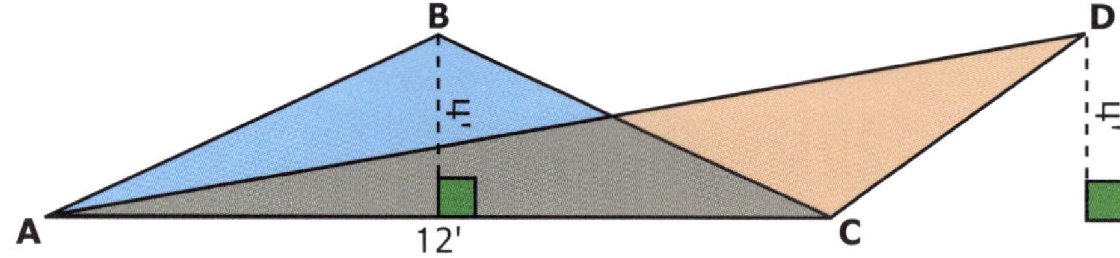

Explain your thinking. ______________________________

____

____

Area of Triangles and Trapezoids (Cont.)

4. Find the altitude of a triangle whose area is 30 square inches and whose base is 20 inches. Always write the formula first.

5. A triangle is inscribed in a rectangle as shown below. Find the area shaded in yellow.

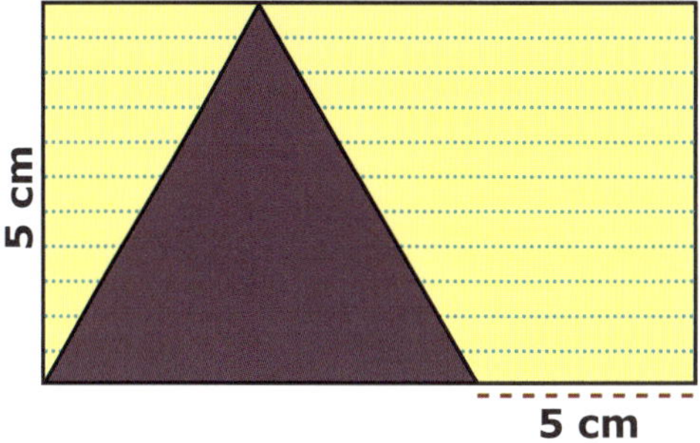

6. Draw an altitude from the vertex opposite the base which is highlighted in yellow.

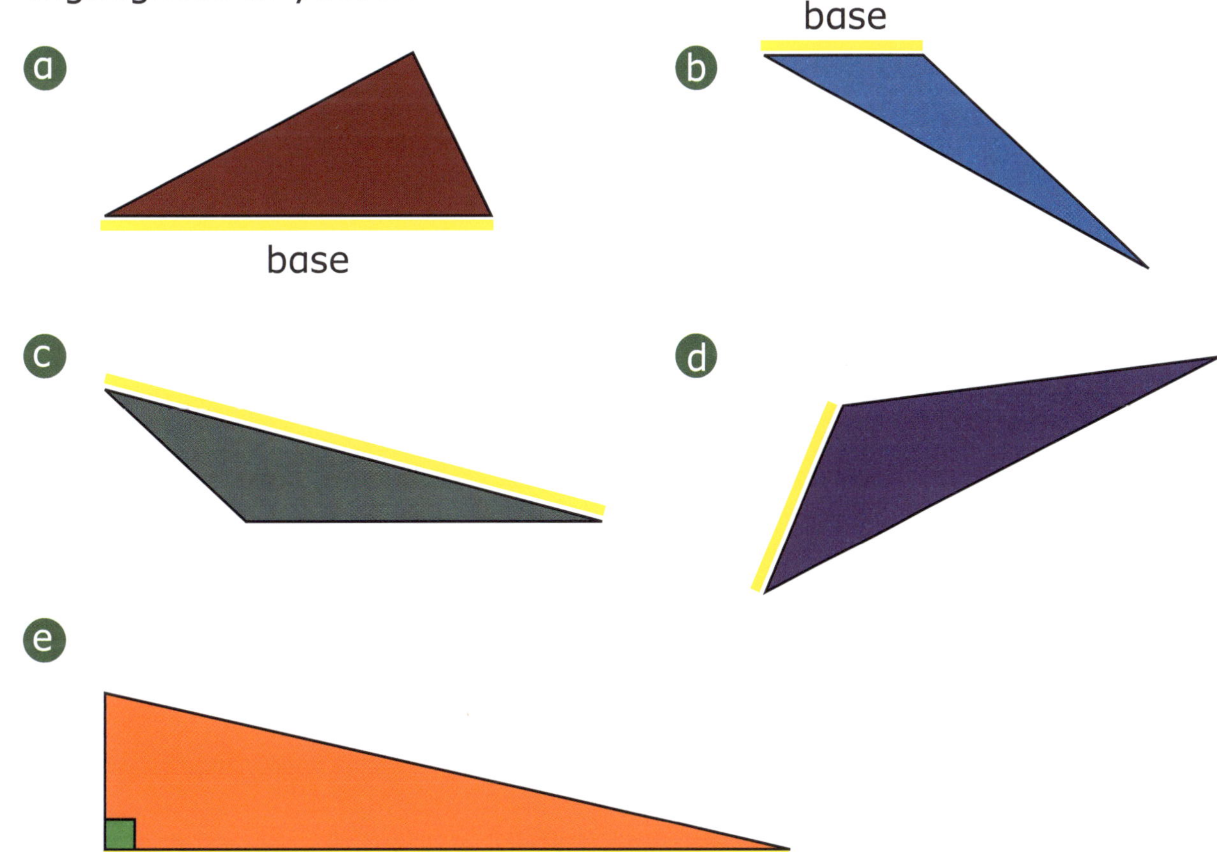

Discovering the Area of a Trapezoid

Country flags around the world are made with many geometric shapes. Kuwait, Philippines, and South African flags include trapezoids in their designs.

Below are two congruent trapezoids A and B.

Trace and cut out trapezoid **B** and try to fit it next to trapezoid **A** to make a parallelogram as shown below. Can you discover the trapezoid formula?

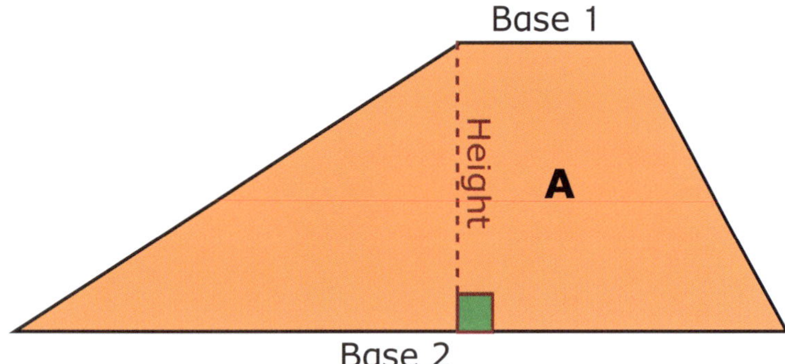

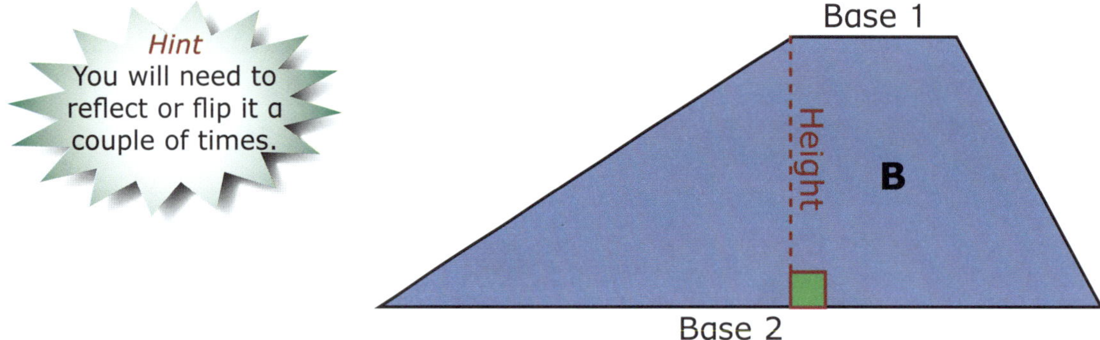

Label Base 1, Base 2, and the Height in ***each*** trapezoid.

Formula: ____

Area of a Trapezoid

To find the area of a trapezoid, use the formula $\boldsymbol{A = \frac{1}{2}h(b1 + b2)}$.

The bases ($b1$, $b2$) are the parallel sides of a trapezoid, and $b1 + b2$ is the sum of the bases. To find the area, multiply the sum of the bases by the height and divide by 2. You can also take half the height, then multiply it by the sum of the bases.

Answer the following questions. Do not forget to write down the formula first.

Do not forget to label.

1. Find the perimeter and the area of this trapezoid.

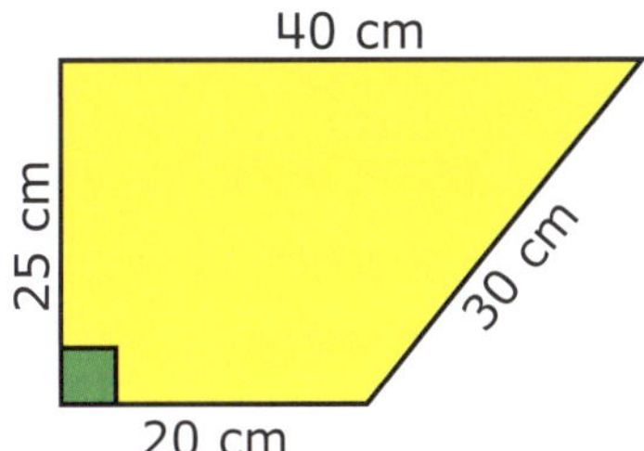

2. The area of a trapezoid is 30 square inches. The smaller base is 5 inches and the larger base is 10 inches. Find the altitude.

3. The area of a trapezoid is 45 square feet. The altitude is 6 feet and one base is 12 feet. Find the other base.

4. Find the area of this trapezoid by using another method besides the trapezoid formula.

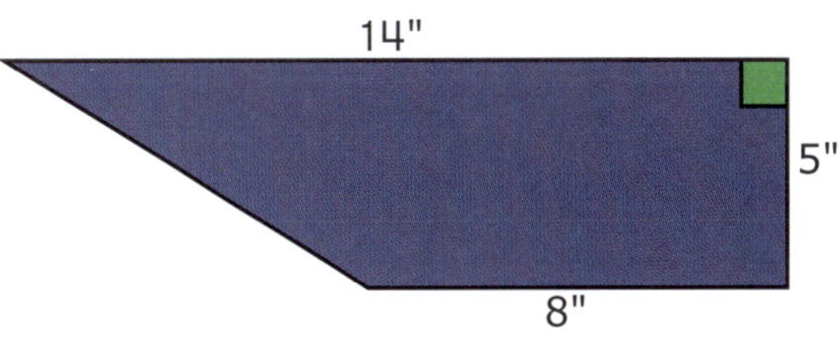

Area of a Trapezoid (Cont.)

5. Find the area of this trapezoid.

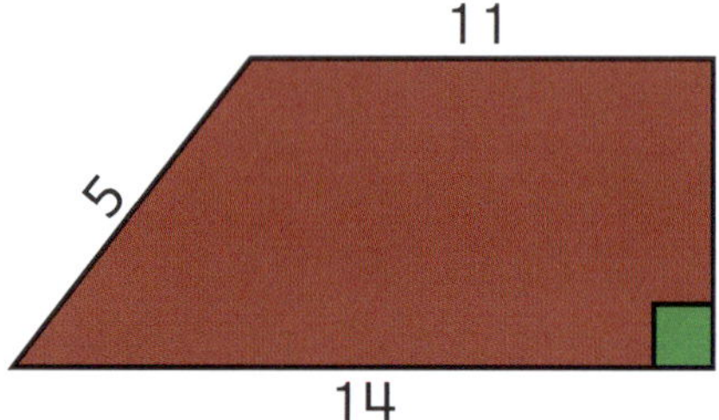

6. Find the perimeter and the area of this isosceles trapezoid. Round both answers to the nearest tenth of a centimeter.

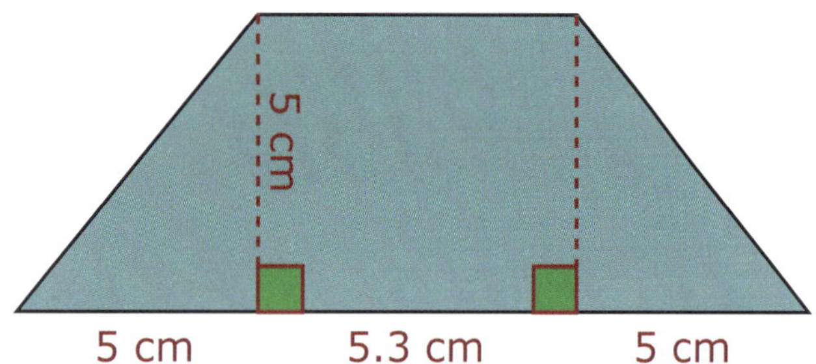

7. The perimeter of an isosceles trapezoid is 76 meters. The bases are 20 meters and 30 meters. Draw the trapezoid, then find the length of its two missing sides and area.

Area of Circles

The formula for the area of a circle is $A = \pi r^2$, where r is the radius of the circle. The ancient Babylonians computed the area of a circle by using 3 times the square of the radius. But one Babylonian tablet showed 3.125 was the value for pi.

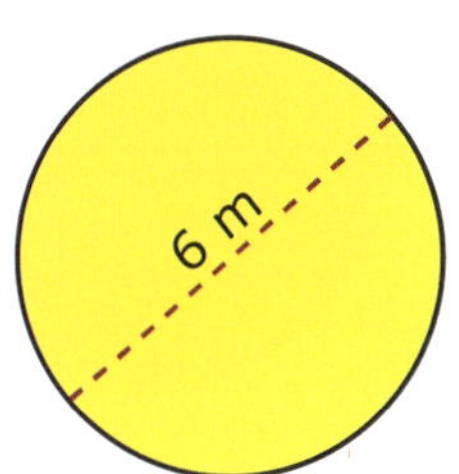

How to remember the first ***seven*** decimal digits of π.

"May I have a large container of apples?"

3. 1 4 1 5 9 2 6 ...

The number of letters in each word in the question equals each digit (3.1415926...).

Answer the following questions. Leave your answer in terms of π unless asked to use 3.14.

1. Find the circumference and area of this circle.

6 m

2. If the area of a circle is 49π square inches, find the radius and the diameter.

3. Find the area of this quarter circle.

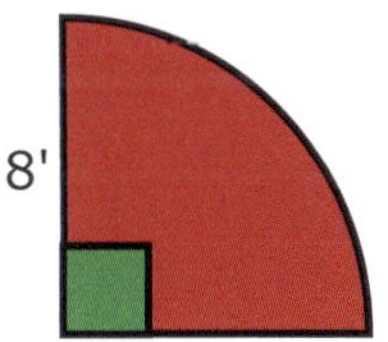

Area of Circles (Cont.)

4. Find the area and perimeter of this semicircle if its diameter is 18 centimeters. Use 3.14 for π. Round your answer to the nearest hundredth.

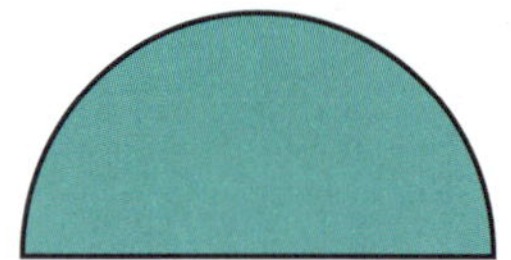

5. All 3 points of this triangle touch the edge of the circle. The base of the triangle equals the diameter of the circle. The radius of the circle is 4 inches. Is it possible to find the area of the triangle?

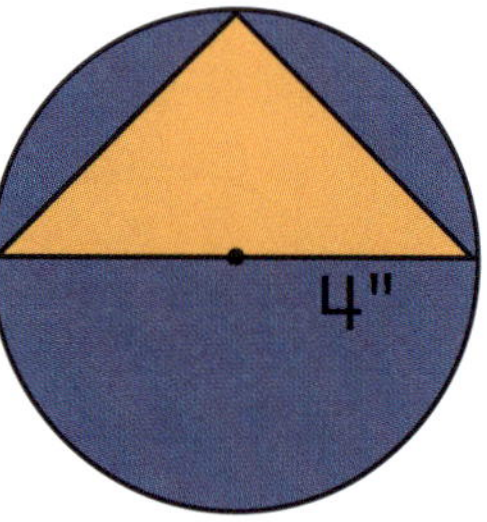

Explain your thinking. ____________________

____

____

6. A circular pool at a park has a diameter of 5 yards. In the center is a fountain with a diameter of 1 yard. Find the area that surrounds the fountain. Round your answer to the nearest square yard. Use 3.14 for π.

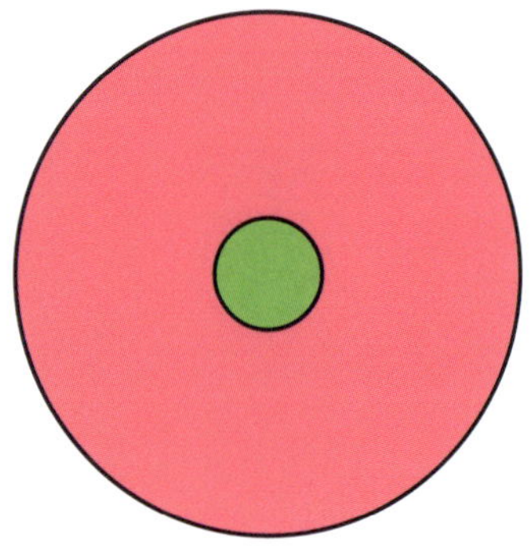

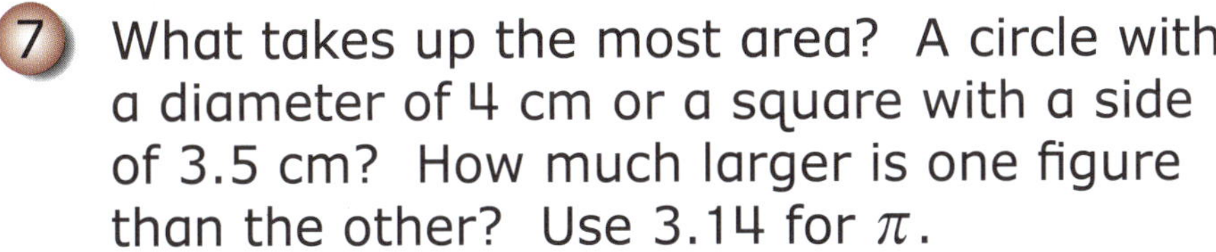

Area of Circles (Cont.)

7. What takes up the most area? A circle with a diameter of 4 cm or a square with a side of 3.5 cm? How much larger is one figure than the other? Use 3.14 for π.

Explain your thinking. ______________________________

____

____

____

8. Two congruent circles are inside a larger circle and **tangent** to each other as shown below. If the larger circle has a diameter of 12 units, find the area inside the larger circle that is ***not*** taken up by the smaller circles. Leave your answer in terms of π.

9. Olga is building a garden shaped by two circles with the same radius that are **tangent** to each other. The distance between the center of circle **A** and the center of circle **B** is 16 ft. Find the area taken up by her garden. Leave your answer in terms of π.

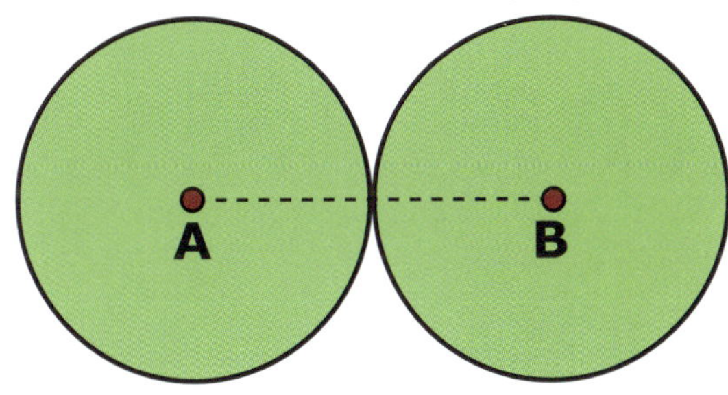

The Arbelos Problem

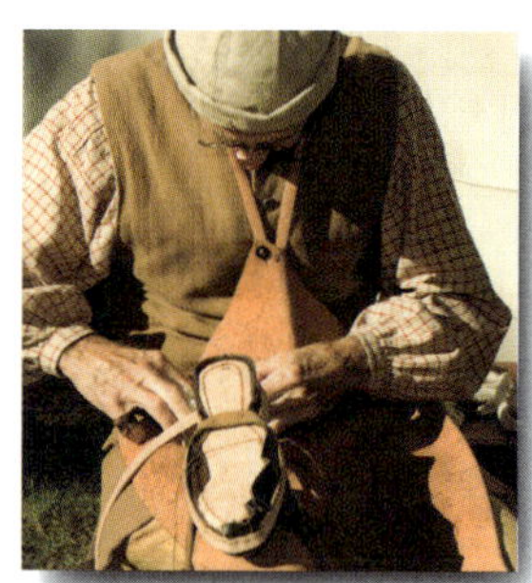

The ancient Greeks studied a shape called the **arbelos**. In Greek, the word means shoemaker's knife because the shape looks like a knife used in ancient times. The **arbelos** is the area shaded in yellow in the figure below. Archimedes is believed to be the one of the first mathematicians to study the arbelos shape.

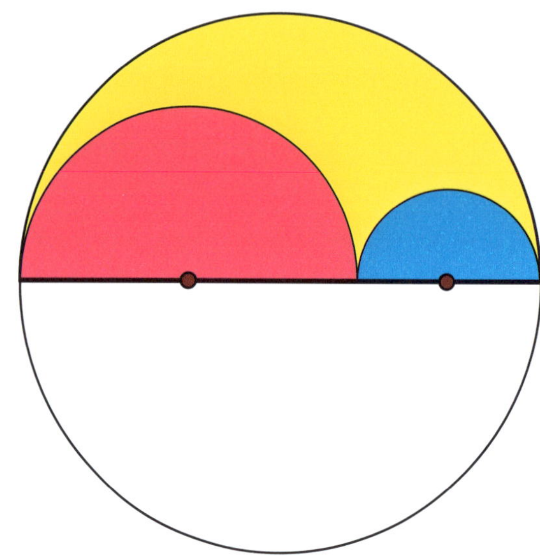

1. Suppose the larger yellow semicircle has a diameter of 12 units and the pink semicircle (which is tangent to the blue circle) has a diameter of 8 units. What is the length of the diameter of the blue semicircle?

2. Find the area of the arbelos above. Leave your answer in terms of π.

To learn more about the properties of the arbelos shape, you can search the Internet.

Chapter 8 - Geometric Constructions

A Geometric Construction

A geometric construction is a drawing of a geometric item done with only a compass and a straightedge. Of course, a good pencil is important. In a classic geometric construction, you are ***not*** allowed to measure or erase. If you make a mistake, it's best you start over.

Before we problem solve and do some *fun thinking* problems with constructions, it is a good idea to review how to do these constructions.

- Bisecting an angle.
- Copying an angle.
- Constructing a perpendicular bisector to a line.
- Constructing a perpendicular bisector to a line from a point on the not on the line.
- Constructing a line parallel to another line through a given point.
- Constructing some popular polygons.

Note

My constructions are actual drawings since they were done on the computer, but if you follow the directions for each of these, you will make *perfect* constructions.

Geometric constructions are used by engineers and designers. They will help you see the beauty of geometry.

For fun, create your own design with a compass and a straightedge. Try to fill up a page of paper with your own design.

How to Bisect an Angle

Using a compass, follow the instructions below.

1. Put the point of the compass at vertex **C** and draw an arc from points **A** to **B**. (Figure a)

2. Put the point of the compass at point **A** and draw an arc in the middle of the angle. From point **B,** do the same without opening or closing the compass so that the arcs intersect. (Figure b)

3. With a straightedge, connect the intersection to vertex **C**. You've constructed the angle bisector (-----) of ∠**ACB**. (Figure c)

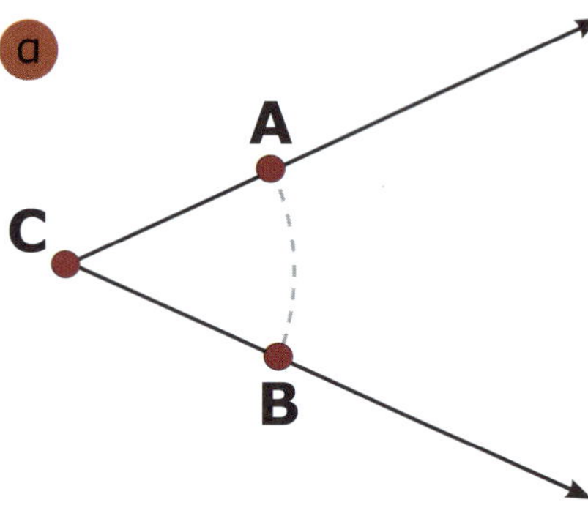

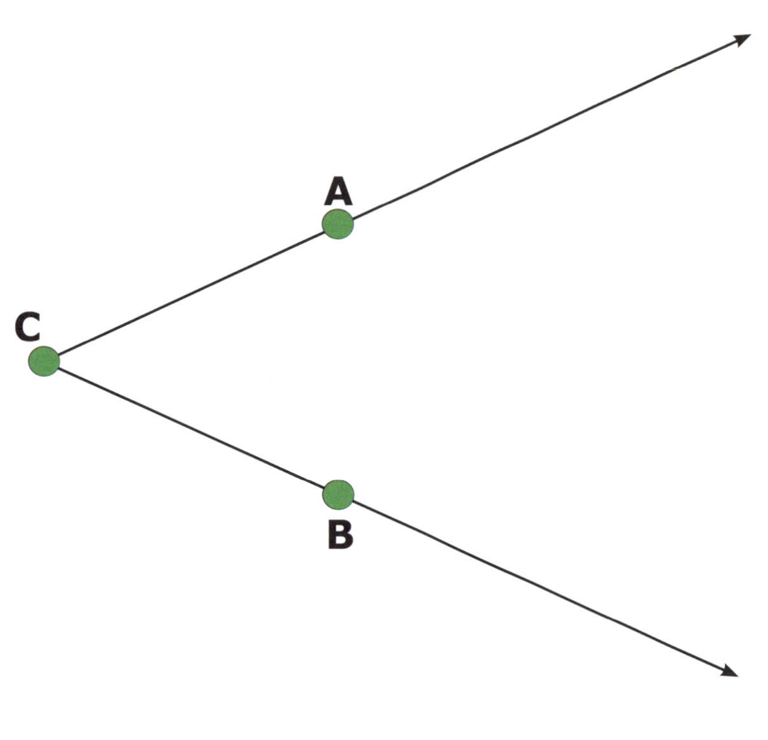

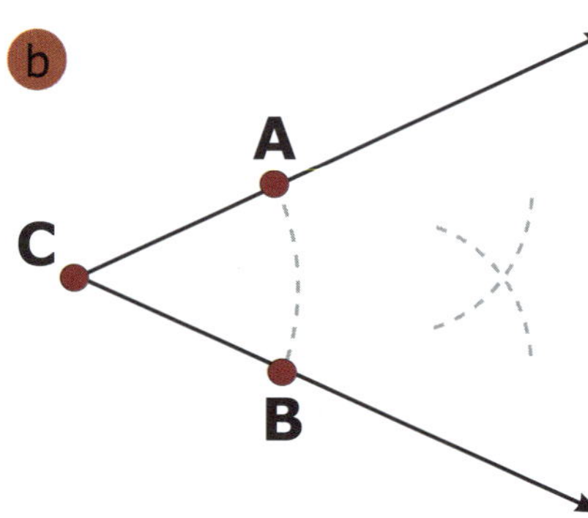

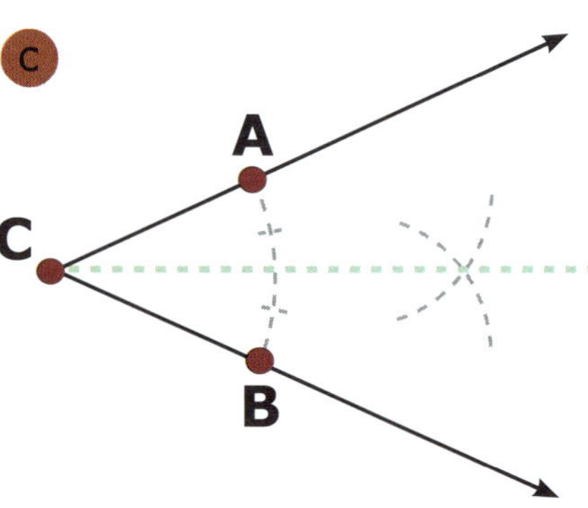

How to Bisect an Angle (Cont.)

Bisect each angle of the triangle below. Find the point where all the angle bisectors intersect.

The intersection of the bisectors is called the **incenter** of the triangle.

Using the incenter as the center point, you will now be able to construct a circle that is inscribed in the triangle as shown.

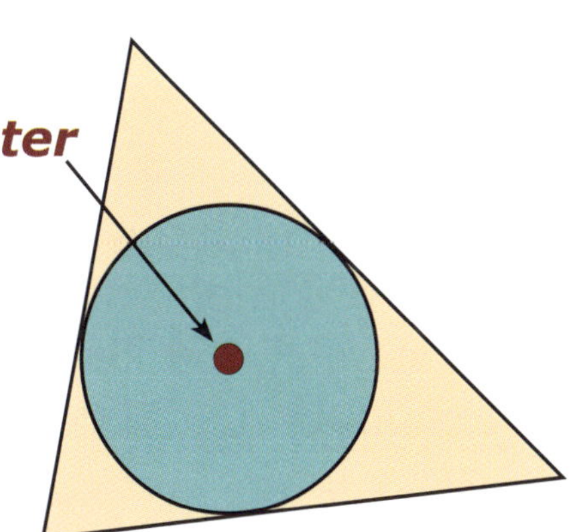

How to Copy an Angle

Suppose you need to copy this angle using the given segment below. Use the examples and follow the steps to make your copy of this angle.

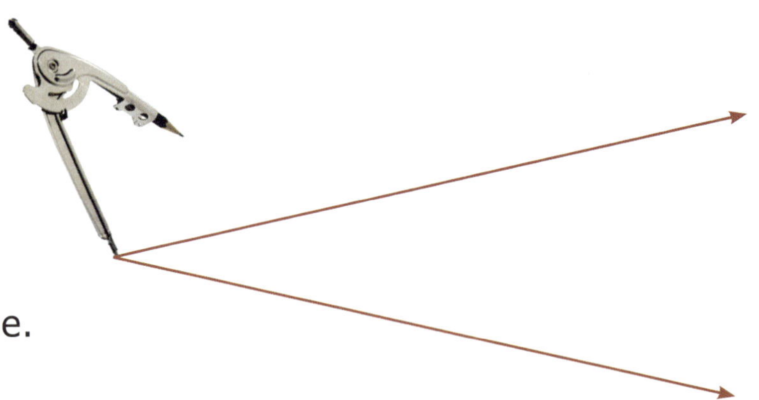

1. First, you may have to extend the segment using a straightedge. (Figure a)
2. From the vertex of the angle above, draw an arc. (Figure b)
3. On the segment, go to one endpoint and draw the same arc. (Figure c)

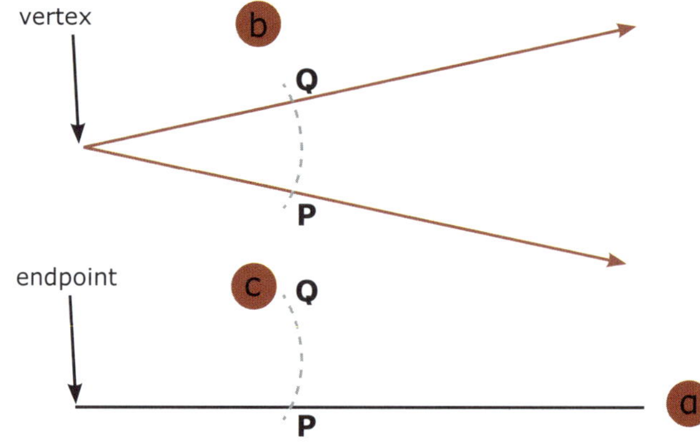

4. With your compass (not a ruler), measure the distance between **P** and **Q** on the angle. Make a mark on the angle you are copying. (Figure d)
5. Make the same mark on the arc you made on the segment (Figure e) and join **Q** to the endpoint using a straightedge. (Figure f)

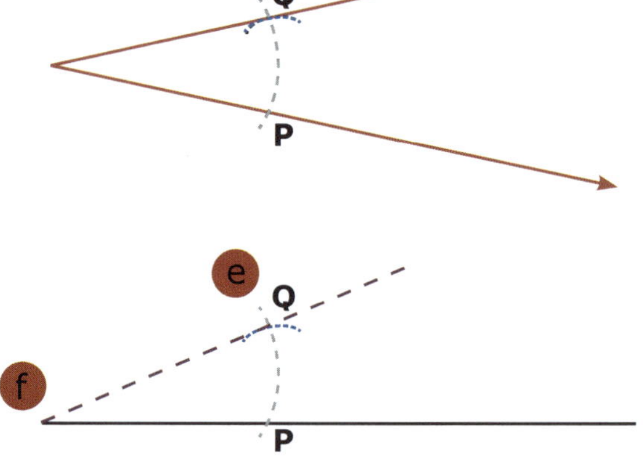

How to Construct a Perpendicular to a Line

A **perpendicular** line is one of the ***most*** important constructions used in architectural drawings and other fields where designing is important.

Follow the steps and examples below to create a perpendicular to the line segment above.

1. Put the compass at one endpoint of the given segment and open your compass to more than half way the length of the segment. (Figures a)

2. From each endpoint make two arcs, one above and one below the segment making sure they intersect. (Figures b)

3. With a straightedge, connect the intersection of the arcs. (Figure c)

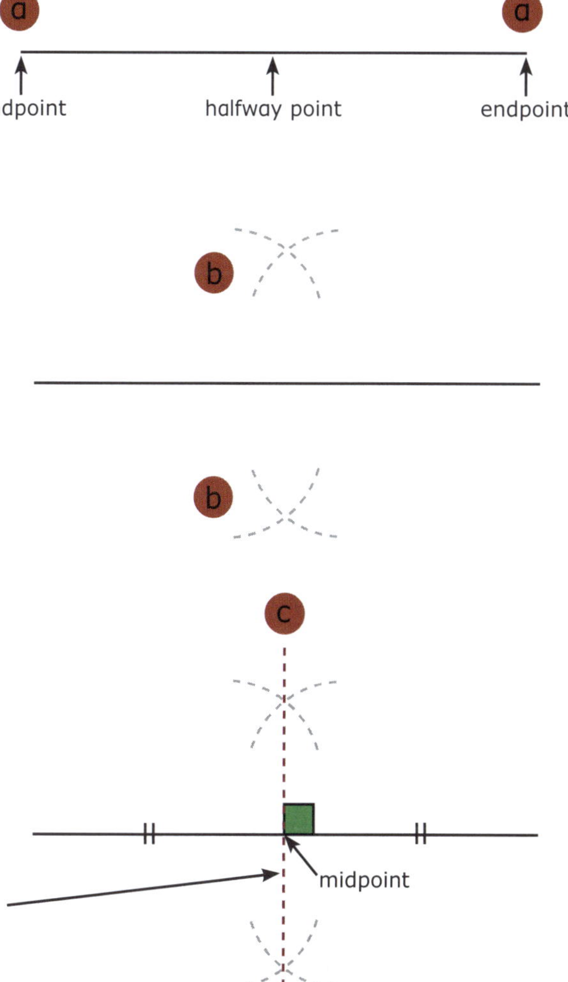

A **perpendicular line** is a segment that is perpendicular to the given segment and also bisects it.

How to Construct a Perpendicular to a Line (Cont.)

Construct a perpendicular line to each side of this triangle. Find the intersection of the three perpendicular lines.

This point of intersection (or point of concurrency) is called the **circumcenter**.

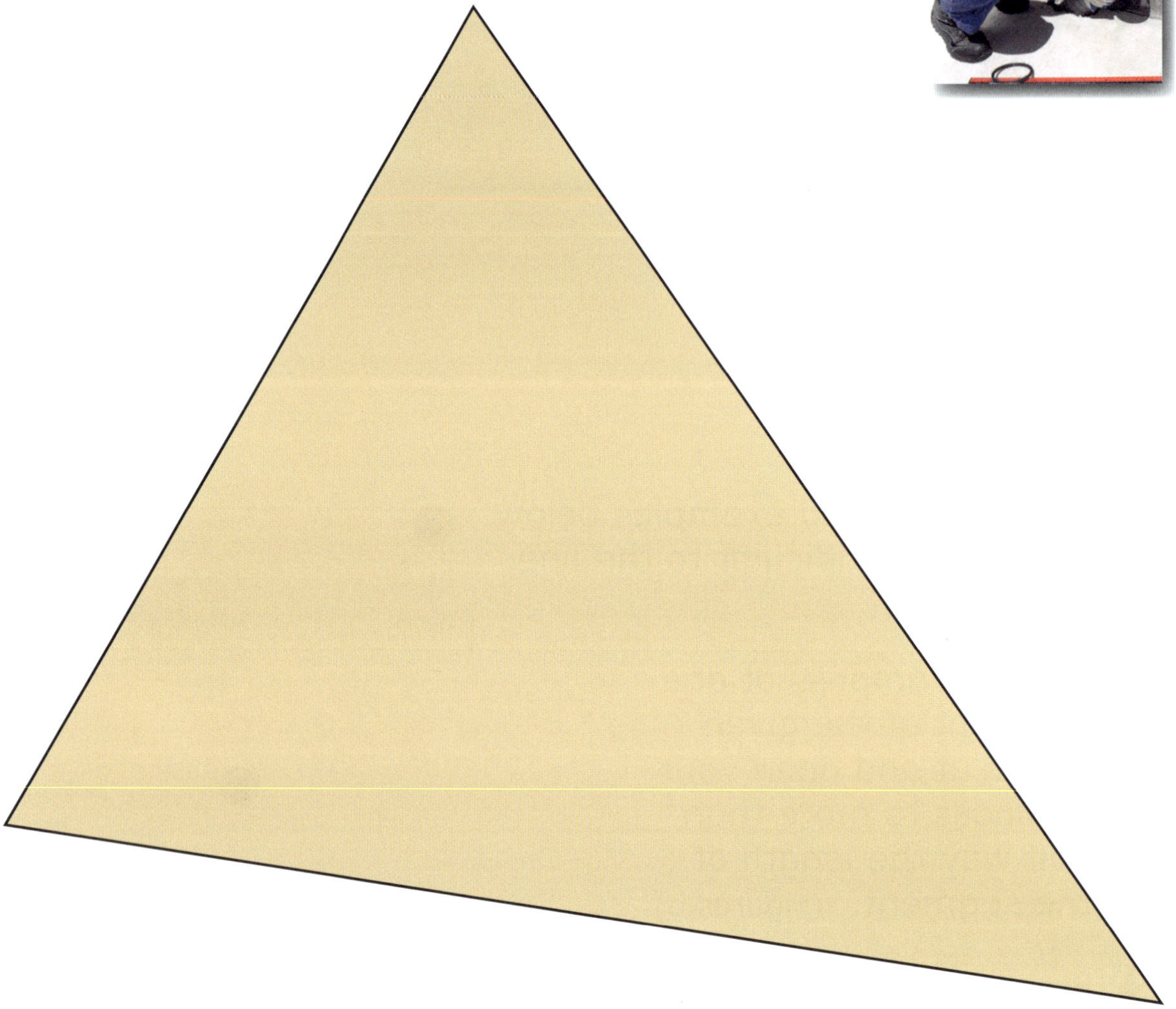

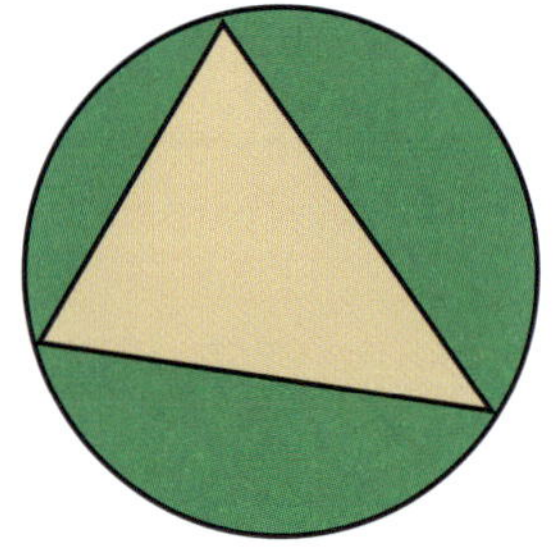

Using the circumcenter as your center, construct a circle that circumscribes the triangle as shown here.

How to Construct a Perpendicular to a Line (Cont.)

To construct a perpendicular to a segment through a point ***not*** on the segment, follow the steps and examples below.

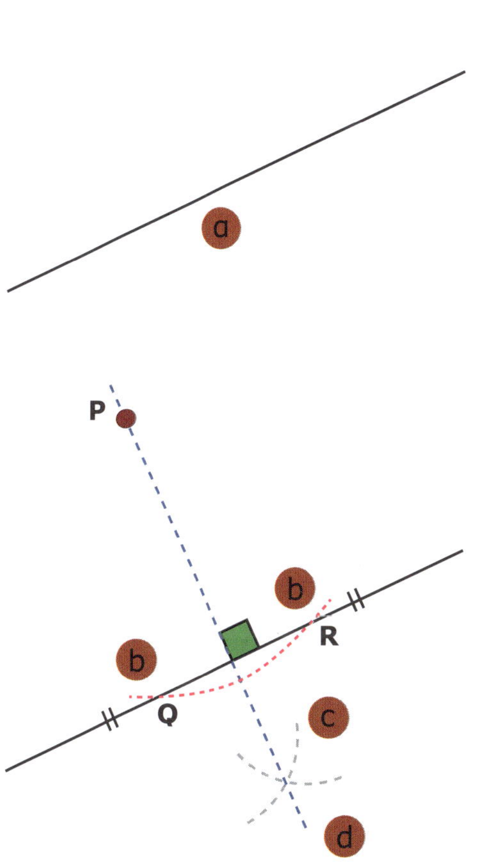

1. You might have to extend the segment on one side. (Figure a)

2. With the compass at point **P**, draw an arc that intersects the segment at two points as shown here. (Figures b)

3. From **Q** and **R** draw two arcs that intersect (Figure c), then connect that intersection to point **P**. (Figure d)

Finding the Median in a Triangle

The median is the segment that connects the midpoint of a side of a triangle to the vertex of the angle opposite that side.

1. What construction would you use to find the midpoint of the side of a triangle? ____________________

2. How many medians does a triangle have? ____________________

3. Using the triangle below, find the midpoint of each side by using a construction. After you find all midpoints, connect each midpoint to the vertex of the opposite angle.

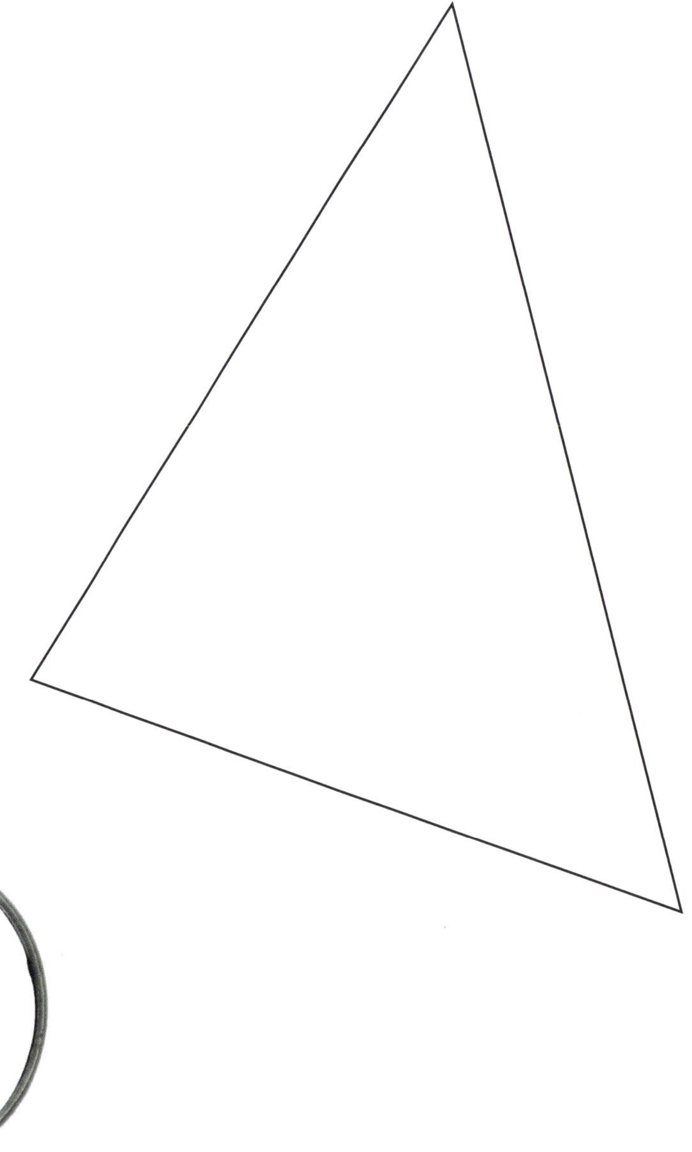

Hint
You only need to find the midpoints so do not draw the perpendicular bisectors.

Finding the Median in a Triangle (Cont.)

The three **medians** intersect at a point called the **centroid**. This is the center of gravity of the triangle.

How to Remember

Think of a **median** on a road. It's in the middle. The median in a triangle goes from the vertex of each angle to the midpoint of the side opposite that angle.

A freeway in Florida with a grass median. Freeways in the United Sates have different kinds of medians.

Find the centroid.

4. On heavier paper, draw your own triangle and find the centroid. Cut the triangle out and try balancing it using the centroid.

5. Measure the distance (this time with a ruler) from the centroid to each vertex of the triangle. What seems to be true?

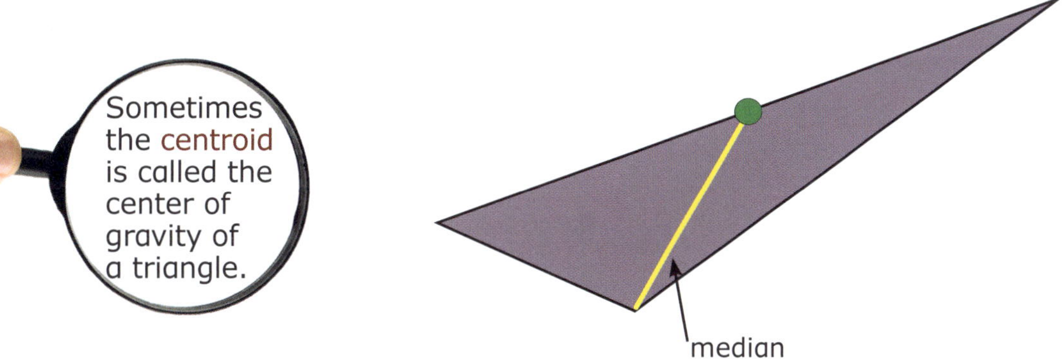

Explain your thinking.

___

___

___

How to Construct a Line Parallel to Another Line

Construct a line parallel to another line through a given point.

P

Engineers of the Edinburgh Railway used geometric constructions to design these train lines.

Follow the steps and examples below.

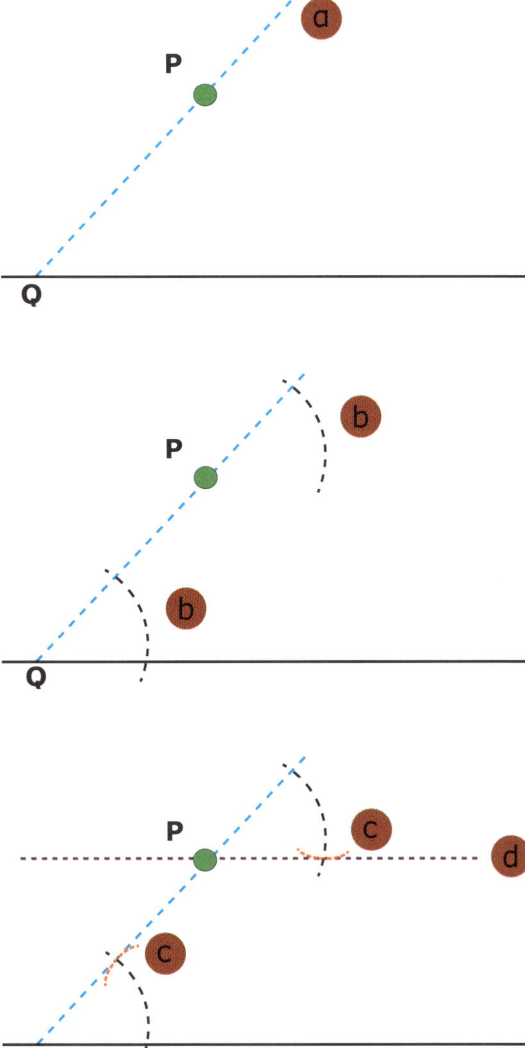

1. With a straightedge, draw a line from a point on the given segment going through point **P**. Drawing the line at an angle is better. (Figure a)
2. From point **Q,** draw an arc, then draw the same arc from point **P** as shown. (Figures b)
3. Copy the bottom angle on the arc above. (Figures c)
4. Draw the line. (Figure d)

Geometric Construction Review

Answer the following questions.

1. How many lines can be parallel to another line in space? ____________

2. How many lines are parallel to another line through a given point?

   Explain your thinking. ____________

3. On the last construction, what is the mathematical property that is used to prove the lines are parallel?

   Explain your thinking. ____________

4. What is the reason why a protractor is not a tool used in a geometric construction?

   Explain your thinking. ____________

5. Point **A** is on segment $\overline{\mathbf{TR}}$. On a plane, how many lines are perpendicular to $\overline{\mathbf{TR}}$ going through point **A**? Is your answer also true in three dimensions?

   Explain your thinking. ____________

Problem-Solving With Geometric Constructions

1 Paulo needs to put another fence post perpendicular to this board below. The post must also be in the center of the board. Use a construction to show where the post should go.

2 

Lucy is a civil engineer and she needs to design a road that goes from the park through the center of town. The road must be equidistant from the existing roads below which form an angle. Use a construction to design the new road.

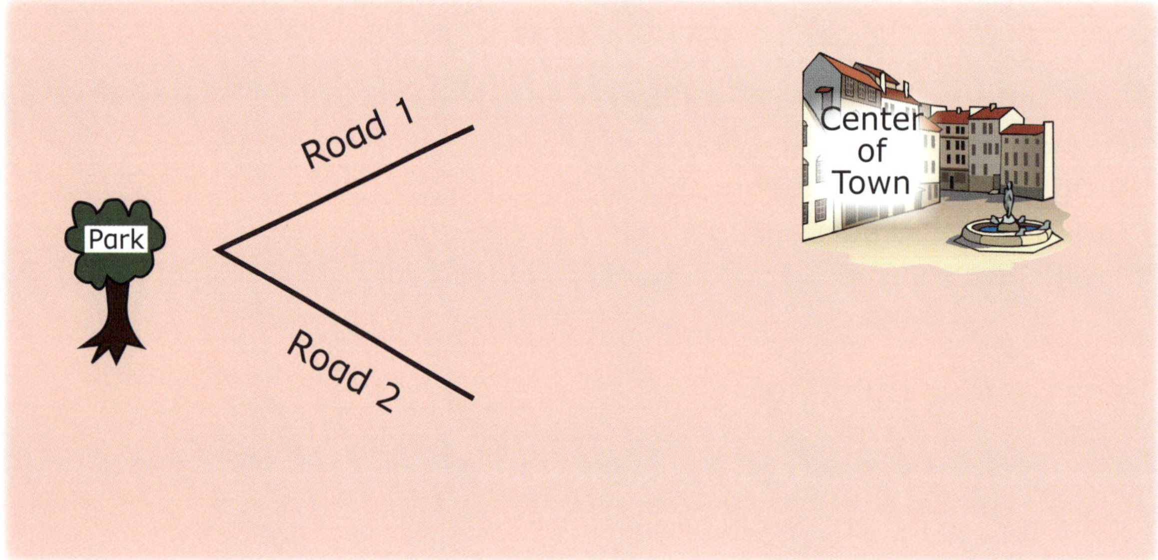

Problem-Solving With Geometric Constructions (Cont.)

3. Follow these steps and examples to construct a regular hexagon on the next page.

1. Use your compass to draw a circle making sure you know where the center is located. (Figure a)

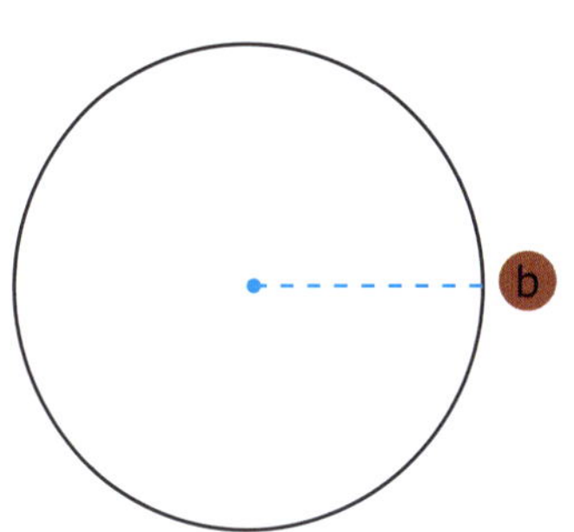

2. Using your compass, open it to the distance of the radius. (Figure b)

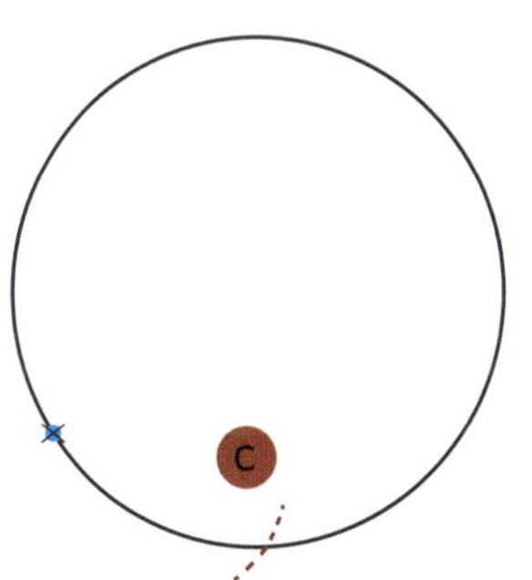

3. Then put the point of the compass on the circle (distance of the radius) and make a small arc as shown. (Figure c)

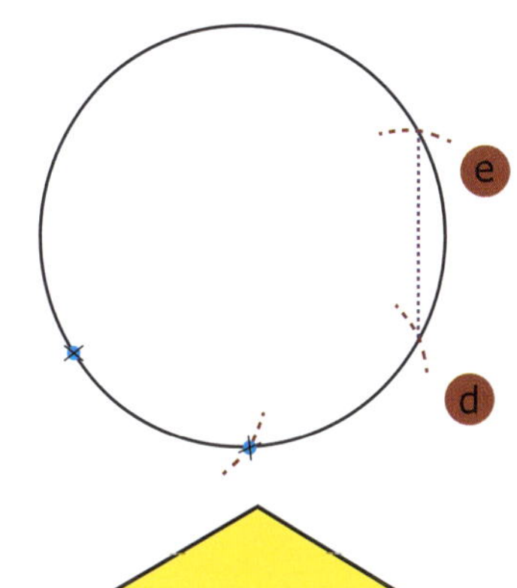

4. From the point where the arc intersects with the circle, make another mark and continue doing until you come to the first point. (Figure d)

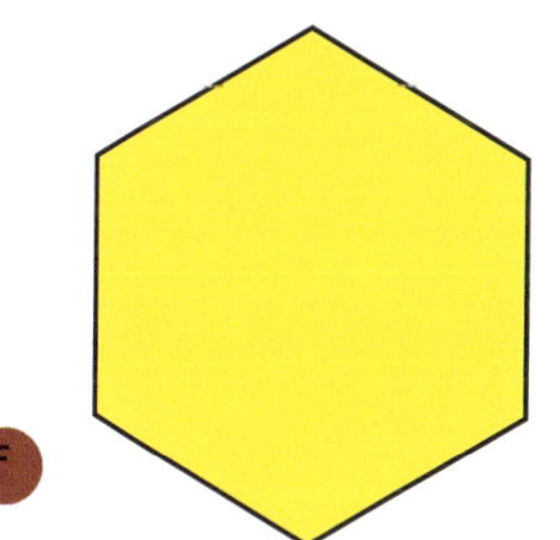

5. Connect those points (Figure e) and you will construct a regular hexagon. (Figure f)

Problem-Solving With Geometric Constructions (Cont.)

4 Now construct your own regular hexagon, then answer the following questions.

a Connect the opposite vertices of your hexagon. What type of triangles, and how many, are created?

____

b Construct a 30° angle. Explain how you know it is a 30° angle without using a protractor.

____

____

____

____

c How would you construct a 15° angle?

____

d How would you construct a 120° angle?

____

Problem-Solving With Geometric Constructions (Cont.)

5. Mr. Baker is a lawyer who conducts business in three different New York towns; Trumansburg, Ithaca, and Alpine. He wants to build a house exactly the same distance from all three cities in order to save time and gas. Where exactly should he build his house? Draw his house below. A geometric construction will help.

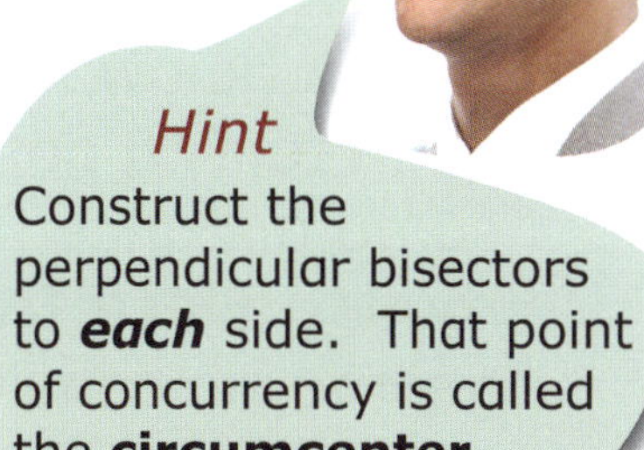

Hint
Construct the perpendicular bisectors to ***each*** side. That point of concurrency is called the **circumcenter**.

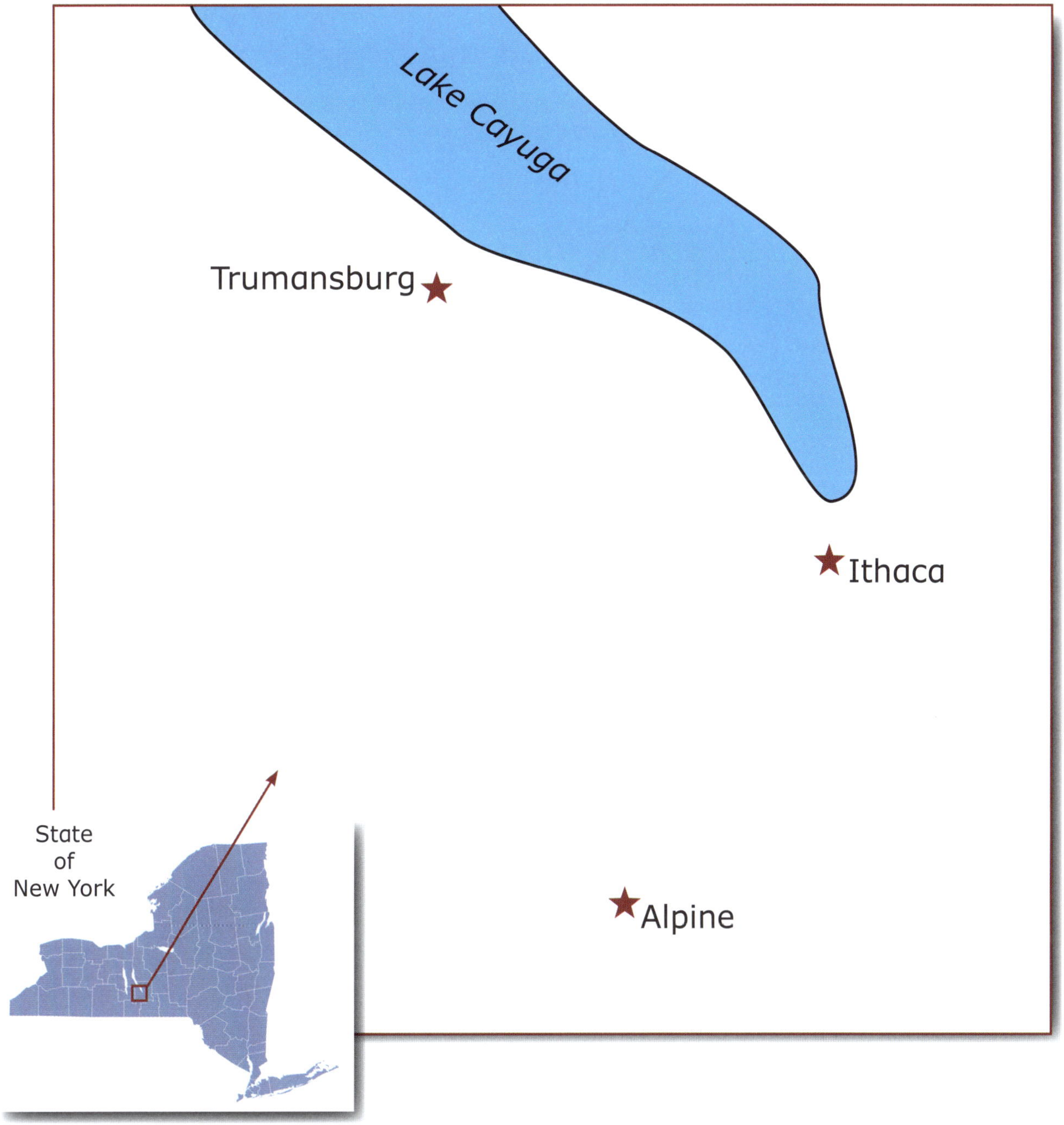

Lake Cayuga

Trumansburg ★

★ Ithaca

★ Alpine

State of New York

Problem-Solving With Geometric Constructions (Cont.)

Hint
Find the incenter.

6. Two bank robbers are fleeing in a stolen automobile. The police know that they will take one of three main roads shown below. Trooper Alice Brown has been told to position a base camp the same distance from each of these main roads. Since Trooper Brown knows her geometric constructions, she finds the exact spot for her base camp. Mark that position below.

HIGHWAY PATROL

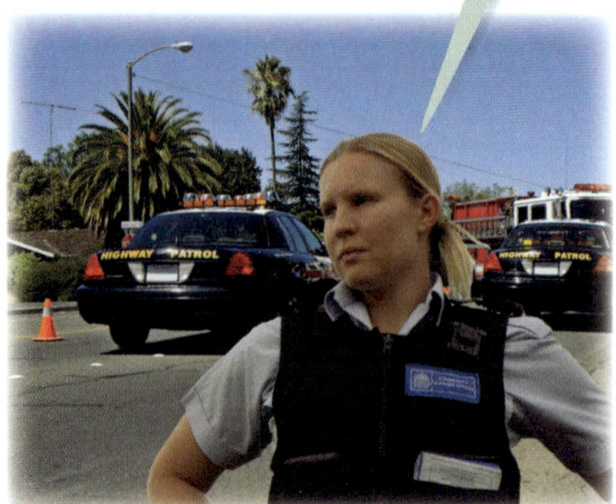

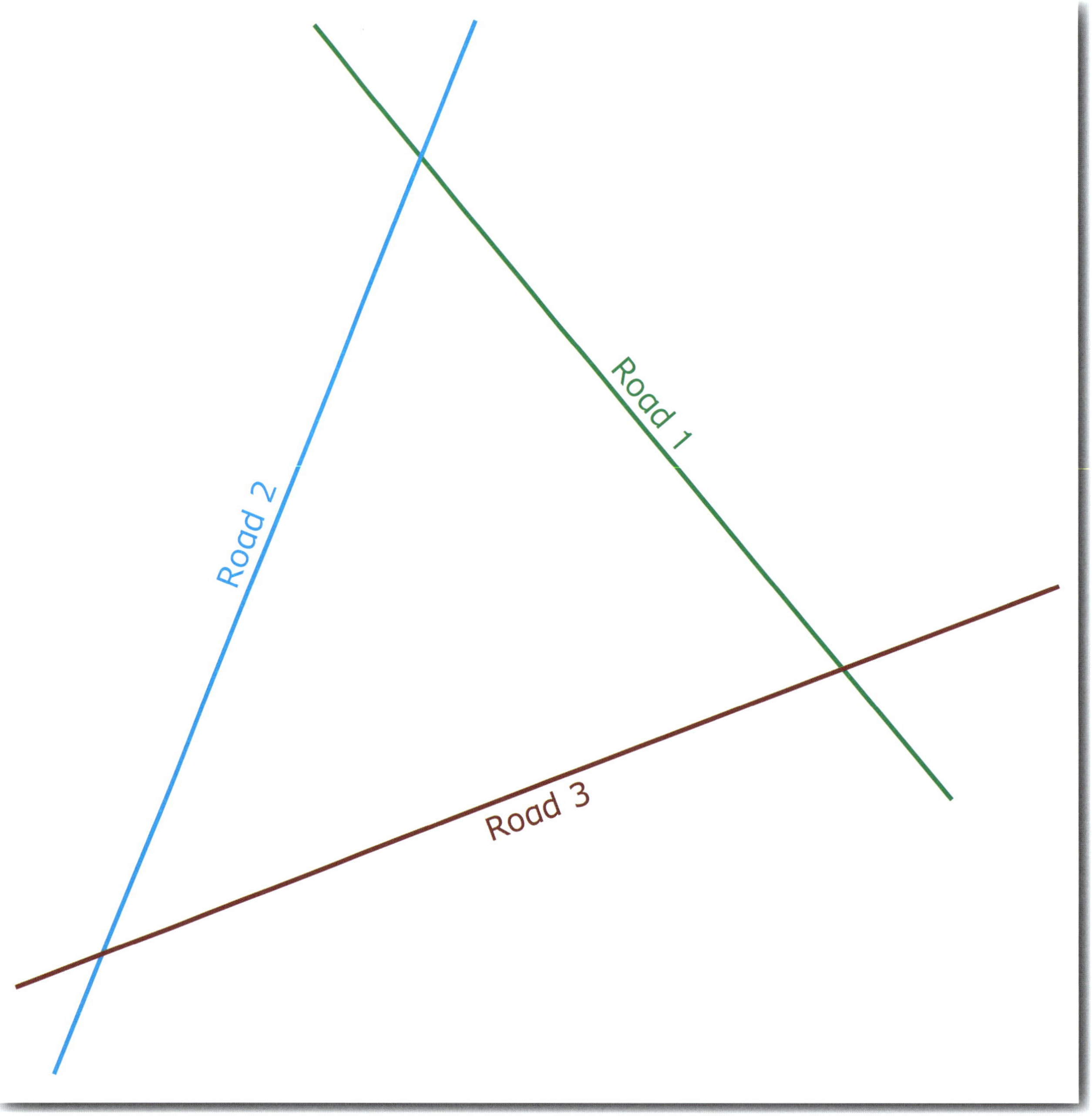
Road 1
Road 2
Road 3

Problem-Solving With Geometric Constructions (Cont.)

Plato (*428-347 BC*), a famous Greek philosopher and mathematician, discovered that many constructions can be made with only a compass and no straightedge. Those constructions are now called Mascheroni constructions in honor of Italian mathematician Lorenzo Mascheroni (1750-1800) who wrote a book called *The Geometry of Compasses*.

Ancient Greek philosopher drawing his theorem in the sand.

7 Using *only* a compass, given segment $\overline{\mathbf{AB}}$, construct segments that are 2, 3, and 4 times bigger than $\overline{\mathbf{AB}}$.

A B

Remember
You ***cannot*** use a straightedge so you can only show the points that mark such distances.

8 I lost the center of *My Circle* construction below. If you draw a circle and forget where the center is, draw two non-parallel chords. Construct the perpendicular bisectors of each chord and where the perpendicular bisectors meet is your missing center. Try it!

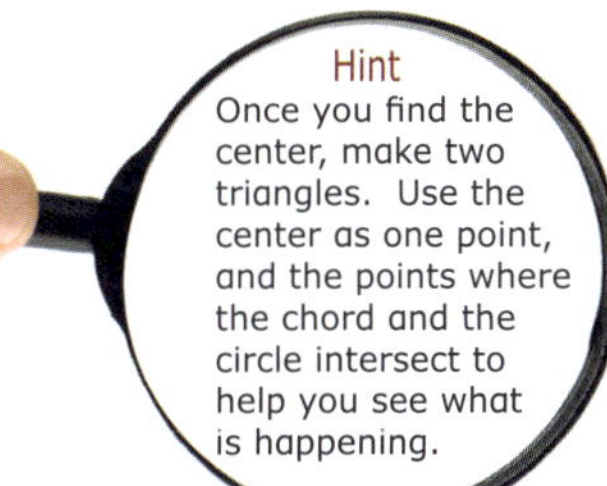

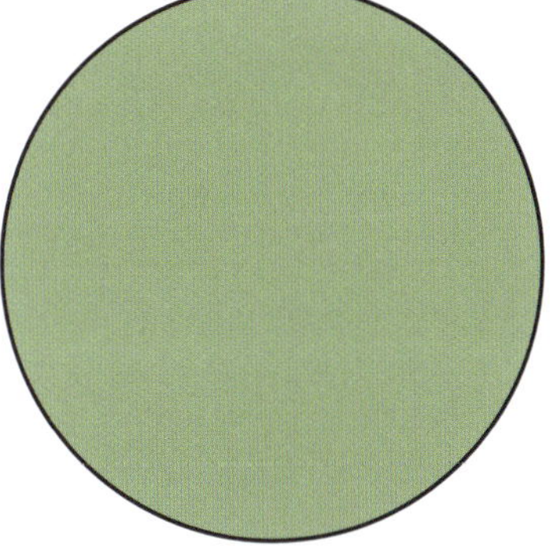

Why does this work? Explain your thinking. ____________________

____

____

Problem-Solving With Geometric Constructions (Cont.)

The intersection of the three altitudes ( ) of a triangle is called the **orthocenter**.

Find the orthocenter of each triangle. In which of these triangles would the orthocenter lie outside the triangle?

a

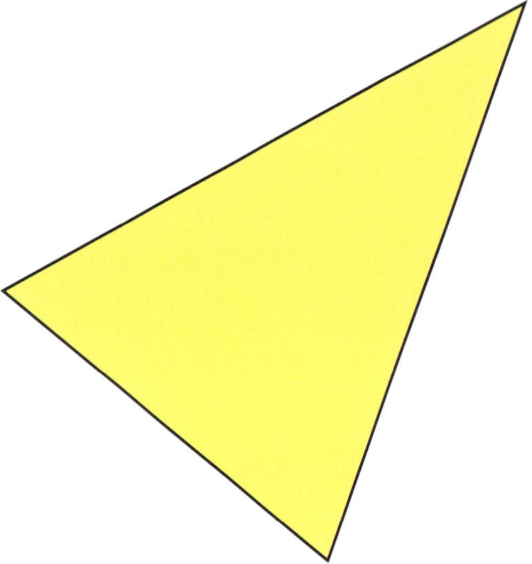

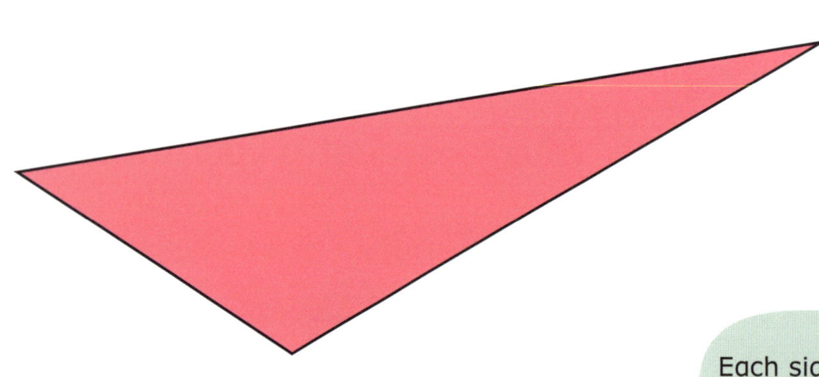

Hint
Each side is the line, and the point not on the line is the vertex of the angle across from that side. (See Construction IV - Constructing a perpendicular to a line from a point not on the line.)

Problem-Solving With Geometric Constructions (Cont.)

10 The following are the directions to inscribe a square in a circle. Do the construction, then answer the questions below.

1. On the circle, mark and label the center **O**.
2. Draw a diameter and label the points where the diameter intersects the circle as points **A** and **B**.
3. Construct a perpendicular bisector to $\overline{\mathbf{AB}}$.
4. Label where the perpendicular bisector intersects the circle as points **P** and **Q**.
5. Connect **P**, **A**, **Q**, and **B** to make a square.

a 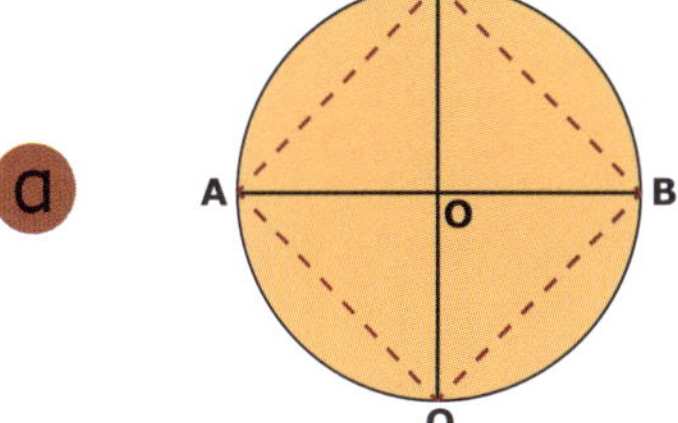

Assume your labels look like those in this picture. What type of triangle is Δ**ABP**? ____________________

b What type of triangle is Δ**ABQ**? ____________________

c Draw several circles, then inscribe a triangle in each semicircle (using the diameter as one side). What seems to be true?

Explain your thinking. ______________________________________

____

Problem-Solving With Geometric Constructions (Cont.)

11. How would you construct a regular octagon inscribed in a circle?

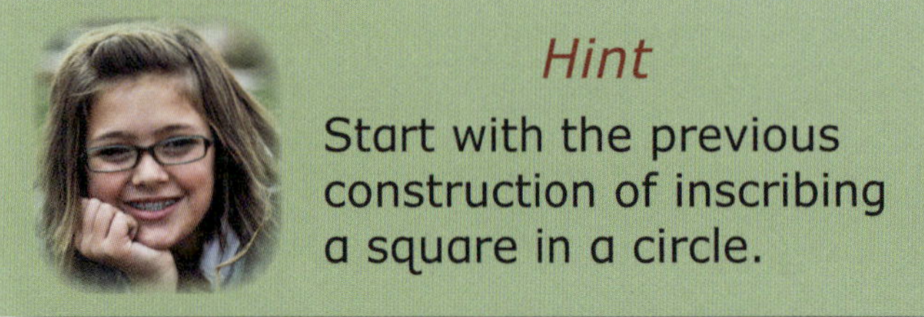

Hint

Start with the previous construction of inscribing a square in a circle.

A spiral staircase and an octagon window at Vatican City.

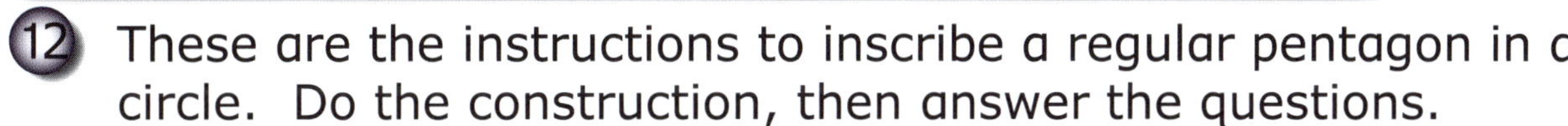

Problem-Solving With Geometric Constructions (Cont.)

12 These are the instructions to inscribe a regular pentagon in a circle. Do the construction, then answer the questions.

1. In the circle **P**, draw diameter **AC.**
2. Construct a perpendicular bisector to **AC**. Label this diameter **QR**.
3. Bisect **PC** and label its midpoint **M**.
4. Put your compass at **M** then using distance **MQ** as your radius, draw an arc that intersects **AP** at point **F**. **FQ** is the length of each arc needed to make your pentagon.
5. Start anywhere on the circle making five arcs the length of **FQ**. Connect their intersection to make a regular pentagon.

a What is the measurement of each angle in the regular pentagon?

____

____

b Explain what you would do to inscribe a regular decagon in a circle.

____

____

Problem-Solving With Impossible Constructions

All the constructions we have done and many others were successfully done by the ancient Greeks. However, there were many constructions that were not solved until later.

One example is that of inscribing a regular 17-gon in a circle. In 1796, mathematician **C. F. Gauss** was able to construct it. He also proved that it was impossible to inscribe a regular nonagon in a circle.

The ancient Greeks also struggled trying to come up with a construction to trisect an angle. French mathematician, **Pierre Wantzel**, proved in 1837 that trisecting an angle was *impossible*. While some angles can be trisected, there are no steps to trisect just any angle like there is for bisecting.

Answer these questions.

1 What is wrong with this construction?

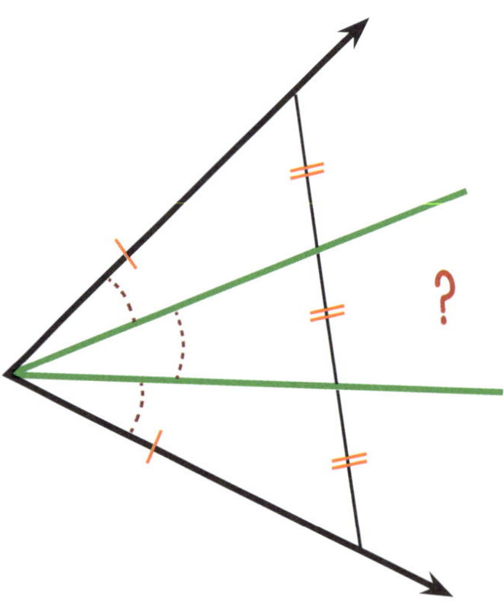

Explain your thinking. ______________________________

____

____

____

Problem-Solving With Impossible Constructions (Cont.)

Trisect a 90° angle. It is possible to do so?

Remember

Classic geometric construction only allows a compass and a straightedge.

Hint

It will help if you construct a 90° angle, then construct an equilateral triangle in that angle.

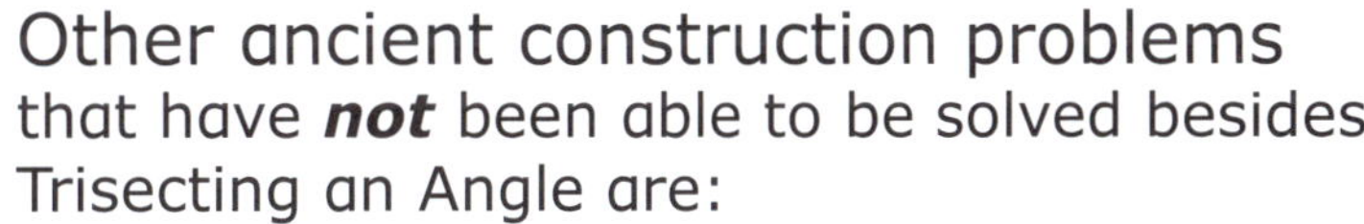

Other ancient construction problems that have ***not*** been able to be solved besides Trisecting an Angle are:

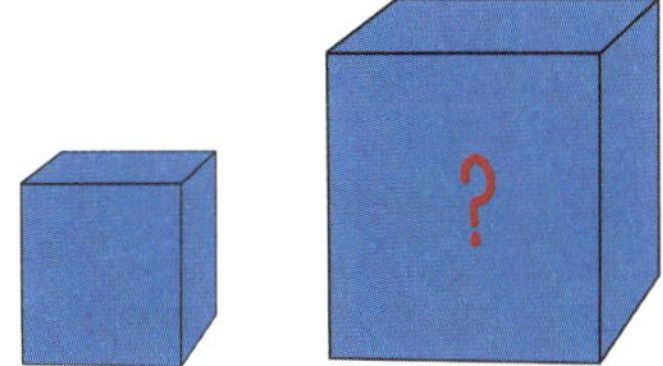

Duplicating a Cube means that given the side of a cube, you are to use a geometric construction to make a cube with twice the volume of the original cube.

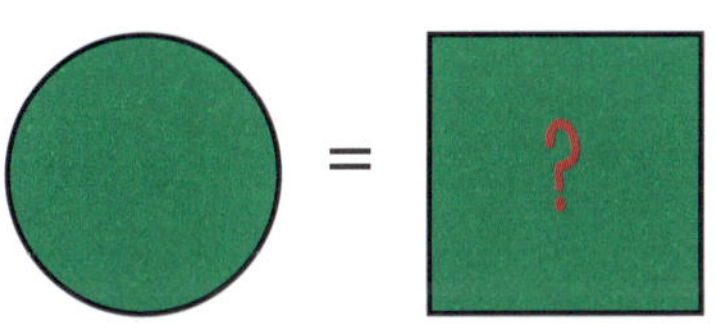

Squaring a Circle, mathematicians have tried unsuccessfully to take the radius of a circle and construct a square with the same area as the circle.

If something is hard to do, it does not mean it is impossible. Sometimes it is, but in mathematics, it is ***not*** impossible until someone proves it is impossible. *So never stop trying!*

Chapter 9 - The Geometry of Three Dimensional Shapes

3D Shapes - Prisms

Right prisms are polyhedra (polygons 2-D, polyhedra 3-D) with two polygon bases that are congruent and parallel. The other faces of a right prism are parallelograms that are perpendicular to the bases. You can name a prism by the type of polygon that makes up its base.

The volume of a prism is ***V* = *BH*** where ***B*** stands for the total area of one of the BASES of the prism and ***H*** stands for the ALTITUDE (sometimes called depth) of the prism.

To understand how to find the volume of a prism, you need to understand one basic principle. If you slice each prism with cuts parallel to one of the parallel bases, you will have ***n*** number of congruent slices. So, find the area of one polygonal BASE, and multiply it by the ALTITUDE of the entire prism.

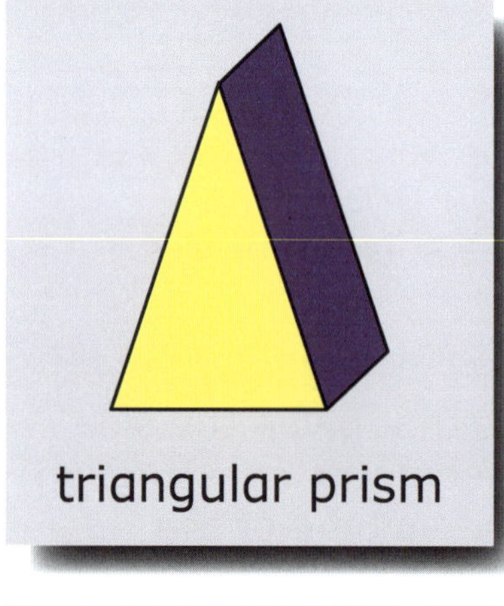
triangular prism

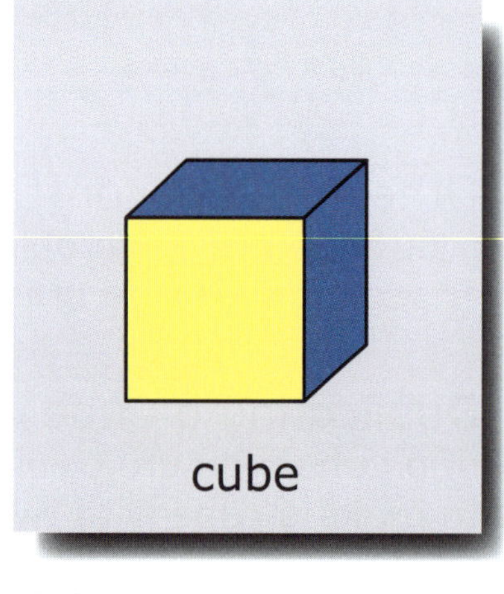
cube

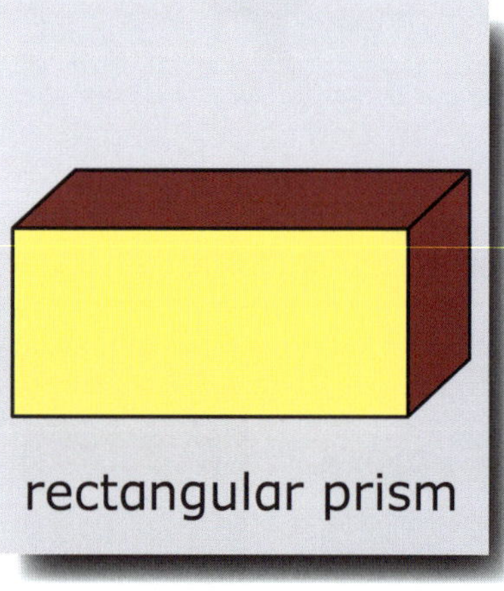
rectangular prism

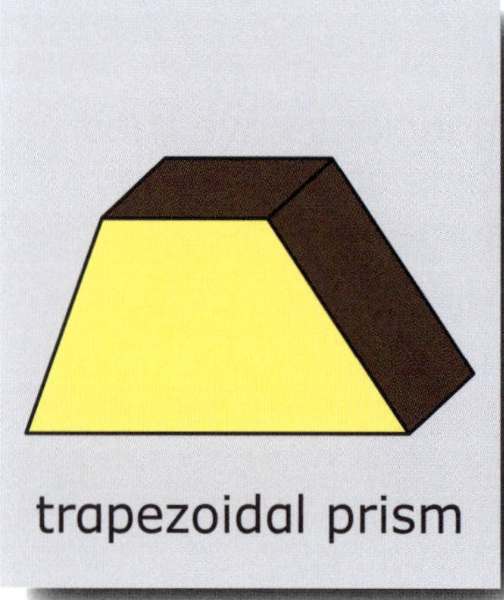
trapezoidal prism

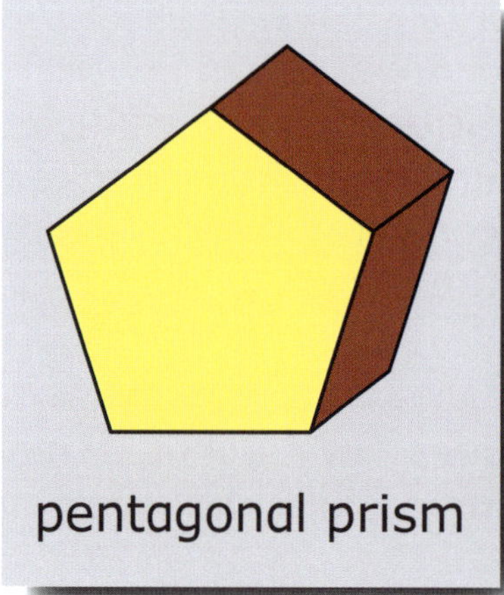
pentagonal prism

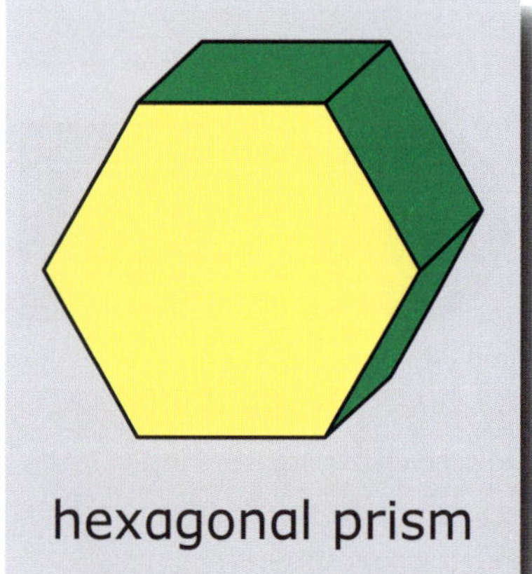
hexagonal prism

3D Shapes - Prisms (Cont.)

To find the volume of this cube, you can either use the formula ***lwh*** *(length x width x height)* or find the area of the BASE (*25*) times the ALTITUDE (*5*). In both cases, the answer is 125 cubic feet.

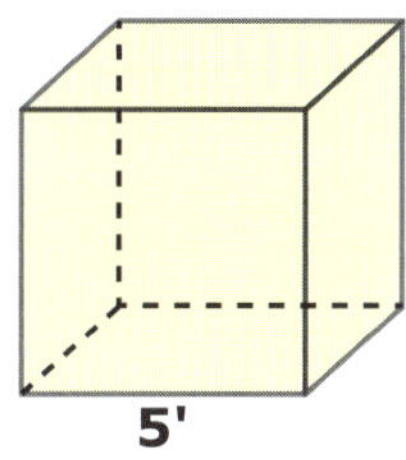

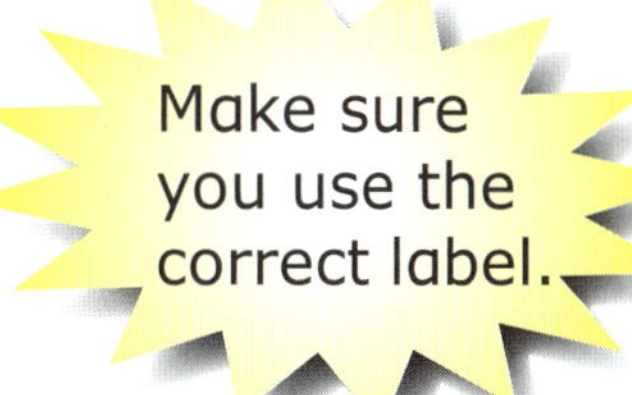

Answer the following questions.

1. A cube has a volume of 216 cubic centimeters. Find one side.

2. For a volume problem, Todd got the correct answer of 512 cubic feet, but he wrote his answer as 512'³. What is wrong with his label? How would you write Todd's answer?

3. Find the volume of this hexagonal prism. The BASE is a regular hexagon.

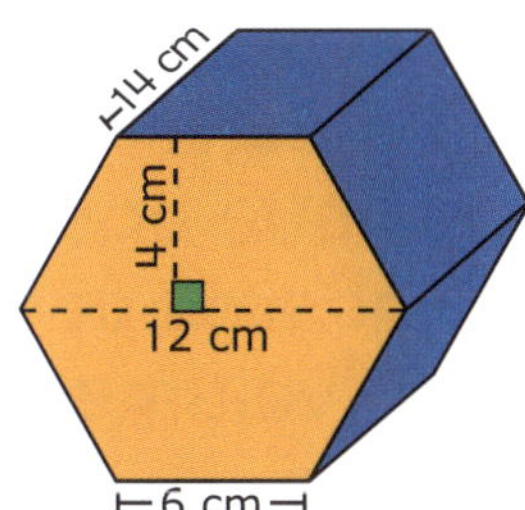

4. The BASE of the pentagonal prism shown is 50 square meters. If the ALTITUDE is 5 meters, find the volume.

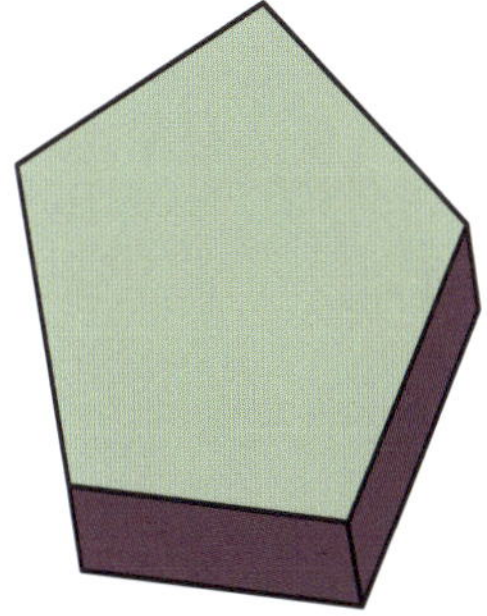

3D Shapes - Prisms (Cont.)

5. The Chocolate House at a fair is shown below. Find its volume.

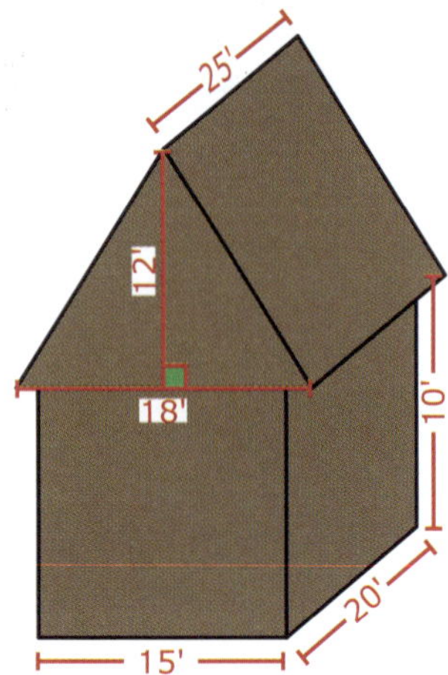

6. A cube is inside another cube. The inner cube has a side of 2 inches. and the outside cube has a side of 3 inches. Find the volume that is left after removing the inside cube from the outer cube.

7. Italian mathematician **Cavalieri** (*1598-1647*) claimed that these solids have the same volume. As long as the oblique prism has the same ALTITUDE and the same cross-sectional area at every level, then they have the same volume. Find the volume of both solids if they both have a BASE of 20 square inches.

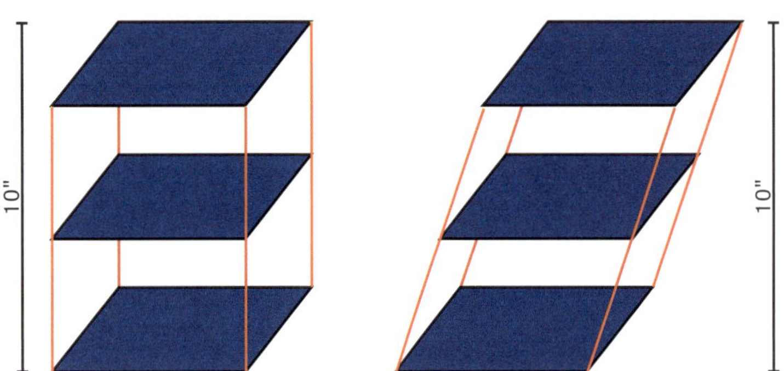

The Volume of Cylinders

The formula for the volume of a cylinder is $V = \pi r^2 H$. This formula is based on the same principle as the volume of a prism. It is the area of the BASE (this time the BASE is a circle) times its ALTITUDE (H), but remember a cylinder is not a prism because it does not have polygonal faces.

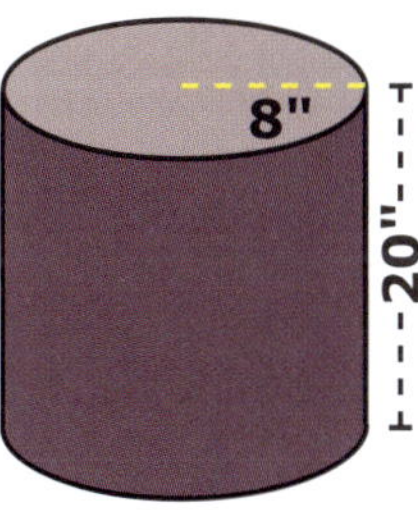

$V = \pi r^2 H$
$V = (64)(20)(\pi)$
$V = 1{,}280\pi$ cubic inches

Answer these questions. Leave your answers in terms of π unless asked to use 3.14.

1. Find the volume of this cylinder.

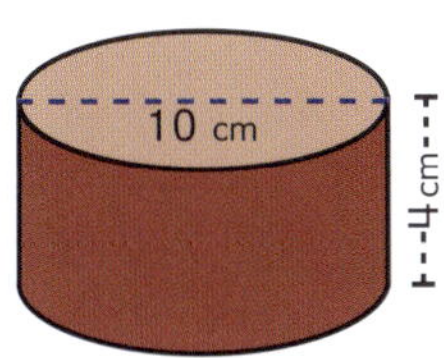

2. If the volume of a cylinder is 395.64 cubic inches and its ALTITUDE is 14 inches, find its radius. Use π = 3.14. Round your answer to the nearest inch.

3. Which solid has the greater volume? Use π = 3.14. Figures ***not*** to scale. Explain your thinking.

____

____

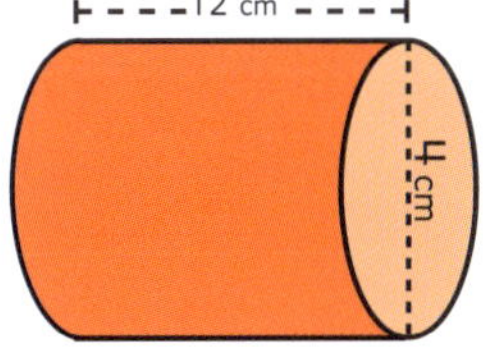

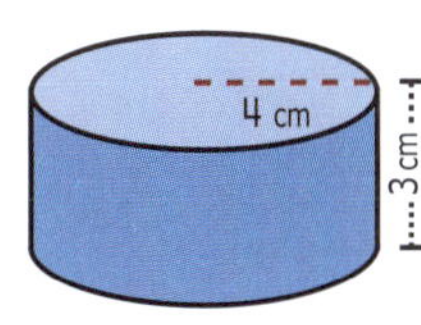

The Volume of Cylinders (Cont.)

4. A pipe has a thickness of 1 inch and an ALTITUDE of 5 feet. Find its volume. Use 3.14 for π.

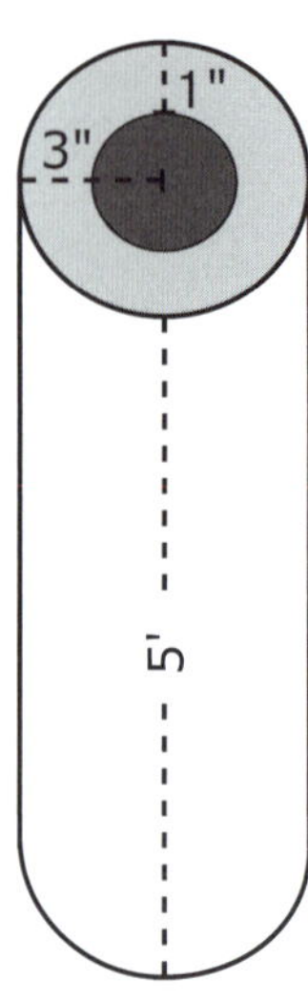

5. A student in your class computed the volume of this cylinder by showing this work. Describe the error and correct it.

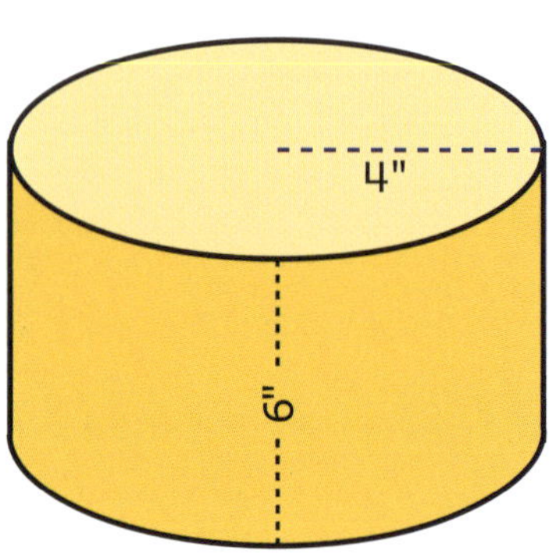

$V = \pi r^2 H$

$V = \pi(8)(6)$

$V = 48\pi$ cubic inches

Volumes of Pyramids and Cones

A pyramid is a polyhedron with a polygon BASE whose other faces are triangles. These triangular faces intersect at a point called the **apex**. A **tetrahedron** is a polyhedron with four triangular faces.

The Perito Moreno Glacier in Patagonia, Argentina forms natural ice pyramids.

To find the volume of a pyramid, take $\frac{1}{3}BH$ (one-third of the BASE times the height or ALTITUDE).

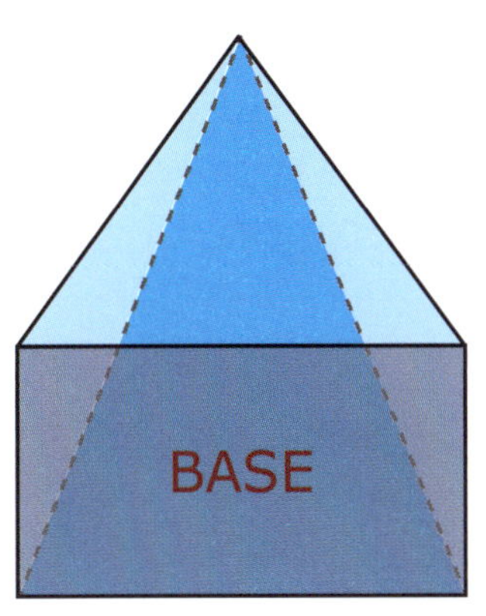

rectangular pyramid

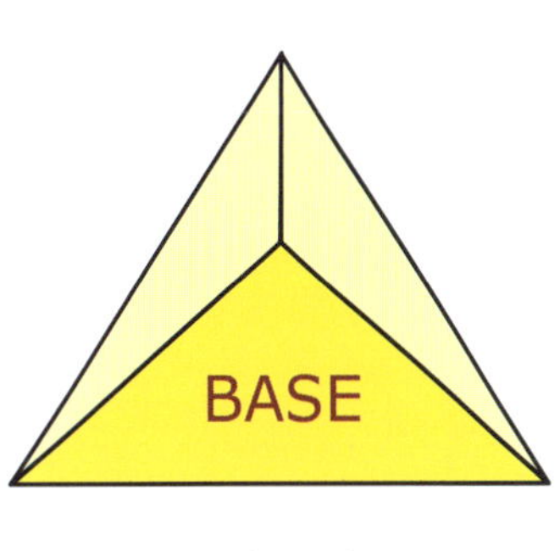

tetrahedron

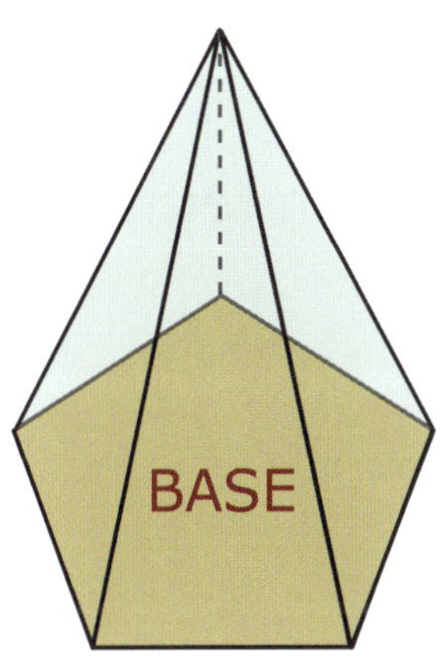

pentagonal pyramid

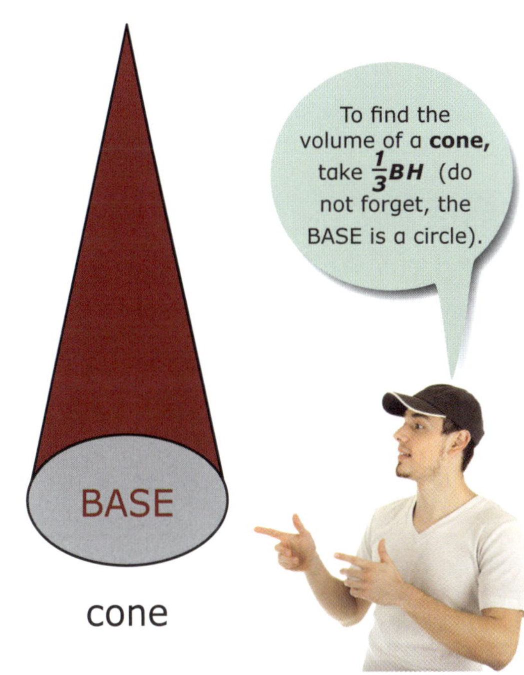

cone

Volumes of Pyramids and Cones (Cont.)

Answer these questions.

1. How many times greater is the volume of this cylinder compared to the volume of this cone?

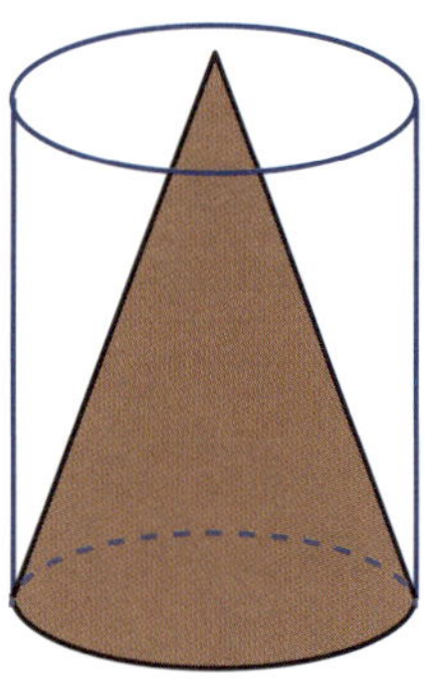

Explain your thinking. ______________________________

____

2. A regular pyramid has a BASE which is a regular polygon. Its faces are isosceles triangles.

What is the name of this regular pyramid? ____________

Find its volume.

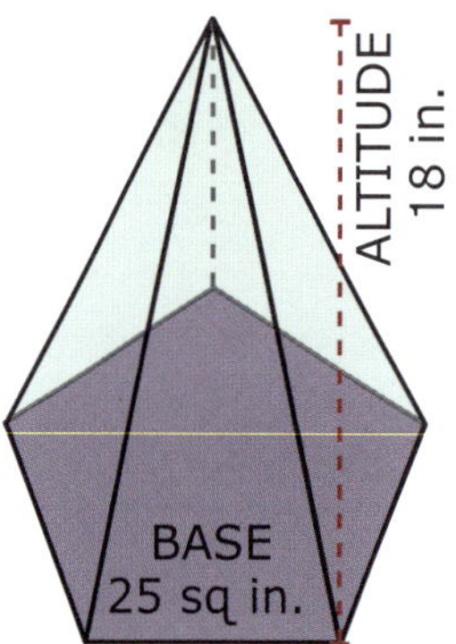

3. Find the volume of an ice cream cone with a diameter of 2 inches. and an ALTITUDE OF 6 inches. Leave your answer in terms of π.

Turn Up the Volume!

Answer these questions.

1. Maria's dad wants to build a new storage chest that is taller than this one, but he wants to keep the same volume as the one he now has which is shown here. Choose some measurements to help Maria's dad.

2. A chef wants to store several cans of soup into a box to save space in her kitchen. How many cans can fit inside the box? And how much space in the box is not taken up by the cans? Use $\pi = 3.14$.

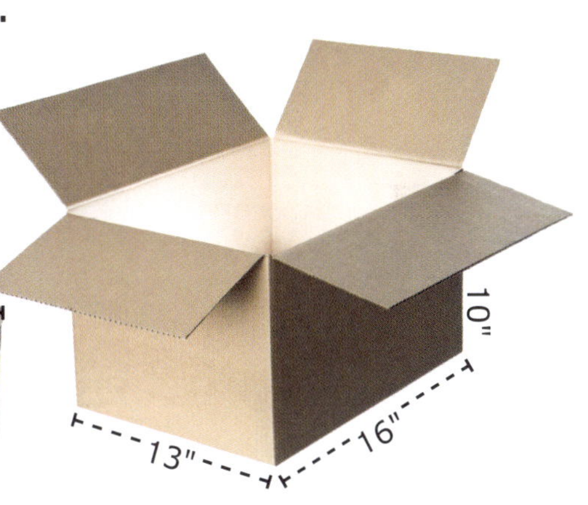

Explain your thinking. ______________________________

____

____

3. The volume of a triangular pyramid is 32 cu cm. The BASE is a triangle of base 6 cm and height 4 cm. Find the ALTITUDE of the triangular pyramid. Draw a picture.

Turn Up The Volume! (Cont.)

4. The volume of a cylinder is 1,846.32 cubic inches. The ALTITUDE of the cylinder is 12 inches. Using $\pi = 3.14$, find the circumference of the BASE.

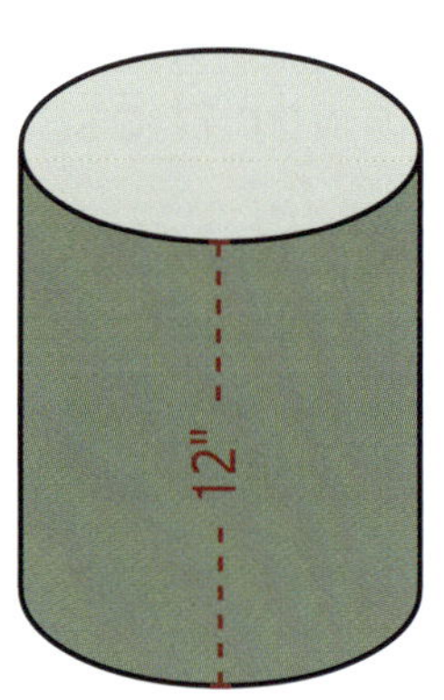

5. John told Maria if the side of a cube is increased by 20%, then the volume of a cube is increased by 60%. Maria thinks if the side is increased by 20%, then the volume is increased by 72.8%. Who is right?

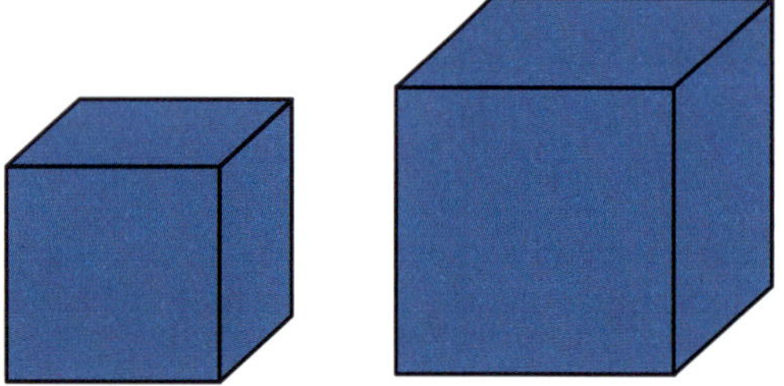

Hint
Create your own measurement to help you.

Explain your thinking. ______________________________

____

____

6. Which volume is larger: a cone with radius 8 inches and an ALTITUDE of 20 inches, or a rectangular prism that is 20 inches by 10 inches by 5 inches? Use $\pi = 3.14$.

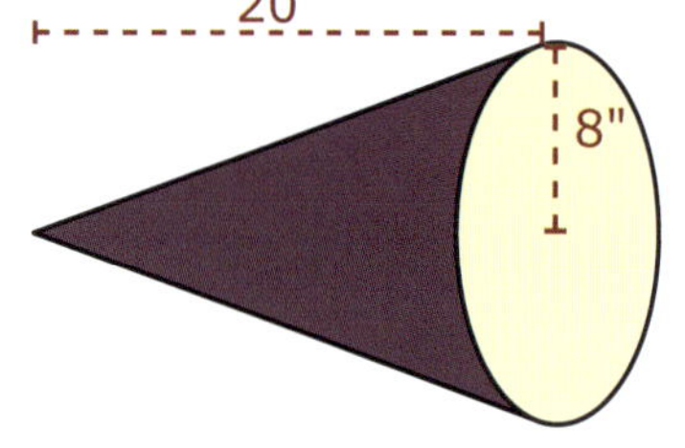

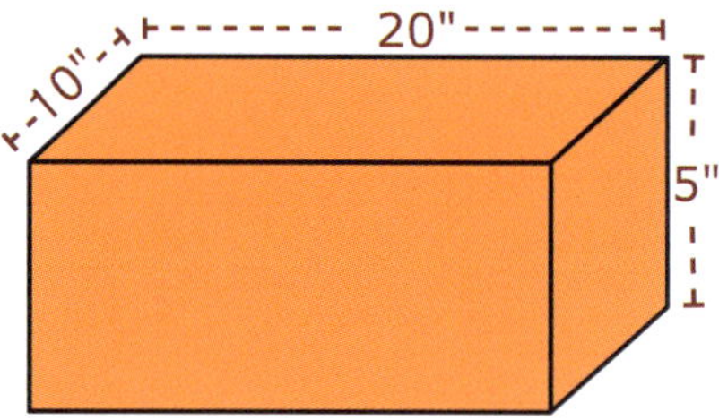

Explain your thinking. ______________________________

____

Volume of a Sphere

The volume of a sphere is found by using this formula, $V = \frac{4}{3}\pi r^3$.

The formula for the volume of a sphere was derived by Archimedes. It takes a higher level of mathematics to explain why it works.

Finding the volume of this sphere with the answer in terms of π.

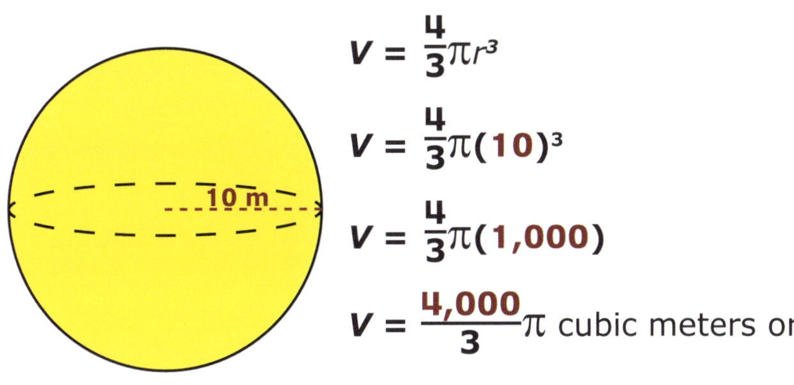

$V = \frac{4}{3}\pi r^3$

$V = \frac{4}{3}\pi(10)^3$

$V = \frac{4}{3}\pi(1{,}000)$

$V = \frac{4{,}000}{3}\pi$ cubic meters or

$1{,}333\pi$ rounded to the nearest meter

Answer the following questions.

1. Find the volume of these spheres. Round your answers to the nearest centimeter. Use 3.14 for π.

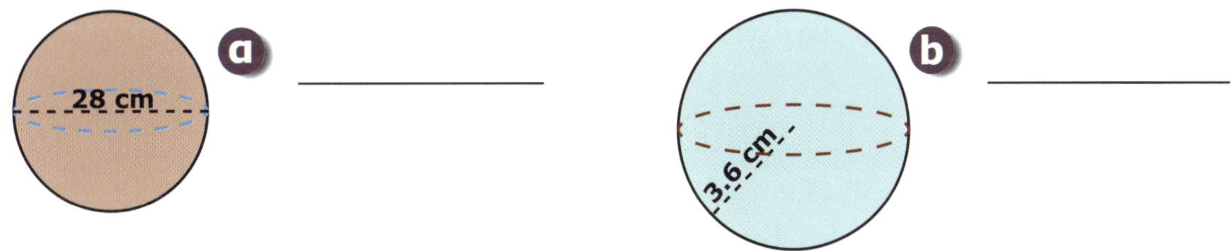

a ____________ b ____________

2. If the volume of a sphere is 36π cubic feet, find its radius.

Volume of a Sphere (Cont.)

Sphere Inscribed in a cylinder problem.

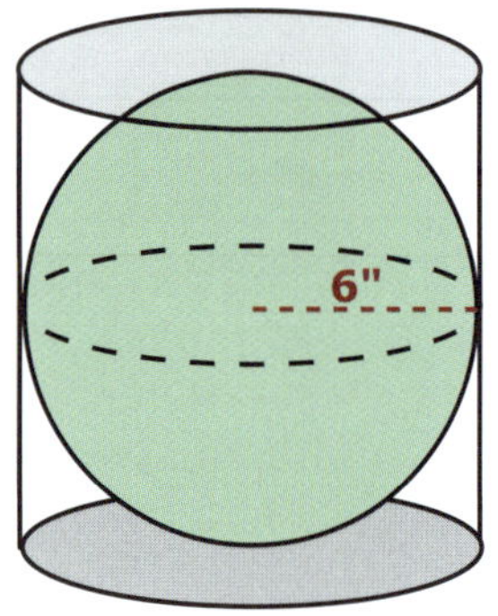

At Gettysburg, a civil war cannon and the cannon balls were made using sphere inscribed in a cylinder geometry.

Use the inscribed sphere above to answer the following questions.

1. If the sphere above is inscribed in the cylinder, what is the radius of the cylinder if the radius of the sphere is 6 inches?

2. What is the ALTITUDE of the cylinder?

3. Find the volume of the sphere. Leave your answer in terms of π.

4. Find the volume of the cylinder. Leave your answer in terms of π.

5. Archimedes discovered that the volume of an inscribed sphere is always $\frac{2}{3}$ the volume of the cylinder that circumscribes it. He always considered this discovery one of his major achievements. Show that this works in the example above.

Surface Area of Prisms

To find the surface area (**SA**) of any prism, you must find the sum of the areas of every face in the prism.

Note
If you are asked to find the **lateral area** (**LA**, the area of the sides only), then you do not need to add the two BASES to your answer.

Find the surface area of these prisms. Make sure you organize your work. Figures are ***not*** to scale.

1 ____________________

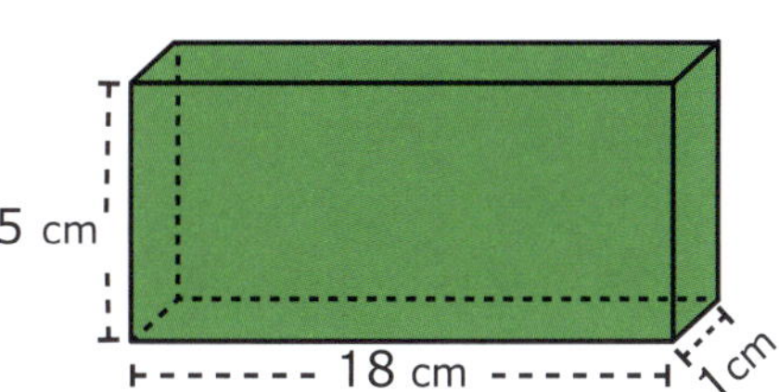

2 ____________________

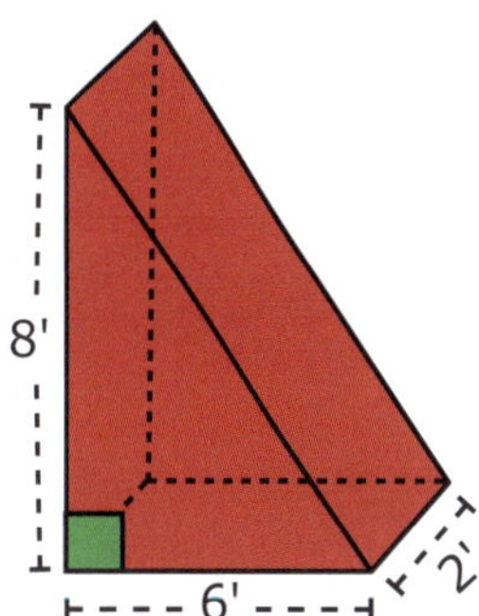

3 The volume of a cube is 8 cubic inches. Find its surface area.

Explain your thinking. ____

____

4 Find the surface area (**SA**) and the lateral area (**LA**) of this rectangular prism. The volume is 60 cubic feet.

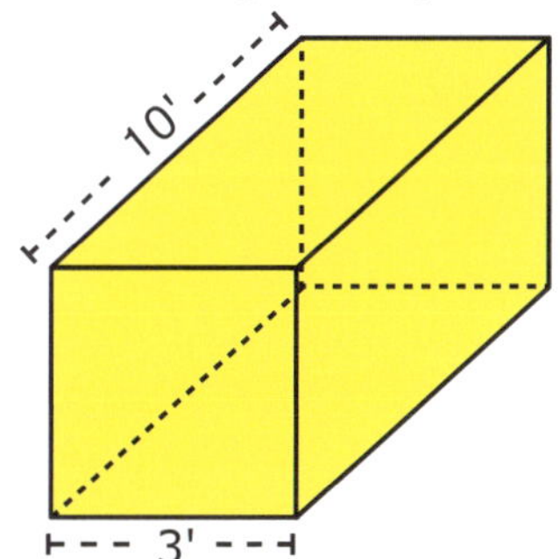

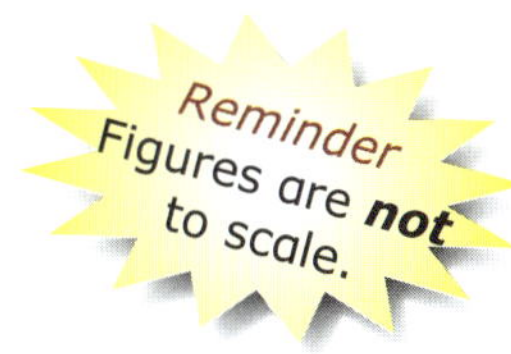

Surface Area of a Cylinder Activity

Take the wrapper off a can and lay it flat. You should notice that the wrapper forms a rectangle. One side is the ALTITUDE of the can and the other side is the **circumference** because that is the side that went around the can. Add to the area of the rectangle the area of both lids.

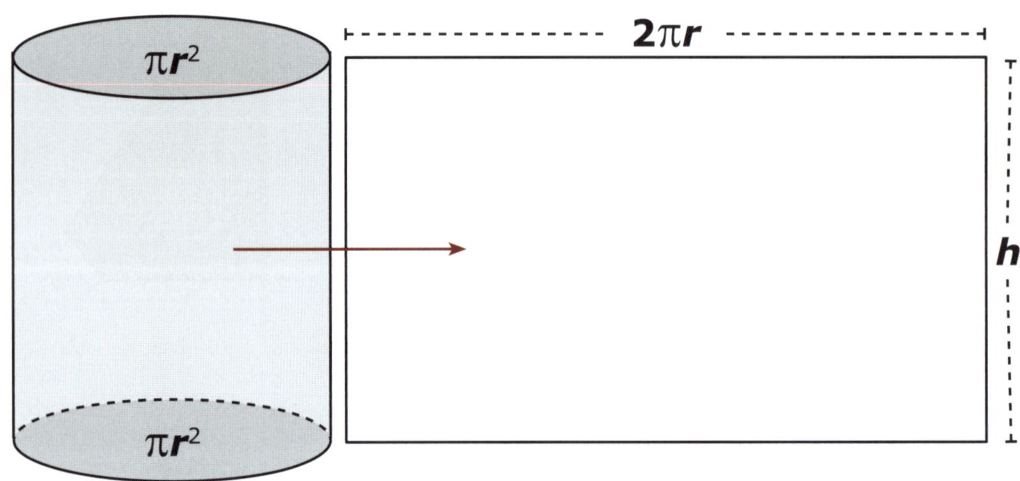

1. Write the formula.

2. If the radius is 3 inches and the height (or ALTITUDE) is 4.5 inches, find the surface area of the cylinder. Leave your answer in terms of π.

Finding Surface Area

Find the Surface Area. Match the problem with the answer. Use 3.14 for π and round your answer to the nearest inch.

1. ______

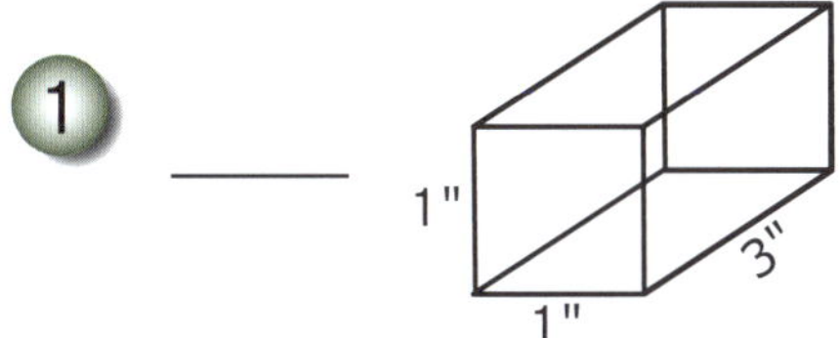

2. ______

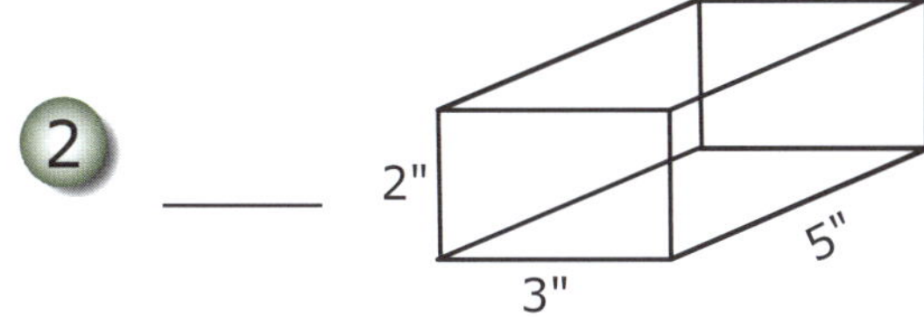

3. ______

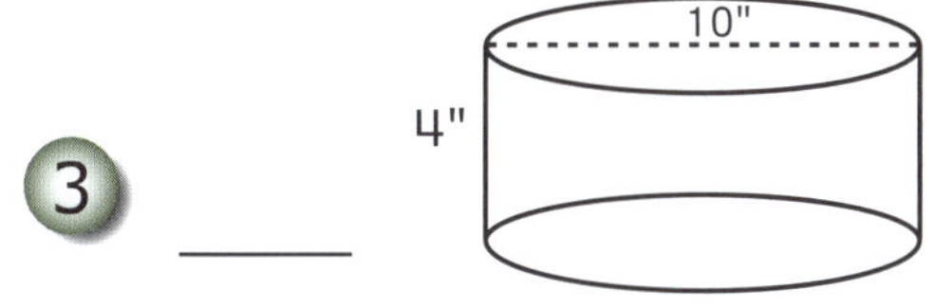

4. ______

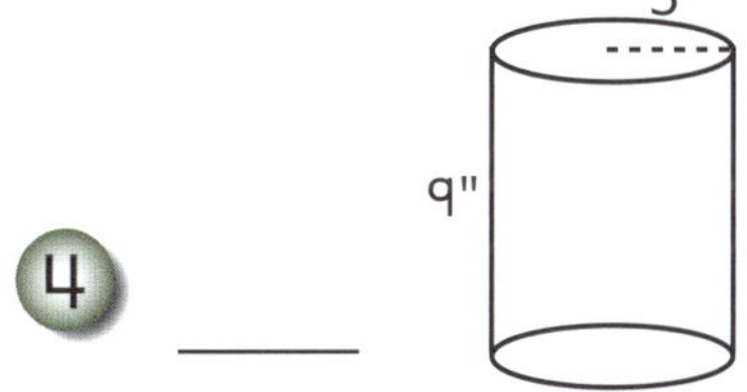

5. ______

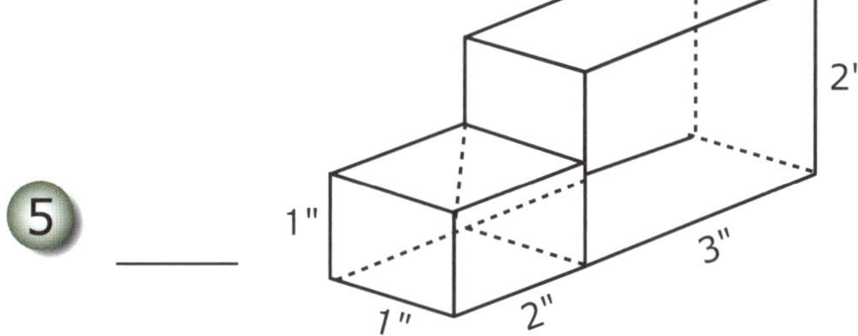

6. ______

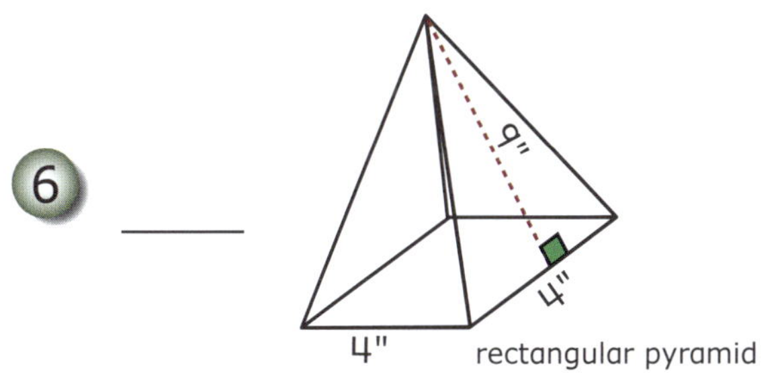

rectangular pyramid

- a) 283 sq in.
- b) 62 sq in.
- c) 88 sq in.
- d) 30 sq in.
- e) 226 sq in.
- f) 14 sq in.

Euler's Formula

Leonhard Euler (*1707-1783*), a Swiss mathematician discovered a formula we now call Euler's Formula.

As you know, a **polyhedron** is a three-dimensional solid with polygon faces.

In the chart below, count the faces, vertices, and edges in each polyhedron to see if you can discover his formula. Then write the formula.

Euler's Formula: ____________________

		Faces	Vertices	Edges
1	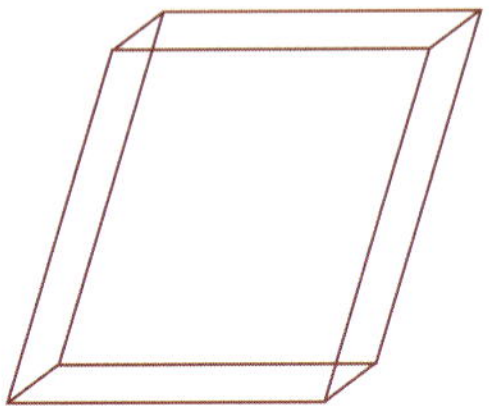			
2	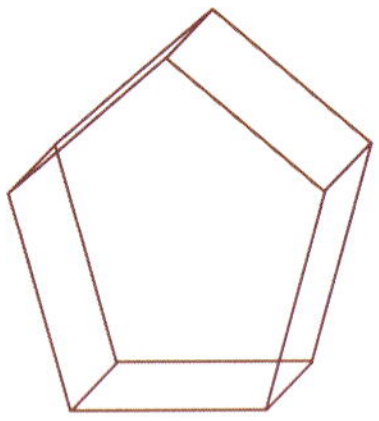			
3	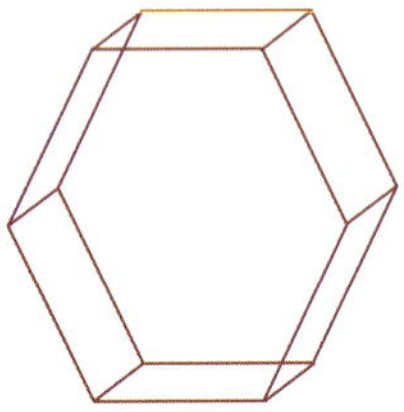			
4	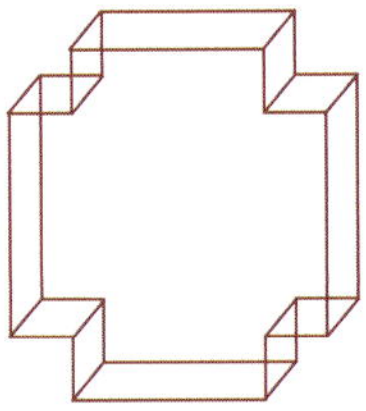			

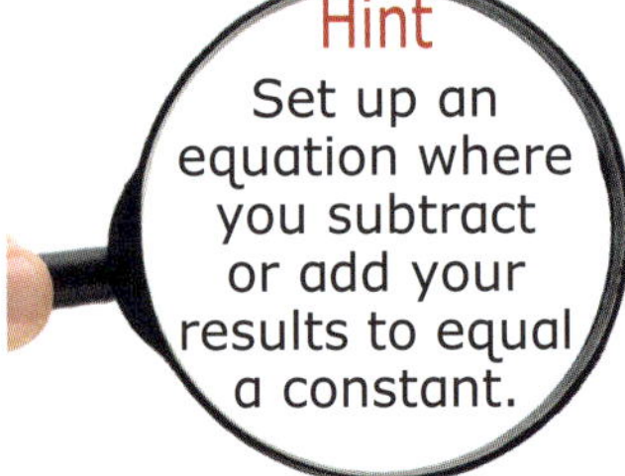

Cumulative Review – Chapters 7-9

Use a separate sheet of paper if needed.

1. If a square has an area of 121 sq in., find its perimeter. _______
2. In a rectangle the length is twice the width. If the perimeter is 120 feet, find its area. _______
3. A circle has a circumference of 50π; find its radius. _______
4. A circle has an area of 144π; find its diameter. _______
5. Explain how two triangles can have the same area and not be congruent.

____

____

6. A trapezoid has an area of 50 sq ft. It the bases are 16' and 4', find the height of the trapezoid. _______
7. Bisect the following angle.

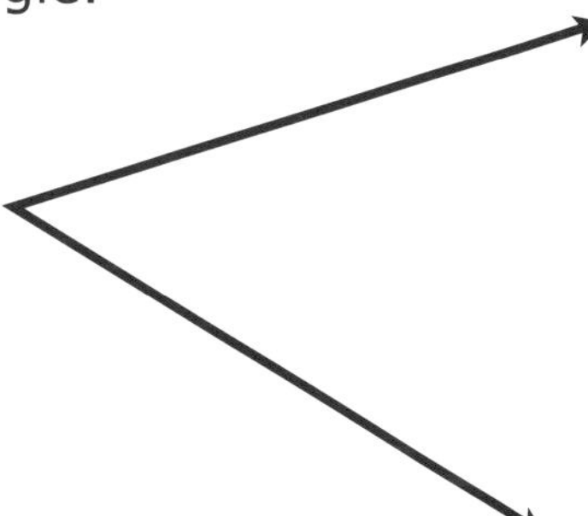

8. Construct a perpendicular bisector to this line segment.

9. Construct an equilateral triangle inside this circle. See the construction on page 113 to help you.

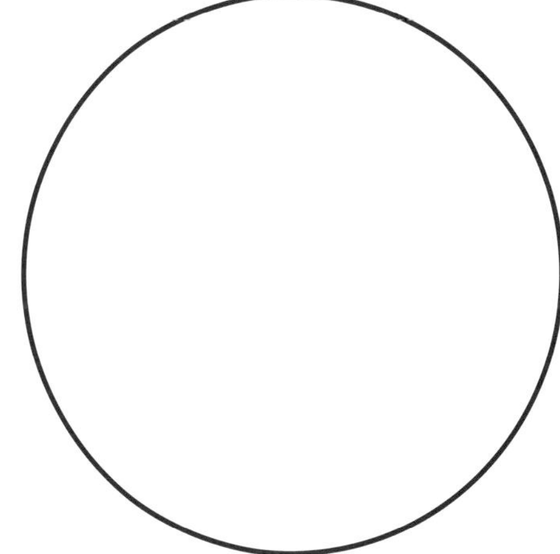

10 Find the missing side if the volume of each rectangular prism below is 100 cubic units.

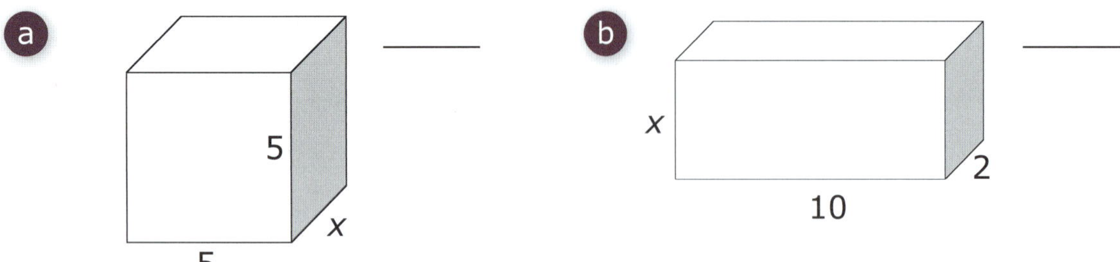

11 Find the volume of this triangular prism.

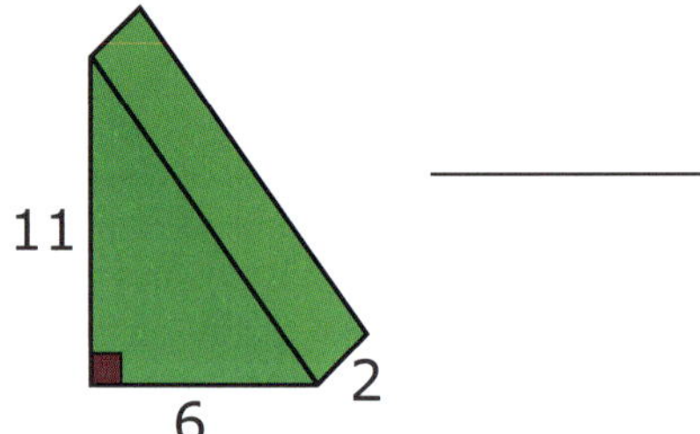

12 How much smaller is the volume of the cylinder than the volume of the trapezoidal prism? Use 3.14 for π.

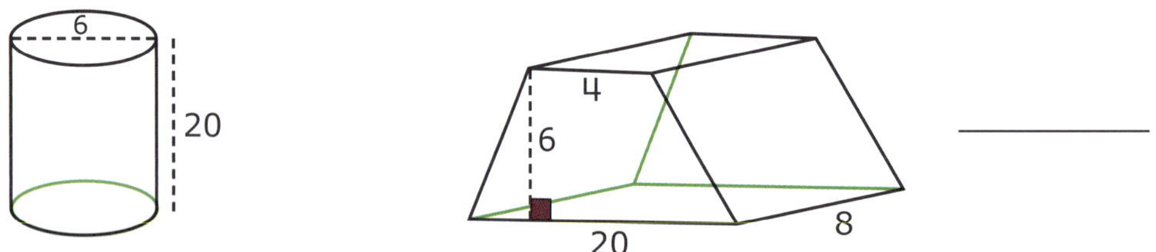

13 Which is larger: the volume of a sphere with a radius of 3 or the volume of a cone with a radius of 3 and a height of 9? Use 3.14 for π. Draw your own pictures on a separate sheet of paper.

____

14 Find the volume and the surface area of this rectangular pyramid. The height of the pyramid is 9 units.

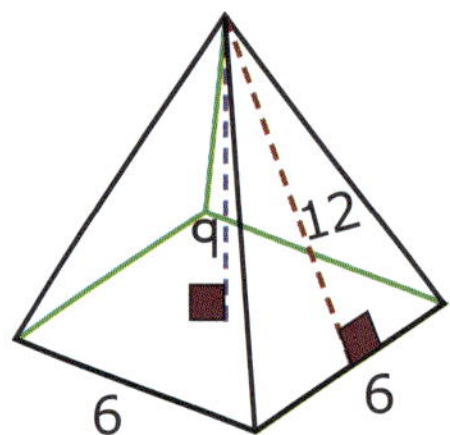

Chapter 10 - Symmetry and Transformations

What Is Vertical, Horizontal, and Point Symmetry?

Symmetry adds beauty to our world.

There are three kinds of symmetry that we are exploring in this chapter, vertical symmetry, horizontal symmetry, and point symmetry.

The letters **M**, **A**, **T**, and **H** have vertical symmetry. If you draw an imaginary vertical line down the middle, you get a mirror image on each side.

Horizontal symmetry means that if you draw an imaginary horizontal line across the center of the figure, you get mirror images above and below the figure. The letter **H** has both vertical and horizontal symmetry. The imaginary line (the blue line) is called the **line of symmetry**.

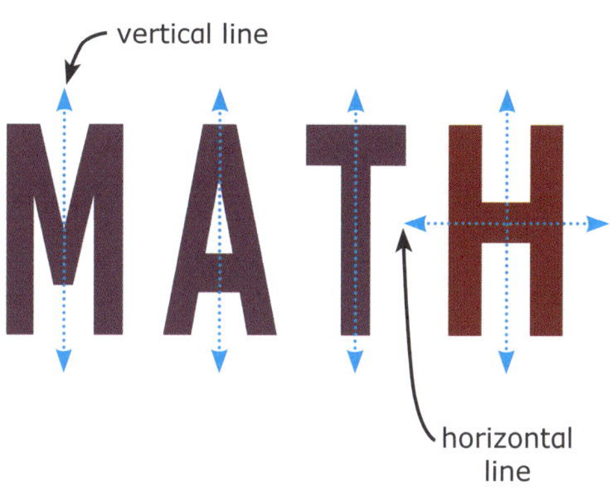

In addition, the letter **H** has point symmetry. Point symmetry means that every point on the figure is the same distance from a central point as another point but in the opposite direction.

Look at the letter **S**. It also has point symmetry. An easy test to check for point symmetry is to turn the image upside down. If you get the same image, then it has point symmetry.

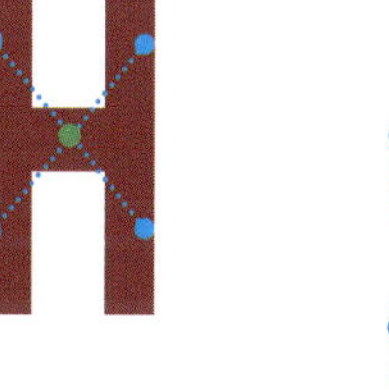

Answer the following.

1. How many lines of symmetry are in the block letter **O**?

2. Name five other block letters in the alphabet that have point symmetry besides the letter **S**.

What Is Vertical, Horizontal, and Point Symmetry? (Cont.)

3. What type of symmetry does this playing card have and why?

Explain your thinking. ____________________

____

____

4. State what type of symmetry is found in each of the polygons below.

	Most Specific Name for This Polygon	Type of Symmetry
a		
b		
c		

What Is Vertical, Horizontal, and Point Symmetry? (Cont.)

5. Is this a true statement? Each regular polygon has as many lines of symmetry as it has sides.

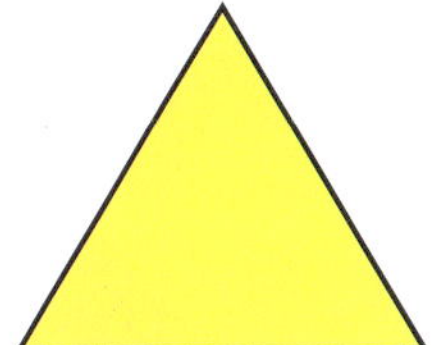  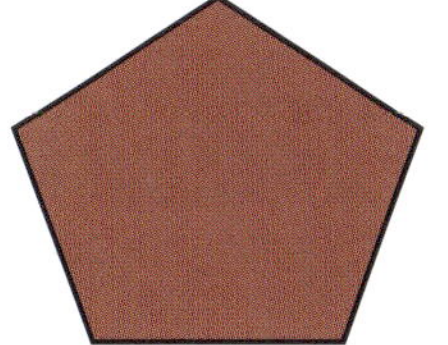 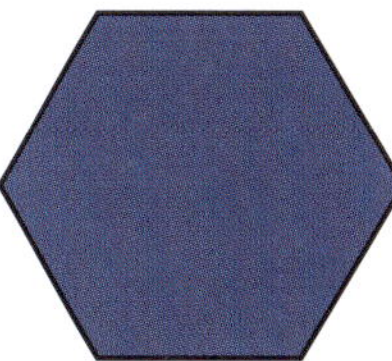

Explain your thinking. ______________________________

____

____

6. Does this figure have point symmetry?

Explain your thinking. ______________________________

____

____

7. A snowflake is a single crystal of water. Describe the symmetry of this snowflake.

____

____

____

____

Transformations - Reflections

There are four kinds of transformations (or movements) that can be done to a figure in a plane.

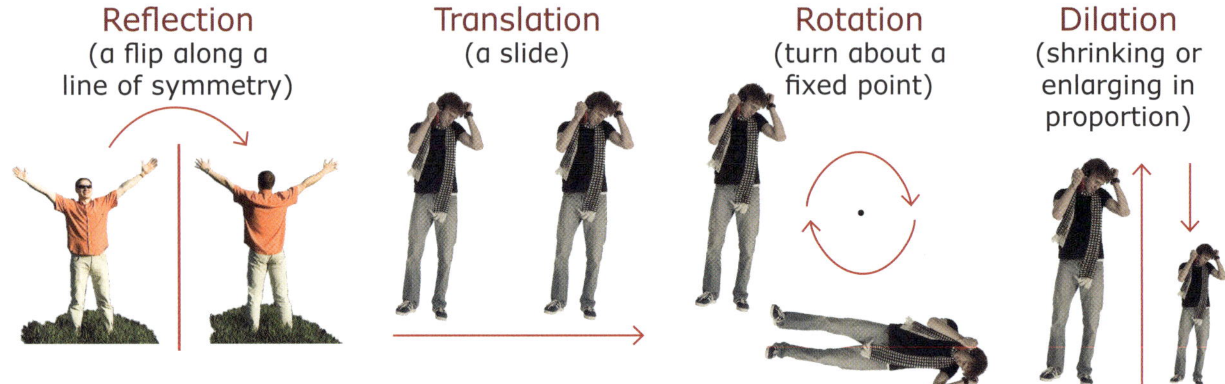

Reflections - The following is a reflection of Δ**ABC** in the *x*-axis. Δ**ABC** is called the **preimage**. The end result is called the **image** and the new triangle is labeled **A′B′C′**.

Another way to say or write, "reflect in or about the *x*-axis," is $r_{x\text{-axis}}$.

A = (-5,4)
B = (-1,3)
C = (-3,1)

Notice how the ordered pairs changed.

A′ = (-5,-4)
B′ = (-1,-3)
C′ = (-3,-1)

1. When a figure is reflected in the *x*-axis, which value changed, the *x* value or the *y* value?

   Why? Explain your thinking. ______________________________

   ____

   ____

Transformations - Reflections (Cont.)

2. Plot and label the points **C**(0,2), **D**(1,4), **E**(5,4), and **F**(4,2). Connect the points in order. Now, perform the transformations $\boldsymbol{r}_{y\text{-axis}}$. What are the ordered pairs of the image?

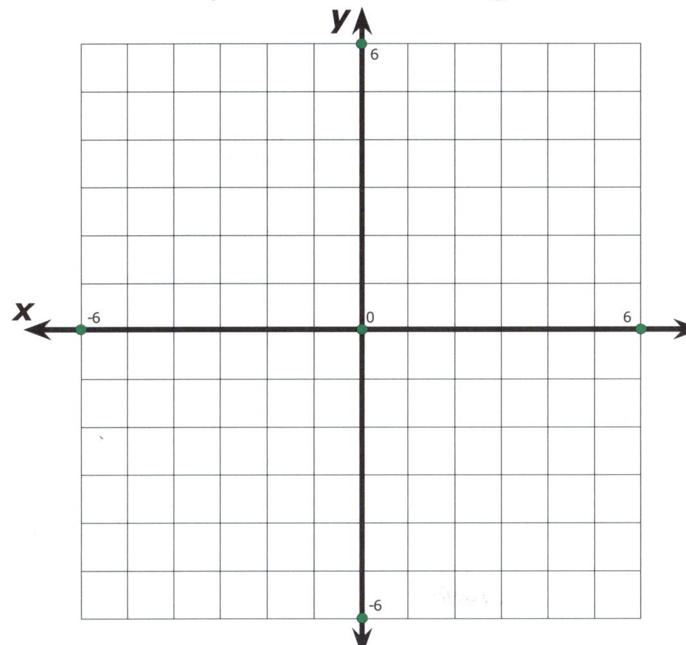

C′ = ______

D' = ______

E′ = ______

F′ = ______

How did the ordered pairs change? ____________________

3. The preimage of a point is **A**(5,-4). If you reflect it in the *y*-axis (**A′**), and then reflect **A′** in the *x*-axis, what is the end result (**A″**)?

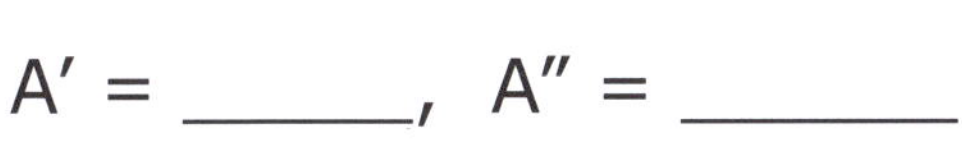

A′ = ______, A″ = ______

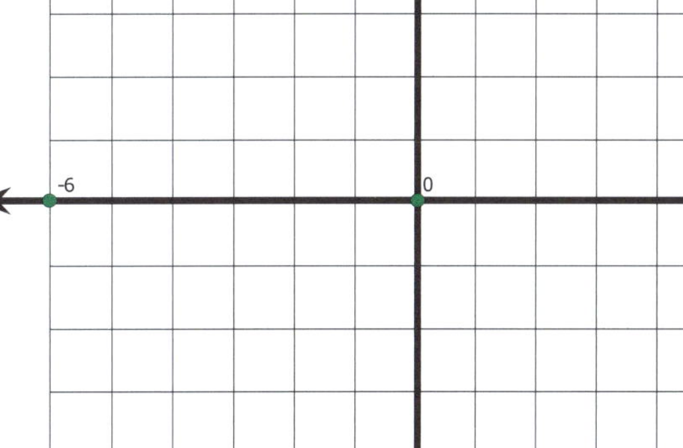

Explain your thinking. ____________________

____

____

Transformations - Reflections (Cont.)

4. Reflect Δ**ABC** across the line $y = x$. Draw and label the image then fill out the new ordered pairs below.

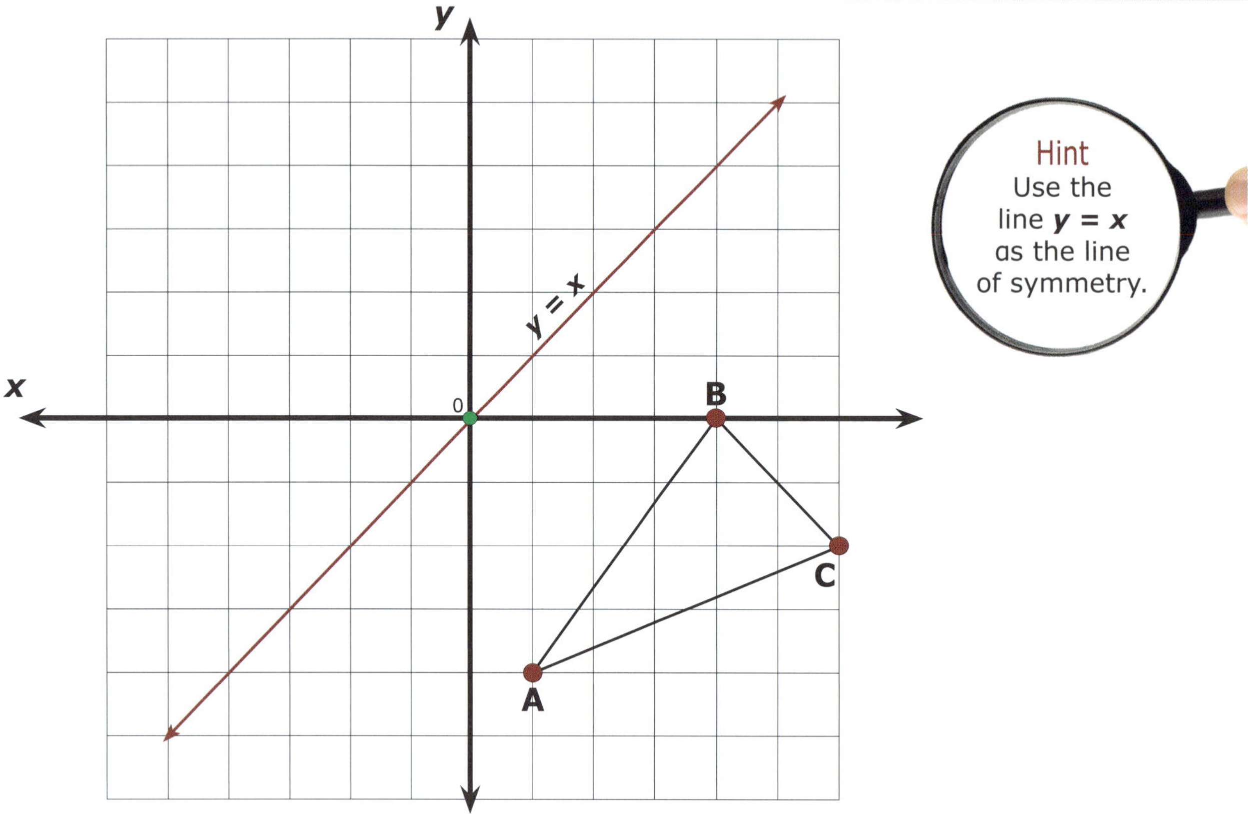

Hint
Use the line $y = x$ as the line of symmetry.

$r_{y=x}(1,-4) =$ _______, $r_{y=x}(4,0) =$ _______, $r_{y=x}(6,-2) =$ _______

5. How did the ordered pairs of the preimage compare to the corresponding ordered pairs of the image?

Explain your thinking. ____

____

Transformations - Reflections (Cont.)

A reflection in or through a point is another type of reflection demonstrated in the graph below. This reflection shows the end result as Δ**WZR** reflected in the **origin**. Notice how the corresponding ordered pairs change in this type of reflection.

The **origin** is the point (**0,0**).

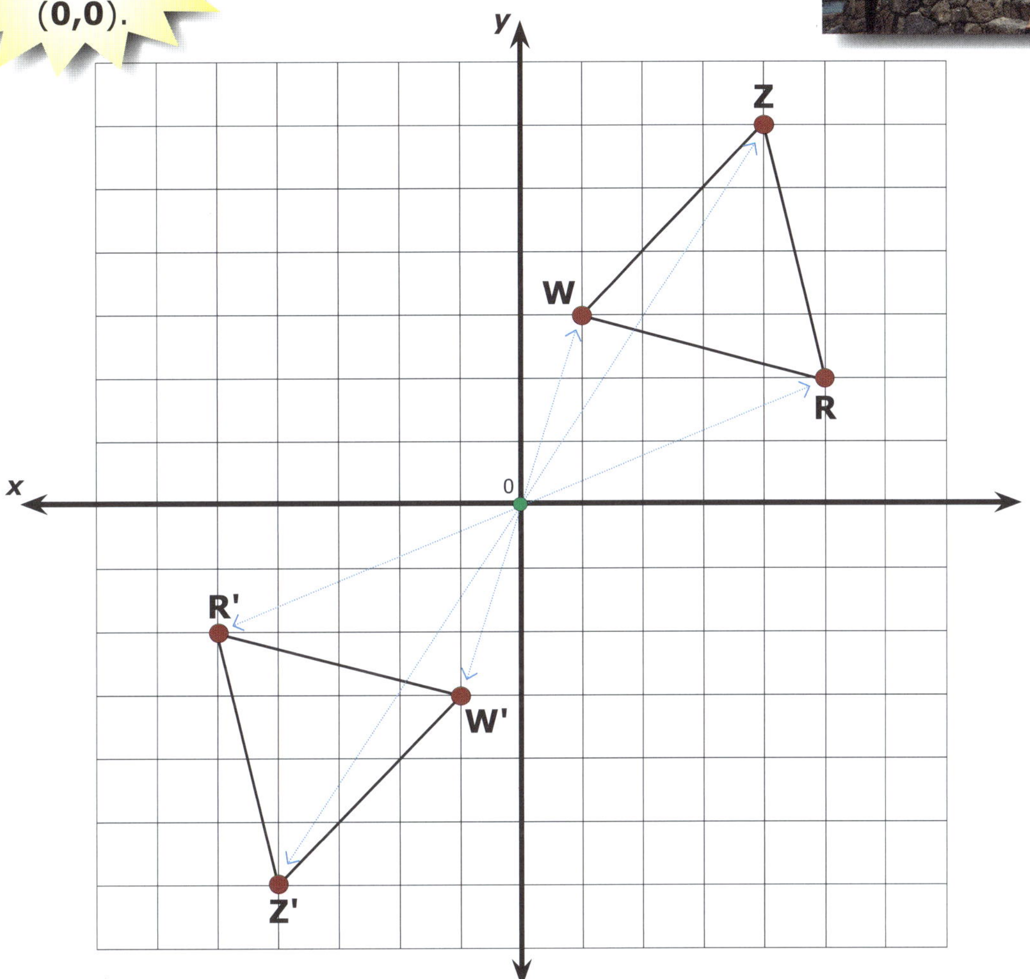

1. Find the ordered pairs that created the transformation above.

W = _______, **Z** = ________, and **R** = ________

W′ = _______, **Z′** = ________, and **R′** = ________

Explain how the values of *x* and *y* changed under a reflection in the origin.

____

Transformations - Reflections (Cont.)

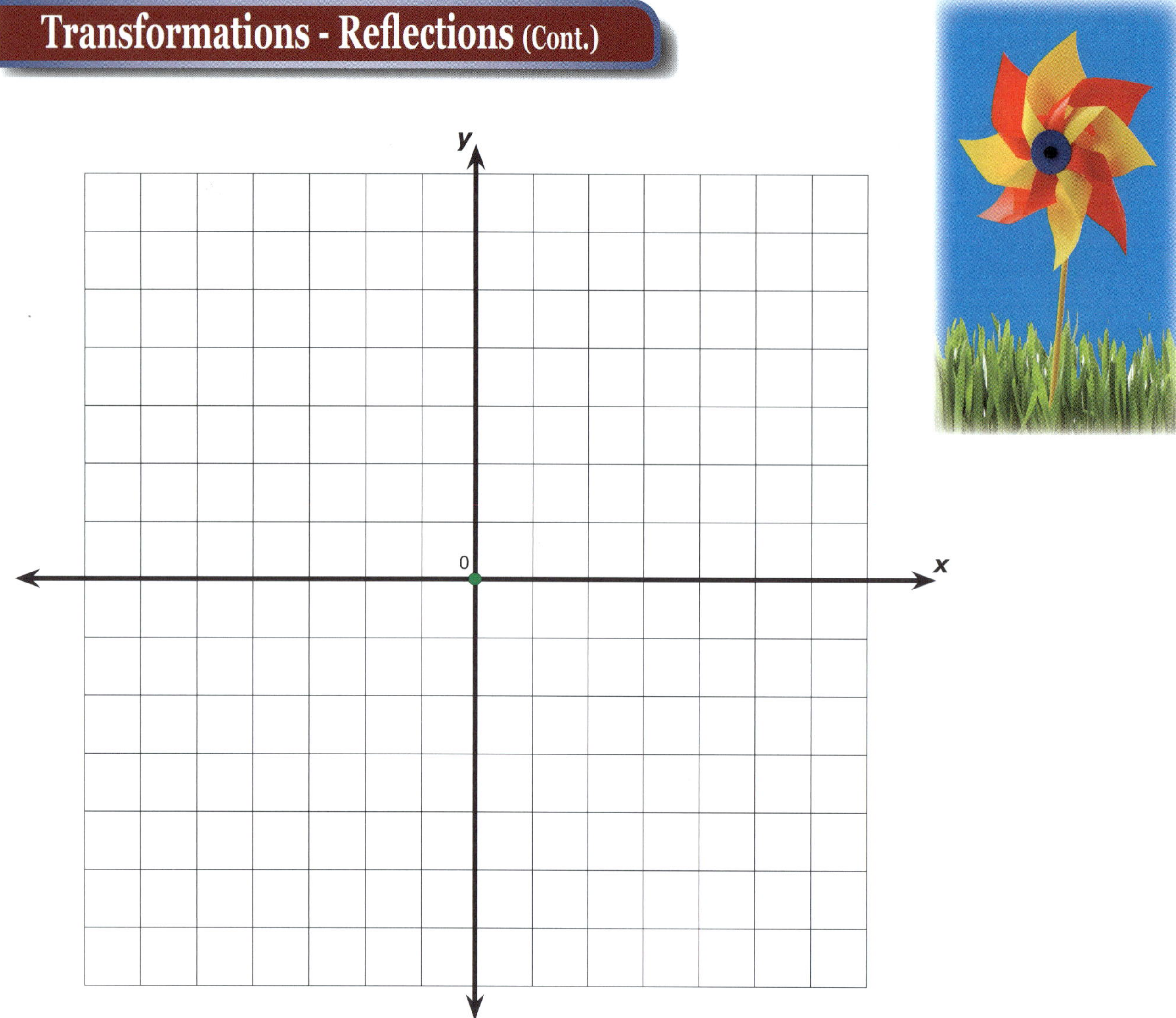

Use the graph above to answer the questions.

2. What are the coordinates of **P**(-3,5) under a reflection in the **origin**? ____________.

3. Is a reflection in the origin the same as a reflection in the *x*-axis followed by a reflection in the *y*-axis?

   Graph one point, then explain your thinking.

   ____

   ____

Transformations - Reflections (Cont.)

4. Graph the preimage **M**(-5,4), **A**(-5,7), **T**(-1,7), and **H**(-1,1) below.

a. What is the most specific name for this type of polygon? ______________________

Why? ______________________

b. Reflect the figure in the origin and label the image **M′ A′ T′ H′**.

The figure goes from quadrant ________ to quadrant ________.

c. Write the coordinates of the image.

M′ = ________, **A′** = ________, **T′** = ________, **H′** = ________

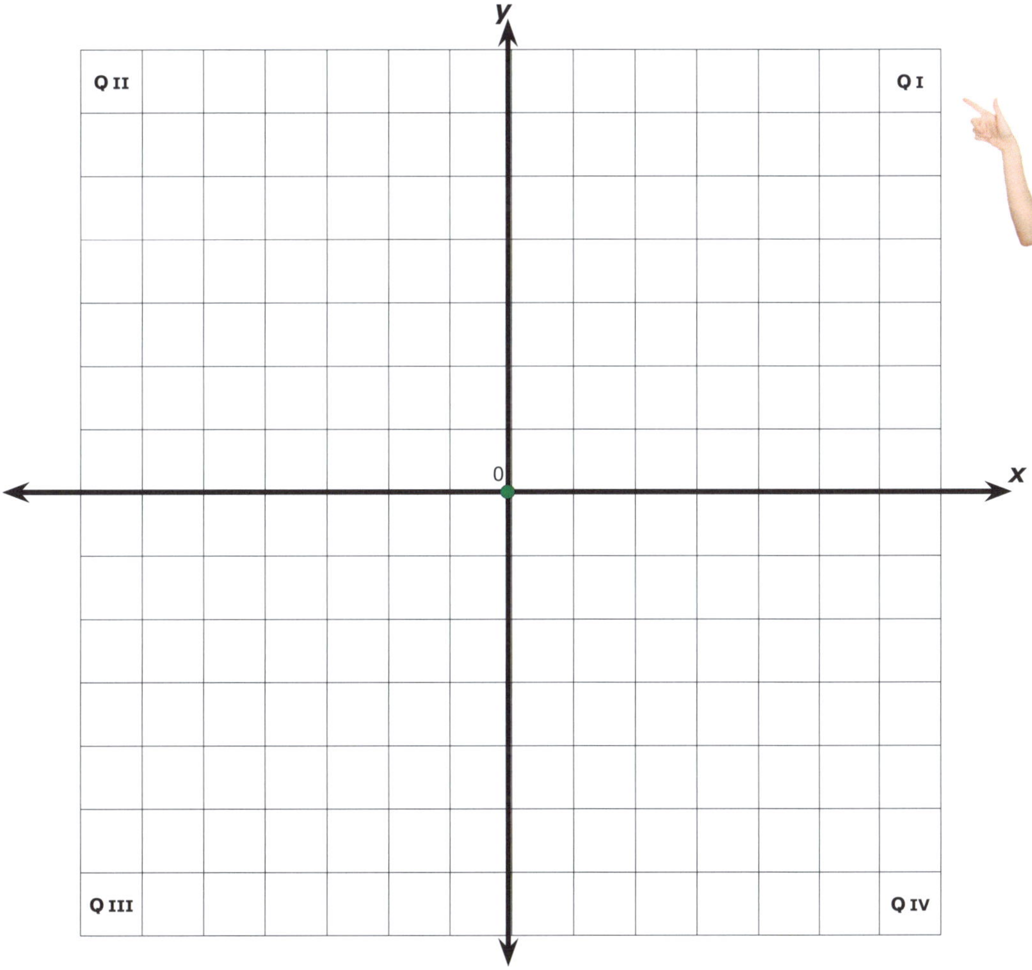

Q II Q I
y
0 x
Q III Q IV

Remember
Quad means four. This is Quadrant I (**Q I**)

Transformations - Translations

A translation is a transformation where every point in the plane is moved the same distance in the same direction. Sometimes a translation is called a **slide**.

The **notation** for a **translation** is $\mathbf{T}_{a,b}(x,y)$. You add ***a*** to the *x* value and *b* to *y* value to get the image $(x + a, y + b)$.

In the graph below, is the image of Δ**ABC** under $\mathbf{T}_{5,-3}$. For example, point **C**(-1,2) becomes **C′**(4,-1).

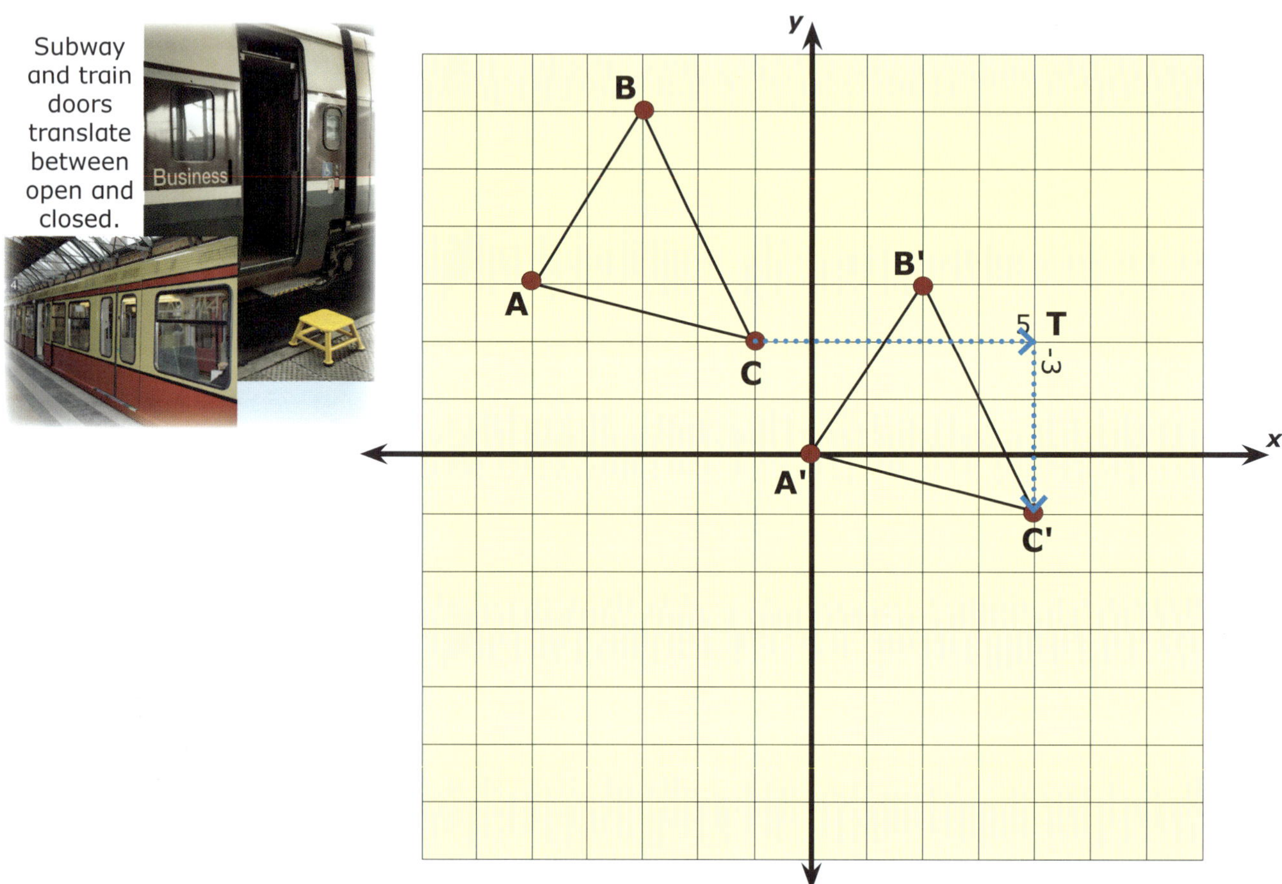

Subway and train doors translate between open and closed.

1. Find the rest of the ordered pairs for the vertices of Δ**A′B′C′**, the image of Δ**ABC** under $\mathbf{T}_{5,-3}$.

   A = ______ becomes **A′** = _______

   B = ______ becomes **B′** = _______

2. Under a translation is the image congruent to the preimage? ______

   Explain your thinking. ____

   ____

Transformations - Translations (Cont.)

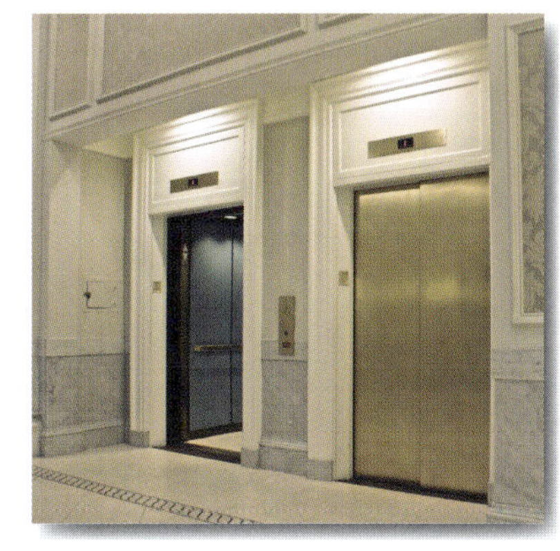

3. In the graph below, the coordinate plane has the points shown. Under a translation, the image of **M** is **Q**.
Find the image of the points under the same translation.

a. M → Q, b. A → ______, c. T → ______,

d. H → ______, e. G → ______, f. E → ______, g. O → ______

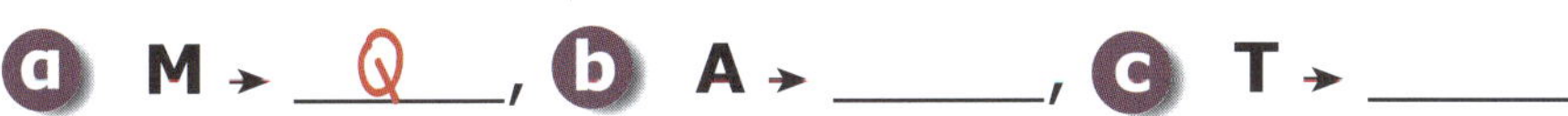

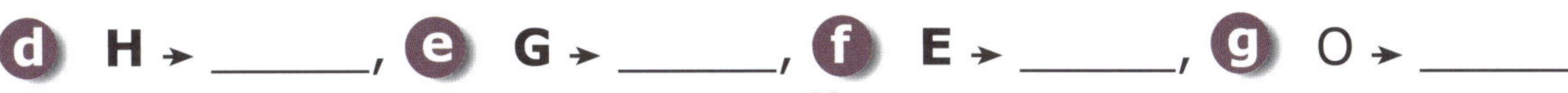

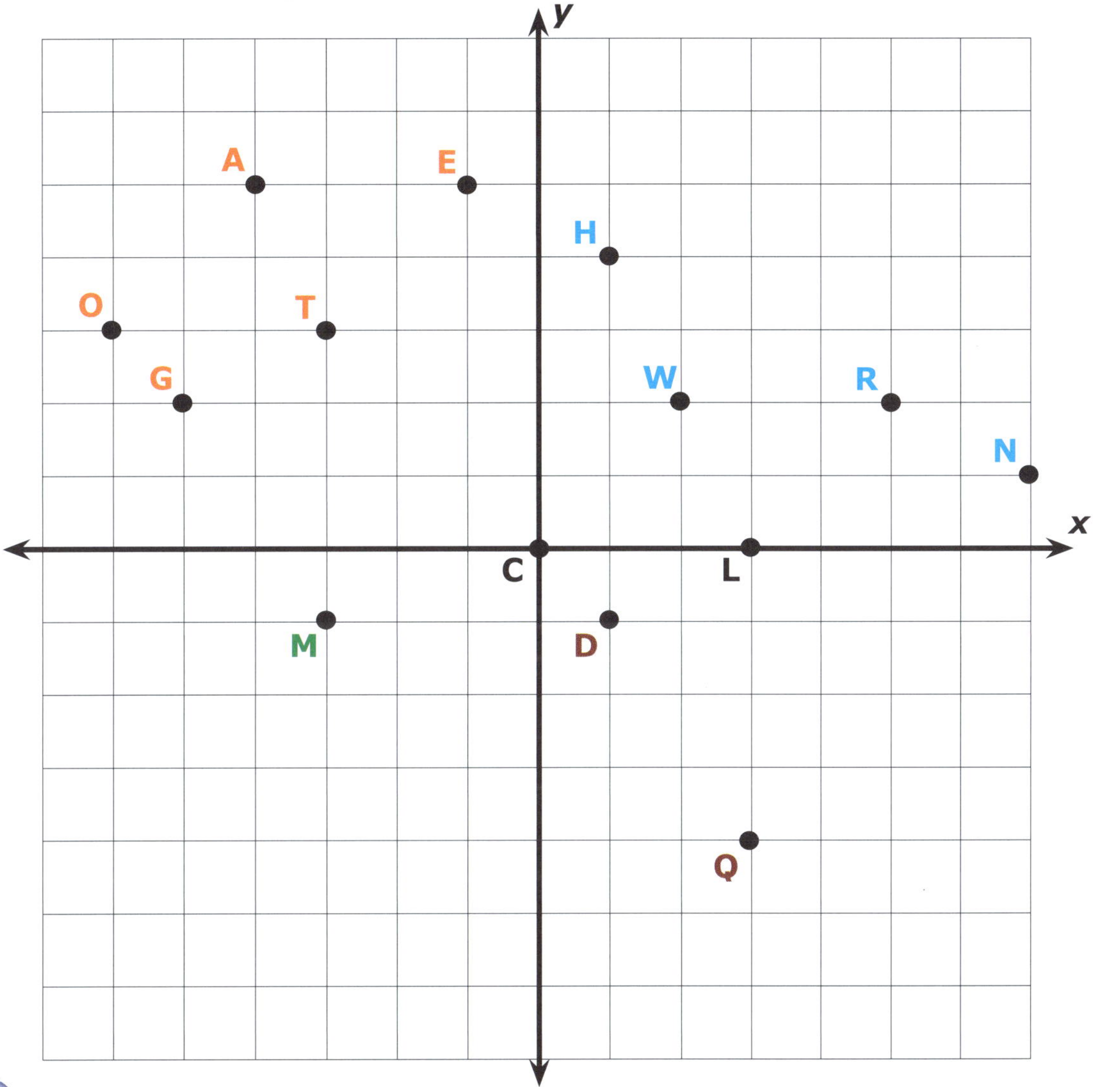

4. In a translation, every point only moves 10 units down. Write this translation using the following notation. $(x,y) \rightarrow (x + a,\ y + b)$.

____

5. Find $\mathbf{T}_{9,-2}(1,5)$. Is this the same image as $\mathbf{T}_{1,5}(9,-2)$? ________

____

Transformations - Translations (Cont.)

6. Graph ΔFGH. The vertices are **F**(-4,-7), **G**(-3,-1), and **H**(-2,-7).

Answer the following.

a. What is the most specific name for this triangle? ____________

b. What quadrant is Δ**FGH** in? ____________

c. Perform the following transformation and label the triangle **F′G′H′**. $(x,y) \rightarrow (x + 7, y + 1)$

d. Reflect Δ**F′G′H′** in the x-axis. What are the coordinates of Δ**F″G″H″**.

F″ = ________, **G″** ________, **H″** ________.

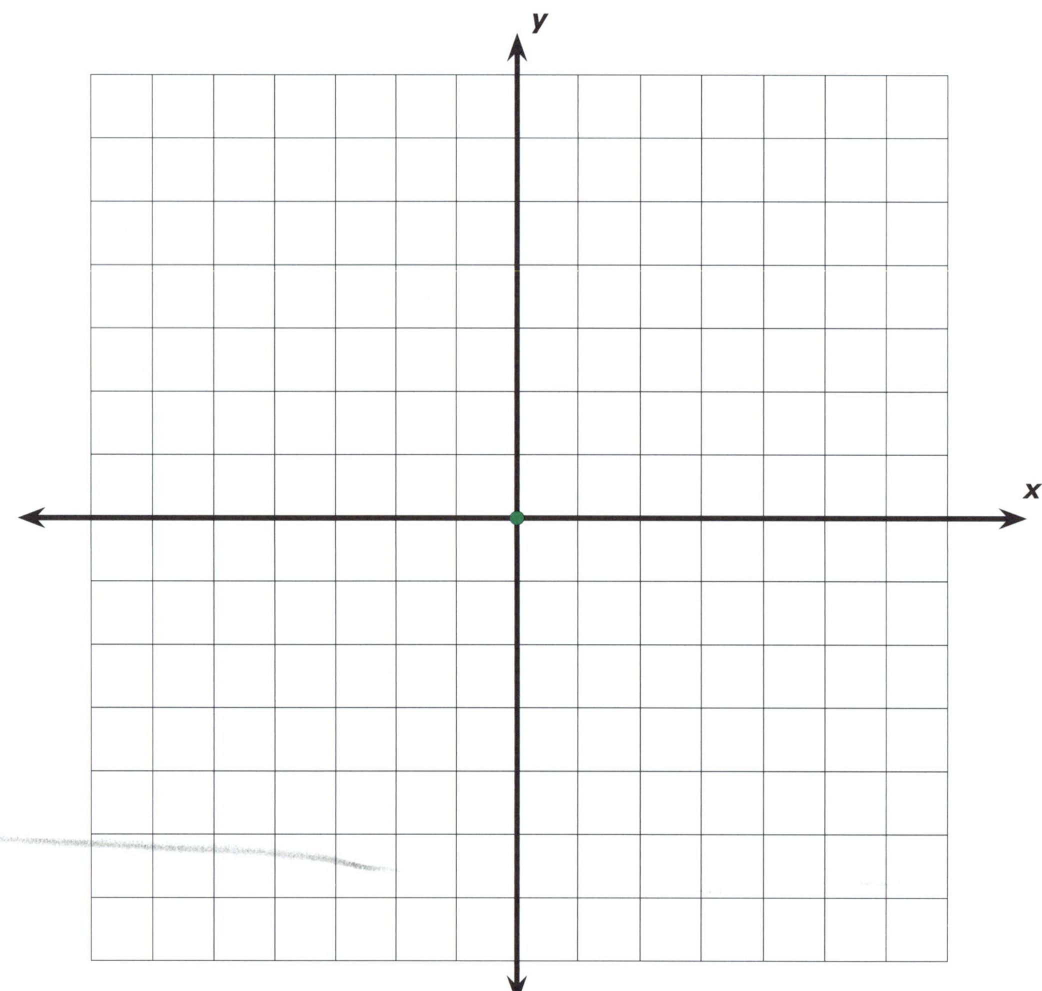

Transformations - Translations (Cont.)

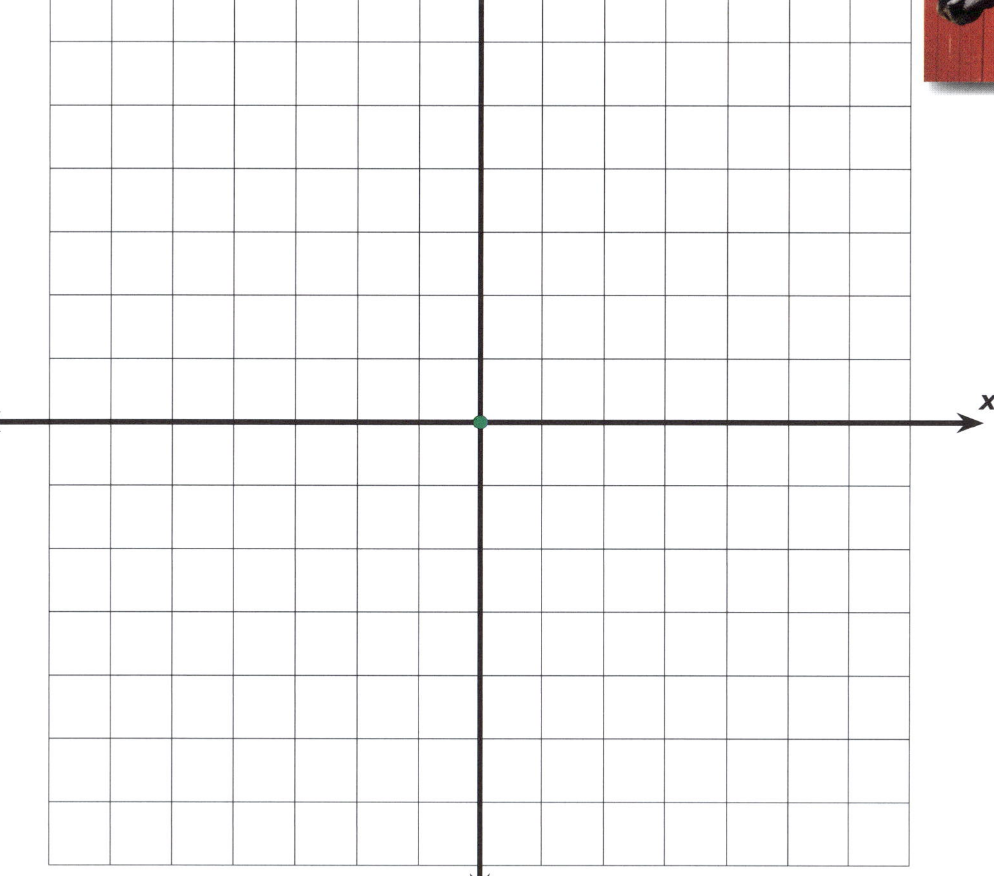

7. After the translation $T_{3,-5}$, a point moved from **P**(x,y) to **P′**(1,-1). What is the ordered pair **P**(x,y)?

   Explain your thinking. ____________________

   ____

8. Graph and label the following points **W**(0,0), **R**(3,0), and **S**(0,3). Answer the following.

   a. What is the most specific name for this figure? __________

      Why? ____________________

   b. What translation would you make to have Δ**W′R′S′** sit on top of Δ**WRS** so that **W′** and **S** become the same point?

      ____

Transformations - Rotations

A rotation is a transformation where a figure in a plane is rotated about a fixed point a given number of degrees. The most common angles of rotation are 90°, 180°, and 270°. You can rotate clockwise or counterclockwise.

Note

When you see the notation $\mathbf{R}_d$ (**R** for rotation and *d* for degree), you will turn the figure **counterclockwise** if *d* is positive. All rotations in this book use the origin as the fixed point.

Using Δ**ABC** as the preimage, perform the transformation $\mathbf{R}_{90}$ about the origin. The fixed point (0,0) is the origin.

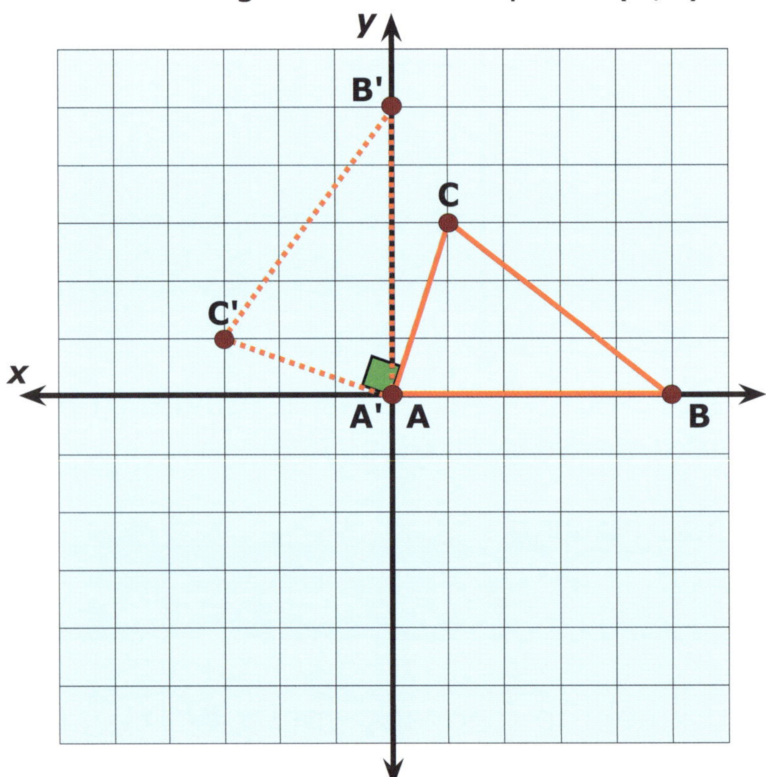

If you trace Δ**ABC** and turn it using point (0,0) as your fixed point, you will see how the preimage coordinates change.

A(0,0) remains **A'**(0,0),
B(5,0) becomes **B'**(0,5),
C(1,3) becomes **C'**(-3,1)

In general, a rotation 90° about the origin results in **P**(*a*,*b*) becoming **P'**(−*b*,*a*).

Transformations - Rotations (Cont.)

1 Graph and label rectangle **ABCD**. The vertices are **A**(0,2), **B**(4,2), **C**(4,0), and **D**(0,0). Perform the following transformations $\mathbf{R}_{90°}$, $\mathbf{R}_{180°}$, and $\mathbf{R}_{270°}$ about the origin.

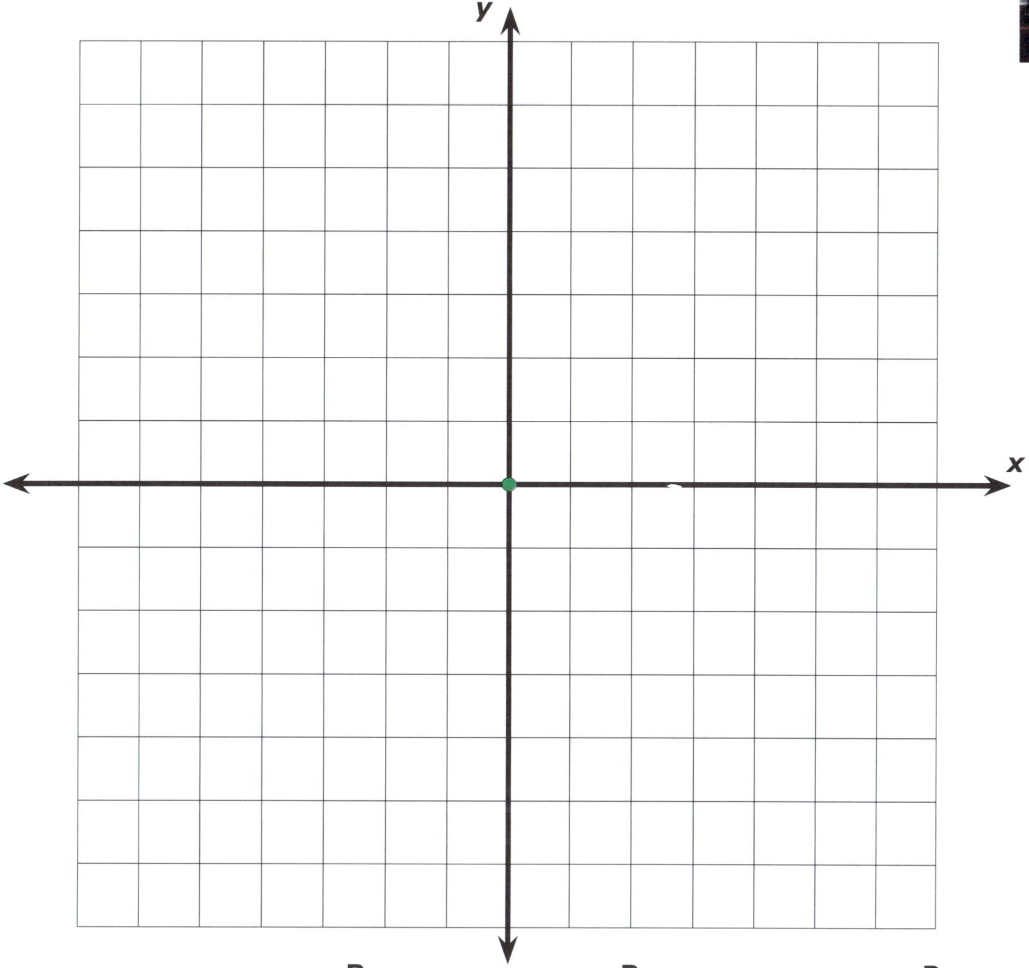

	$\mathbf{R}_{90°}$	$\mathbf{R}_{180°}$	$\mathbf{R}_{270°}$
A(0,2),	**A′** ______	**A″** ______	**A‴** ______
B(4,2),	**B′** ______	**B″** ______	**B‴** ______
C(4,0),	**C′** ______	**C″** ______	**C‴** ______
D(0,0),	**D′** ______	**D″** ______	**D‴** ______

2 Look at the results above. If you reflected **ABCD** in the origin, how would your image compare to any of the images above?

Explain your thinking. ______________________________

____

Transformations - Rotations (Cont.)

3. Graph the polygon **DEFG**. The vertices are at **D**(-5,4), **E**(-2,4), **F**(-2,1), and **G**(-7,1).
   a. What is the most specific name for this polygon?
   b. Perform the following transformation, $\mathbf{R}_{180°}$ about the origin and label your image **D′E′F′G′**.
   c. Write a rule to show how (a,b) changes when it is rotated 180° about the origin.

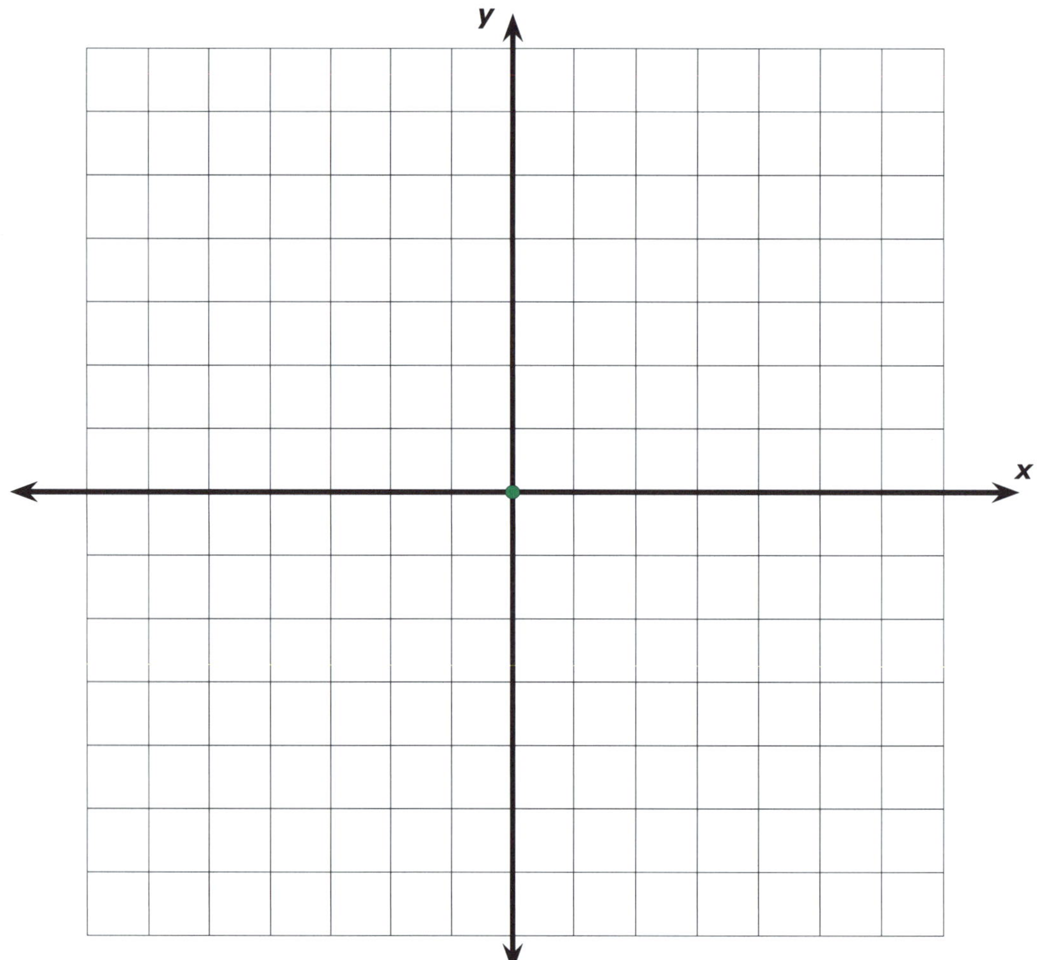

4. Without graphing, find the image of **P**(-2,5) under:
   a. $\mathbf{R}_{90°}$ ____________,
   b. $\mathbf{R}_{180°}$ ____________,
   c. $\mathbf{R}_{270°}$ ____________

Transformations - Rotations (Cont.)

5. Use tracing paper to rotate the following figure 270° about the origin.

The yellow point has been done for you!

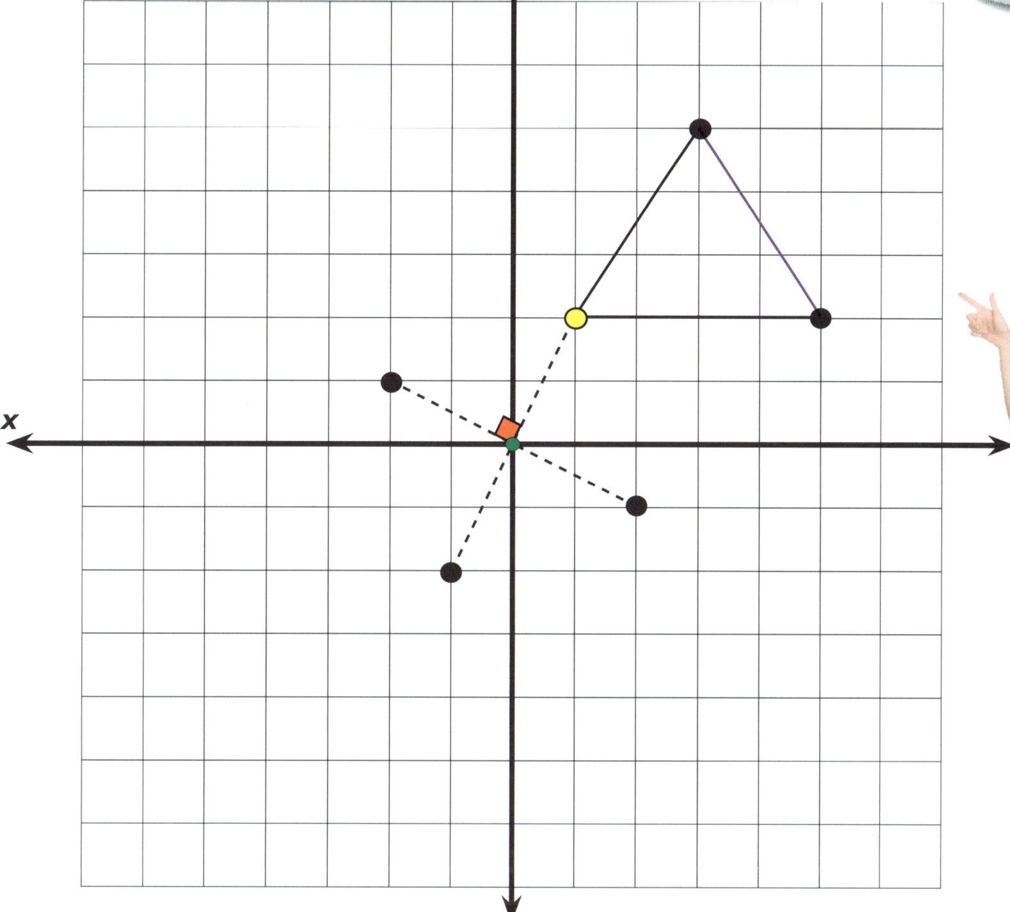

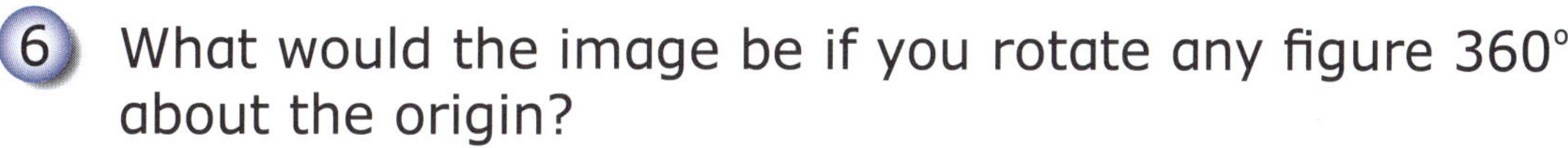

6. What would the image be if you rotate any figure 360° about the origin?

Explain your thinking. ______________________________

____

7. Many artists have produced drawings using the principles of transformations. In this drawing, what transformation is being used?

Explain your thinking. ______________________

____

Transformations - Rotations (Cont.)

A figure can be rotated any number of degrees.

In fact, many figures have their own **rotational symmetry**. A figure is said to have rotational symmetry when the image becomes the preimage under a rotation where the center of the figure is the fixed point.

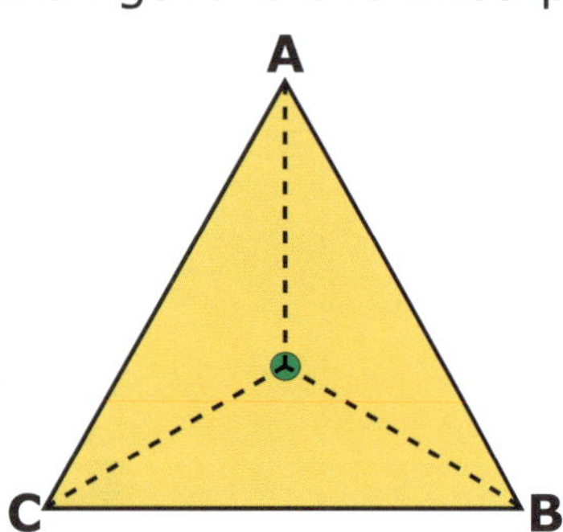

The equilateral triangle shown here has 120° rotational symmetry. For point **B** to rotate to point **A**, and then to point **C**, while keeping the center fixed, point **B** would travel 120° each time, and so would each vertex.

Measure the angle shown with a protractor. Keep in mind that measuring is ***not*** always exact.

All regular polygons have **rotational symmetry**. If a full turn is 360°, the degree of rotational symmetry is determined by this formula, **360°/*n***, where *n* is the number of sides.

Try to determine how many degrees of rotation it would take for the image of each of these regular polygons to become their preimage. Use tracing paper to verify your results.

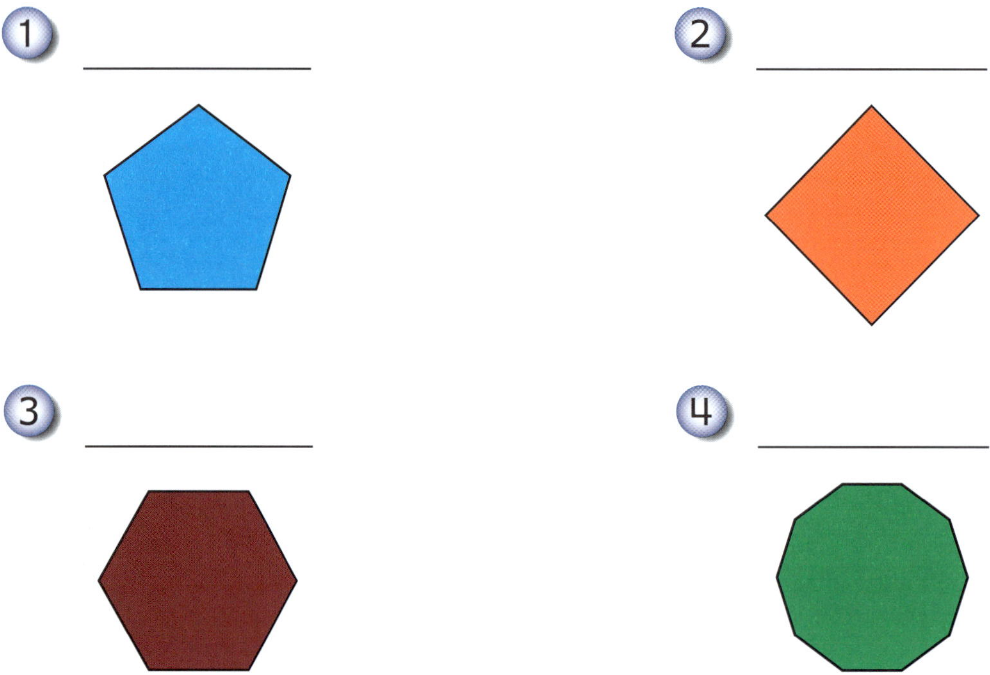

Transformations - Rotations (Cont.)

The number of times a figure matches itself is called the **symmetry order**. The block letter **H** (H) has rotational symmetry of order 2 since it matches itself twice. If an object matches itself only once it is ***not*** considered to have rotational symmetry.

5. What is the symmetry order number for each of these figures?

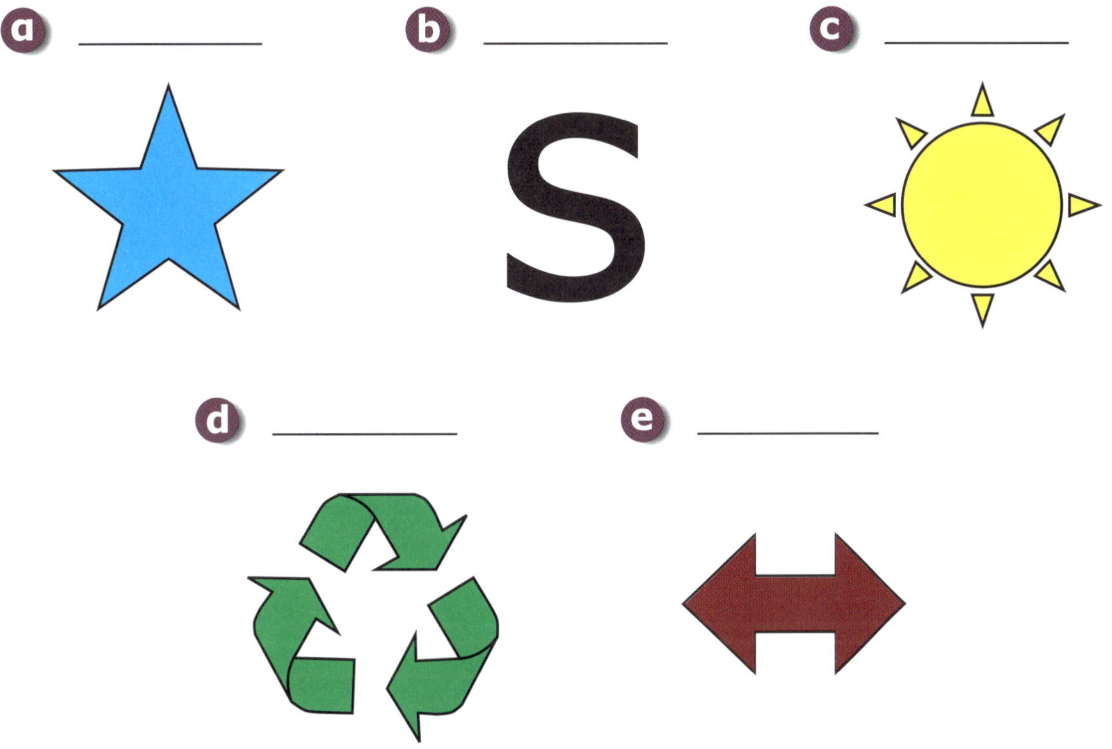

6. What is the rotational symmetry order for any figure with point symmetry? Give an example to explain your thinking.

____

____

7. This is a picture of a hub cap on a car. Look at the hub cap of your family car and find its symmetry order.

Transformations - Dilations

A dilation is a transformation where a figure shrinks or enlarges in proportion. Translations, reflections, and rotations preserve distance, meaning that the image after the transformation has the same distance between the vertices as the preimage.

A transformation that preserves distance is called an **isometry** (the image is congruent to the preimage).

A dilation is ***not*** an isometry because dilations do not preserve the distance between the vertices. The image is ***not*** congruent to the preimage (unless it is dilated by a factor of 1). But, under a dilation, corresponding angles remain congruent. The image and the preimage are therefore ***not*** congruent, but *similar*.

The notation for a dilation is D_k where k stands for the scale factor (what each number will be multiplied by).

For example, $\mathbf{D_2}(x,y)$ means $(2x,2y)$.

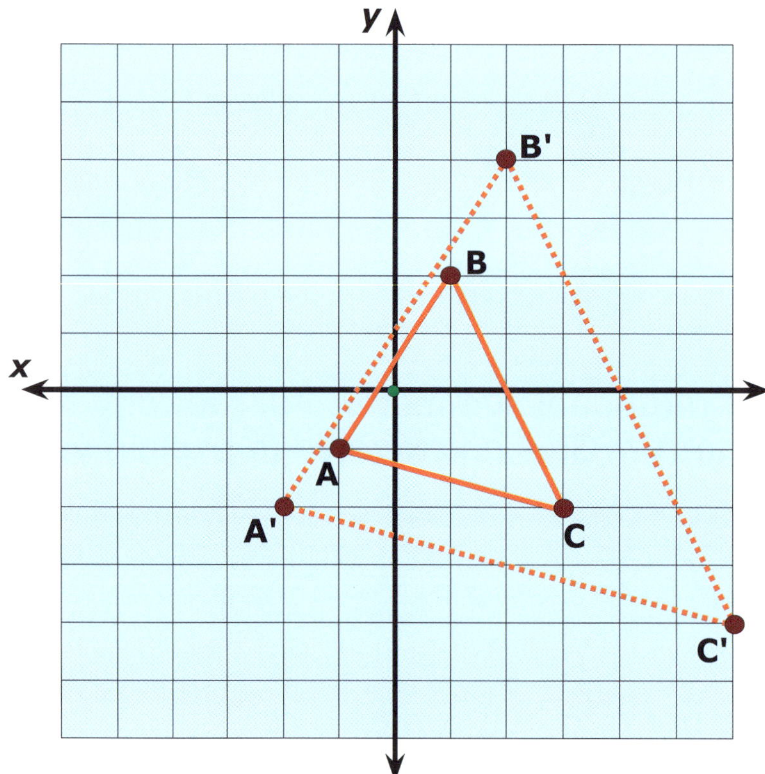

Notice

If **A** = (-1,-1), **B** = (1,2), and **C** = (3,-2), then $\mathbf{D_2}$ enlarges the preimage by a factor of 2.

A′ = (-2,-2), **B′** = (2,4), and **C′** = (6,-4).

Transformations - Dilations (Cont.)

Answer the following questions about dilations.

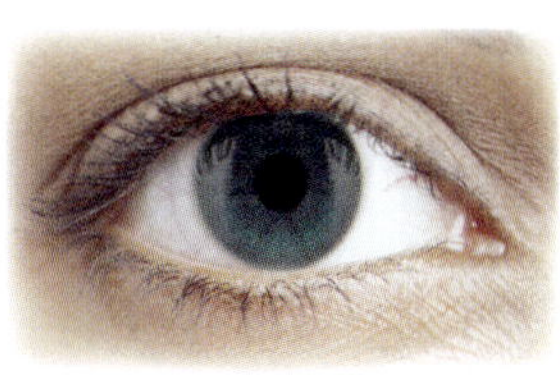

The pupils in your eyes dilate due to the light. Your pupils shrink when the light is too bright and enlarge in the dark.

1. Using the triangle **ABC** below as your preimage, perform the transformation $\mathbf{D}_{\frac{1}{4}}$ graph and write the coordinates of the new image, **A′**, **B′**, and **C′** below.

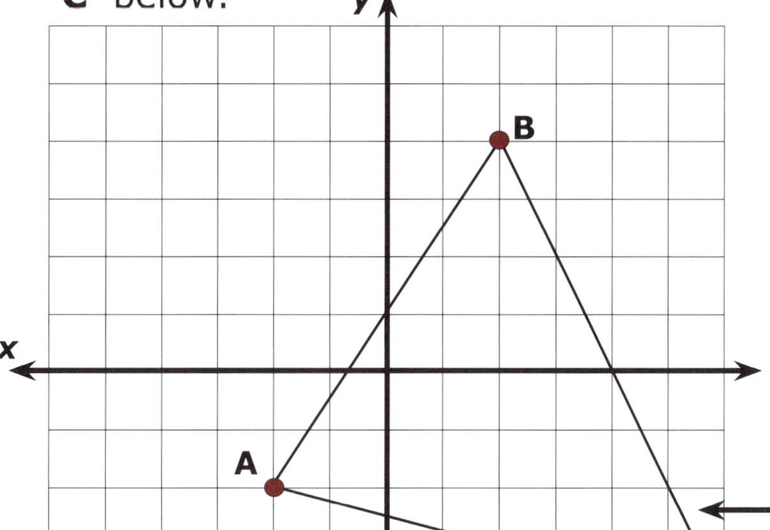

A′ = ________,

B′ = ________,

C′ = ________

preimage

2. Shown here is the image **D′E′F′G′** which is the result of this dilation, $\mathbf{D}_{\frac{1}{3}}$.

Draw and label the coordinates of the preimage **DEFG**.

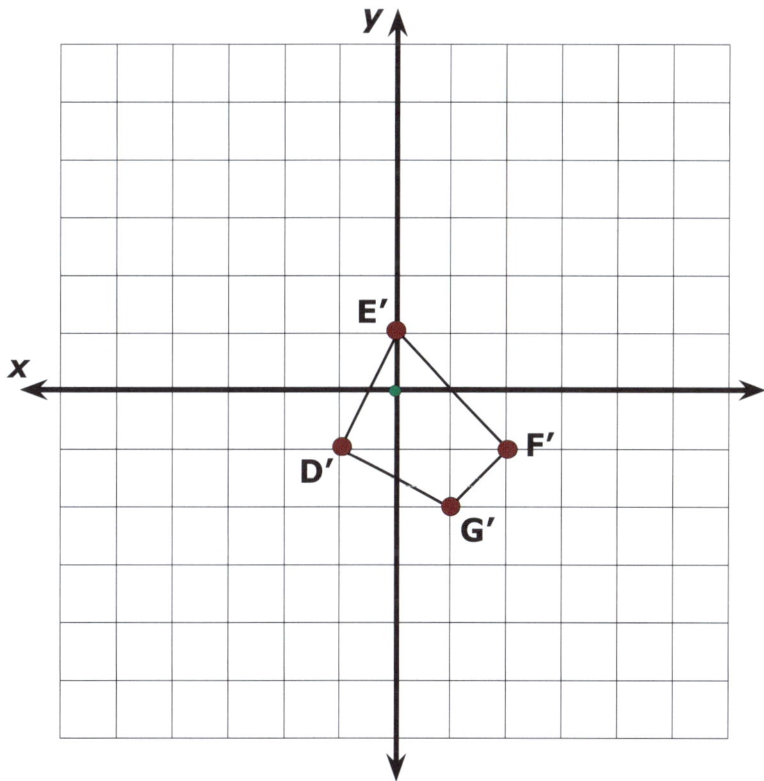

Transformations - Dilations (Cont.)

3. Draw the figure **MATH**. **M**(-2,-2), **A**(-2,4), **T**(6,4), **H**(6,-2). Answer the following questions.

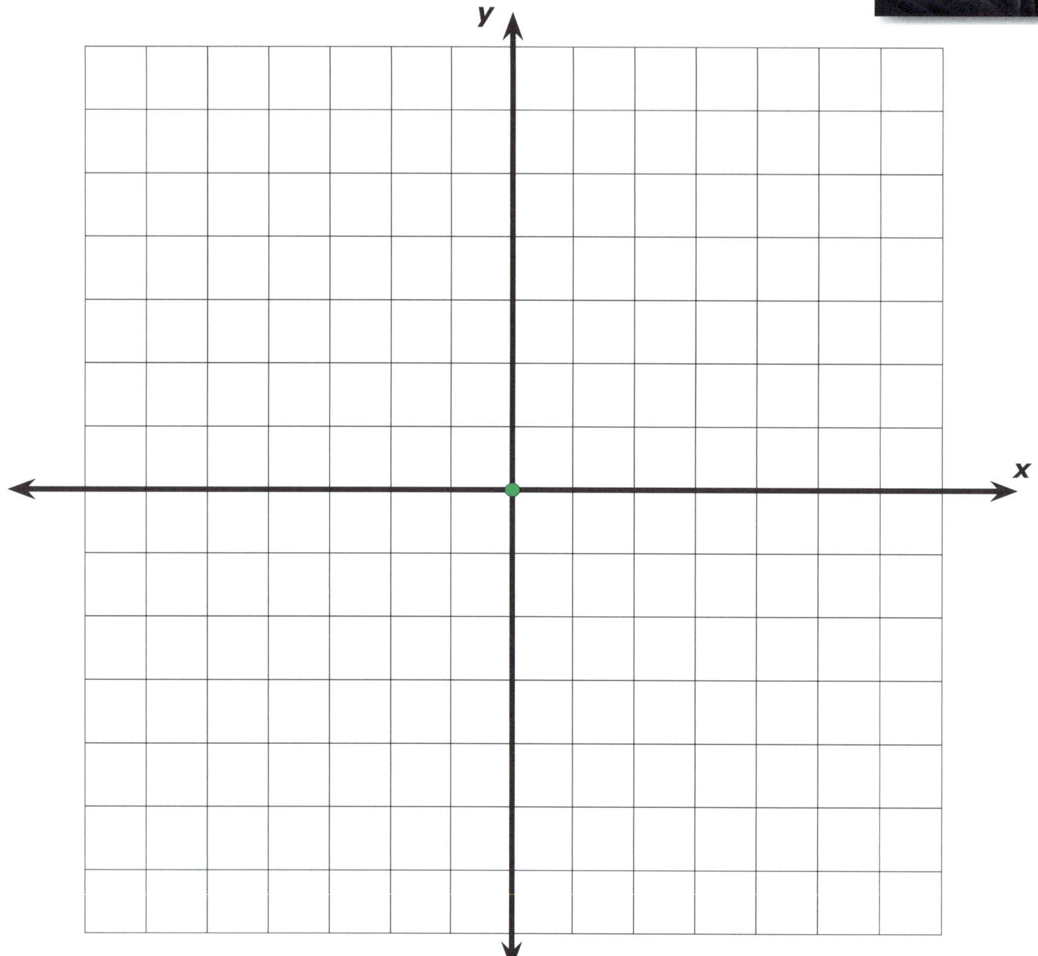

a. What is the perimeter of the figure **MATH**? ________________

b. Perform the transformation $\mathbf{D}_{\frac{1}{2}}$. Label **M′A′T′H′**.

c. Find the perimeter of **M′A′T′H′**. ________________

d. Find the ratio of the perimeter of **M′A′T′H′** to the perimeter of **MATH**. ________________

How does your answer compare to the dilation factor?

Explain your thinking. ________________________________

e. Find the ratio of the area of **M′A′T′H′** to the area of **MATH**. (Do not forget to reduce.) ________________

f. How does the ratio of the areas compare to the ratio of the perimeters?

Explain your thinking. ________________________________

Transformations - Dilations (Cont.)

4. Graph and label the following triangle on the grid provided. **X** = (-2,-1), **Y** = (-2,2), and **Z** = (2,-1). Then answer the questions below.

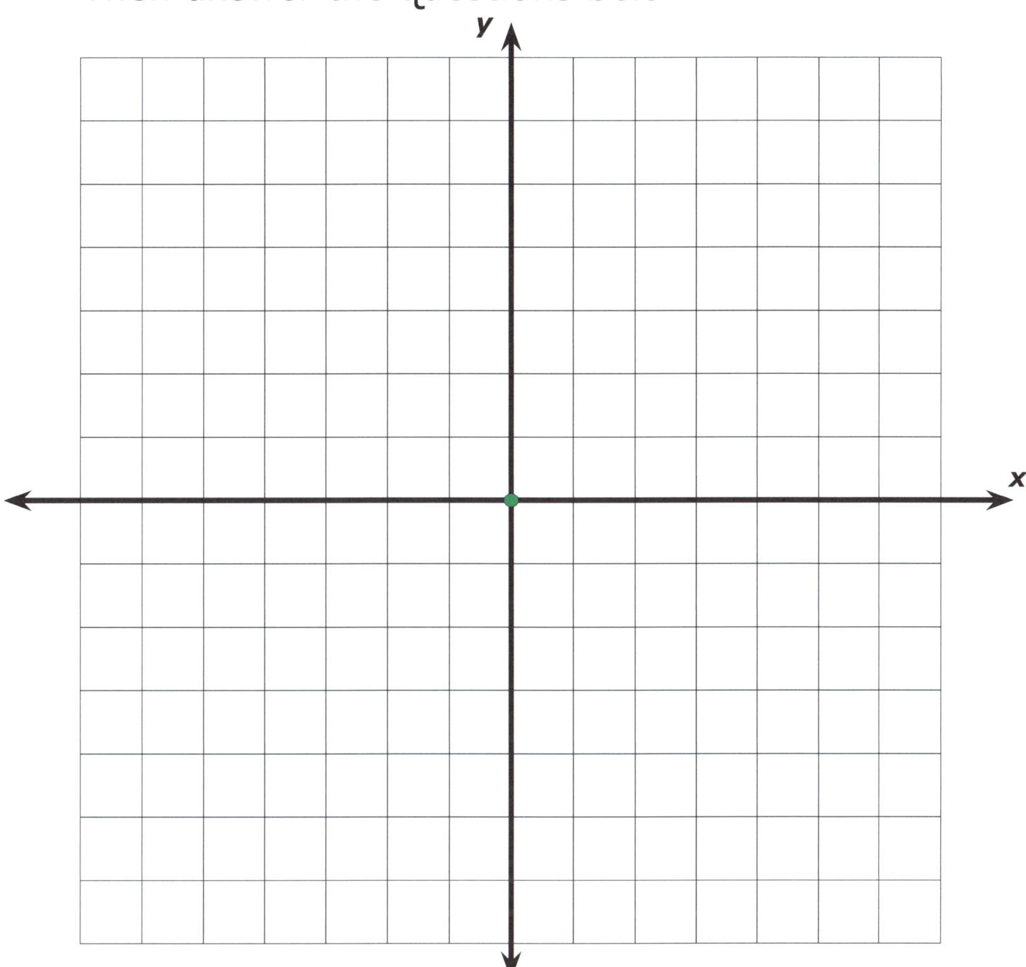

a. What type of triangle did you draw? ____________________

b. Perform the following transformation, $\mathbf{D_2}$. Label your image **X'Y'Z'**.

c. Find the ratio of the perimeter of Δ**X'Y'Z'** to the perimeter of Δ**XYZ**. (Do not forget to reduce.) ________________

d. Find the ratio of the area of Δ**X'Y'Z'** to the area of Δ**XYZ**. (Do not forget to reduce.) ________________

e. Based on your results of this problem and the previous problem (Question #3), what conclusions can you make about how the scale factor relates to the ratio of the perimeters and the ratio of the areas of similar figures?

Explain your thinking. ____________________________________

____

Glide Reflections and Compositions

A **glide reflection** is a reflection followed by a translation, or a translation followed by a reflection. A glide reflection is **commutative**, meaning that the order in which you do each transformation results in the same final image.

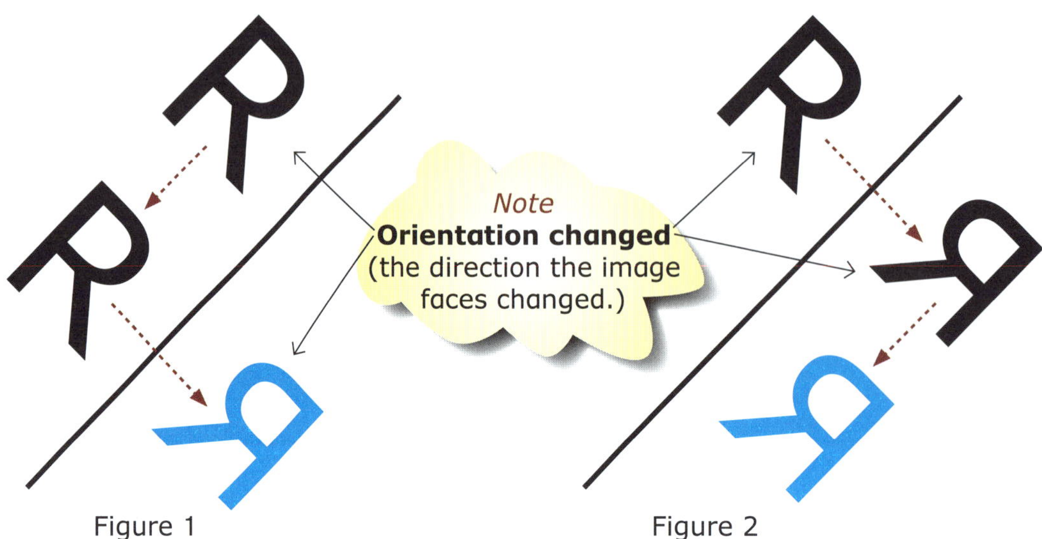

Figure 1

Figure 2

Figure 1, the **R** was translated first, then reflected.

Figure 2, the **R** was reflected first, then translated.

The end result (**Я**) is the same.

Notice how the end result changes the orientation of the initial preimage.

Many wallpaper designs are made with glide reflections. Native American art, for example, is full of glide reflections. Many different cultures have used symmetry in their rugs, baskets, and quilts.

Glide Reflections and Compositions (Cont.)

1. Do these transformations represent a glide reflection?

   Explain your thinking. ______________________________

   ____

2. Do these transformations represent a glide reflection?

   Explain your thinking. ______________________________

   ____

3. Copy the preimage **B** to finish the glide reflection started below.

Glide Reflections and Compositions (Cont.)

- Graph and label triangle **ABC**. **A**(1,1), **B**(1,3), and **C**(6,1)
- Perform this transformation, $\mathbf{r}_{x\text{-}axis}$.
- Label this image **A'B'C'**.
- Then perform this transformation, $\mathbf{T}_{-8,0}$.
- Label this final image **A"B"C"**.

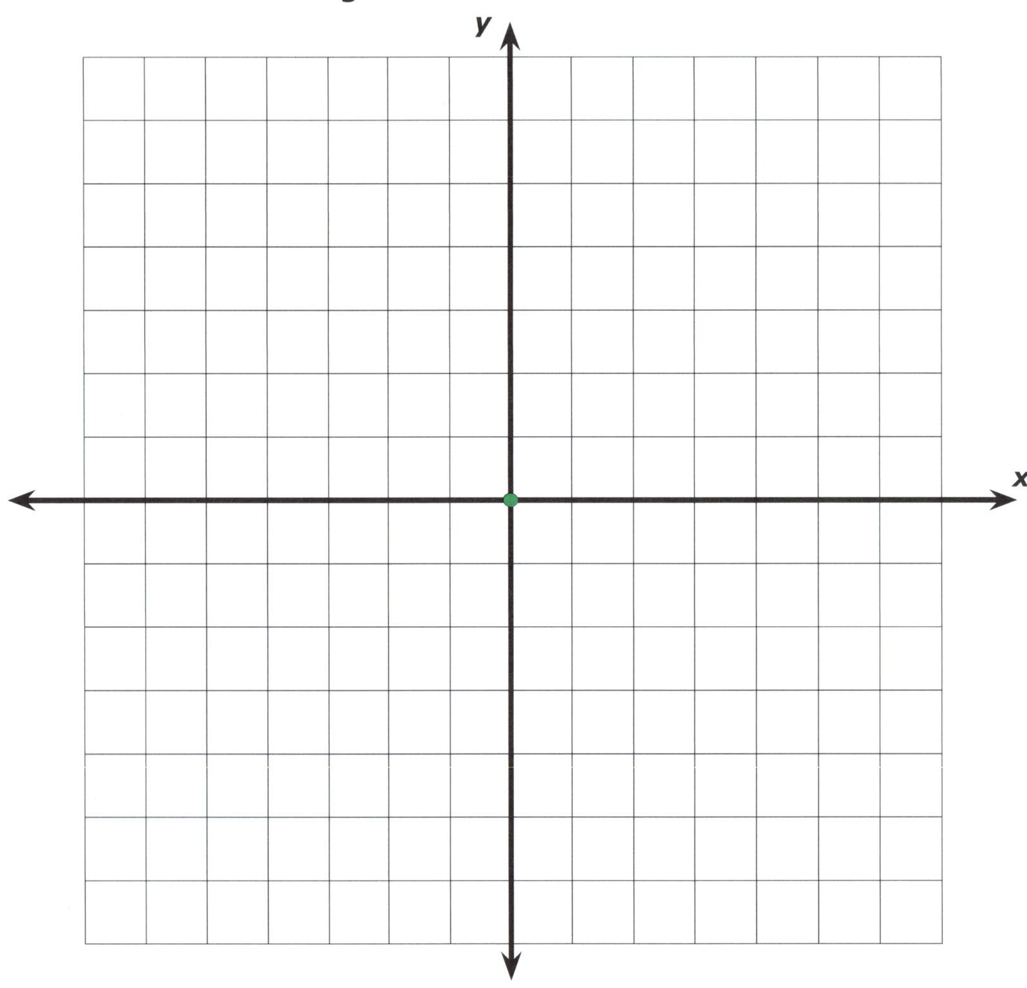

a) Explain why the transformations above result in a glide reflection.

____

____

b) Would you get the same results if you had done the translation first and then the reflection? *Try it!*

Explain your thinking. ______________________________

____

Glide Reflections and Compositions (Cont.)

A glide reflection is a type of composition. A composition is a set of transformations where the first transformation is done to the preimage, then another transformation is done to the image.

The notation for a composition is an open circle, ∘. When you see the notation for a composition, the transformation is done from right *to* left, ***not*** from left to right.

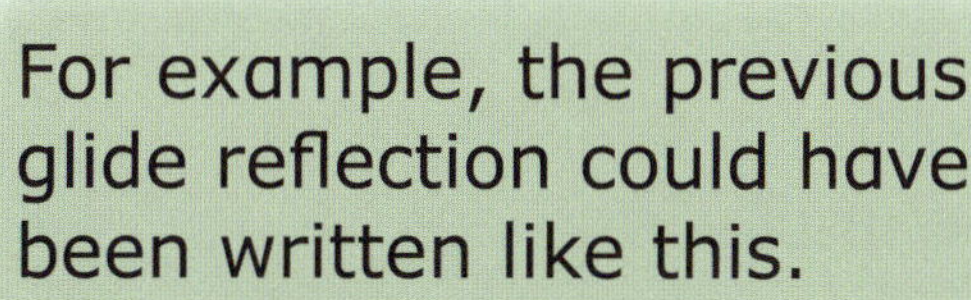

Start on the right side.
Even though the order does not matter in a glide reflection, when you see the notation for a composition, remember to start on the right side and go left.

Perform this composition, $\mathbf{D}_{\frac{1}{2}} \circ \mathbf{T}_{1,-6}(5,4)$, below.

1. Plot **P**(5,4).
2. Translate $(x + 1, y + -6)$ resulting in **P′**(6,−2).
3. Dilate $\frac{1}{2}$ resulting in **P″**(3,−1).

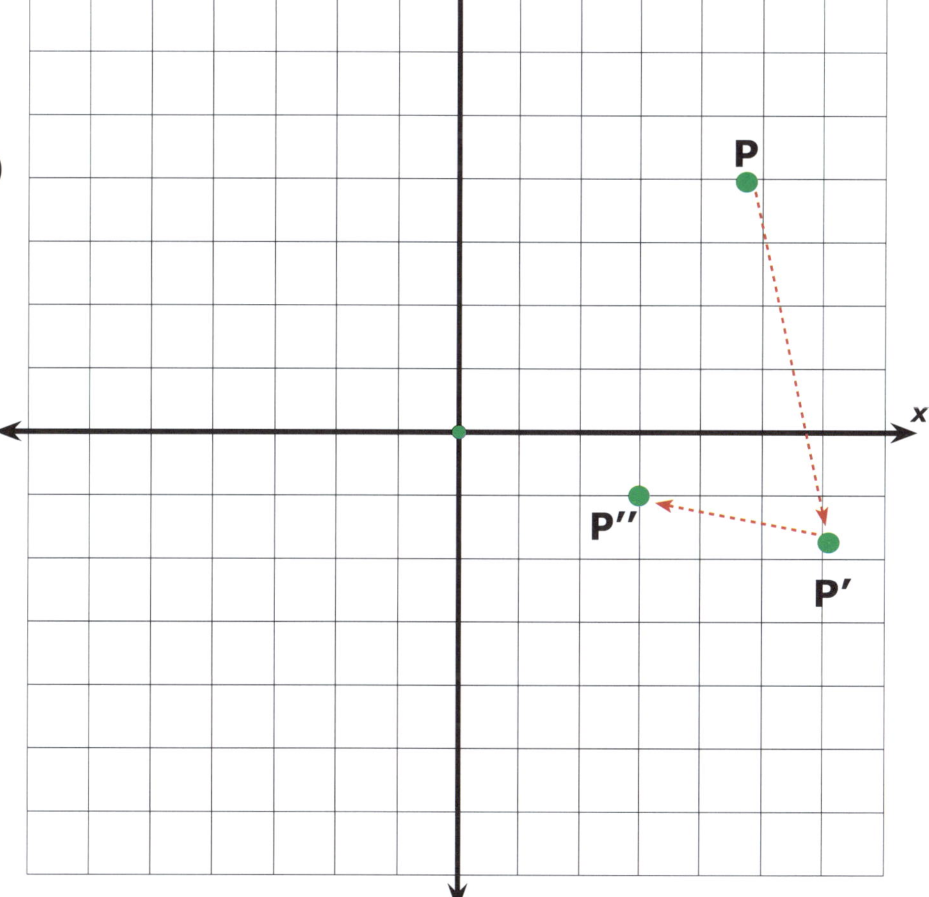

Glide Reflections and Compositions (Cont.)

1. Using the point (x,y), how would you write a dilation of 3 followed by a translation that then moves a point two units to the right and three units down?

   ____

2. Using the point (a,b), how would you write a reflection over the y-axis and then a translation two units to the left?

   ____

3. On the grid below, perform the following composition, $\mathbf{r}_{y\text{-}axis} \circ \mathbf{T}_{2,3} \circ \mathbf{R}_{180°}(1,5)$. Label the point $(1,5)$ as **P**.

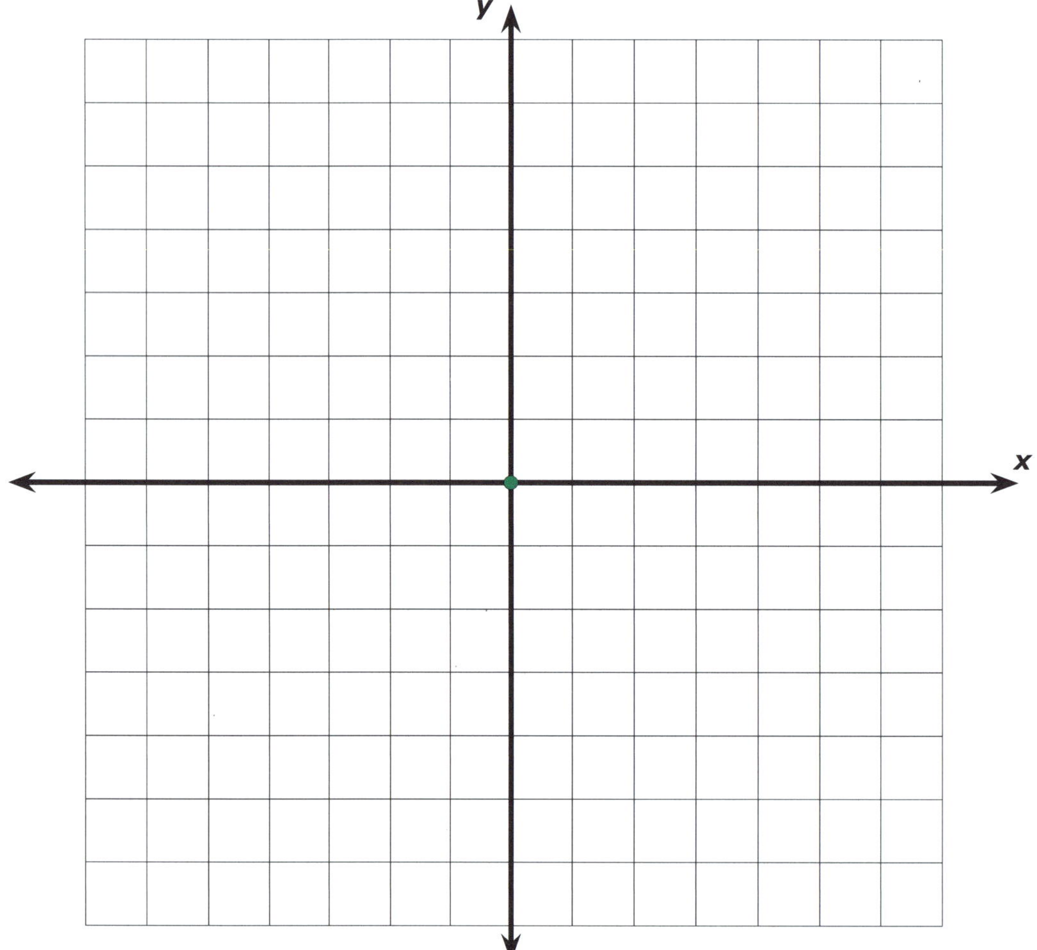

Glide Reflections and Compositions (Cont.)

4. Circle the letter of the following composition that would be a rule for a dilation of 4 followed by a translation of 3 units up.

a. $\mathbf{D}_4 \circ \mathbf{T}_{0,3}(x,y) = (4x, 4y)$

b. $\mathbf{T}_{0,3} \circ \mathbf{D}_4(x,y) = (4x + 3, 4y)$

c. $\mathbf{T}_{0,3} \circ \mathbf{D}_4(x,y) = (4x, 4y + 3)$

d. $\mathbf{D}_4 \circ \mathbf{T}_{0,3}(x,y) = (4x, 4y + 3)$

Explain why the answer you chose is the correct one. ____________

____

____

5. Perform this composition. $\mathbf{R}_{90°} \circ \mathbf{T}_{-3,1}$

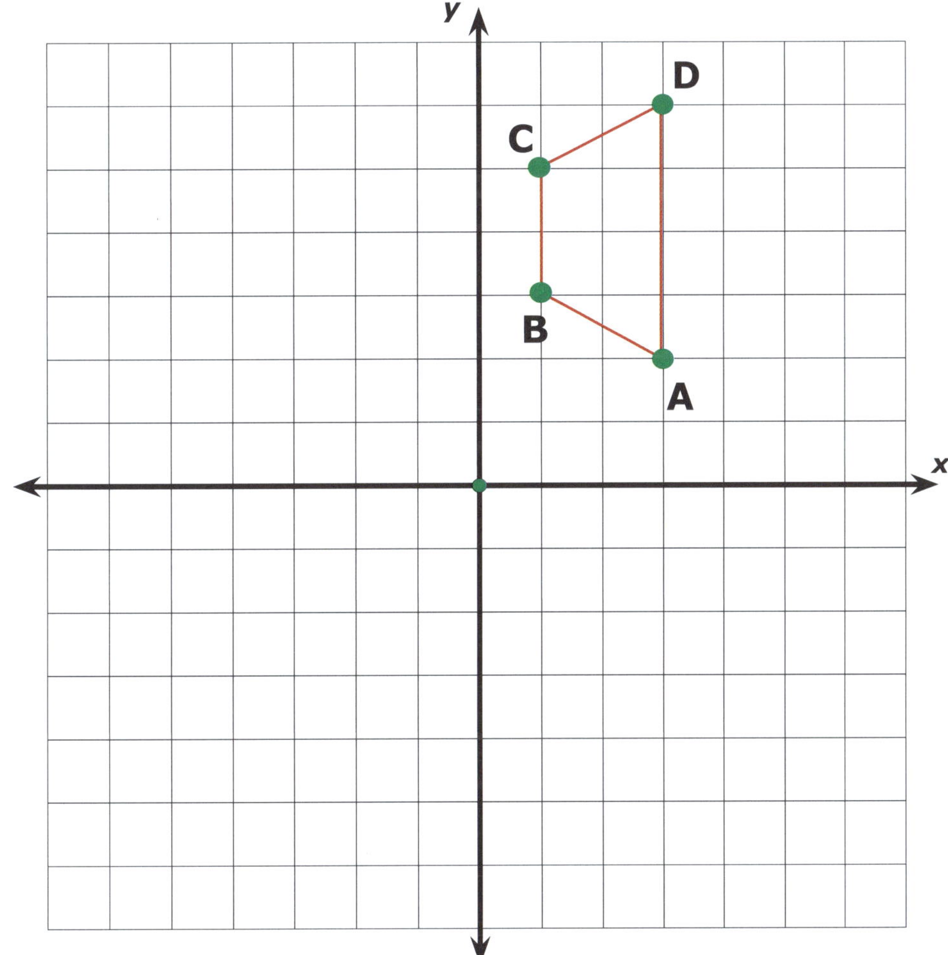

Glide Reflections and Compositions (Cont.)

6. Describe a 2 step composition that could result in ΔABC becoming ΔA″B″C″. ______________________

____

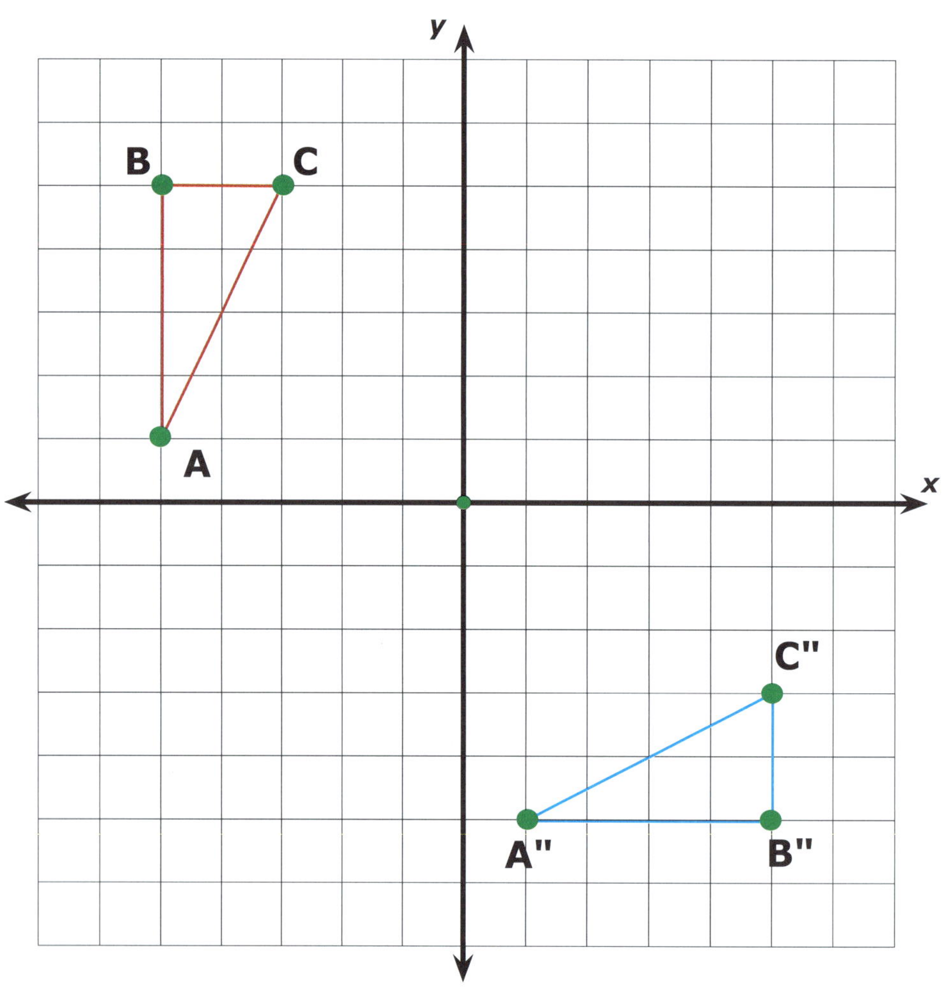

7. Can you describe another 2 step composition that could result in ΔABC becoming ΔA″B″C″ in the picture above? (Use tracing paper to help you if needed.)

____

____

8. Could ΔABC become ΔA″B″C″ using only one transformation?

Explain your thinking. ______________________________

____

Tessellations

A tessellation is a tiling on the plane where a figure is repeated over and over so that there are no spaces or gaps between each figure. Some polygons tessellate and some ***do not***. Look at the following polygons below.

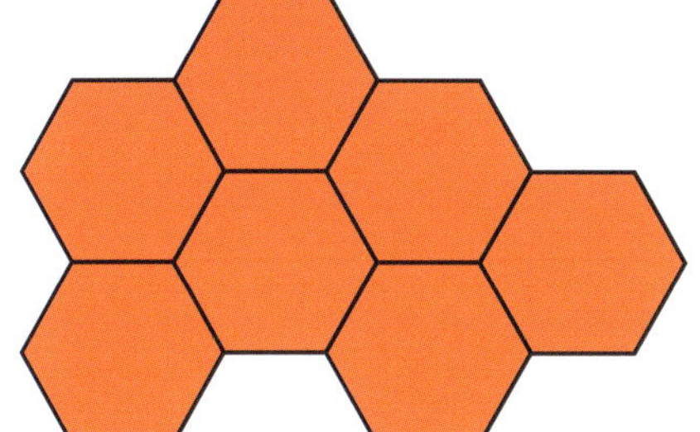

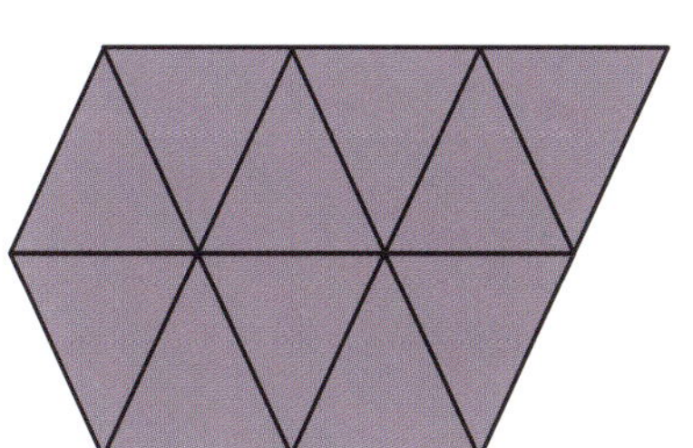

1. Does a regular pentagon tessellate?

   Explain your thinking. ______________________________

   ____

2. Name another regular polygon that tessellates.

   ____

3. You can also combine more than one polygon to tessellate the plane. Try making a design below that combines squares with regular octagons.

Tessellations (Cont.)

Solar panels installed on the roofs of homes for alternative energy create designs that tessellate.

Steps to create your own tessellation.

1. Cut a square from a piece of oak tag paper (or heavy paper). This will be your stencil.
2. Make a design on one side of the square. (Figure 1)
3. Carefully cut your design and tape it to the opposite side keeping the same distance from the top. (Figure 2)
4. Use this stencil and trace all around it. Match and keep tracing it over and over on a large piece of paper to tessellate the plane.
5. You can make a more fancy design by cutting pieces from more than one side and doing the same as below. (Figure 2)
6. Do not forget to see what your design resembles and color it.

Figure 1

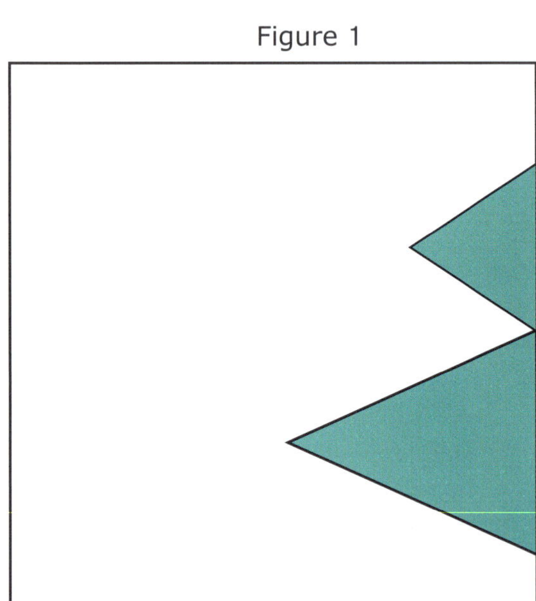

Figure 2

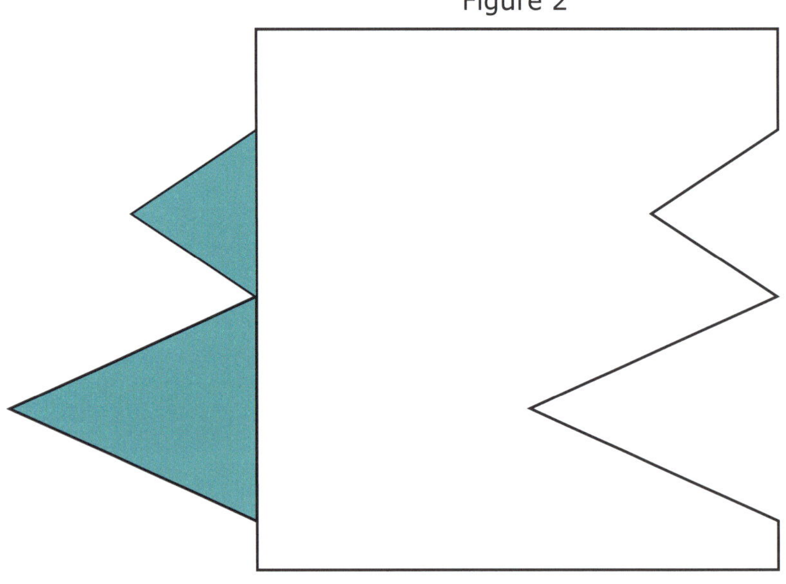

Tessellations (Cont.)

7. Now tessellate your figure by covering the plane with your stencil.

Review – Chapter 10

Use a separate sheet of paper if needed.

1. Which of these capital letters have point symmetry? H, A, T, S _______

2. Given the pre-image, a rectangle **ABCD** where **A** = (-2, 4), **B** = (1, 4), **C** = (1, 2) and **D** = (-2, 2), answer questions a-d below. Graphing is optional.

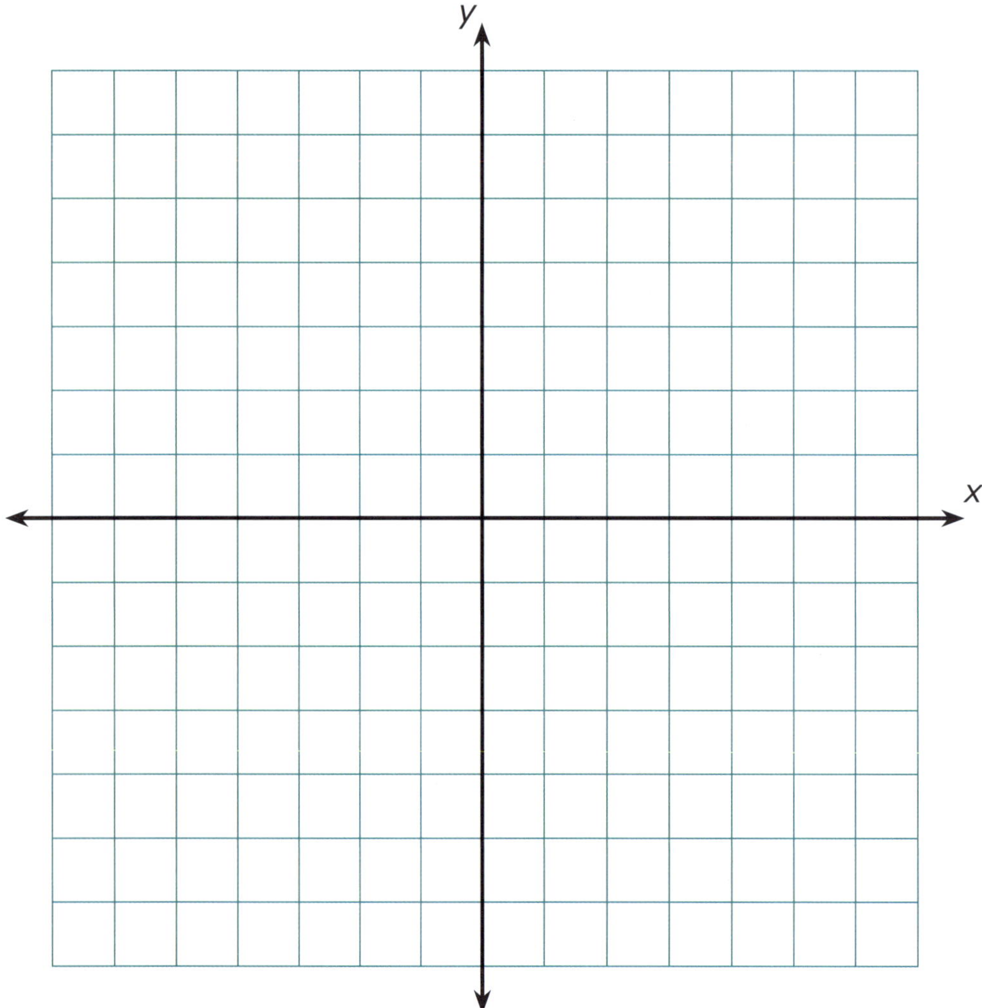

a. What are the coordinates of the image after the original rectangle is reflected about the *x*-axis? _______________

b. What are the coordinates of the image after the original rectangle is rotated 180° about the origin? _______________

c. What are the coordinates of the image after the original rectangle is dilated by a factor of 2? _______________

d. What are the coordinates of the image after the original rectangle is translated as $\mathbf{T}_{3,-1}$? _______________

3. Perform the following composition on point **Q** = (-3, 5). Remember to start on the right and go left.

$$\mathbf{r}_{y\text{-axis}} \circ \mathbf{T}_{-2,4} \circ \mathbf{R}_{90^\circ}(-3, 5)$$

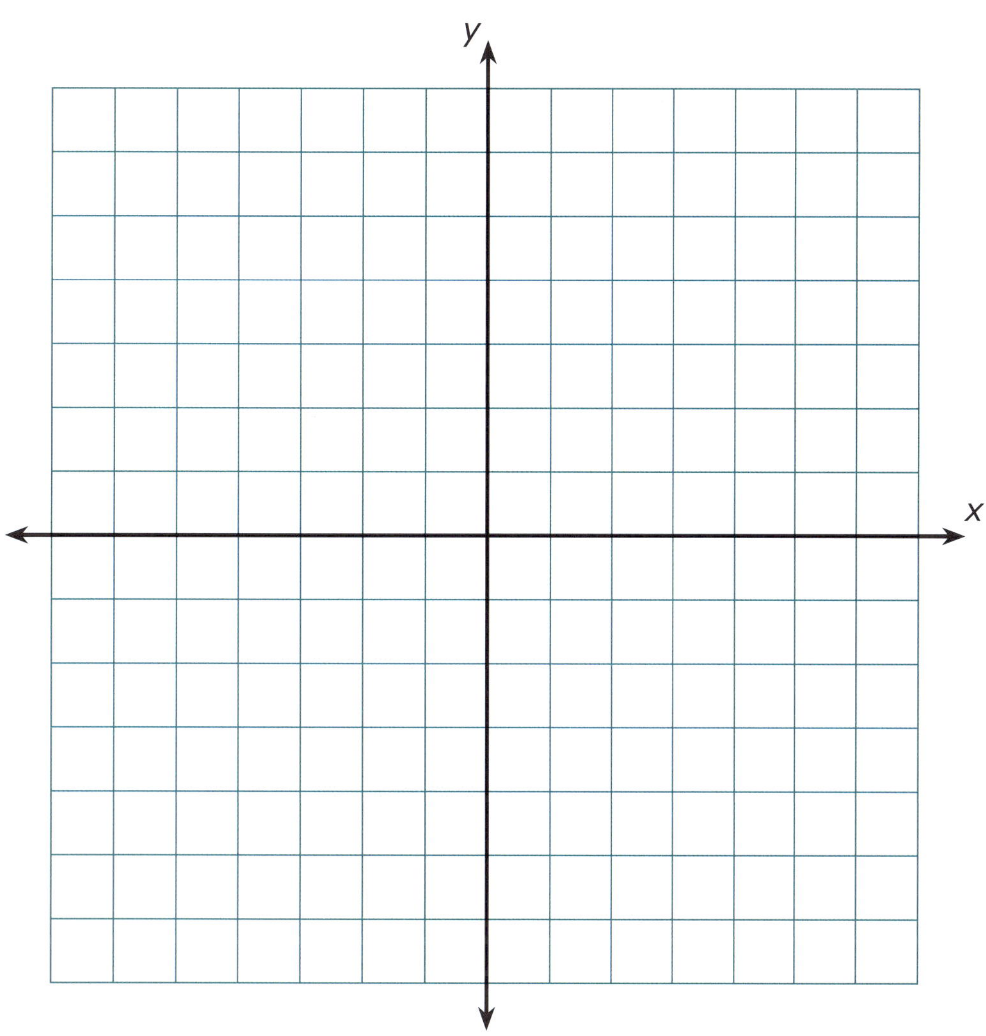

Chapter 11 - Proving Triangles Congruent

Introduction to Proofs - Congruency

The two triangles below are congruent.

They are identical to each other. We can write **ΔABC ≅ ΔDEF**.

Notice

The triangles' corresponding sides are congruent and their corresponding angles are also congruent.

The order in which you write **ΔABC ≅ ΔDEF** is important.

Without even looking at the pictures. $\overline{AB}$, the first two letters of **ΔABC** indicate that the corresponding congruent segment is $\overline{DE}$, the first two letters of **ΔDEF**.

Also, $\overline{AC}$, the first and third letters indicate that segment $\overline{AC}$ corresponds to $\overline{DF}$, first and third letters of **ΔDEF**.

The same is true of the angles, ∠**B**, second letter of **ΔABC** corresponds to ∠**E**, second letter of **ΔDEF**, and so on.

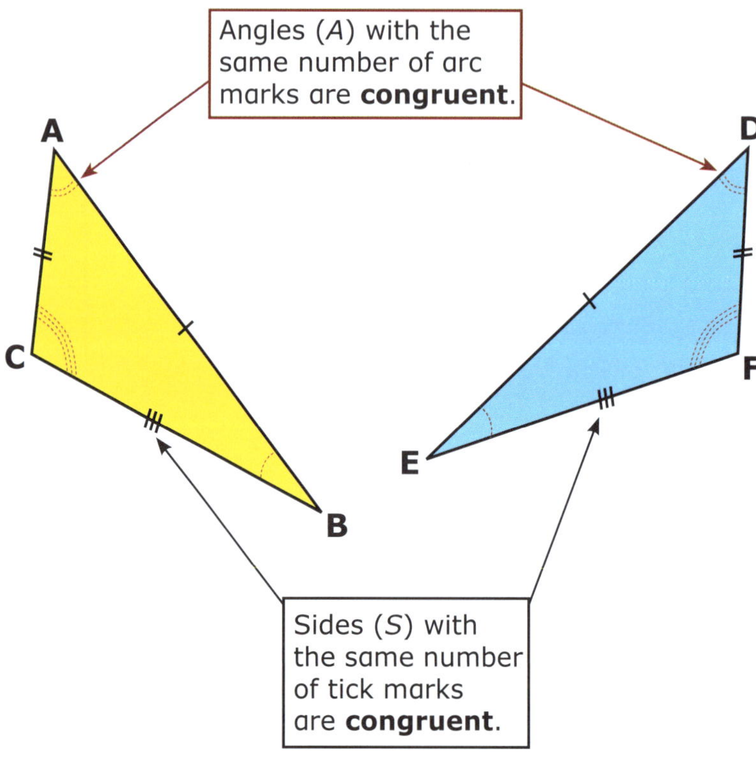

Remember

If two triangles are congruent, then their corresponding parts must be congruent.

The abbreviation for this statement is **cpctc**. (corresponding parts of congruent triangles are congruent.)

We will see how we use cpctc later when we learn how to write a proof.

Introduction to Proofs - Congruency (Cont.)

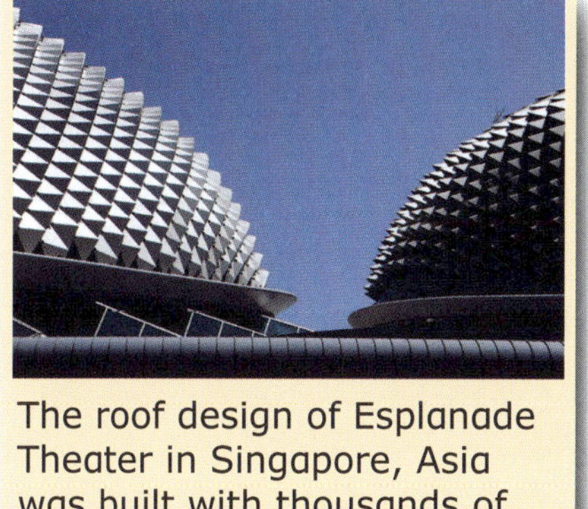

The roof design of Esplanade Theater in Singapore, Asia was built with thousands of congruent triangle shape tiles.

Answer the following questions. **Given** means the fact is stated in the picture or in the information.

1. Given that Δ**FRQ** ≅ Δ**GJW**. Complete the following list of six congruent facts about the triangles.

a. ∠**F** ≅ ∠**G**; b. $\overline{FQ}$ ≅ $\overline{GW}$;

c. ∠**W** ≅ ________; d. ∠**R** ≅ ________;

e. $\overline{WJ}$ ≅ ________; f. $\overline{FR}$ ≅ ________

2. Given that Δ**RST** ≅ Δ**WEB**, finish the labels on both triangles. Show tick marks on the sides.

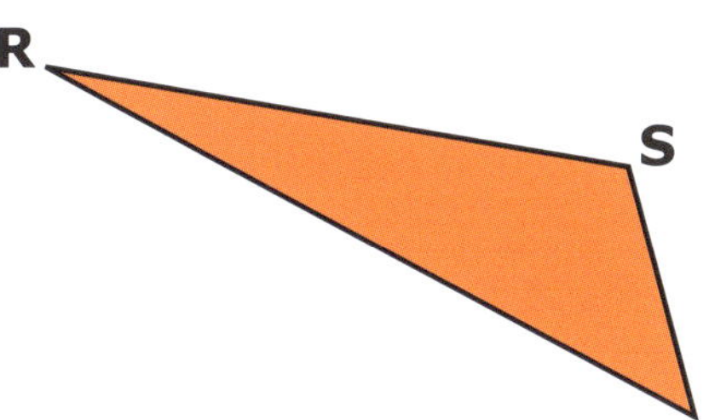

3. These triangles are congruent. Write a congruence statement and list all corresponding angles and sides.

____

____

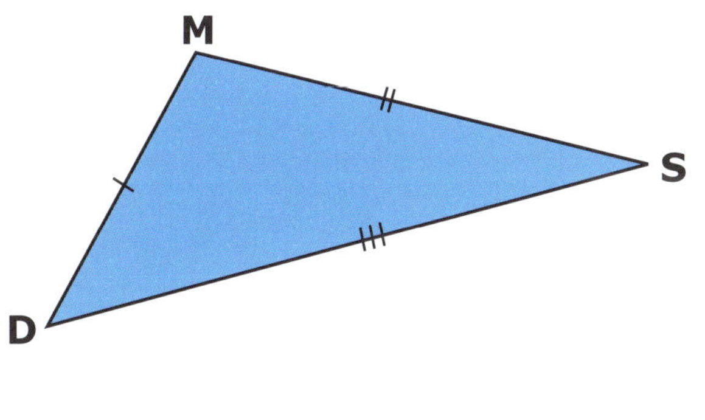

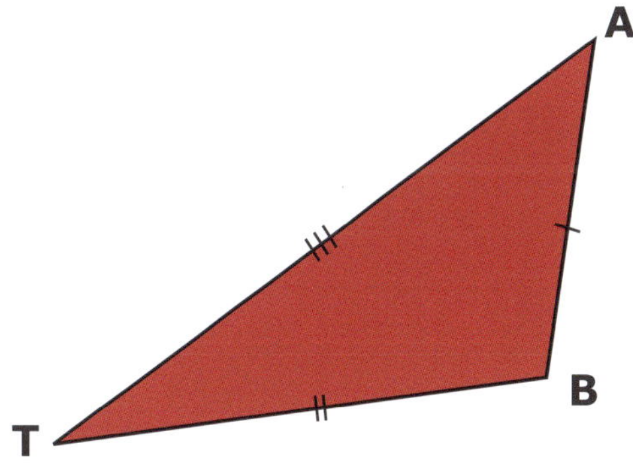

SSS Activity

Are you wondering what is the minimum number of facts needed to prove that two triangles are congruent to each other? Do we need all six facts (three corresponding angles and three corresponding sides)? Let's examine these questions.

1. Supposing we know three sides (***SSS***) of a triangle are congruent to the three sides (***SSS***) of another triangle, is that enough to prove the triangles congruent?

Explain your thinking. ______________________________

____

2. 

Take three plastic straws or stir sticks and cut them into the measurements 2 in., 3 in., and 4 in. Make a triangle using these lengths. Now, make another triangle using the same lengths. Are the triangles congruent?

2"

3"

4"

Remember
You can use your own measurements as long as the sum of two sides is more than the third side.

Explain your thinking. ______________________________

____

____

SAS Activity

When three sides of one triangle are congruent to three sides of another triangle (***SSS***), then the triangles are congruent. Three other ways of proving triangles congruent are **SAS**, **ASA**, or **AAS**.

1. In **SAS**, you know that two sides and the angle included between the two sides are congruent to two sides and the included angle of another triangle. Is this information enough to prove the two triangles are congruent?

Explain your thinking. ____

____

2. Use a protractor and create a specific angle of 40°. Make one ray of the angle 3 in. and the other ray 4 in. Make a triangle. Now repeat the directions to make a second triangle. Try it!

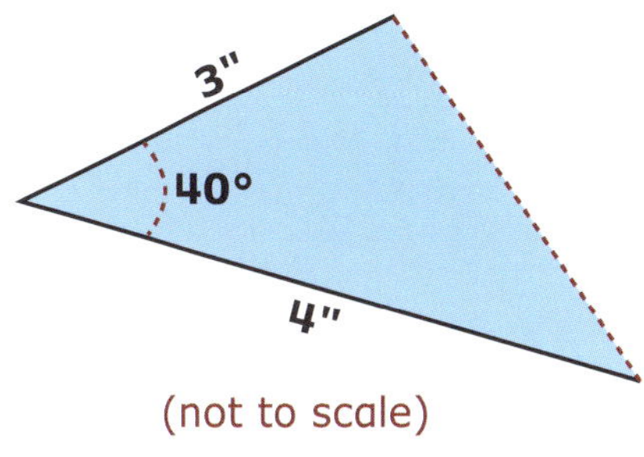

(not to scale)

Is your second triangle congruent to the first one? __________

ASA and AAS Activities

In **ASA**, two angles and the included side (between those two angles) of one triangle are congruent to two angles and the included side of another triangle.

Draw a line of 3 in., then use a protractor to make an angle of 20° and an angle of 50° at each endpoint of that side. Complete the triangle. Now repeat the directions to make a second triangle. You should end up with congruent triangles.

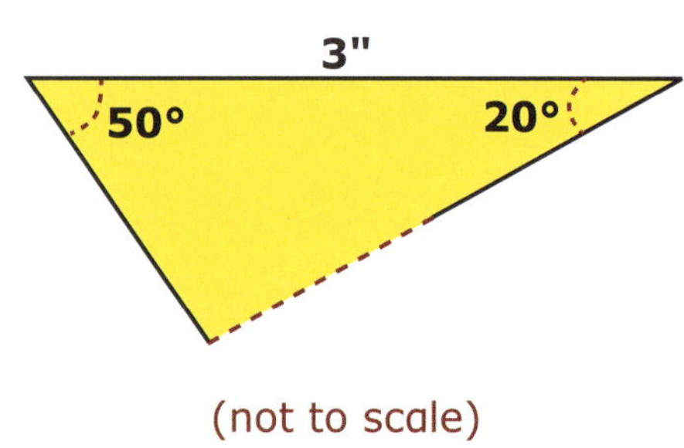

(not to scale)

Now try it with different measurements making sure the fixed side is between the two fixed angles. You should end up with two congruent triangles.

Why would **AAS** be the same as **ASA**?

Explain your thinking. ______________________________

____

____

SSA Activity

So far, to prove two triangles congruent, you see that you can use **SSS**, **SAS**, **ASA**, or **AAS**. What about **SSA**?

Does knowing two sides of one triangle and an angle not included between the two sides guarantee congruency?

Look at this picture.

Can you see that ΔABC is ***not*** congruent to ΔABD?

That is because the angle, in the example 40°, is ***not*** in between congruent sides.

SSA or **ASS** (sometimes called the donkey theorem) cannot be used to prove triangles are congruent.

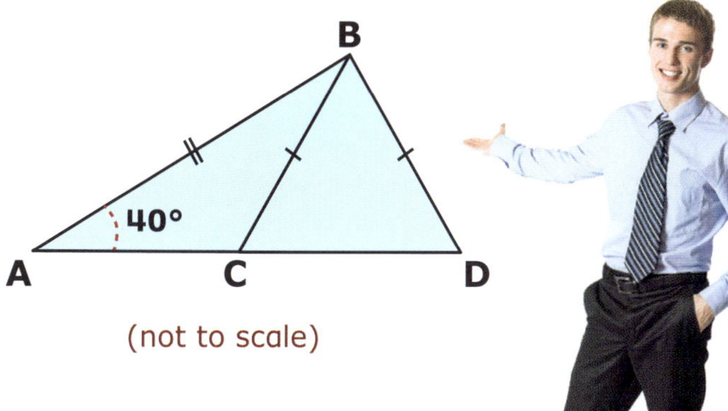

(not to scale)

What about **AAA**? Would two triangles with corresponding congruent angles give you congruency?

Review the section on dilations in the previous chapter on symmetry.

  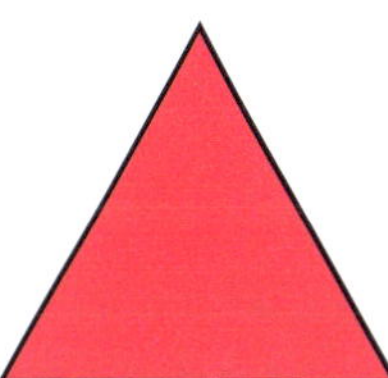

Above are three equilateral triangles. Explain why these drawings prove that **AAA** does ***not*** guarantee congruency.

____

____

SSS, **SAS**, **ASA**, and **AAS** are called **postulates**. Postulates are statements that need no formal proof. We will use these postulates to write simple geometry proofs in the next section.

There is one more way of proving triangles congruent. In right triangles, we can use **H-L** (Hypotenuse/Leg). We will investigate this theorem later.

The Essence of a Good Geometric Proof

To be successful with proofs, it is important to review some of the most important geometric properties studied so far and learn some new ones.

In some properties, the converse is also true. If a statement is *if p then q*, then the converse is *if q then p*.

Sketch a drawing for each of these properties.

Description	Drawing
1 Vertical angles are congruent (≅).	
2 If lines are parallel (ll), then alternate interior angles are congruent (≅). Converse: If alternate interior angles are congruent (≅), then lines are parallel (ll).	
3 If lines are parallel (ll), then corresponding angles are congruent (≅). Converse: If corresponding angles are congruent (≅), then lines are parallel (ll).	
4 If two sides of a triangle are congruent (≅), then the angles opposite those sides are congruent (≅). Converse: If two angles of a triangle are congruent (≅), then the sides opposite those angles are congruent (≅).	

The Essence of a Good Geometric Proof (Cont.)

Description	Drawing
5 If two lines are perpendicular (⊥), then they intersect to form right angles.	

Here are some other important properties frequently used in geometric proofs.

Properties of Equality

Description	Drawing
6 Reflexive Property of Equality A quantity is equal to itself. **BD** = **BD** or $\overline{BD} \cong \overline{BD}$	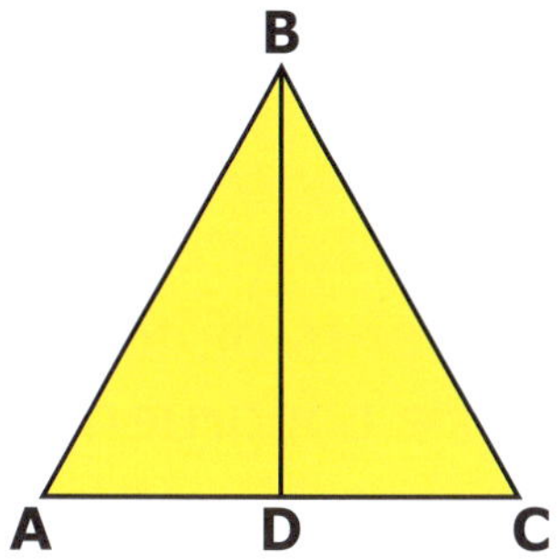 B, A, D, C
7 Symmetric Property of Equality An equality may be expressed in either order. If m∠**E** = m∠**Q**, then m∠**Q** = m∠**E**.	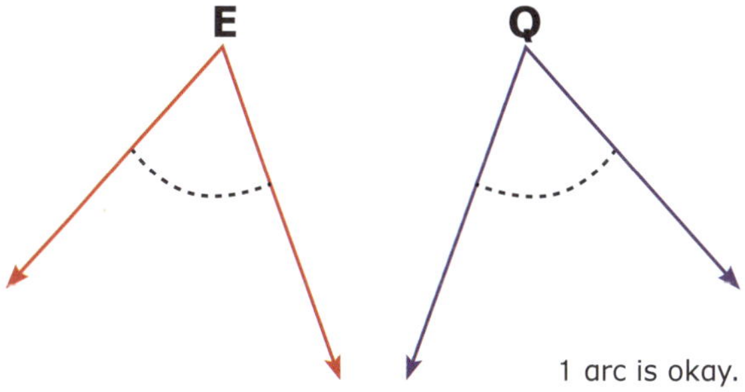 E, Q 1 arc is okay.
8 Transitive Property of Equality Quantities equal to the same quantity are equal. If m∠**3** = m∠**2** and m∠**2** = m∠**1** (vertical angles are congruent), then ∠m**3** = ∠m**1**.	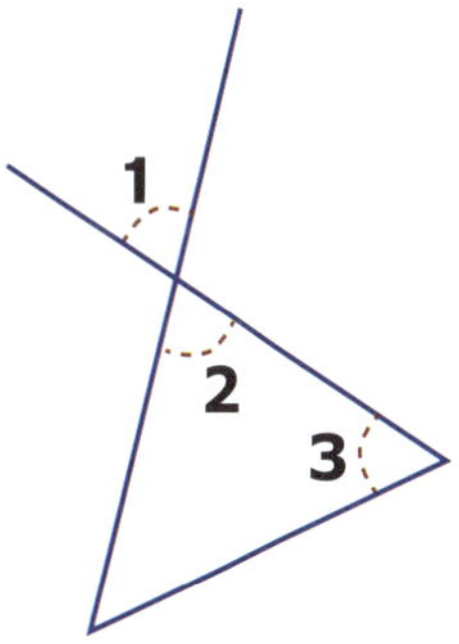 1, 2, 3

The Essence of a Good Geometric Proof (Cont.)

Description	Drawing
9 Addition Postulate If **R** is between **M** and **P**, then **MR** + **RP** = **MP**.	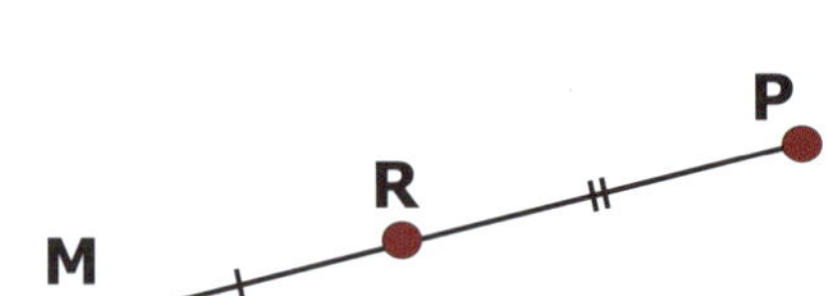
10 Supplements of congruent angles are congruent. If ∠**1** ≅ ∠**2**, then ∠**3** ≅ ∠**4**.	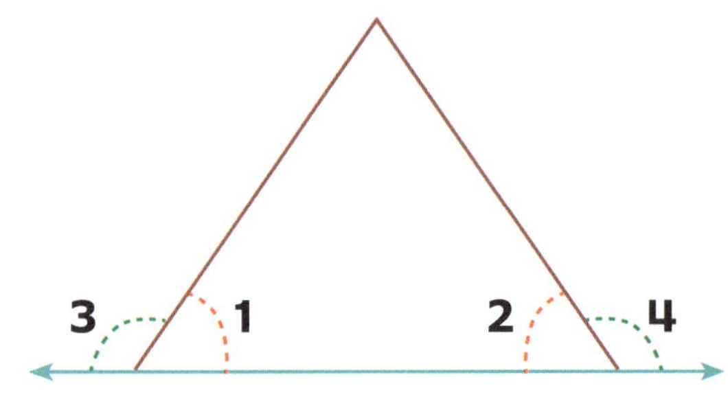
11 Complements of congruent angles are congruent. If ∠**3** is the complement of ∠**2** and ∠**1** is the complement of ∠**2**, then ∠**1** ≅ ∠**3**.	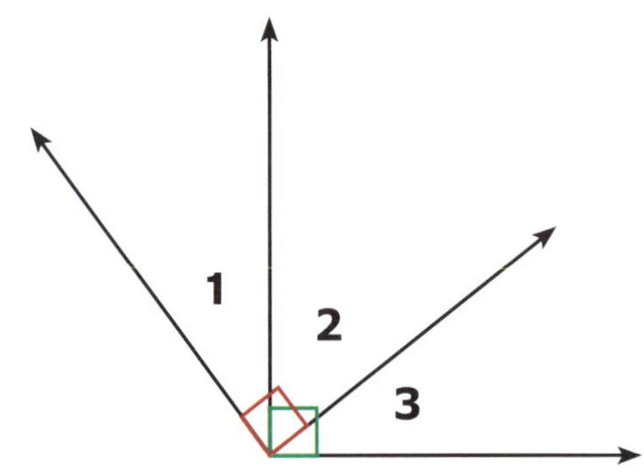
12 Third Angle Theorem (A **theorem** is a property that can be proven with steps.) If two angles of a triangle are congruent to two angles of another triangle, then the third pair must be congruent. If ∠**A** ≅ ∠**E** and ∠**C** ≅ ∠**F**, then ∠**B** ≅ ∠**D**.	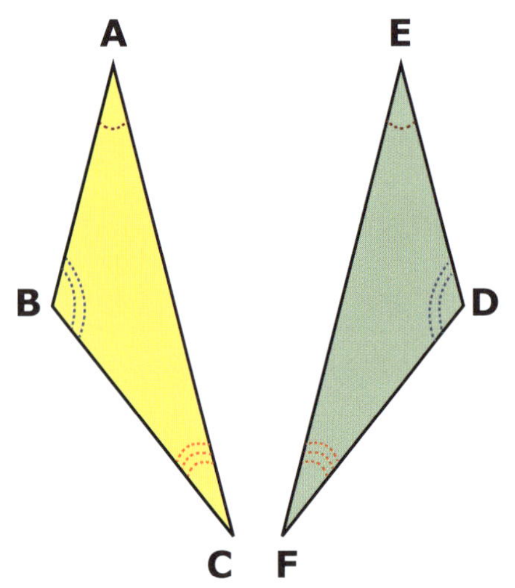

Picture, Statement, and Reason

Refer to the picture and write a reason for each statement.

	Statement	Reason
1 B A D C	a $\overline{AB} \cong \overline{CB}$	a Given (The fact is stated in the picture or in the information.)
	b $\angle A \cong \angle C$	b ______ ______ ______
2 T V R W	a $\overline{TV} \cong \overline{TV}$	a ______ ______ ______
3 2 1	a $\angle 1 \cong \angle 2$	a ______ ______ ______

Picture, Statement, and Reason (Cont.)

Refer to the picture and write a reason for each statement.

	Statement	Reason
4	 (a) ∠GFA ≅ ∠CEA	 (a) ______________ ______________
	(b) $\overline{CE} \parallel \overline{GF}$	(b) ______________ ______________ ______________
 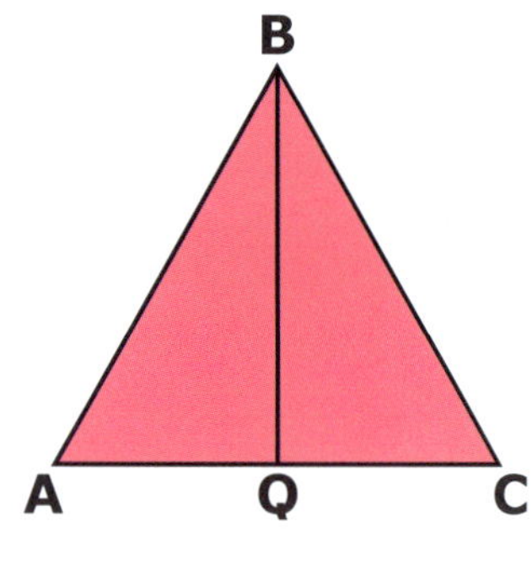 Given: (BQ ⊥ AC)	(a) $\overline{BQ} \perp \overline{AC}$	(a) Given
	 (b) ∠BQA and ∠BQC are right angles.	(b) ______________ ______________
	(c) ∠BQA ≅ ∠BQC	(c) ______________ ______________ ______________
6 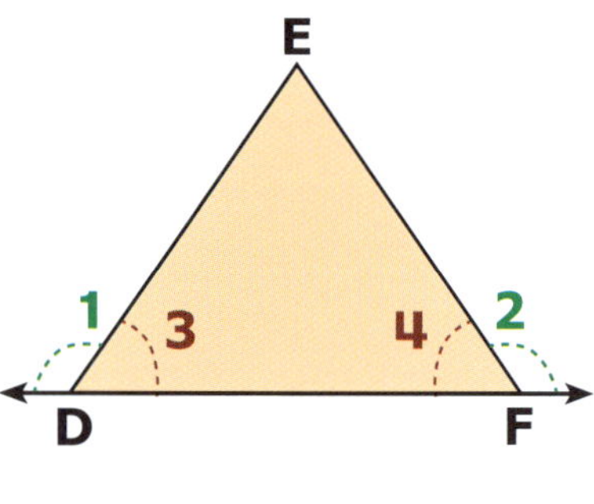 Given: (∠1 ≅ ∠2)	(a) ______________	(a) Given
	(b) ∠3 ≅ ∠4	(b) ______________ ______________
	(c) $\overline{DE} \cong \overline{FE}$	(c) ______________ ______________
	(d) ΔDEF is isosceles.	(d) ______________ ______________

Finding Congruent Triangles

Are these triangles congruent? Write Yes or No. If Yes, then give a reason **SSS**, **SAS**, **ASA**, or **AAS**. Rely on the information given.

Before starting this section, please review the ways we can prove triangles congruent (***SSS***, ***SAS***, ***ASA***, or ***AAS***).

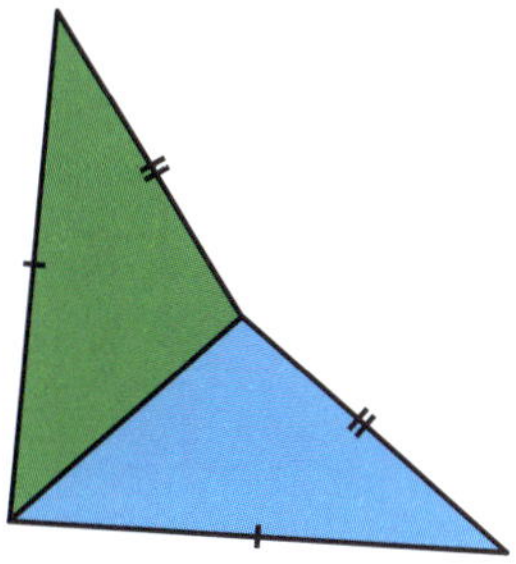

1. ______________

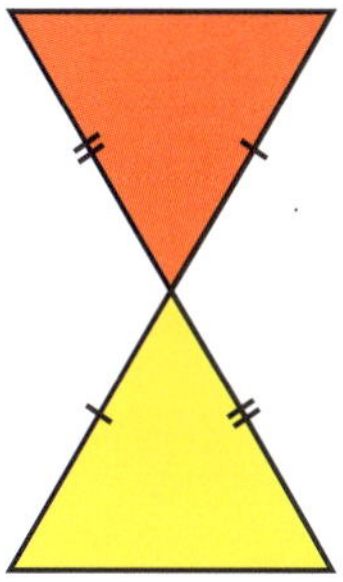

2. ______________

3. ______________

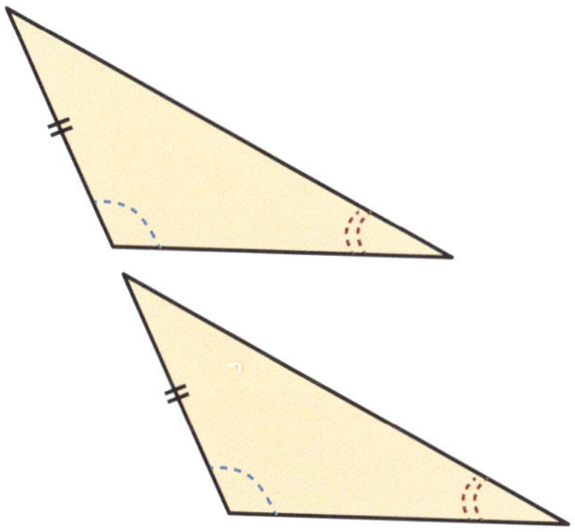

4. ______________

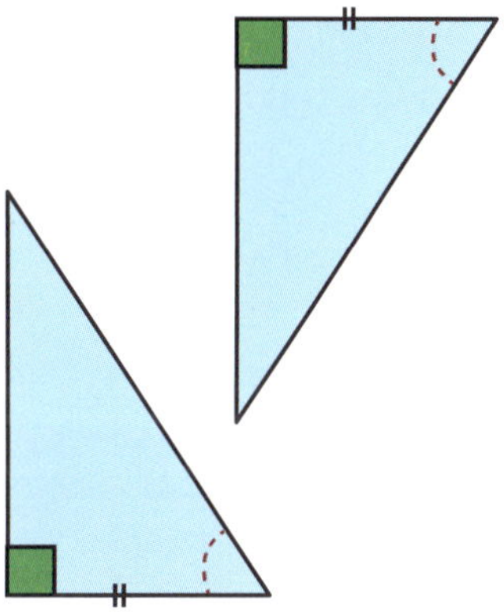

5. ______________

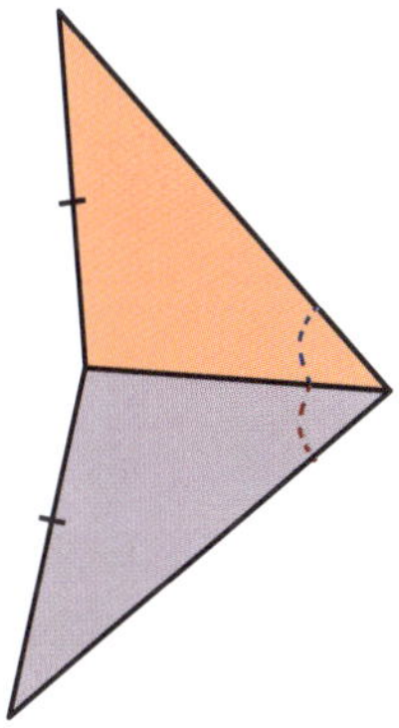

6. ______________

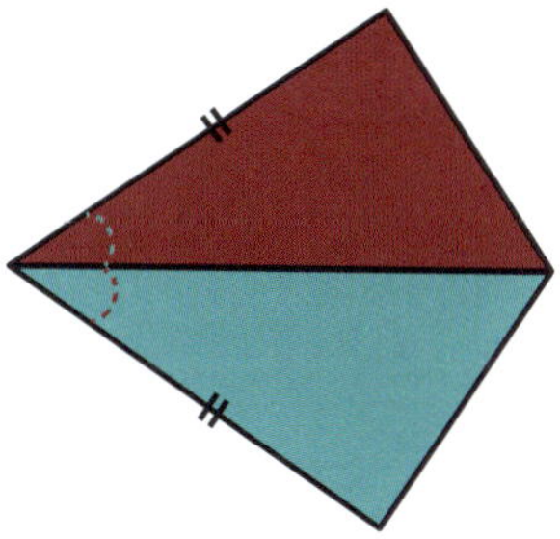

7. ______________

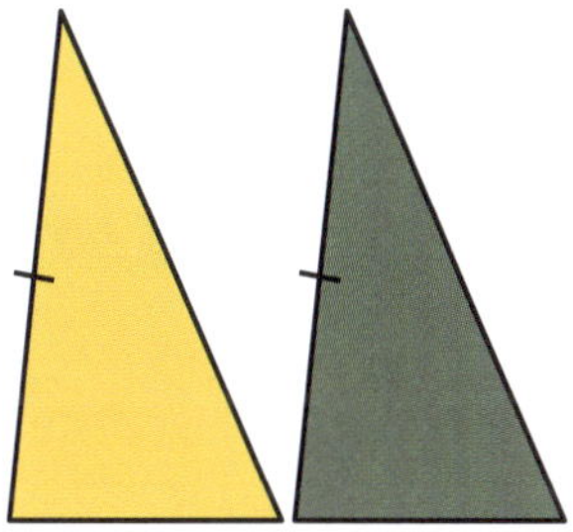

8. ______________

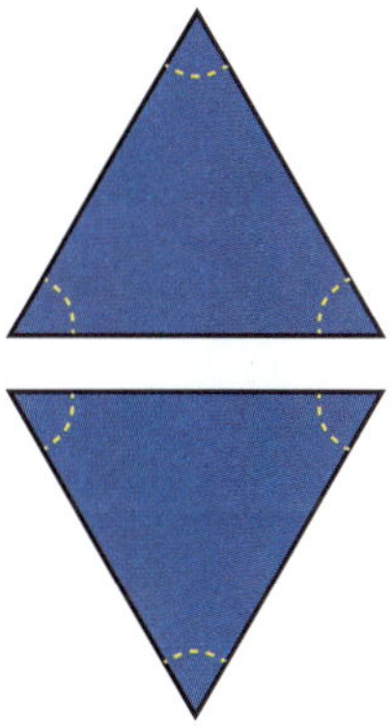

9. ______________

Two Column Proofs

Refer to the picture and fill in the missing reasons or statements for each proof.

Proof 1

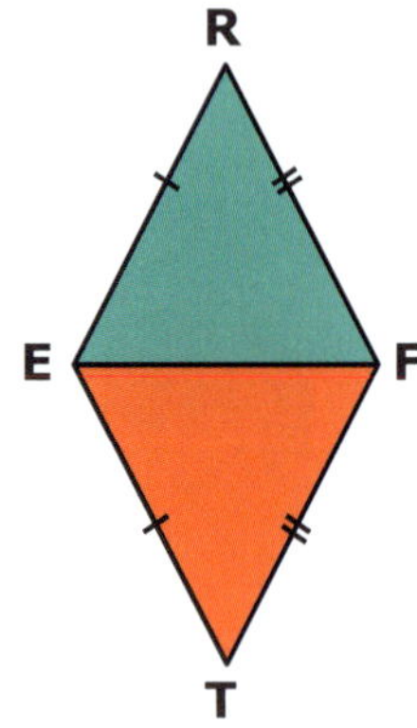

Given: $\overline{ER} \cong \overline{ET}$ and $\overline{RF} \cong \overline{TF}$

Prove: $\Delta ERF \cong \Delta ETF$

Statement	Reason
1 $\overline{ER} \cong \overline{ET}$	1 ____________ ____________
2 ____________	2 Given
3 $\overline{EF} \cong \overline{EF}$	3 ____________ ____________
4 $\Delta ERF \cong \Delta ETF$	4 ____________ ____________

Proof 2

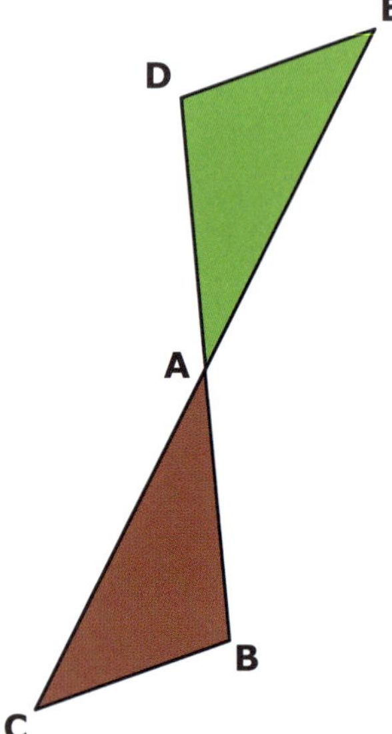

Given: $\overline{BA} \cong \overline{DA}$ and $\overline{CA} \cong \overline{EA}$

Prove: $\angle E \cong \angle C$

Statement	Reason
1 $\overline{BA} \cong \overline{DA}$	1 ____________ ____________
2 $\overline{CA} \cong \overline{EA}$	2 ____________ ____________
3 $\angle CAB \cong \angle EAD$	3 ____________ ____________
4 $\Delta CAB \cong \Delta EAD$	4 ____________ ____________
5 $\angle E \cong \angle C$	5 cpctc (corresponding parts of congruent triangles are congruent.)

Two Column Proofs (Cont.)

Refer to the picture and fill in the missing reasons or statements for each proof.

Proof 3

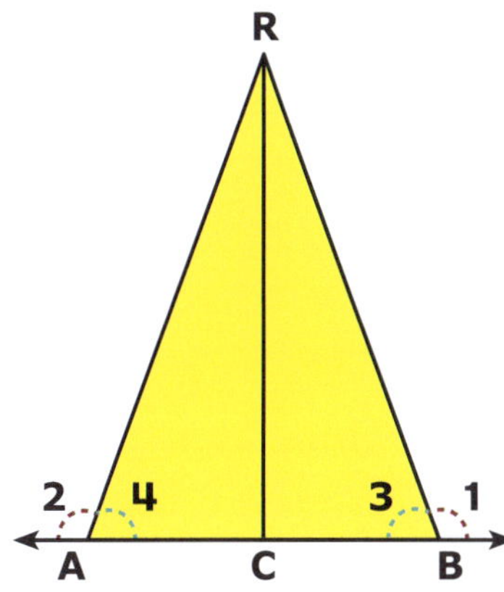

Given: $\overline{RC} \perp \overline{AB}$ and $\overline{AC} \cong \overline{BC}$

Prove: $\angle 1 \cong \angle 2$

Statement	Reason
1 ________________	1 Given
2 ________________	2 Given
3 $\angle$**ACR** and $\angle$**BCR** are right angles.	3 ________________
4 ________________	4 All right angles are congruent.
5 $\overline{RC} \cong \overline{RC}$	5 ________________
6 $\Delta ACR \cong \Delta BCR$	6 ________________
7 $\angle 3 \cong \angle 4$	7 ________________
8 $\angle 1 \cong \angle 2$	8 ________________

Proof 4

A B
W R L H

Given: $\overline{WR} \cong \overline{HL}$, $\angle W \cong \angle H$, $\angle ALW \cong \angle BRH$

Prove: $\angle \Delta AWL \cong \Delta BHR$ and $\angle A \cong \angle B$

Statement	Reason
1 ________________	1 Given
2 ________________	2 Given
3 ________________	3 Given
4 $\overline{RL} \cong \overline{RL}$	4 ________________
5 $\overline{WL} \cong \overline{HR}$	5 ________________
6 $\Delta AWL \cong \Delta BHR$	6 ________________
7 $\angle A \cong \angle B$	7 ________________

Two Column Proofs (Cont.)

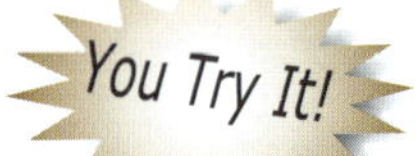

Do the following proofs. Remember to always look first at what you are trying to prove. Then try to find what properties can be useful to arrive at a conclusion.

Proof 5

Given: ∠**A** ≅ ∠**D**, ∠**C** ≅ ∠**F**, and $\overline{AB} \cong \overline{DE}$

Prove: △**ABC** ≅ △**DEF**

Statement	Reason
1 ______	1 ______
2 ______	2 ______
3 ______	3 ______
4 ______	4 ______

Proof 6

Given: **E is the midpoint of** $\overline{DC}$**.** ∠**1** ≅ ∠**2**, and ∠**3** ≅ ∠**4**

Prove: $\overline{DA} \cong \overline{CB}$

Statement	Reason
1 ______	1 ______
2 ______	2 ______
3 ______	3 ______
4 ______	4 ______
5 ______	5 ______
6 ______	6 ______
7 ______	7 ______

Two Column Proofs (Cont.)

Do the following proof. Remember to always look first at what you are trying to prove. Then try to find what properties can be useful to arrive at a conclusion.

Proof 7

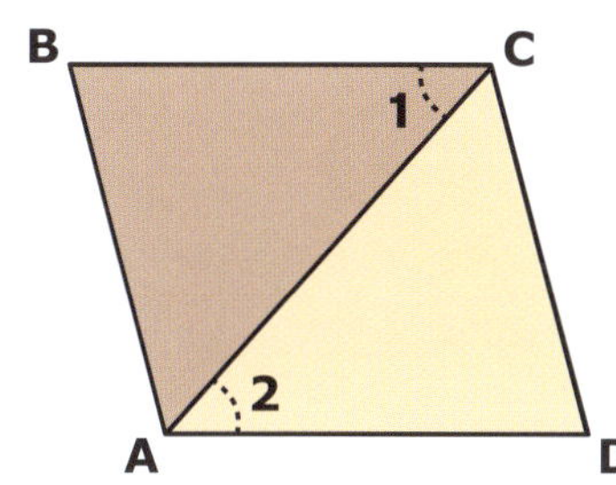

Given: $\overline{BC} \parallel \overline{DA}$ and $\angle B \cong \angle D$

Prove: $\triangle ABC \cong \triangle ADC$ and $\overline{BA} \cong \overline{DC}$

Statement	Reason
1 __________	1 __________
2 __________	2 __________
3 __________	3 __________
__________	__________
4 __________	4 __________
5 __________	5 __________
6 __________	6 __________

Investigate Hypotenuse - Leg Theorem

Use the Pythagorean Theorem to show that if the hypotenuse and a leg of one right triangle are congruent to the hypotenuse and the leg of another right triangle, then the triangles are congruent.

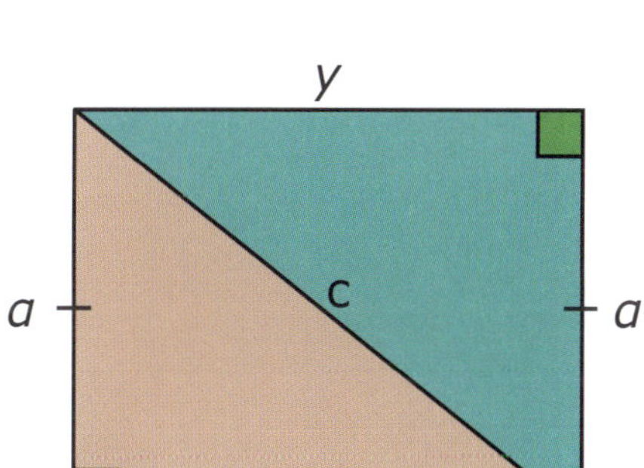

Investigate Hypotenuse - Leg Theorem (Cont.)

Are these triangles congruent by the Hypotenuse-Leg Theorem?

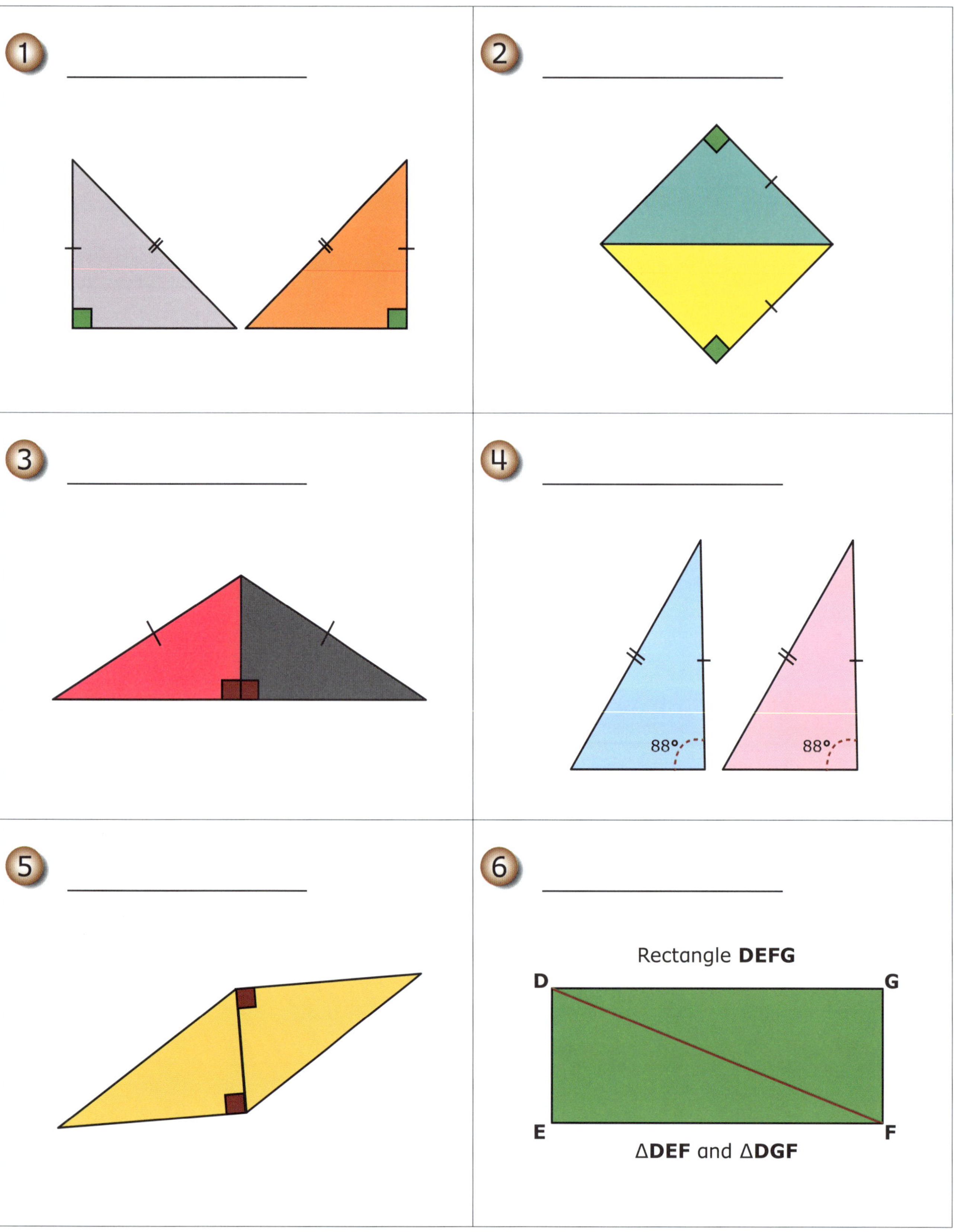

Similar Figures and Introduction to Similarity Proofs

Similar figures are figures that look the same but are not necessarily the same size. One figure can be the reflection of the other or a rotation of the other. When a figure is dilated the end result is similar to the original. (Refer to the section on dilations in the chapter on transformations.)

The symbol for **similar** is a tilde (~).

In Geometry, when a figure is similar to another, their corresponding angles remain congruent and their corresponding sides are in **proportion**.

Remember, a proportion is two ratios that are equal.

For example:

Figure A

2'
w
y
q
88°
6'
7'
50°

~

Figure B

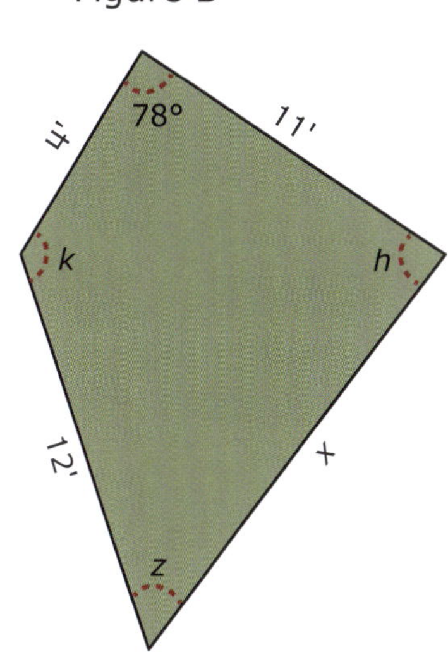

1 The quadrilaterals above are similar. Find the missing sides and angles.

a $x =$ ______, b $y =$ ______, c $m\angle z =$ ______,

d $m\angle h =$ ______, e $m\angle q =$ ______, f $m\angle k =$ ______,

g $m\angle w =$ ______

2 a Find the perimeter of Figure A ________.

b Find the perimeter of Figure B ________.

c How does the ratio of perimeters compare to the ratio of the sides?

Explain your thinking. ____

____

Similar Figures and Introduction to Similarity Proofs (Cont.)

When two figures are similar you can set up a proportion to find any of the missing sides. For example:

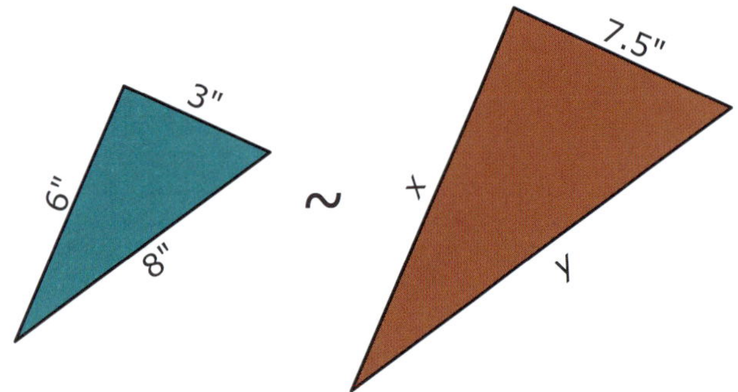

$$\frac{3}{7.5} = \frac{6}{x}$$

$$3x = 45$$

$$x = 15 \text{ in.}$$

1. In the example above, find y by using a proportion.

   y = ________

2. Are these hexagons similar?

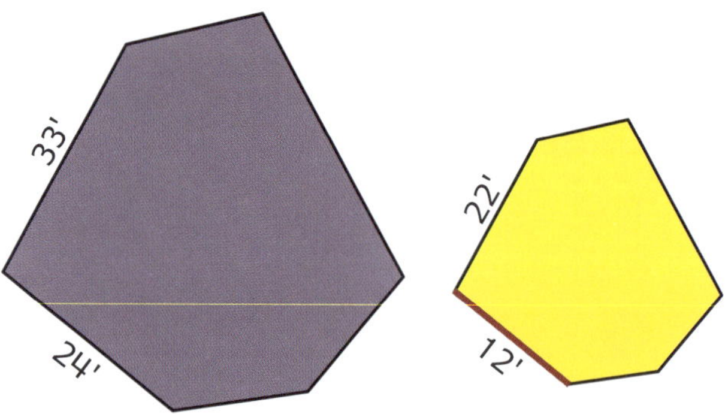

   Explain your thinking. ________________________________

   ____

   ____

3. If you were to make both hexagons similar by making all their corresponding sides in proportion, what should the side marked with red be? Show your work. ________

Similar Figures and Introduction to Similarity Proofs (Cont.)

4. Study the corresponding angles of Δ**ADE** and Δ**ABC** below. What can you conclude if $\overline{DE} \parallel \overline{BC}$?

   Explain your thinking. ____________

   ____

   ____

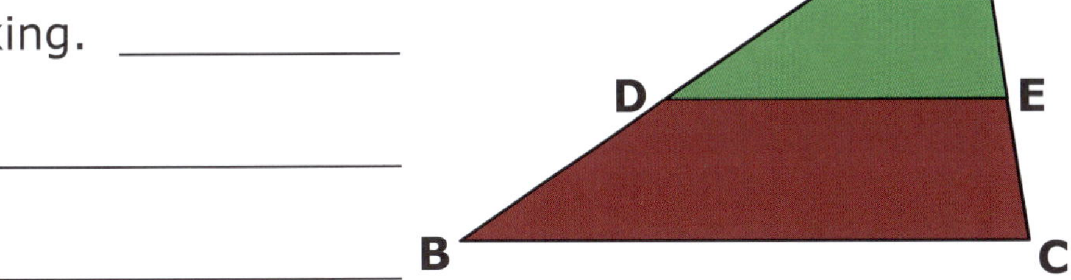

5. Are all equilateral triangles similar? ________

   Explain your thinking. ________________________________

   ____

6. Are all right triangles similar? ________

   Explain your thinking. ________________________________

   ____

   Show a drawing to support your answer.

7. If two triangles have only two corresponding angles that are congruent, are the triangles similar? ________

   Explain your thinking. ________________________________

   ____

8. Are all congruent triangles also similar? ________

   Explain your thinking. ________________________________

   ____

Proving Triangles Similar

To prove triangles are similar, prove that two triangles have corresponding angles congruent (***AA***) or corresponding sides in proportion (***SSS*** similarity). Look at the information given below and tell if the triangles are similar. If yes, state the reason (***AA*** *or* ***SSS*** similarity).

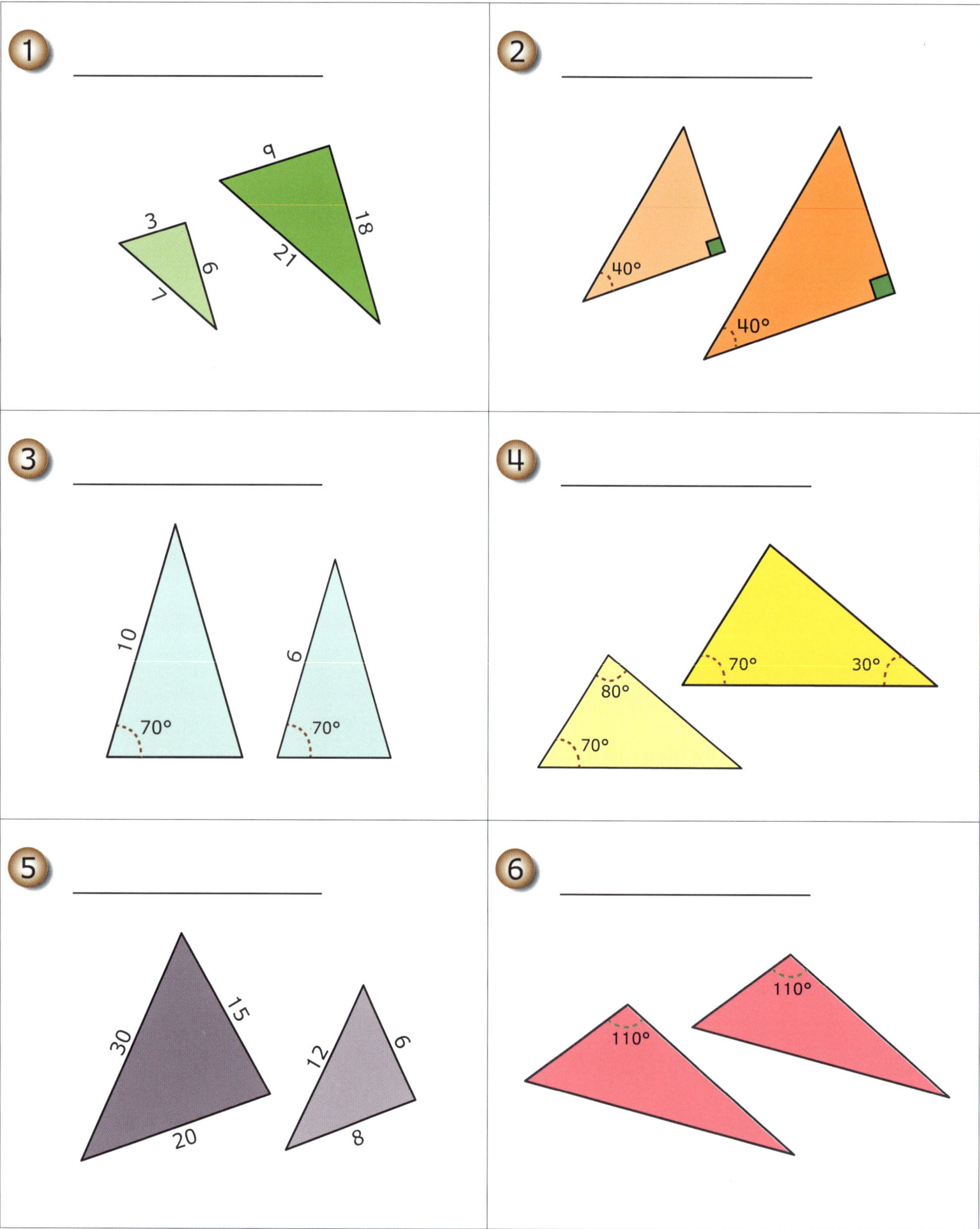

Proving Triangles Similar (Cont.)

Similarity Investigation

Draw or trace ΔABC with one side **AB** = 1 inch and **AC** = 1.5 inches. If you make your own triangle on a separate paper, make the included angle **A** any measurement you wish. Extend $\overline{AB}$ and $\overline{AC}$ by a scale factor of 3 to create a new triangle Δ**ABC**. Make sure that ∠**A** remains unchanged as you extend $\overline{AB}$ and $\overline{AC}$ by a factor of 3. Use a protractor to measure the new angles and compare those to the original corresponding angles. Measure side **BC**.

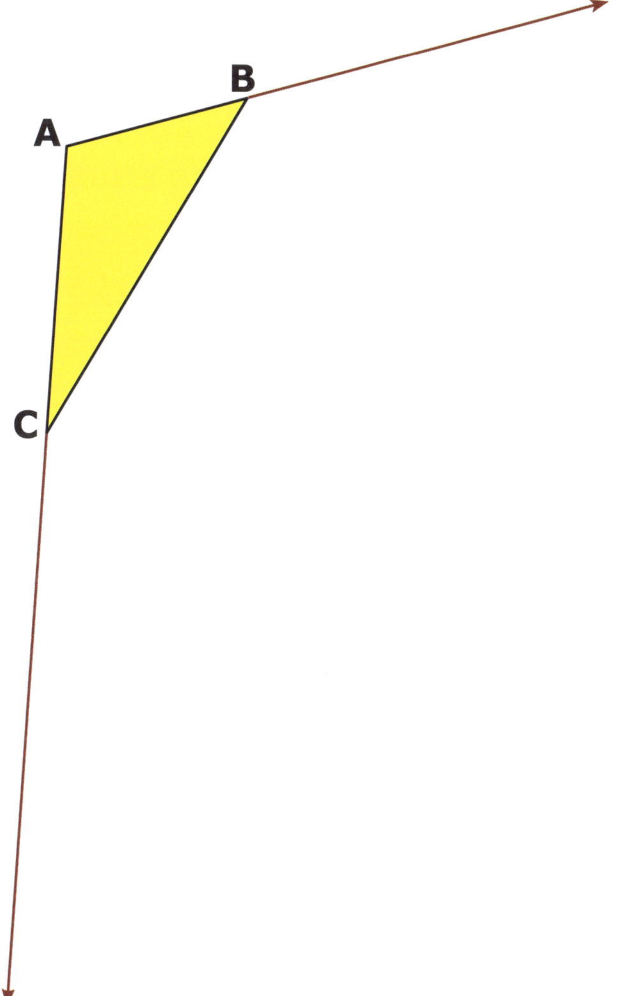

Is the new triangle similar to the original? ________

Are all corresponding sides in proportion? ________

Explain your thinking. ______________________________

____

Test Your Reasoning Skills

Answer the following questions True (T) or False (F).

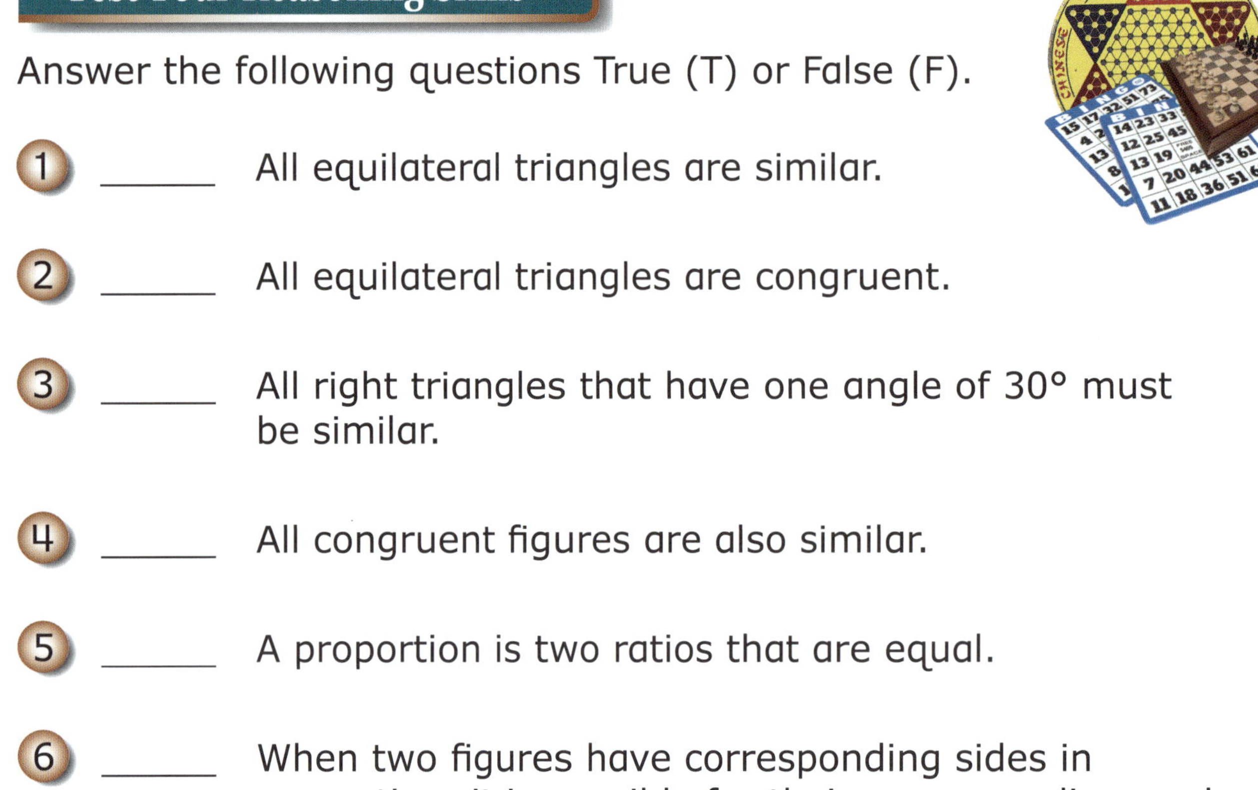

1. ______ All equilateral triangles are similar.

2. ______ All equilateral triangles are congruent.

3. ______ All right triangles that have one angle of 30° must be similar.

4. ______ All congruent figures are also similar.

5. ______ A proportion is two ratios that are equal.

6. ______ When two figures have corresponding sides in proportion, it is possible for their corresponding angles to have different measurements.

7. ______ All regular hexagons are similar to each other.

8. ______ If two angles of one triangle are congruent to two angles of another triangle, then the triangles must be similar.

9. ______ All squares are similar.

10. ______ All rectangles are similar.

11. ______ If two sides of one triangle are in proportion to the corresponding sides of another triangle and their included angles are congruent, then the triangles must be similar.

12. ______ A triangle with sides 3 in., 4 in., and 5 in. is similar to a triangle with sides 18 in., 24 in., and 32 in.

Review – Chapter 11

Use a separate sheet of paper if needed.

1. Given that ΔABC iand ΔBDC are both isosceles, does that guarantee that both triangles are congruent? Explain your thinking.

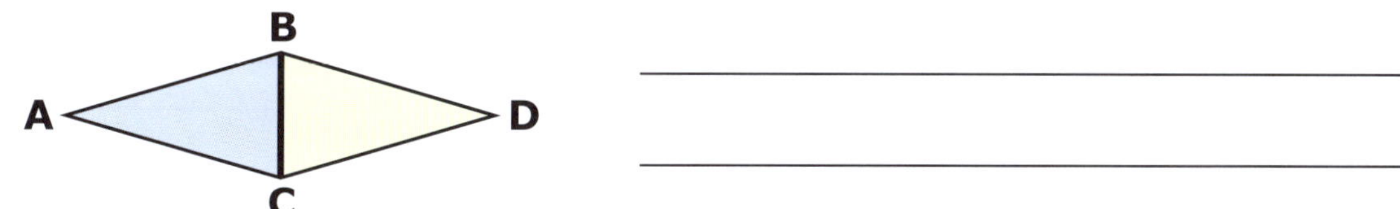

2. Given ∠1 ≅ ∠2 and both triangles are isosceles, prove ΔABC ≅ ΔADC.

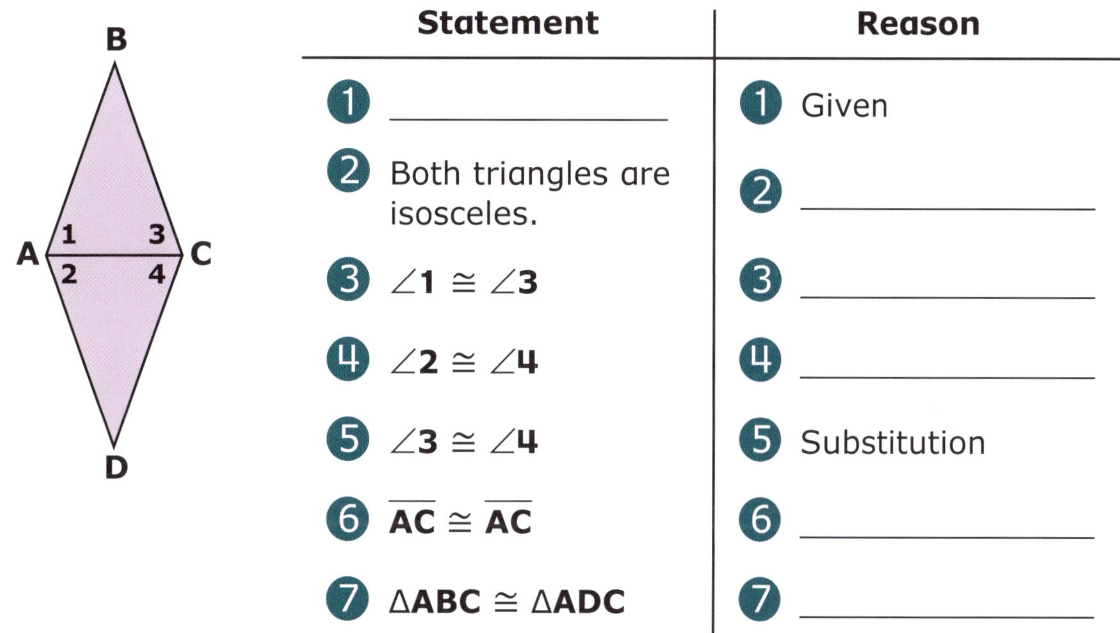

Statement	Reason
1 ________________	1 Given
2 Both triangles are isosceles.	2 ________________
3 ∠1 ≅ ∠3	3 ________________
4 ∠2 ≅ ∠4	4 ________________
5 ∠3 ≅ ∠4	5 Substitution
6 $\overline{AC} \cong \overline{AC}$	6 ________________
7 ΔABC ≅ ΔADC	7 ________________

3. Given ∠E ≅ ∠H and F is the midpoint of $\overline{EH}$, prove ΔGEF ≅ ΔQHF and ∠G ≅ ∠Q.

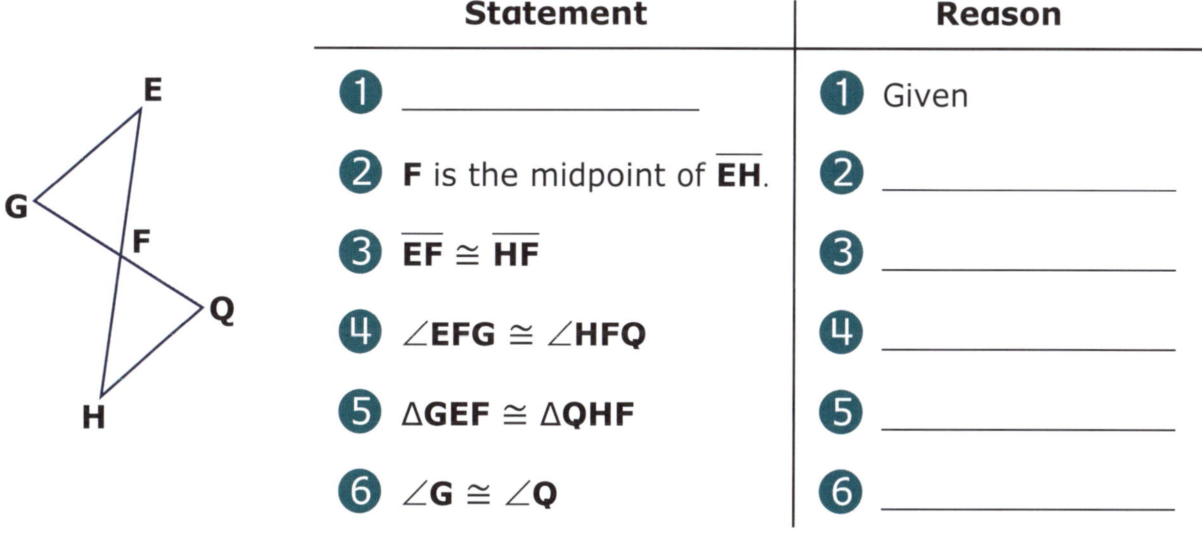

Statement	Reason
1 ________________	1 Given
2 F is the midpoint of $\overline{EH}$.	2 ________________
3 $\overline{EF} \cong \overline{HF}$	3 ________________
4 ∠EFG ≅ ∠HFQ	4 ________________
5 ΔGEF ≅ ΔQHF	5 ________________
6 ∠G ≅ ∠Q	6 ________________

4. $\overline{\mathbf{PR}}$ is the perpendicular bisector of $\overline{\mathbf{AB}}$. Prove that **ΔAPR ≅ ΔBPR**.

Statement	Reason
1. $\overline{\mathbf{PR}}$ is the perpendicular bisector of $\overline{\mathbf{AB}}$	1. ____________
2. ∠**ARP** and ∠**BRP** are right angles.	2. ____________
3. ∠**ARP** ≅ ∠**BRP**	3. ____________
4. $\overline{\mathbf{PR}} \cong \overline{\mathbf{PR}}$	4. ____________
5. $\overline{\mathbf{AR}} \cong \overline{\mathbf{BR}}$	5. ____________
6. **ΔAPR ≅ ΔBPR**	6. ____________

P

A R B

5. Why is **ΔABC** similar to **ΔFQR**? Both triangles are equilateral. Explain your thinking.

6. Are these two triangles similar? Explain your thinking.

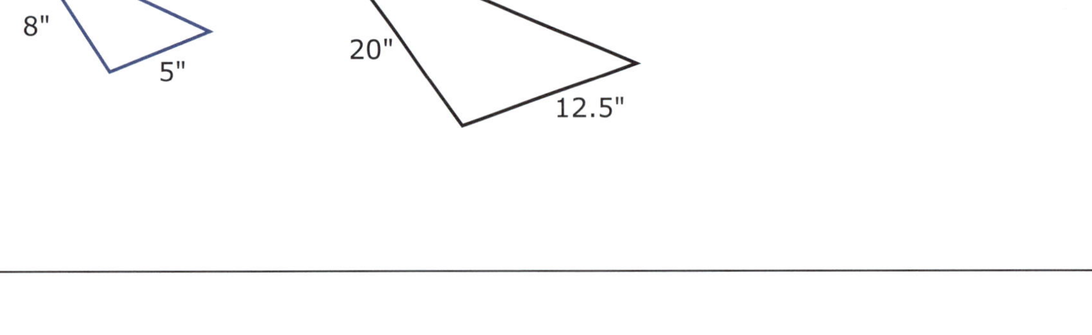

____

____

Chapter 12 - Coordinate Geometry

What is the Slope of a Line?

Graphing on the coordinate plane can help us solve many problems in geometry and in real life. In this chapter, we will learn some new tools to prove many properties learned so far. Our first tool is understanding what we mean by the slope of a line or line segment.

Slope is the steepness of a line or line segment. It is often defined as rise/run or the vertical change divided by the horizontal change.

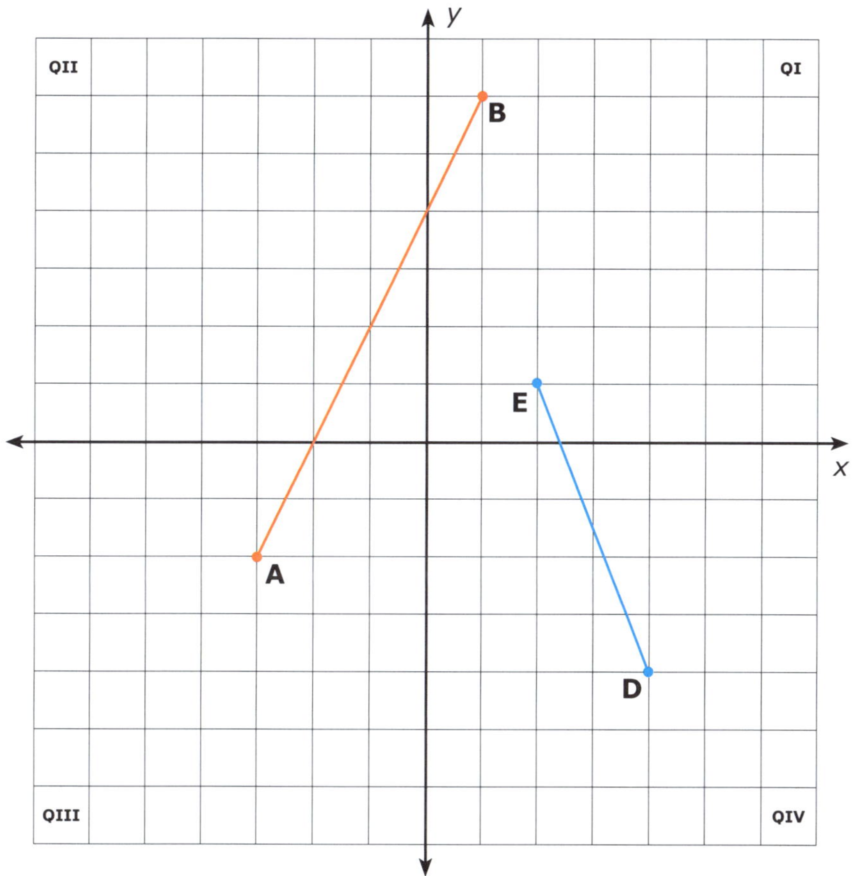

Example 1: Finding the slope of line segment $\overline{AB}$ on the coordinate plane above.

It connects (–3,–2) and (1,6). To find the slope from **A** to **B,** you go up 8 units and right 4 units. So the slope is 8/4 or 2/1.

If you count from **B** to **A**, you go down 8 and left 4. Again, the slope is –8/–4 or 2/1.

Example 2: Finding the slope of line segment $\overline{DE}$ using the same coordinate plane above.

From **D** to **E**, you count up 5 units and left 2 units. So the slope is 5/–2. Notice that from **E** to **D**, you go down 5 units and right two units so the slope is –5/2 which is the same answer.

Slope Formula

To find the slope, you can start with either y value for y_1 as long as you use its matching x value.

$$\frac{(y_2) - (y_1)}{(x_2) - (x_1)} = \text{slope } (m)$$

$$\frac{(1) - (-4)}{(2) - (4)} = (-5/2)$$

To find slope (m), you can use the slope formula. This formula helps you find the slope when the numbers are too big to fit on a grid. Since slope (m) is defined as the change in y's (Δy, pronounced delta y) over the change in x's (Δx), use this formula to find slope.

Using the coordinates for the line segment $\overline{\textbf{DE}}$, **D** = (4,–4) and **E** = (2,1), we can use the slope formula to find the slope.

Find the slope of the segment (-5,3) and (2,-1). Use the slope formula and verify your answer on the graph.

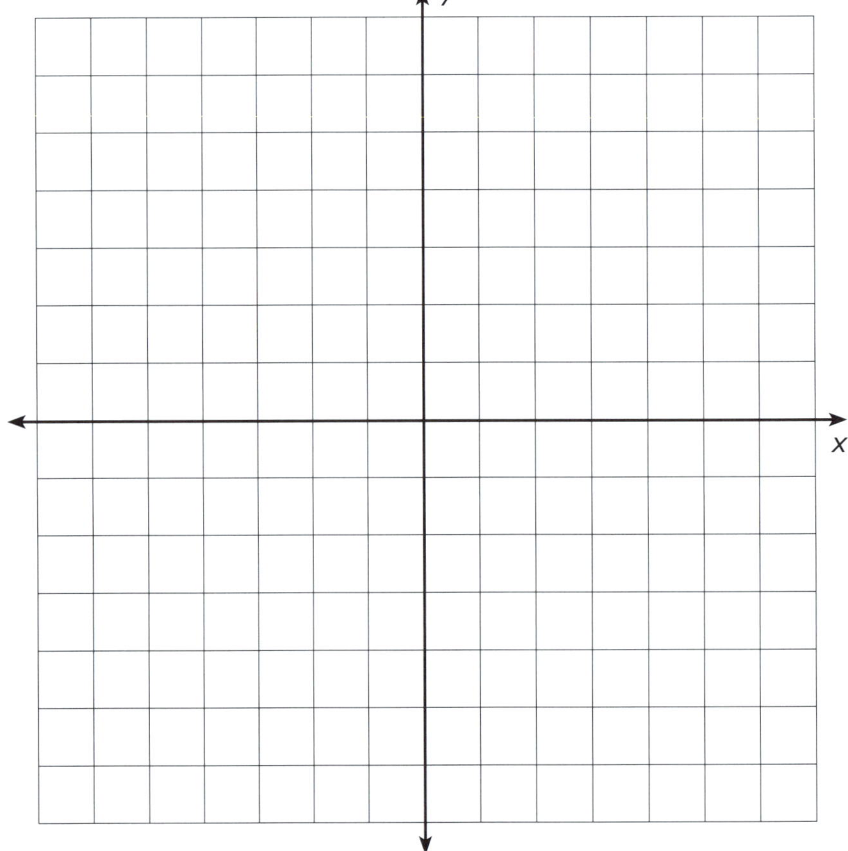

Slope Formula (Cont.)

Answer the following questions. If needed, use the coordinate plane on the previous page to help you answer the next two questions. If more grids are needed, you can copy the blank grid on the next page. Additional grids are provided for following lessons.

A bridge designed with many slopes crosses over the Missouri River.

1. Find the slope of a line or line segment that is horizontal.

   Explain how you determined your answer. ______________________

   ____

   ____

2. Find the slope of a line or line segment that is vertical.

   Explain how you determined your answer. ______________________

   ____

   ____

3. Use the slope formula to find the slope of line segment $\overline{\mathbf{QR}}$ with endpoints **Q**(-1,5) and **R**(2,-1). Show work.

4. What is the slope of the line $y = x$?
   Hint: Find some points where x always equals y.

   Explain your thinking. ______________________________

   ____

   ____

Slope Formula (Cont.)

5. On the following coordinate plane, graph segment $\overline{AB}$ with endpoints **A**(-3,1) and **B**(3,4) and also graph segment $\overline{DE}$ with endpoints **D**(-4,-3) and **E**(2,0).

   a. Find the slope of $\overline{AB}$. ________ (reduce)

   b. Find the slope of $\overline{DE}$. ________ (reduce)

   c. Why would both slopes be equal?

      Explain your thinking. ______________________________

      ____

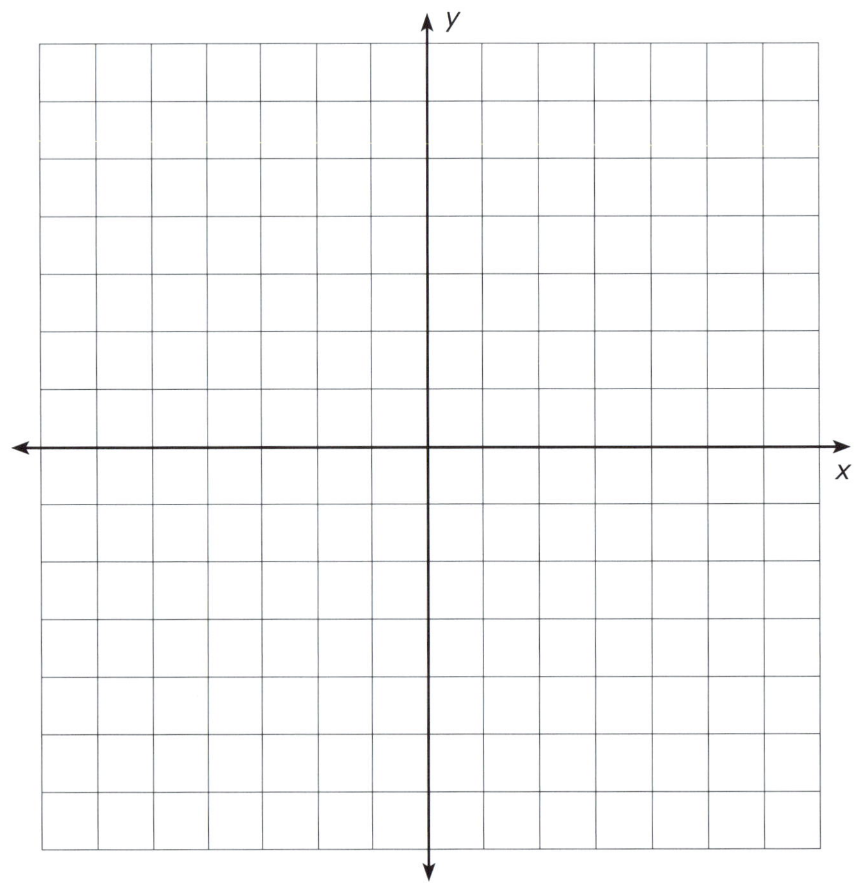

Slope Formula (Cont.)

6. Line segment $\overline{WE}$ has a slope of $\frac{3}{4}$. It is parallel to line segment $\overline{PT}$ which passes through **T**(1,1) and **P**(5,*y*). Find the value of *y*. Show work by using the slope formula.

7. Using the coordinate plane provided, find the slopes of the following segments of quadrilateral **ABCD**.

   a. $\overline{AB}$ = ________ b. $\overline{DC}$ = ________

   c. $\overline{BC}$ = ________ d. $\overline{AD}$ = ________

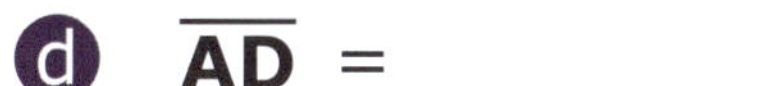

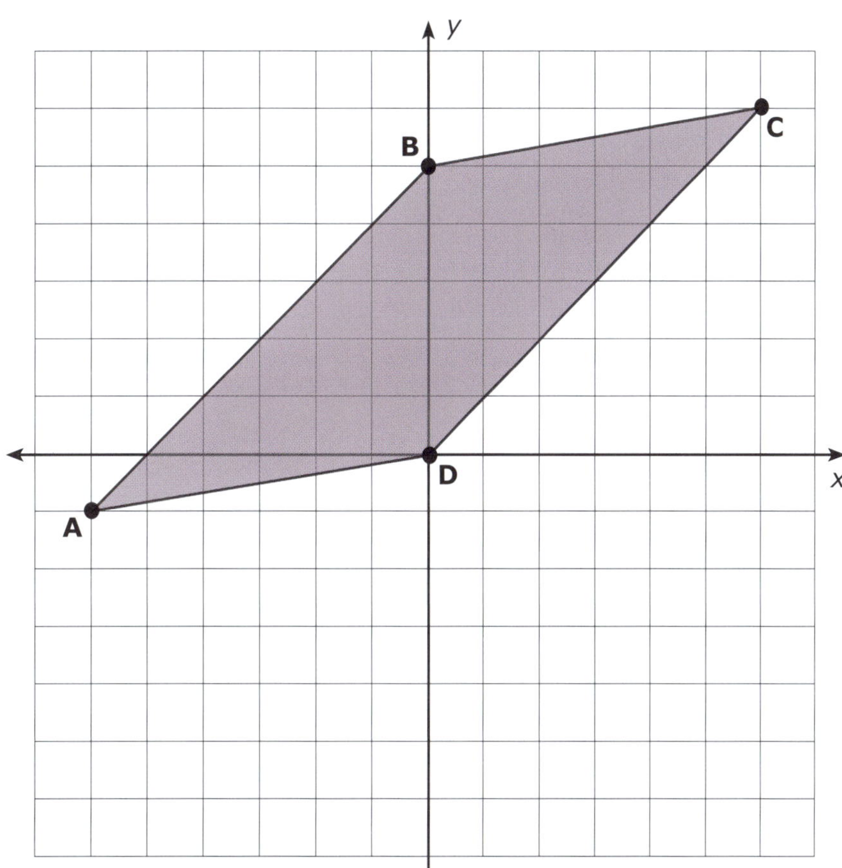

   e. Based on your findings, do your results prove it is a parallelogram?

   Explain your thinking. ______________________________

   ____

Slope Formula (Cont.)

> **Hint**
> Try drawing some segments perpendicular to $\overline{\mathbf{SE}}$ at points **L**, **O**, or **P**.

8. As you know, perpendicular lines intersect to make right angles. Below is line segment $\overline{\mathbf{SE}}$. Find the slope of $\overline{\mathbf{SE}}$, then use your *thinking skills* to determine the slope of a line segment that is perpendicular to $\overline{\mathbf{SE}}$.

   a. Find the slope of $\overline{\mathbf{SE}}$. ______________________

   b. What is the slope of any line segment perpendicular to $\overline{\mathbf{SE}}$? ______________________

   Explain your thinking. ____________________________________

   ____

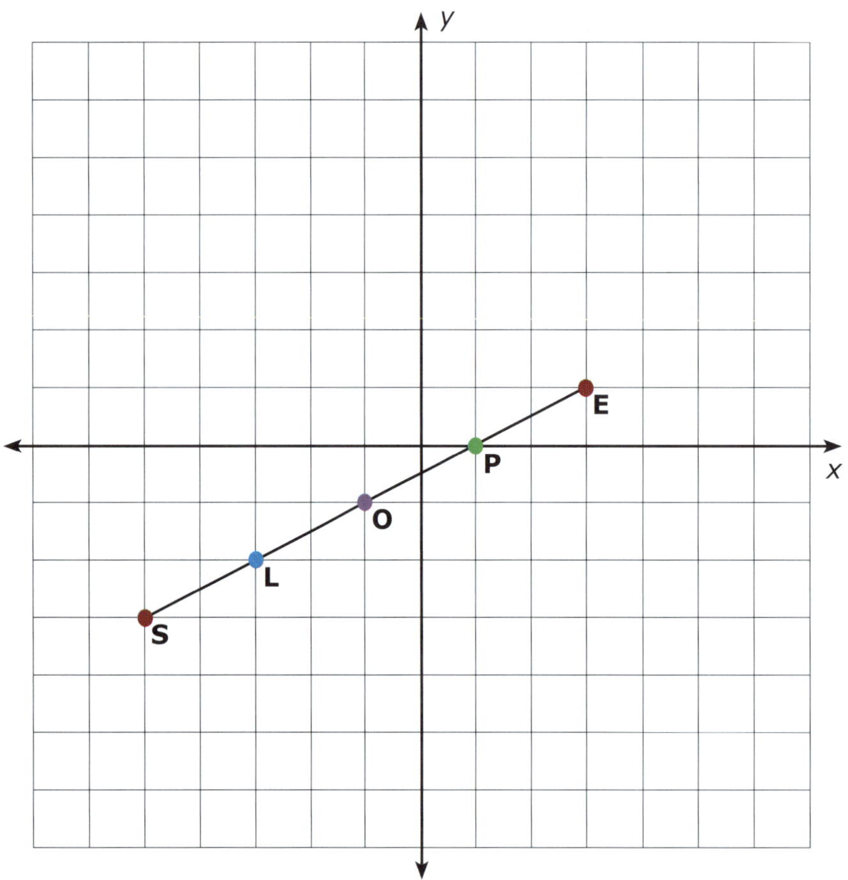

9. Parallel lines have the same slope. What rule or property can you state about the slopes of two perpendicular lines?

____

How to Write an Equation of a Line

Knowing how to find the slope of a line will give you the tools to reason if lines are parallel or perpendicular.

How to Remember the **slope formula.** When you ski down the slope, put your double goggles on.

- Parallel lines have the same slope.
- Perpendicular lines have negative reciprocal slopes.
- Horizontal lines have a slope of 0.
- Vertical lines have no slope or undefined slope.

How to Write an Equation of a Line

You might have learned already how to write the equation of a line. Let us review this as it is important.

$$\frac{(y_2) - (y_1)}{(x_2) - (x_1)} = \text{slope } (m)$$

To write an equation of a line, you need to know the slope and the y-intercept (where the line touches the y-axis). By the way, some lines do not touch the y-axis. We will get to that later.

There are two ways of writing an equation of a line. One is the slope/intercept form and the other way is the point/slope form.

The **slope/intercept form** looks like this: (Where m is the slope and b is the y-intercept.)

$$y = mx + b$$

The **point/slope form** looks like this:

$$y - y_1 = m\,(x - x_1)$$

But if you insert a second point (x_2, y_2) you get:

$$y_2 - y_1 = m(x_2 - x_1)$$

If you divide both sides by the quantity $(x_2 - x_1)$, you get the slope formula:

$$\frac{y_2 - y_1}{x_2 - x_1} = \frac{m(x_2 - x_1)}{(x_2 - x_1)}$$

You can write an equation in slope/intercept form when you know the slope and the y-intercept.

An equation of a line with slope of $\frac{1}{2}$ and a y-intercept of -5 is:

$y = \frac{1}{2}x - 5$ or $y = \frac{1}{2}x + -5$

How to Write an Equation of a Line (Cont.)

Use your *thinking skills* to answer these questions.

1. Write the equation of a line that passes through **A**(-2,4) and **B**(0,8).

   a. Find the slope of $\overleftrightarrow{AB}$ by using the slope formula. ____________________

   b. Write equation in $y = mx + b$ form. ____________________

2. Use the point/slope form to write the equation for $\overleftrightarrow{AB}$ using the slope you found and the given points.

   a. Using point **B**(0,8) and the slope of 2, the point/slope equation is ____________________.

   b. Using point **A**(-2,4) and the slope of 2, the point/slope equation is ____________________.

3. Take both point/slope equations for the line that passes by **A**(-2,4) and **B**(0,8) and show if you solve for *y*, you get the same $y = mx + b$ equation.

$y - 4 = 2(x + 2)$	$y - 8 = 2(x - 0)$

You can always use the $y = mx + b$ form when you have two points by finding the slope, then use either point to solve for *b*. But the point/slope form is a quick way to write an equation of a line.

How to Write an Equation of a Line (Cont.)

Knowing how to find the slope of a line, either by looking at the equation or the graph of the line, will help you prove if lines are parallel, perpendicular, or neither. It is also possible that two equations can represent the same line.

Here is an example: $y = 5x - 10$ and $-2y = -10x + 20$ If you divide the second equation by −2, they are both the same.

Remember
Always solve for y when you are trying to graph an equation. However, if an equation is already in **point/slope form**, then use the point and slope given to graph the equation.

Answer these questions.

1. Write the equation of a line that passes through **A**(-7,8) and **B**(-6,5).

   a. Find the slope. ______________

   b. Write it in point/slope form using point **B**. ______________

   c. Write it in slope/intercept form. ______________

2. Does the line with equation $y = 5x + 6$ pass through the point (-2,-4)?

   Explain your thinking. ______________

   ____

3. If two lines on the coordinate plane have these equations $y = \frac{1}{2}x - 10$ and $y + 2x = 6$, what can you say about these lines?

   Explain your thinking. ______________

   ____

4. On a plane, line **l** is perpendicular to line **m**. Line **n** is parallel to line **l**. What can you say about the slopes of line **n** and line **m**?

   Draw a picture to help you.

   ____

   ____

How to Write an Equation of a Line (Cont.)

5. Graph the line with this equation:
$y + 1 = \frac{2}{3}(x - 3)$.

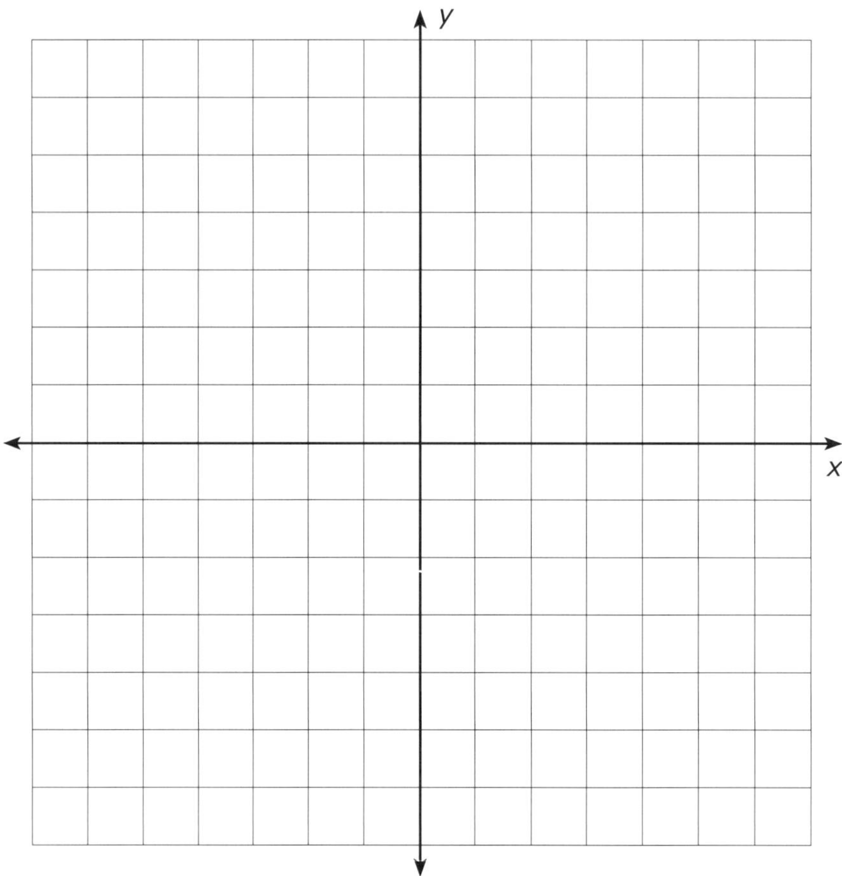

6. Determine the *y*-intercept of the line above. Explain what method you used.

____

____

7. Is the point (6,1) on the line above? How would you know without looking at the graph? Show work and explain your thinking.

____

____

____

How to Write an Equation of a Line (Cont.)

8. A side of a quadrilateral has a slope of 5/4.
The opposite side has a slope of 5/4.
Is the quadrilateral a parallelogram? ____________
Why or why not?
Explain your thinking. ____

____

9. One side of a quadrilateral has a slope of 2 and both adjacent sides to that side have a slope of $-\frac{1}{2}$.
Is the quadrilateral a parallelogram? ____________
Why or why not?
Explain your thinking. ____

____

To prove lines are parallel or perpendicular, use the slope formula.

10. You are a detective and you are told that both opposite sides of a quadrilateral have the same slope. State what else you would need to know to be completely sure you have the following shapes. If no other information is needed, then write proved.

a) parallelogram ____

b) rectangle ____

c) rhombus ____

d) square ____

The Midpoint Formula

The midpoint formula is used to find the middle or center of a line segment on the coordinate plane. The formula is often used to find if segments bisect each other. When line segments are horizontal or vertical, it is easy to find the midpoint. Take a look at $\overline{AB}$ and $\overline{CD}$ below.

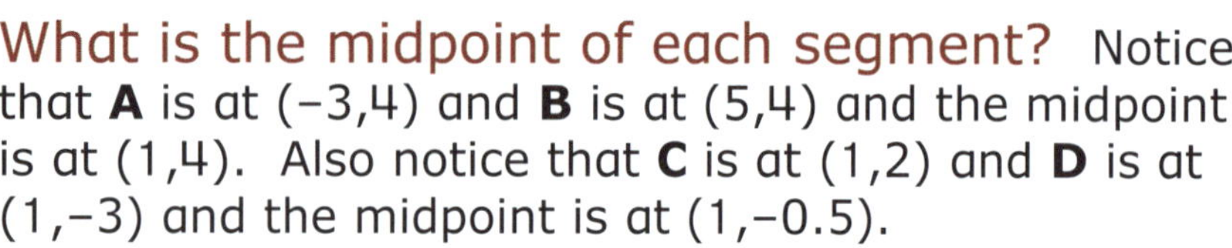

What is the midpoint of each segment? Notice that **A** is at (–3,4) and **B** is at (5,4) and the midpoint is at (1,4). Also notice that **C** is at (1,2) and **D** is at (1,–3) and the midpoint is at (1,–0.5).

You can use this formula to find the midpoint of any segment on the coordinate plane.

$$\frac{x_1 + x_2}{2}, \frac{y_1 + y_2}{2}$$

The **midpoint** is the average of the endpoints.

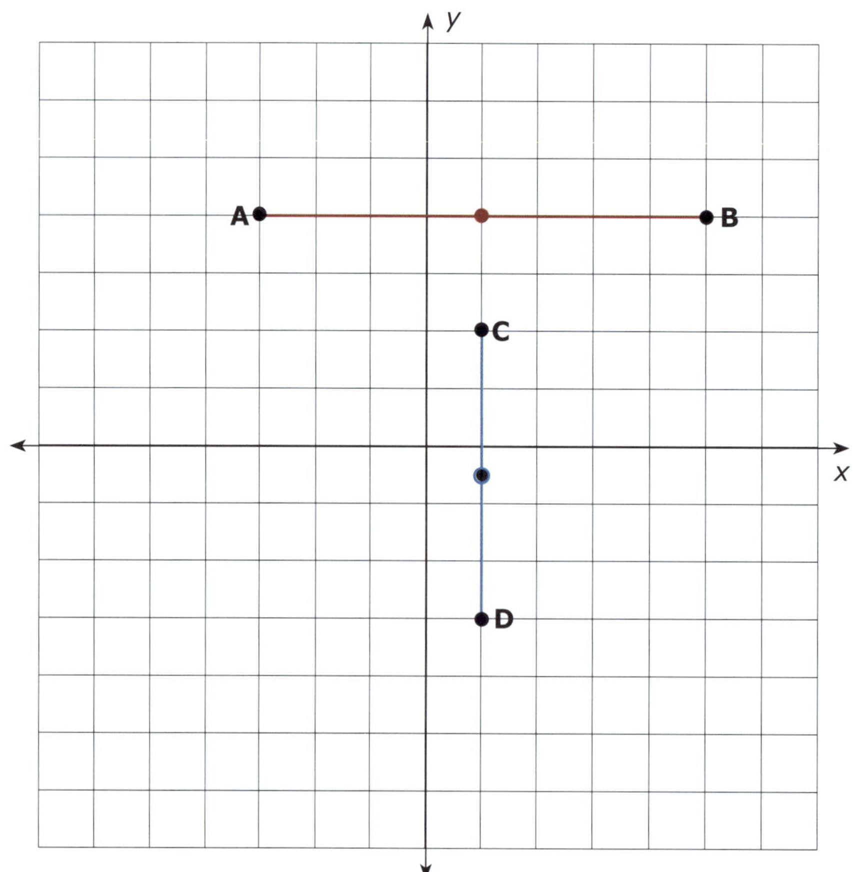

The Midpoint Formula (Cont.)

A midpoint monument for the continent of Europe in Lithuania

Although several locations claim to be the midpoint, this location is the only one listed in the *Guinness Book of World Records* as the geographical center of Europe.

Answer the following questions.

1. What is the midpoint of $\overline{TW}$? Use the formula to find the midpoint, then graph the midpoint.

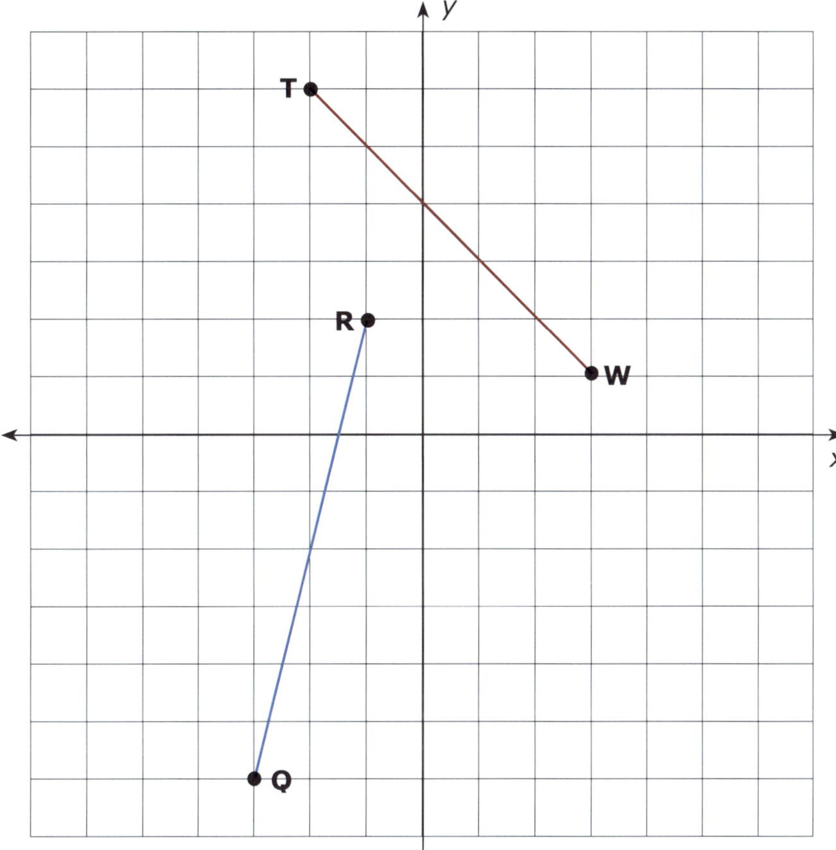

2. What is the midpoint of $\overline{QR}$? Use the formula, then graph the midpoint. It helps to write the coordinates by each point.

3. Does the line $y + x = -4$ bisect $\overline{QR}$?

Explain your thinking. ________________________________

____

____

The Midpoint Formula (Cont.)

Multnomah Falls, Oregon
The midpoint formula can be used to design bridges.

4. A line segment has an endpoint at (-4,4) and a midpoint at (-1,4). Find the other endpoint. Use a grid to help you.

5. Segment $\overline{\mathbf{AT}}$ has endpoint **A** at (-6,-5) and midpoint **M** at (-1,-4). Find the coordinates of **T**. Graph your results below.

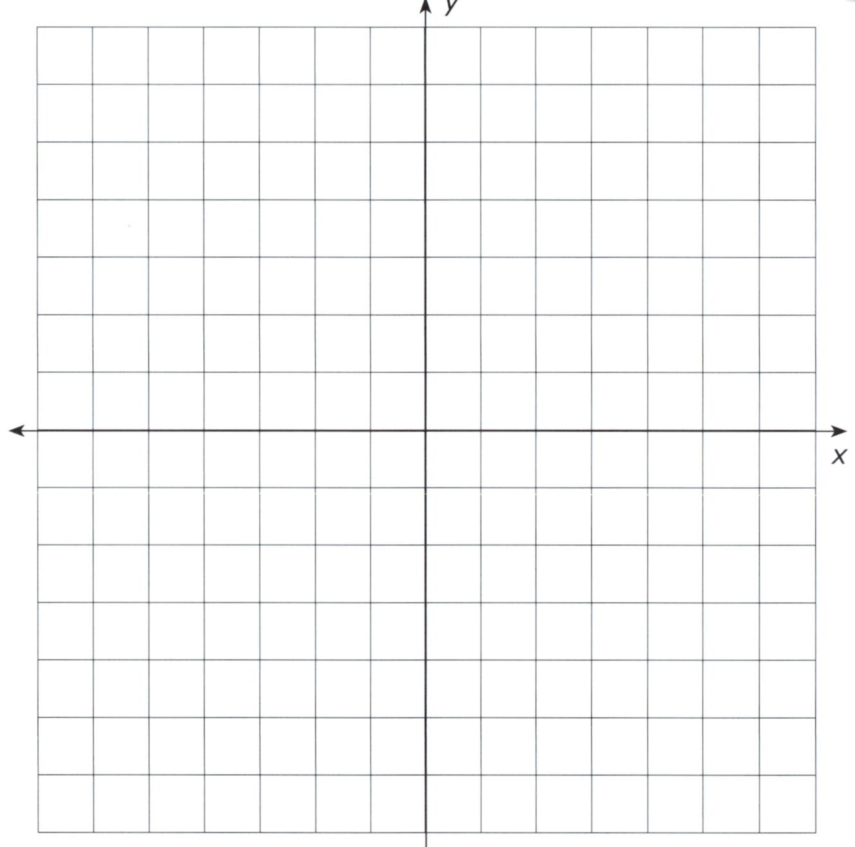

6. Without graphing, can you explain how you would find the coordinates of endpoint **L** in segment $\overline{\mathbf{PL}}$? The endpoint **P** is at (-13,15) and the midpoint of $\overline{\mathbf{PL}}$ is at (3,-4). Find the coordinates of point **L**.

____

____

The Midpoint Formula (Cont.)

One way to prove a quadrilateral is a parallelogram is to prove that its diagonals bisect each other by using the midpoint formula.

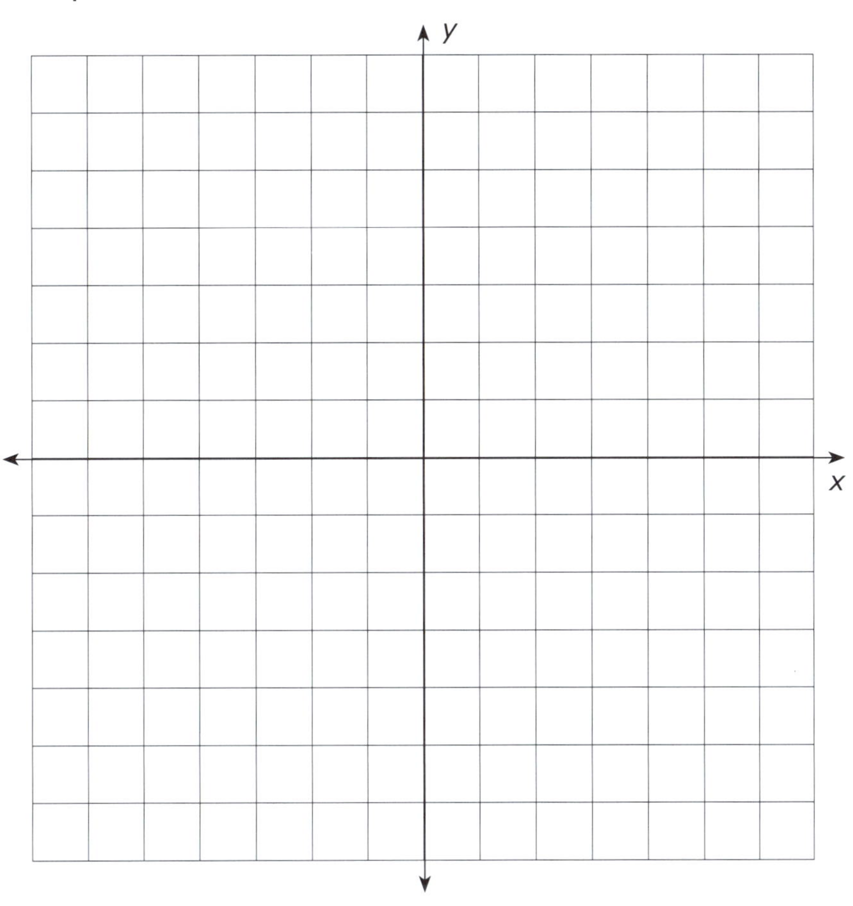

7 Graph parallelogram **ABCD** with vertices **A**(-1,4), **B**(2,6), **C**(3,0), and **D**(0,-2). Draw diagonals $\overline{\mathbf{AC}}$ and $\overline{\mathbf{BD}}$.

a Name the coordinates of the point where the diagonals intersect. ________________

b Find the midpoint of $\overline{\mathbf{AC}}$. ________________

c Find the midpoint of $\overline{\mathbf{BD}}$. ________________

Explain your thinking. ________________________________

____

The Distance Formula

To determine if two segments on a coordinate plane have the same length, we need to know how to find the distance between two points.

The Pythagorean Theorem is a great tool to find the distance between two points on the coordinate plane.

Suppose we have to find the distance between point **A**(3,6) and point **B**(−3,−2). Since the line connecting point **A** to **B** is a diagonal line, we can make $\overline{\textbf{AB}}$ the hypotenuse of a right triangle.

Notice that the distance between **B** and **W** is 6 units and the distance between **A** and **W** is 8 units.

Using the **Pythagorean Theorem** ($a^2 + b^2 = c^2$), you will find that **AB** = 10.

6-8-10 is a Pythagorean triple.

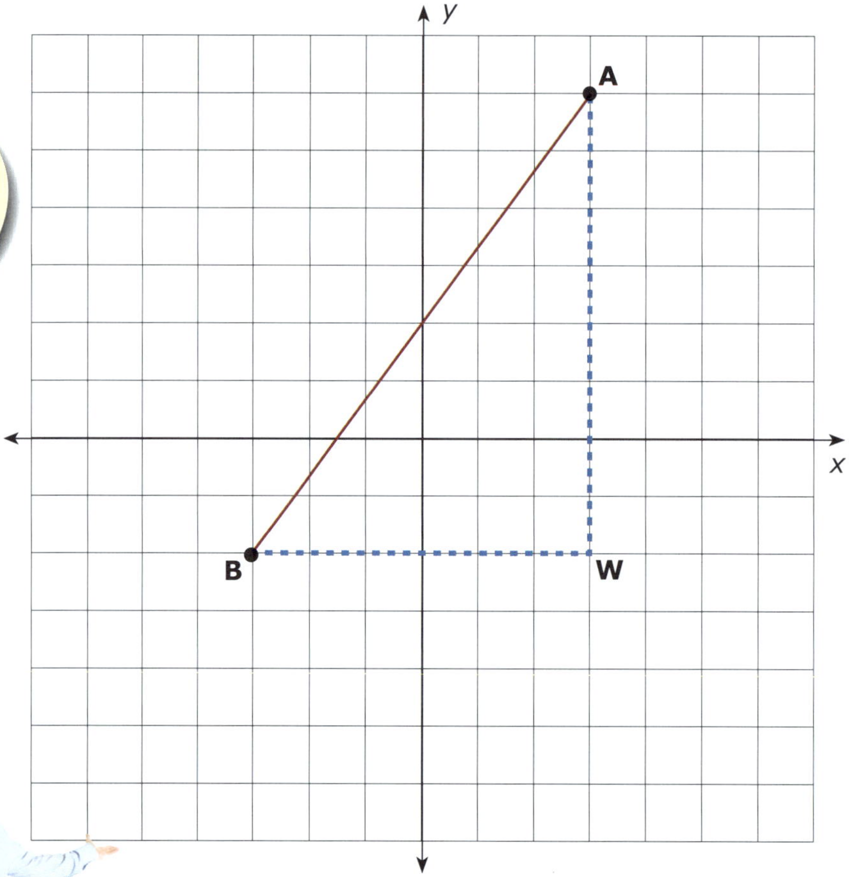

y

A

x

B

W

In the last part of this section, we will discover how a formula we called the **distance formula** is a great way of applying the Pythagorean Theorem. When the points are hard to plot into an ordinary grid, or when we want to find the distance between two points without graphing, the distance formula is a great tool.

The Hoover Dam on the Arizona side shows the penstock towers. The distance formula could be used to find the distance between the towers. The spillway of the dam is seen from the Nevada side.

The Distance Formula (Cont.)

1. An engineer wants to run cable wires between point **H** (Home) and these different points in a city.

S School at 12th St. and Mifflin St.
F Farmer's Market at 13th St. and Snyder St.
I International Specialty Store at 7th St. and Moore St.
P Playground at S. Broad St. and Wolf St.

Plot the points below first, then show your work. Round to the nearest tenth if needed.

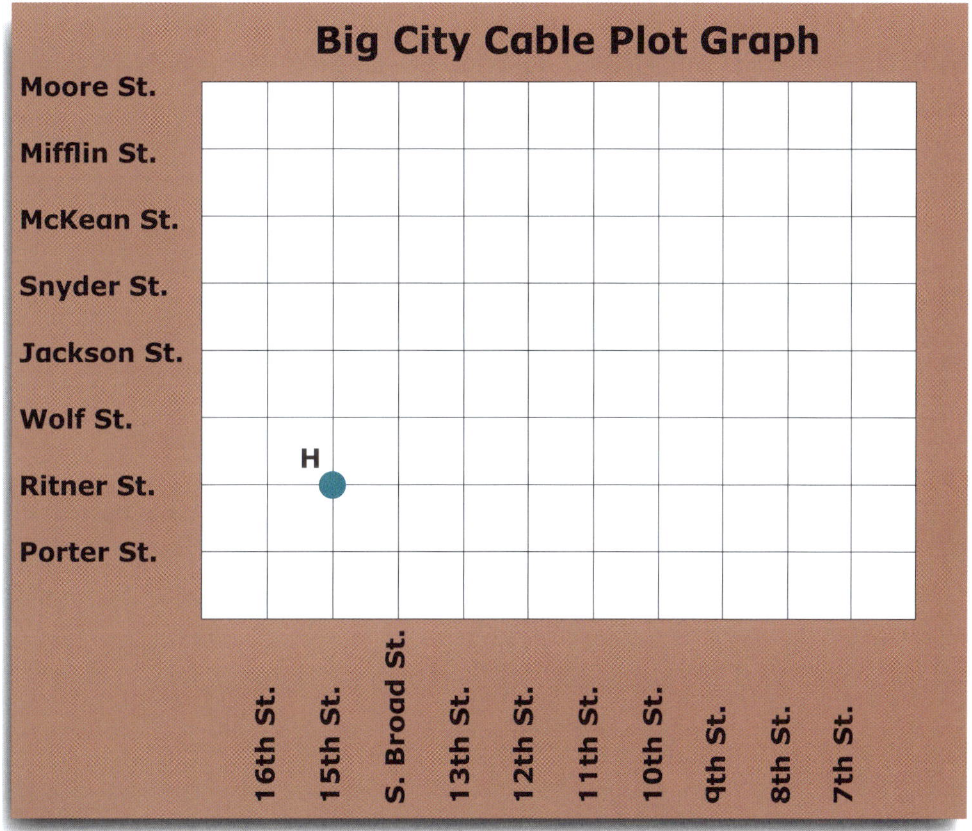

(a) **HS** = ________, (b) **HF** = ________,

(c) **HI** = ________, (d) **HP** = ________

The Distance Formula (Cont.)

2. Quadrilateral **ABCD** is shown below. Find the lengths of each side. Use the Pythagorean Theorem to help you.

   a. **AB** = ______, **BC** = ______, **DC** = ______,

      DA = ______

   b. What is the most specific name for this quadrilateral?

      Explain your thinking. ______________________________

   c. What formula would you use to prove or disprove if the figure is a square?

      Explain your thinking. ______________________________

      ____

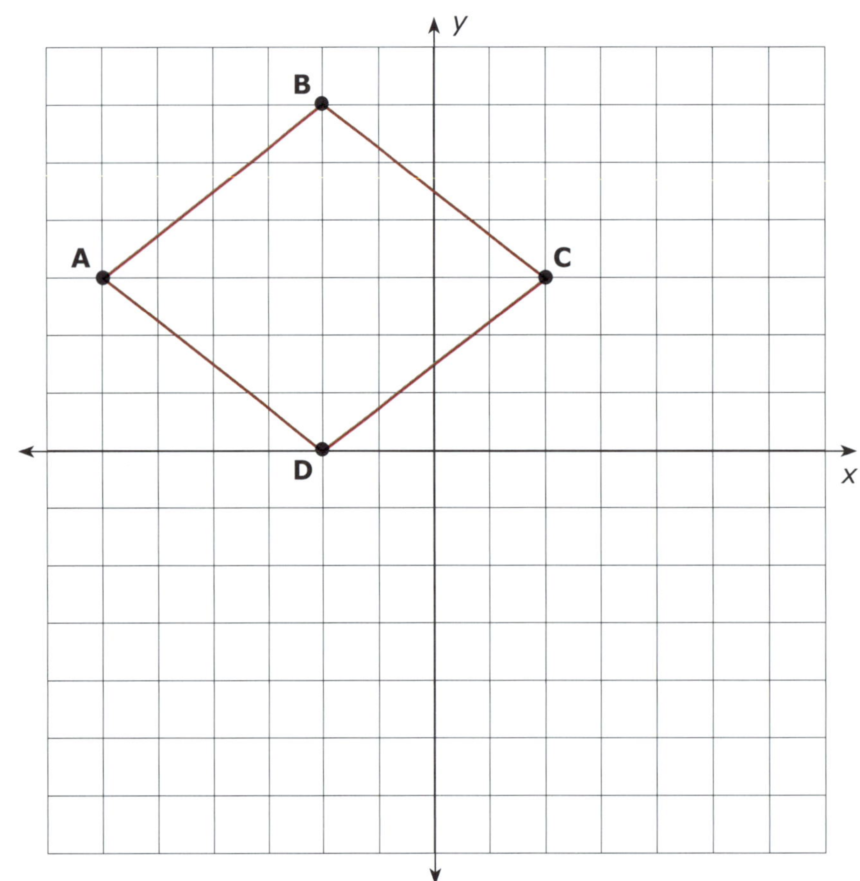

The Distance Formula (Cont.)

3. Draw segment $\overline{QR}$ where **Q** is at (−6,4) and **R** is at (6,−1).

a. What is the difference between the *x*'s (Δx).

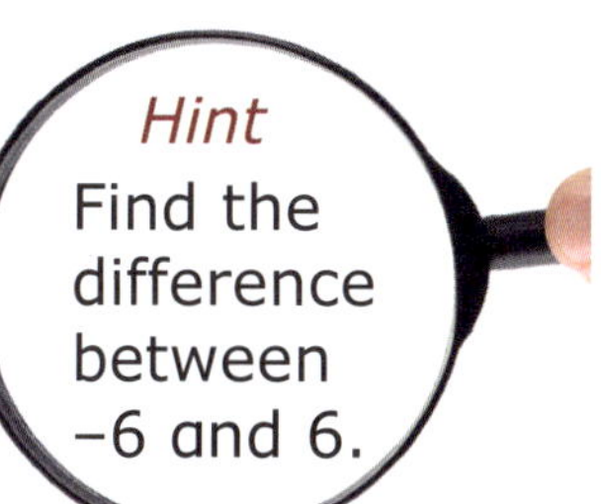

b. What is the difference between the *y*'s (Δy)?

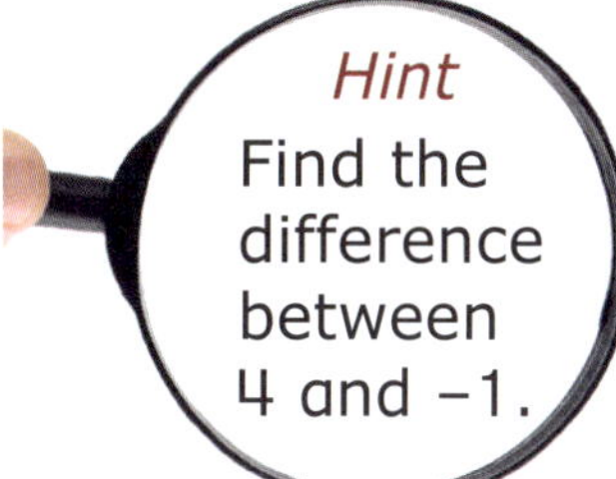

c. Explain why the distance between **Q** and **R** can be written as $\sqrt{(-6-6)^2+(4-(-1))^2}$

____

____

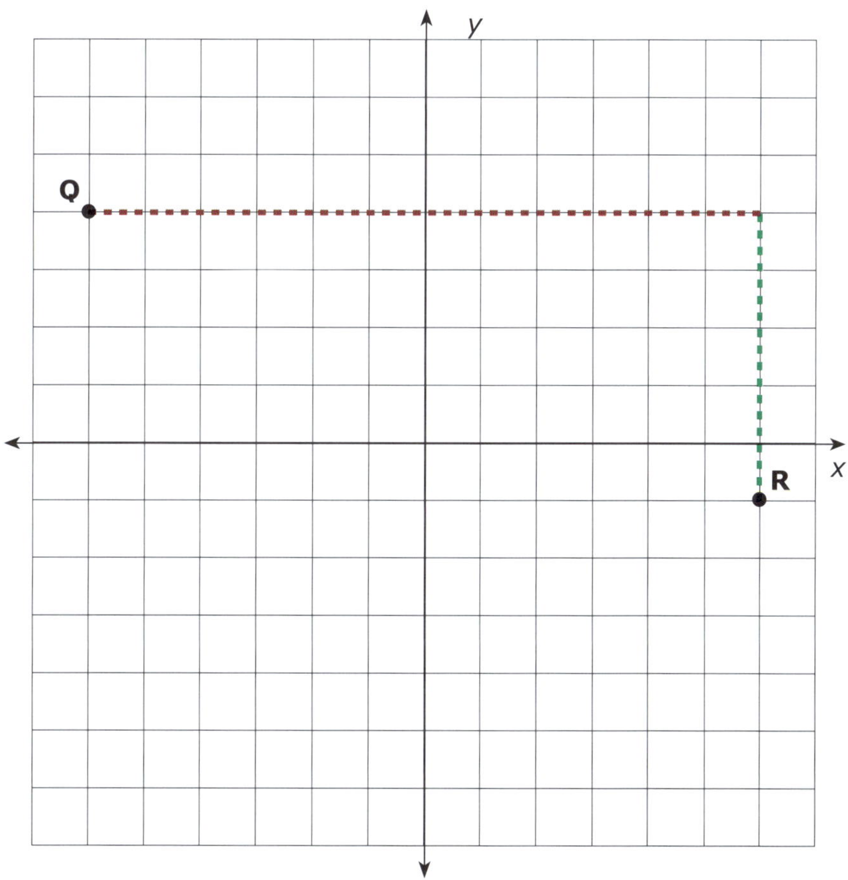

The Distance Formula (Cont.)

Designing airports requires using many different formulas like the distance formula.

The distance formula shown below is useful for finding the distance between two points when the points are too difficult to graph.

For example, if you are asked to find the distance between (–400,200) and (2,900), or if you do not want to graph the points at all, the distance formula can be used. Sometimes if the ordered pairs involve fractions and decimals, this formula becomes very handy.

$$\text{Distance} = \sqrt{(x_2 - x_1)^2 + (y_2 - y_1)^2}$$

Assume we need to find the distance between **A**(x_1, y_1) and **B**(x_2, y_2). The horizontal change (Δx), between **A** and **B** is $(x_2 - x_1)$. The vertical change (Δy) between **A** and **B** is $(y_2 - y_1)$. Using the Pythagorean Theorem, the length of the hypotenuse is the square root of the sum of the squares of the legs of the right triangle.

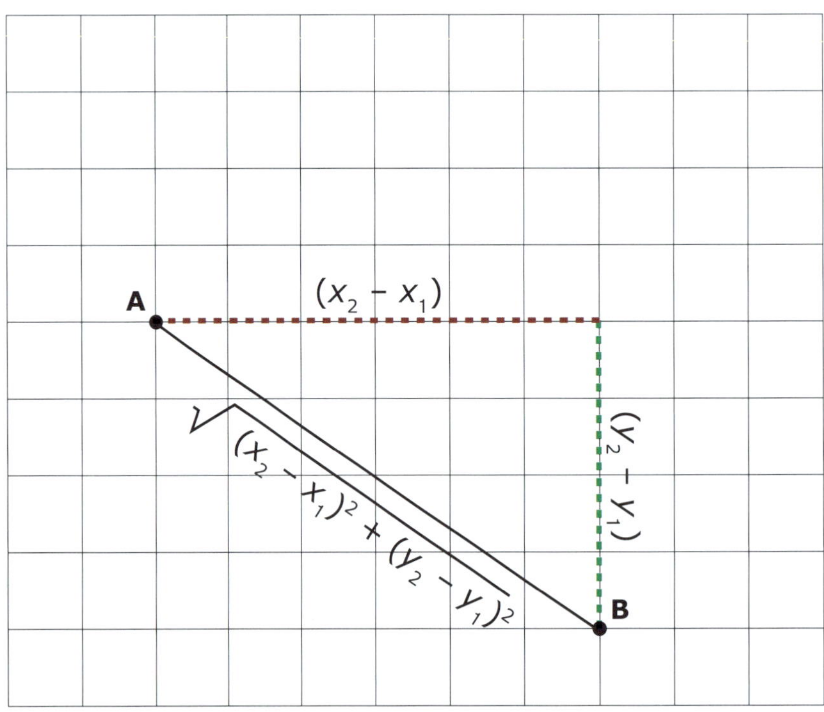

Review Your Formulas

Review your formulas then answer the following questions.

1. Find the distance between (-8,1) and (0,-14). Use the distance formula. Show work.

2. Find the length between (-3,5) and (-6,6). Use the distance formula. Round your answer to the nearest tenth.

3. How far it is from (4,5) to (16,21)? Use the distance formula.

4. Find the slope of the line that passes through (3,-5) and (7,11).

5. What is the slope of a line that is perpendicular to $y = 3x - 4$?

   Explain your thinking. ______________________________

   ____

6. What point is halfway between (-8,4) and (8,-4)?

7. a. If a line segment $\overline{\textbf{AB}}$ cuts $\overline{\textbf{CD}}$ in half, and **C** is at (8,3) and **D** is at (-18,21), then $\overline{\textbf{AB}}$ passes through what point?

   b. If $\overline{\textbf{AB}}$ cuts $\overline{\textbf{CD}}$ in half, then does $\overline{\textbf{CD}}$ also cut $\overline{\textbf{AB}}$ in half? Show a drawing to support your answer.

Review Your Formulas (Cont.)

Slope

$$\frac{(y_2) - (y_1)}{(x_2) - (x_1)} = (m)$$

Midpoint

$$\frac{x_1 + x_2}{2}, \frac{y_1 + y_2}{2}$$

Distance

$$\sqrt{(x_2 - x_1)^2 + (y_2 - y_1)^2}$$

What formula or formulas should you use to answer the following questions?

1. Two sides of a triangle have the same length. ____________

2. Point **B** is halfway between point **A** and **C**. ____________

3. Two sides of a quadrilateral are parallel. ____________

4. Two sides of a quadrilateral are equal. ____________

5. Diagonals of a quadrilateral bisect each other. ____________

6. Adjacent sides of a quadrilateral are not perpendicular. ____________

7. A triangle is equilateral. ____________

8. A rectangle has congruent diagonals. ____________

9. A polygon has all equal sides. ____________

10. A parallelogram is also a square. ____________

Introduction to Coordinate Proofs

This section will help you review many of the properties learned in this book. Follow the first proof as an example of how to outline your reasoning skills.

Prove: Quadrilateral **A**(-3,4), **B**(2,2), **C**(4,-2), and **D**(-1,0) is a parallelogram.

Step 1: Graph and label the points below, then draw the quadrilateral.

Step 2: Remember the properties of a parallelogram. Think of the minimum amount of information you need to prove that a quadrilateral is a parallelogram?

Which formula do you need midpoint, distance, or slope?

Introduction to Coordinate Proofs (Cont.)

Step 3: Show which formula you are using and show your work. Use the slope formula to show if opposite sides are parallel.

Slope (m) of $\overline{\textbf{AB}}$ =

Slope (m) of $\overline{\textbf{DC}}$ =

Slope (m) of $\overline{\textbf{AD}}$ =

Slope (m) of $\overline{\textbf{BC}}$ =

Then write:

Using the slope formula (always say what formula you are using), I found that $\overline{\textbf{AB}}$ and $\overline{\textbf{DC}}$ both have the same slope of $-\frac{2}{5}$. I also found that $\overline{\textbf{AD}}$ and $\overline{\textbf{BC}}$ both have the same slope of −2.

Step 4: Therefore, since segments with the same slope are parallel, and since quadrilateral **ABCD** has both sets of opposite sides parallel, it is a parallelogram.

Coordinate Proof Steps

1. Make sure to graph the points correctly, label them, and write the coordinates by the points.
2. Decide which property will help you prove what is being asked.
3. Decide which formula or formulas (midpoint, slope, or distance) will prove the property you have chosen and show all your work clearly.
4. Write a conclusion. You can say "Therefore, since..."

Introduction to Coordinate Proofs (Cont.)

Answer the following questions.

1. Use the midpoint formula to prove that the same quadrilateral **ABCD** is a parallelogram.

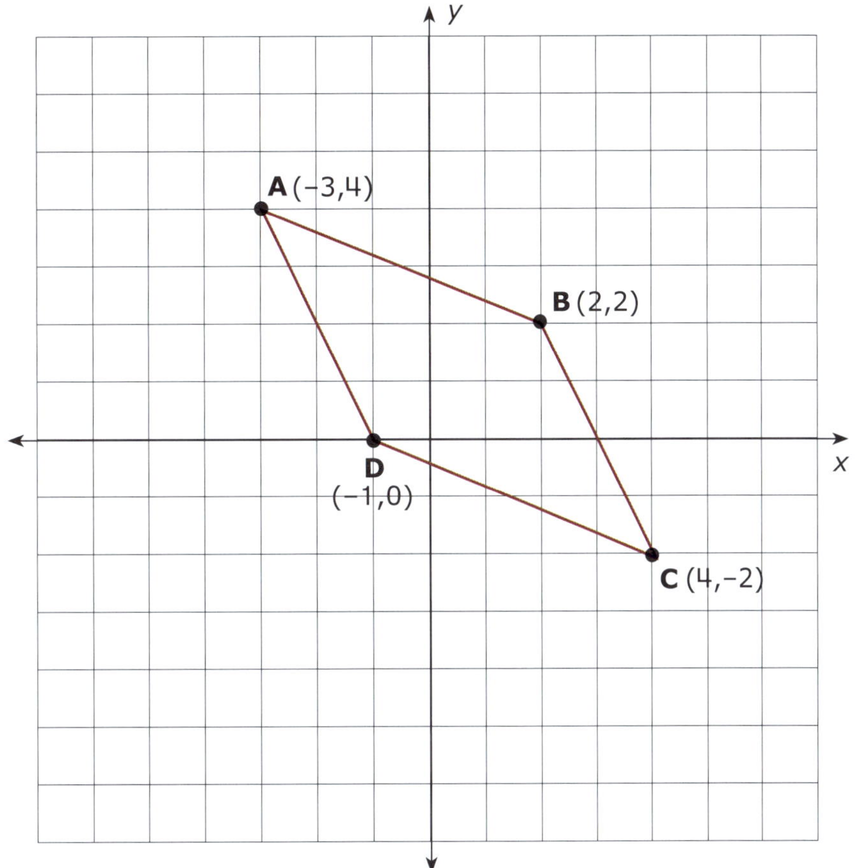

2. Is there another way you could prove that the same quadrilateral **ABCD** is a parallelogram? State what formula or formulas you would use. You do not need to do the full proof.

____

____

____

Introduction to Coordinate Proofs (Cont.)

3. If only one pair of opposite sides of a quadrilateral are congruent and parallel, would that be sufficient to prove the quadrilateral is a parallelogram?

Use a ruler to connect the congruent and parallel segments below to make a quadrilateral. Then make some of your own. Are the resulting quadrilaterals parallelograms?

Explain what you discover.

____

____

____

Introduction to Coordinate Proofs (Cont.)

4. Graph triangle **D**(-4,1), **E**(4,5), and **F**(0,-3). Prove that the triangle is an isosceles.

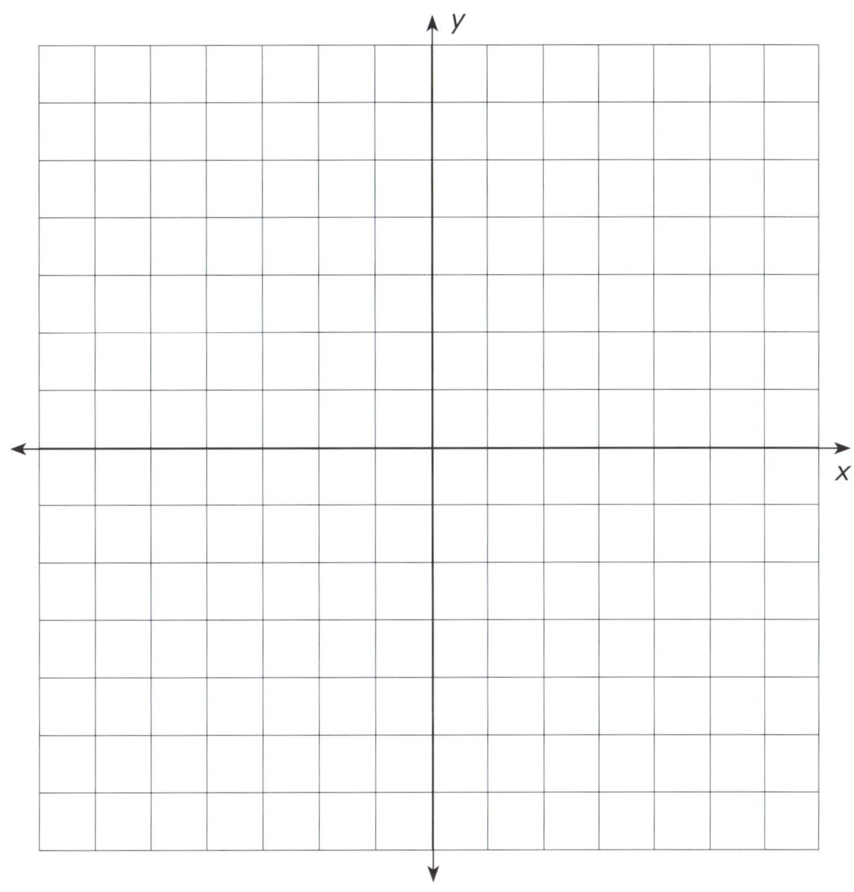

Introduction to Coordinate Proofs (Cont.)

5. Prove quadrilateral R(-2,3), S(1,3), T(2,-1), and U(-5,-1) is a trapezoid.

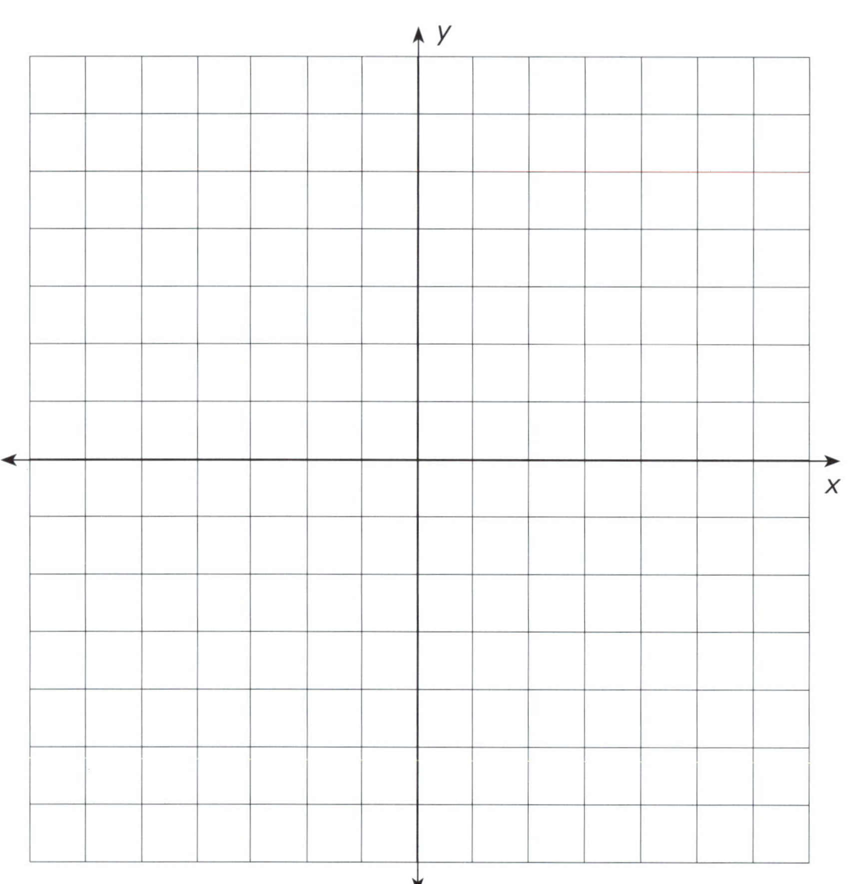

Remember
To prove that a quadrilateral is a trapezoid you must show that two opposite sides are parallel and the other two opposite sides are not.

Introduction to Coordinate Proofs (Cont.)

Proving a quadrilateral is a square. If you had to prove that a quadrilateral is a square, would you have to show the distance formula four times to prove that the sides are equal, then use the slope formula four times to prove that it has 4 right angles?

It is important to find efficient ways to prove certain shapes. Below are some of the most efficient ways to prove these shapes.

Write the formula or formulas that prove these statements.

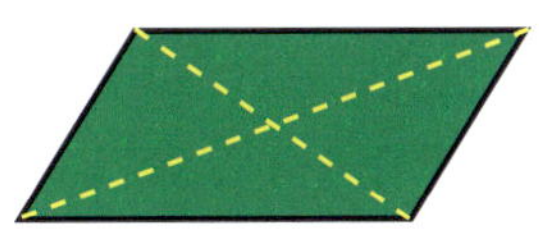

To prove that a quadrilateral is a parallelogram, prove that its diagonals bisect each other.

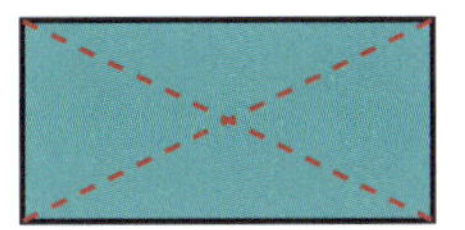

To prove that a parallelogram is a rectangle, prove that its diagonals are equal.

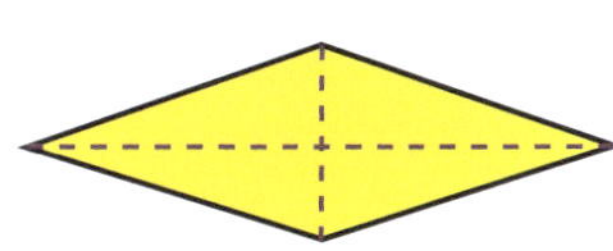

To prove that a parallelogram is a rhombus, prove that its diagonals are perpendicular.

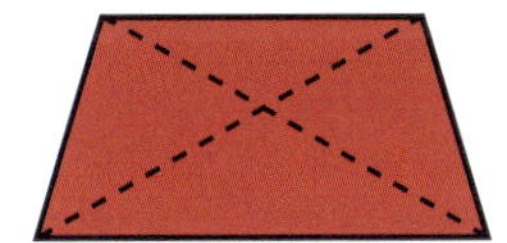

To prove that a trapezoid is an isosceles, prove that its diagonals are equal.

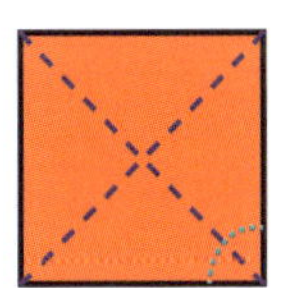

To prove that a quadrilateral is a square, first prove that it is a rhombus, then you only need to prove that it has one right angle.

or

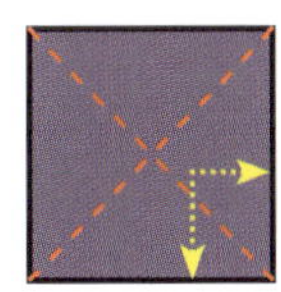

To prove that a quadrilateral is a square, first prove that it is a rectangle, then you only need to prove that one pair of adjacent sides are equal.

Introduction to Coordinate Proofs (Cont.)

1. Why would a rhombus with only one right angle be a square?
   Explain your thinking. ______________________________

   ____

   ____

2. Is it possible to draw a quadrilateral with 4 right angles with only two adjacent sides equal and not make it square? ______ Try it!

   Explain your thinking. ______________________________

   ____

   ____

3. If you had to prove a quadrilateral is a rhombus, is it sufficient to just prove that its diagonals are perpendicular? __________
   Why would you have to prove first that it is a parallelogram? __________
   Draw some quadrilaterals with perpendicular diagonals.

   Explain your thinking. ______________________________

   ____

Introduction to Coordinate Proofs (Cont.)

4. Given that that the figure below is a rhombus, prove that it is also a square.

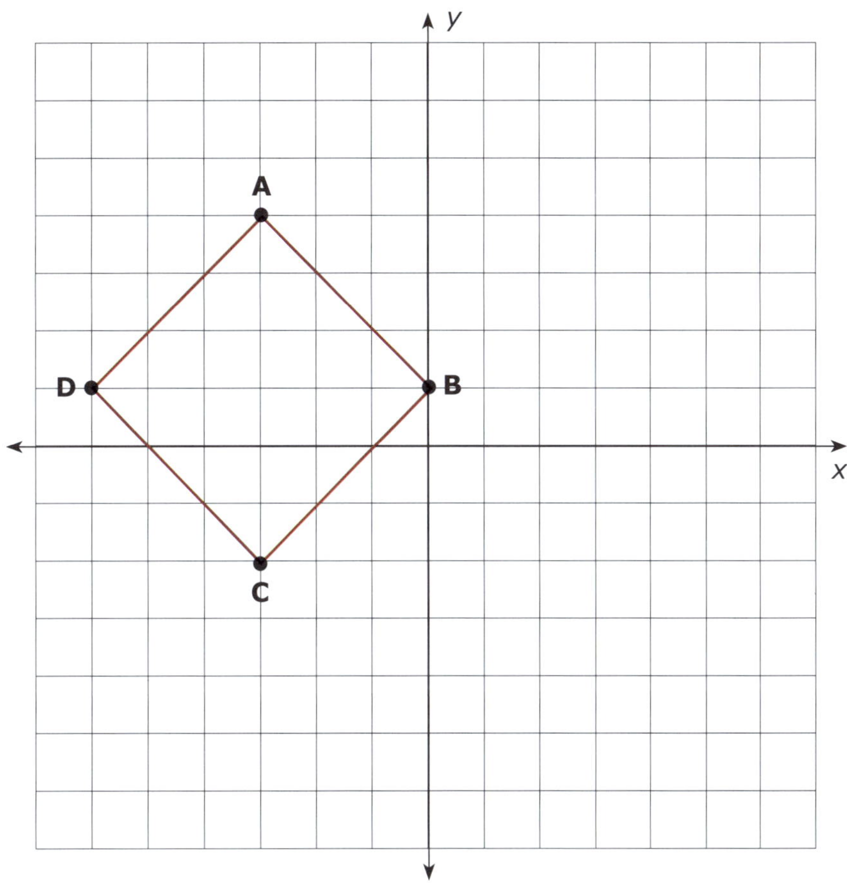

Introduction to Coordinate Proofs (Cont.)

It is important to remember that there are many ways to do a coordinate proof and it does not matter if you take more steps than needed. This is true of all of mathematics. There are often many ways to arrive at a solution. What is important is that you understand what is being asked and you clearly show your *thinking skills* as you solve the problem.

Remember these problem solving skills.

1. Read and re-read the problem carefully to understand what is being asked.

2. If you are not given a drawing, make a good drawing, then make sure you label it correctly. Make a model if needed.

3. If you are given a drawing, remember that it may not be to scale. Rely on the information given and not on the drawing. For example, what may look like a right angle may not be a right angle unless you are given that information.

4. Use the **given** information wisely. There is a reason why what you are given is important.

5. If you do not remember a property or a formula, know where to find it. Good problem solvers are also good researchers.

6. Show all your work clearly and neatly.

7. Always go back to make sure you answered the question being asked.

8. Always check to make sure your answer makes sense. For example, if you end up with a triangle that has angles larger than 180º, then you would know you made an error.

Geometry is the canvas of mathematics. It is the drawing of your thinking and you are the artist!

Review – Chapter 12

Use a separate sheet of paper if needed.

1. Find the slope (m) and the y-intercept (b) of the lines that have these equations. Remember to solve for y when needed.

   a. $y = \frac{3}{4}x - 7$ $m =$ ____ $b =$ ____

   b. $x = 5$ $m =$ ____ $b =$ ____

   c. $2 + y = 3x$ $m =$ ____ $b =$ ____

   d. $3x + 4y = -10$ $m =$ ____ $b =$ ____

   e. $y = -7$ $m =$ ____ $b =$ ____

   f. $2 - y = -5x$ $m =$ ____ $b =$ ____

2. All parallel lines have the ____________ slope and perpendicular lines have ______________________ slopes.

3. Find the slope of a line that passes by (6, 4) and (8, -10). _______

4. Write an equation of a line that is parallel to the line in question 3.

   ____

5. Use the point slope formula to write an equation of a line that has a slope of 5 and passes by (-3, 8).

   ____

6. Find the midpoint of the segment that connects (9, 10) and (3, -12). _______

7. $\overline{\mathbf{PR}}$ is a segment with **M** as its midpoint. If **P** = (-4, 5) and **M** = (3, 8), find the coordinates of **R**. _______

8. Find the distance between the points **A** (1, 4) and **B** (-7, -2). _______

9 Prove that parallelogram **DEFG** is a rhombus.

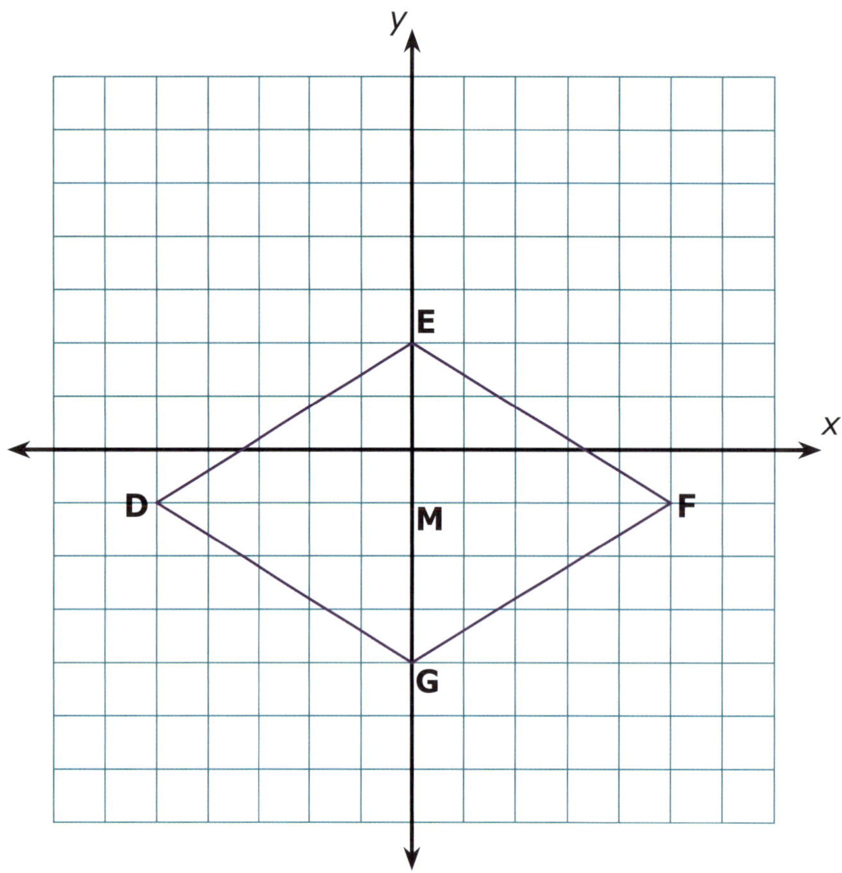

10. Prove that quadrilateral **MATH** is an isosceles trapezoid.

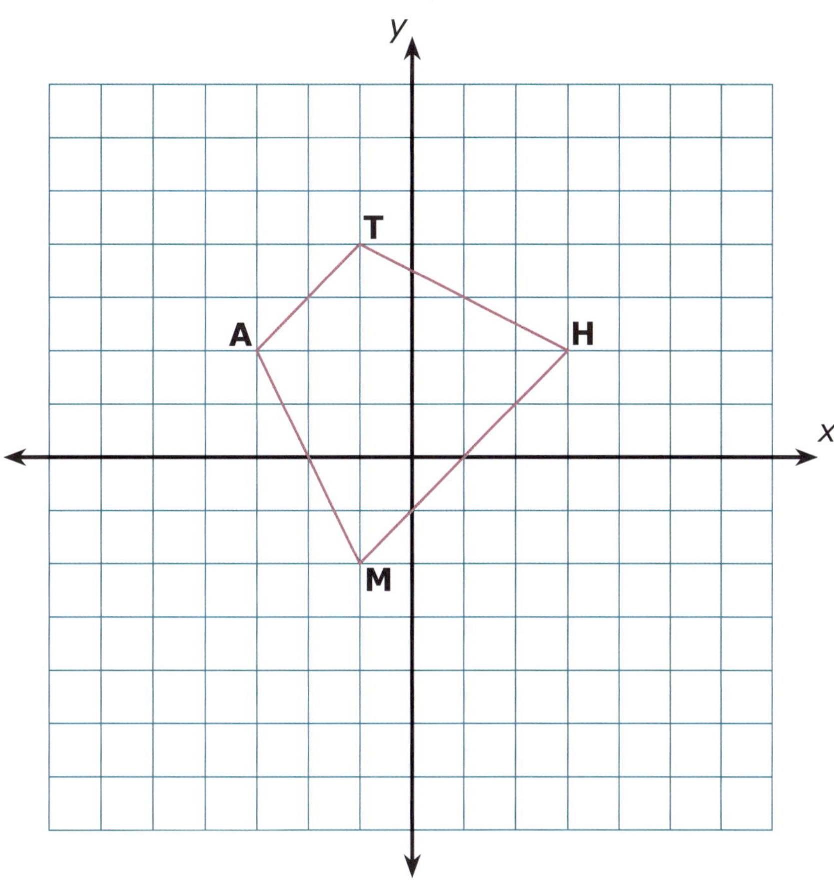

11. Why would a parallelogram with only one right angle be a rectangle? Explain your thinking.

12. To prove a quadrilateral is a parallelogram, a student proved two adjacent sides were congruent. Is this sufficient? Explain your thinking.

Final Review

Use the figure to the right to answer questions 1-2.

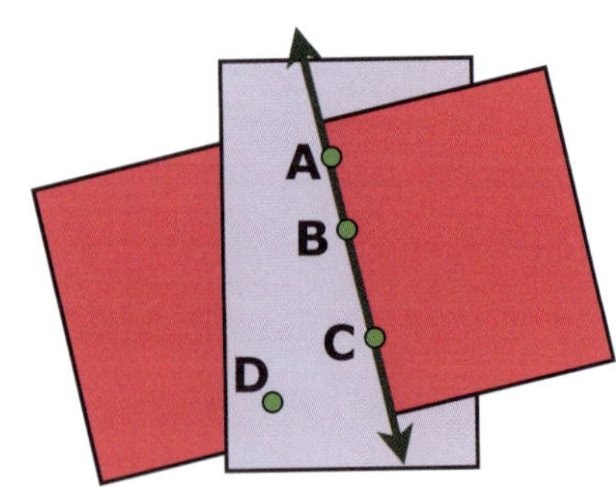

1. What is the intersection of these two planes?

____

2. Which three points determine the purple plane?

____

Use the figure to the right to answer questions 3-8.

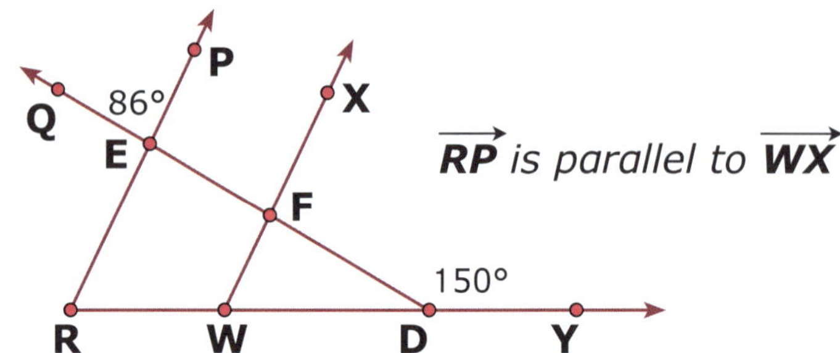

3. Find m∠**RDE**. _______

4. Find m∠**RED**. _______

5. Find m∠**ERD**. _______

6. What type of angles are ∠**WDF** and ∠**YDF**? Explain your thinking.

____

7. What is the complement of ∠**QEP**? Explain your thinking.

____

8. Why is ∠**XFE** ≅ ∠**REF**? Explain your thinking.

____

Answer questions 9-11 about this regular octagon.

9. How many diagonals does it have? What formula can you use?

____

10. What is the sum of all its interior angles? What formula can you use?

____

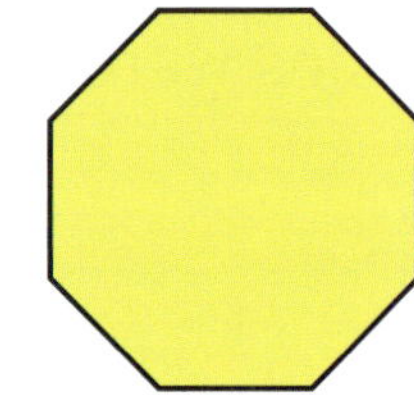

11. What is the sum of all its exterior angles?

____

Which of the following statements are **T**rue or **F**alse? If false, explain.

_____ 12 All quadrilaterals with diagonals that bisect each other are parallelograms.

____

_____ 13 Trapezoids are a type of parallelogram.

____

_____ 14 A nonagon is a seven-sided polygon.

____

_____ 15 A rhombus has perpendicular diagonals.

____

_____ 16 A square is a rectangle with congruent sides.

____

_____ 17 An isosceles trapezoid must have congruent diagonals.

____

ABCD is a parallelogram. Find:

18 the perimeter of **ABCD** _______

19 the area of **ABCD** _______

20 the area of trapezoid **EBCD** _______

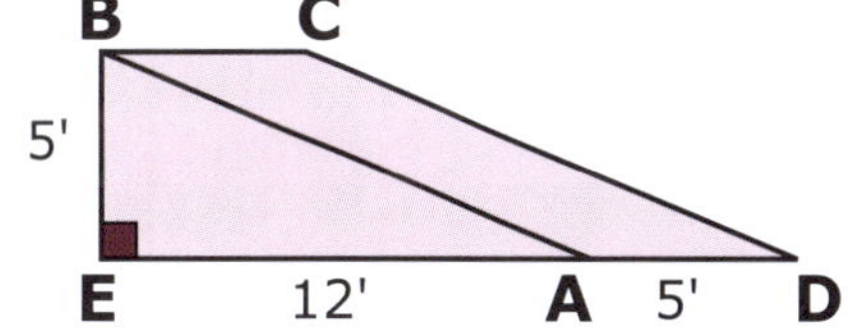

Circle **O** has a radius of 6". Answer questions 21 and 22.

21 the circumference to the nearest tenth (use $\pi = 3.14$). _______

22 the area in terms of π. _______

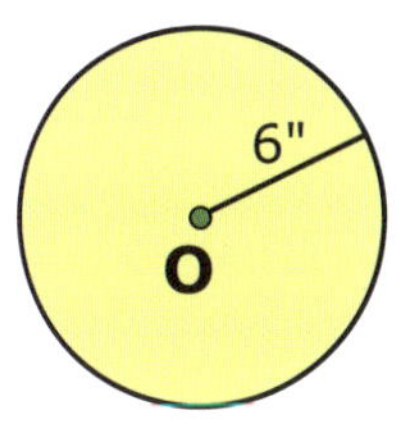

Find the volume of these geometric shapes. Round your answer to the nearest tenth when needed. Use $\pi = 3.14$.

23 _______

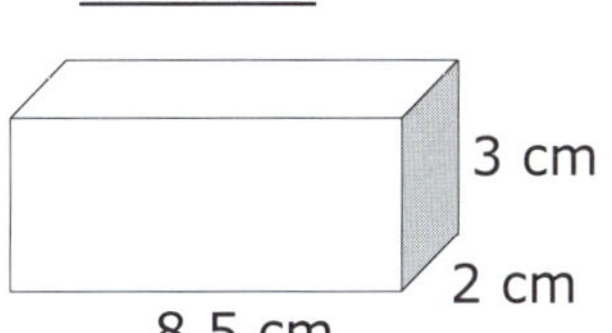

24 _______

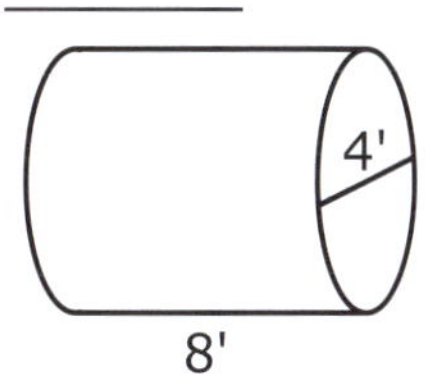

25 _______

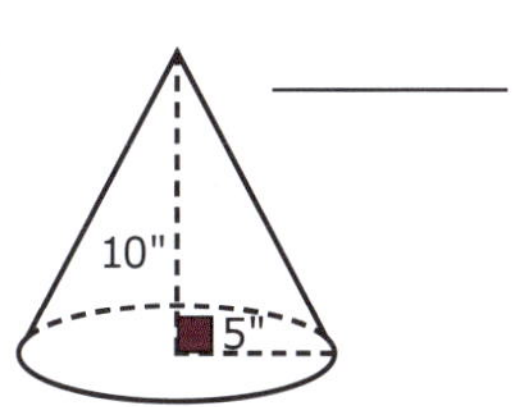

Perform the following constructions using a compass and a straightedge.

26 Bisect this angle.

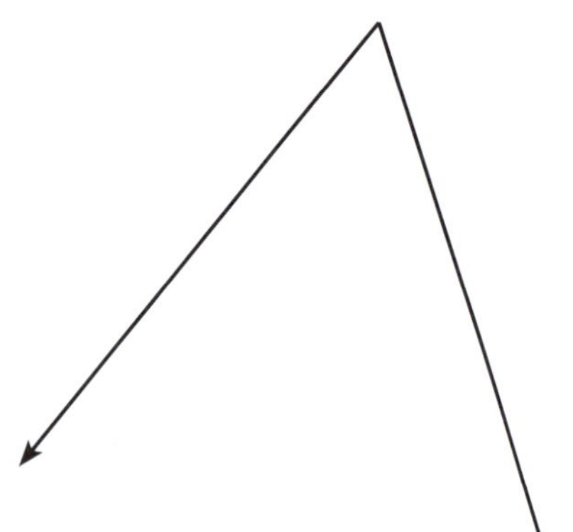

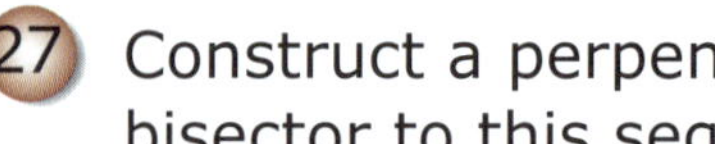

27 Construct a perpendicular bisector to this segment.

Use the figure below to answer questions 28-35.
T = (-2, 2), **A** = (-1, 5), and **P** = (3, 3)

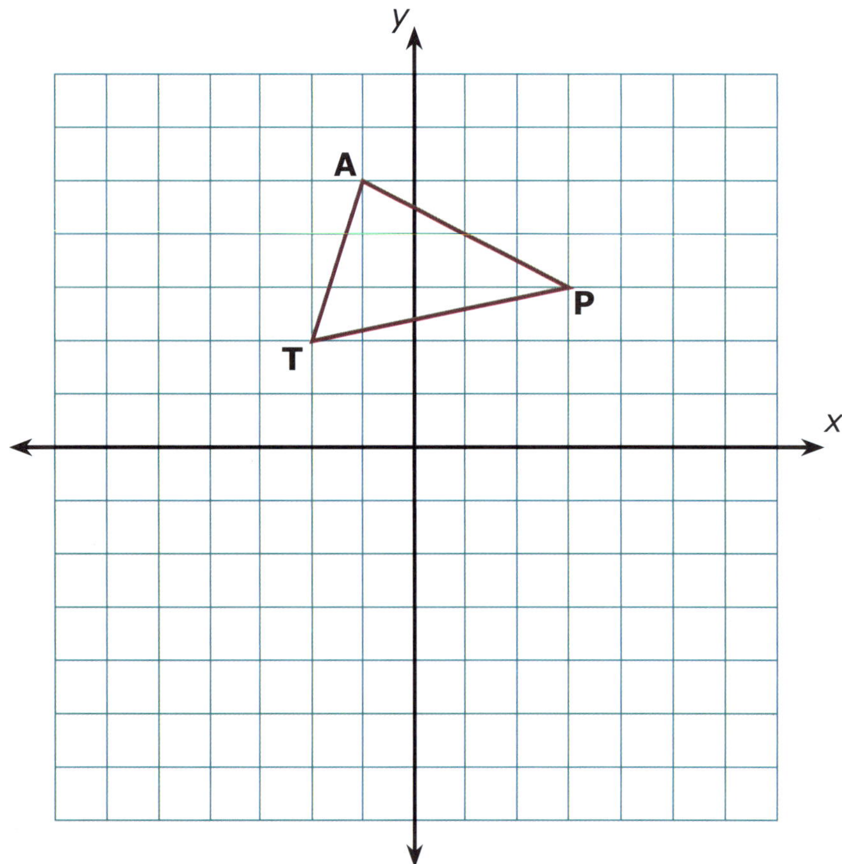

Use the figure on page 238 to answer questions 28-35.

28. What are the coordinates of **ΔTAP** after a reflection about the x-axis?

____

29. What are the coordinates of **ΔTAP** after if you rotate it 270° about the origin?

____

30. What are the coordinates of **ΔTAP** if its dilated by a factor of .5?

____

31. Translate **ΔTAP** by using this transformation: $\mathbf{T}_{-1,-4}$

____

32. What is the slope of $\overline{\mathbf{AP}}$? ________

33. What is the slope of $\overline{\mathbf{AT}}$? ________

34. How does the information from questions 32 and 33 help you determine if $\overline{\mathbf{AP}} \perp \overline{\mathbf{AT}}$. Explain your thinking.

____

____

35. What type of triangle is **ΔTAP**? Use the distance formula to help you. Explain your thinking.

____

____

36. Given these three equations, state which equations represent lines that are parallel or perpendicular. Explain your thinking.

Equation A: $2y = 4x + 10$ ______________________

Equation B: $-y = \frac{1}{2}x + 5$ ______________________

Equation C: $4y - 8x = 4$ ______________________

37. Write the equation of a line that goes through (-10, 4) and (-10, 5). State the slope of this line.

____

38 Find the midpoint of a segment that has endpoints (2, 8) and (10, -6).

______

Use each picture to find the reason you would use in a geometric proof. Explain your thinking.

39 Given ∠**3** ≅ ∠**4**, why is ∠**1** ≅ ∠**2**?

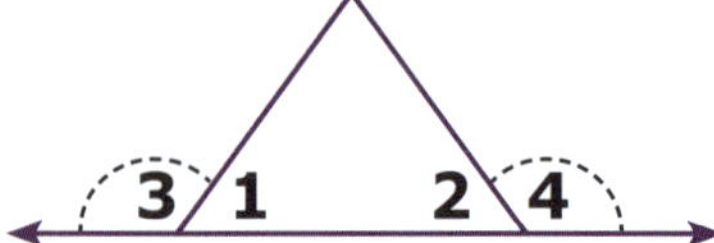

____

____

40 If ∠**A** ≅ ∠**E** and ∠**C** ≅ ∠**Q**, why is ∠**B** ≅ ∠**R**?

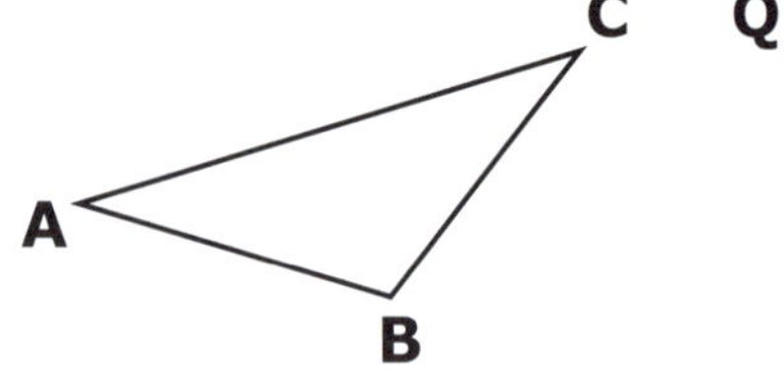

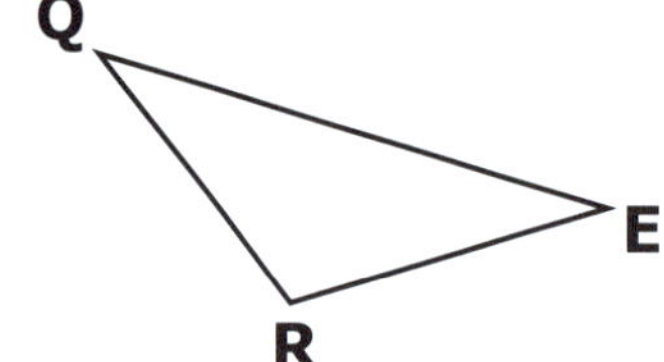

____

____

____

Use this figure to answer questions 41-43.

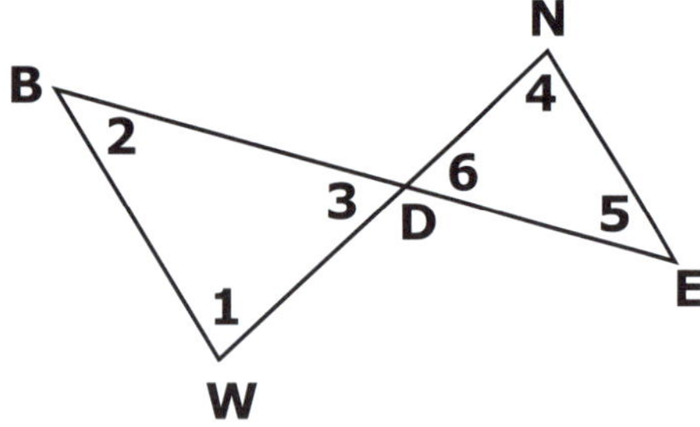

41 Why is ∠**3** ≅ ∠**6**?

____

42 If in the figure above the triangles are similar, why is ∠**2** ≅ ∠**5**?

____

43 Assume the triangles are similar. If $\overline{\textbf{BW}}$ = 12 and $\overline{\textbf{EN}}$ = 6, what is $\overline{\textbf{BD}}$ if $\overline{\textbf{ED}}$ = 5? Explain your thinking.

____

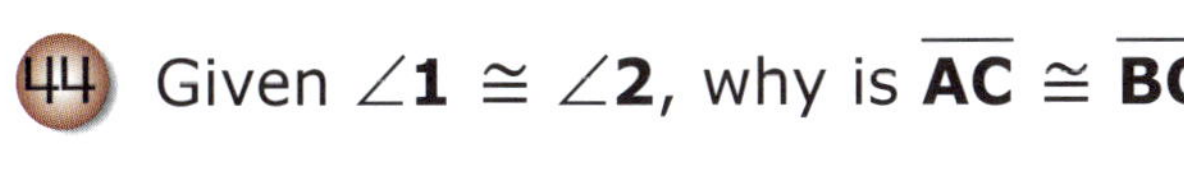

44 Given $\angle 1 \cong \angle 2$, why is $\overline{AC} \cong \overline{BC}$?

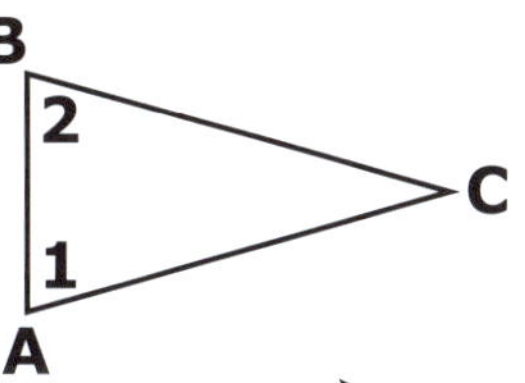

____

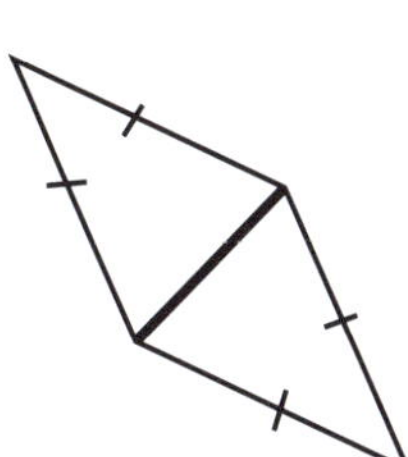

45 By what reason are these triangles congruent?

____

Fill in the steps to the following proof.

Given $\overline{PR} \parallel \overline{FW}$, and $\overline{RQ} \cong \overline{WQ}$, prove $\Delta PRQ \cong \Delta FWQ$.

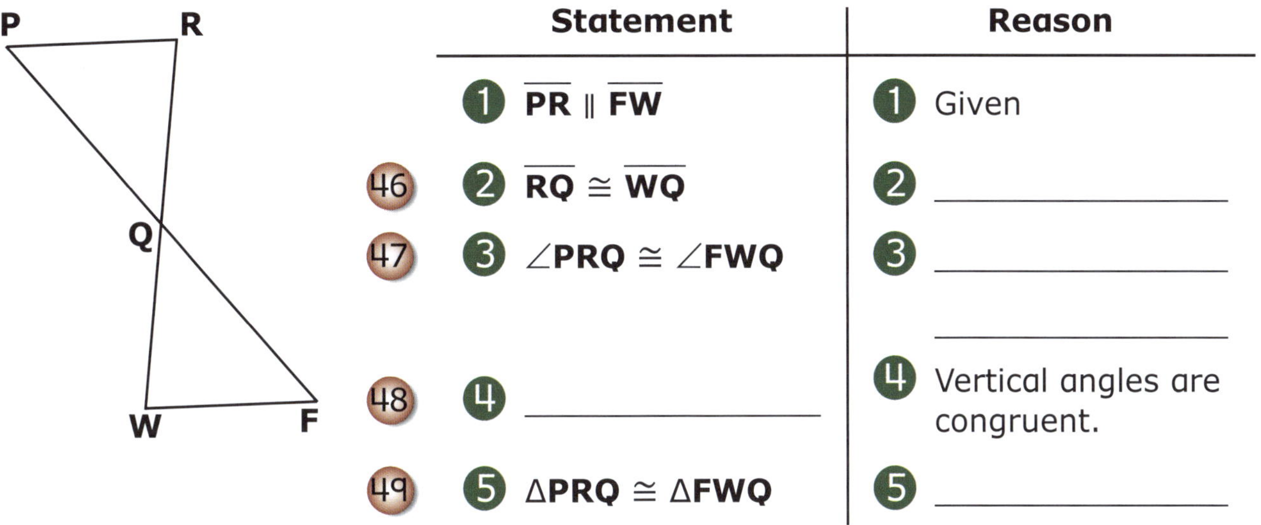

	Statement	Reason
	1 $\overline{PR} \parallel \overline{FW}$	1 Given
46	2 $\overline{RQ} \cong \overline{WQ}$	2 ______________
47	3 $\angle PRQ \cong \angle FWQ$	3 ______________ ______________
48	4 ______________	4 Vertical angles are congruent.
49	5 $\Delta PRQ \cong \Delta FWQ$	5 ______________

50 Compare and contrast the words "median" and "midsegment." Use the diagrams to help you.

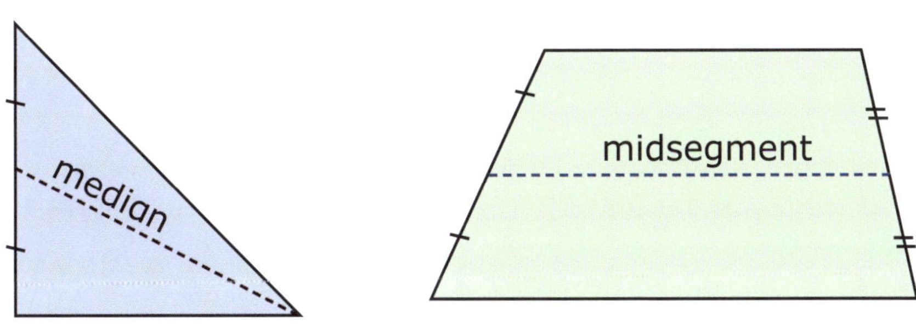

____

____

____

Age Problems

Word problems about peoples' ages can be confusing, but making a chart will help you. However, unlike coin problems it's not always obvious where to place the information and how to arrive at an equation. Here are some great strategies that will help you be successful with these types of word problems.

Age Word Problem Strategies

1. Read the problem carefully to decide which person should be labeled x (the variable).
2. Create a chart with the people on one side and the time periods on the other side.
3. Fill out the "Now" column based on the x if possible. If not possible, then fill out another column based on the x.
4. At this point, stop reading the problem and finish the chart based on your knowledge of how time works. Add the number of years for the future and subtract for past years.
5. Now, go back to the problem and read how the "blocks" on the chart are related according to what the problem says. That is your equation.
6. Solve the equation carefully.
7. Make sure your answer makes sense.

1 Three years from now José will be twice as old as Mike is now. The sum of their ages now is 21. How old is each boy now?

	Now	In Three Years
Mike	x	$x + 3$
José	$2x - 3$	$2x$

Steps 1-3: Read, create a chart, and fill in the information given.

Step 4: Complete the chart. Add three years to x and subtract 3 years from $2x$.

Equation: $x + 2x - 3 = 21$

$3x - 3 = 21$

$x = 8$ Solving the equation.

Step 5: Use the other sentence to write the equation. The sum of their ages is 21.

Answers: Mike is 8 years old, José is 13 years old.

Try to remember that there are many ways to solve a word problem so be ready to justify your method and be open to listen to how others solved the same problem.

2 In five more years, Lucia's grandfather will be eight times as old as Lucia was two years ago. When you add their present ages the sum is 69 years. How old is each one now?

	Two Years Ago	Now	In Five Years
Lucia	$x - 2$	x	$x + 5$
Grandpa	$8(x - 2) - 5 - 2$	$8(x - 2) - 5$	$8(x - 2)$

Steps 1-3: Read, create chart, fill in given information.

Step 4: Complete the chart. Add five years and subtract two years.

Step 5: Use another sentence relating the boxes of the chart to write the equation. Present ages add to a sum of 69 years.

Equation: $x + 8(x - 2) - 5 = 69$

$x + 8x - 16 - 5 = 69$

$9x - 21 = 69$

$x = 10$

Solving the equation.

Lucia is 10 years old, her grandfather is 59 years old

Answer the following questions using a chart. Charts for 1-5 are provided.

1 Sokhem is Chenda's older brother. In six more years Sokhem will be twice Chenda's age now. In six more years the sum of their ages then will be 60 years. How old is each now?

	Now	In Six Years
Chenda	x	
Sokhem		$2x$

Now follow step 4.

Sample 2
Math Analogies™
Level 4

Complete Each Math Analogy

13)

7 faces
15 edges
10 vertices : 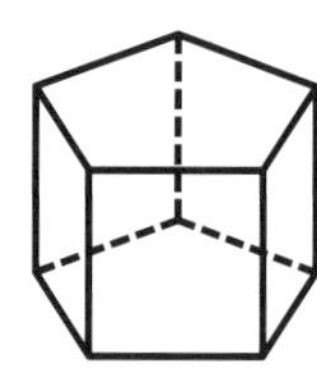 :: 6 faces
12 edges
8 vertices :

14)

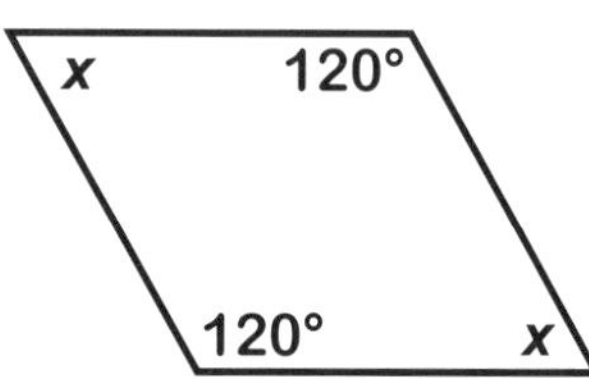

: $x = 60°$ :: 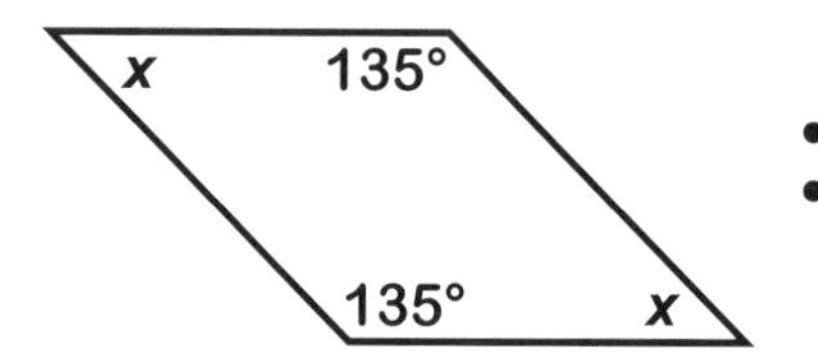

:

15)

hiker descends at a constant rate

minutes into descent	altitude (feet)
25	7,400
55	6,200

: rate of descent is 40 feet per minute ::

hiker descends at a constant rate

minutes into descent	altitude (feet)
37	5,100
87	3,600

:

16)

$\frac{1}{x} + \frac{1}{x} + \frac{1}{x}$: $\frac{3}{x}$ :: $\frac{1}{x} + \frac{2}{x} + \frac{3}{x} + \frac{4}{x}$:

Which answer can replace the question mark?

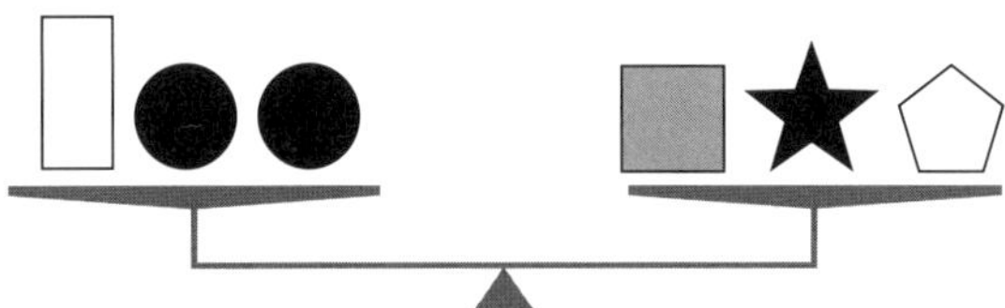

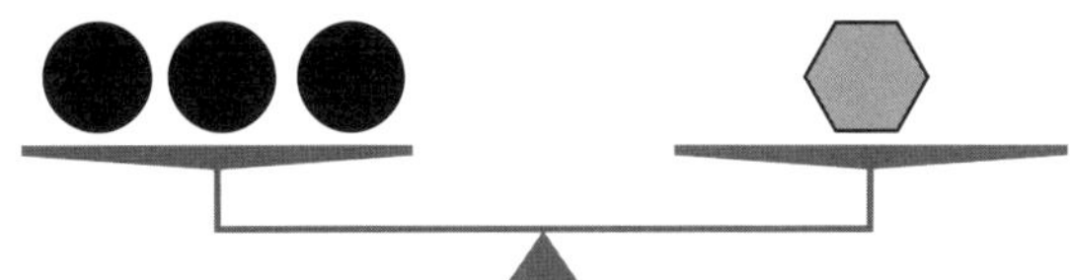

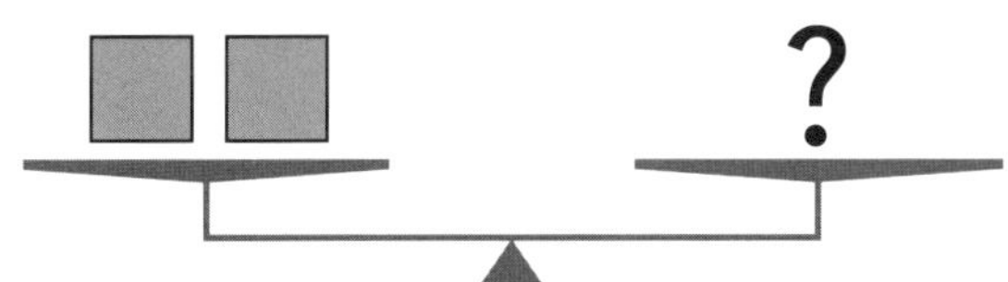

a. b.

c. d.

Hint: On 3rd balance, remove ★ from both pans.

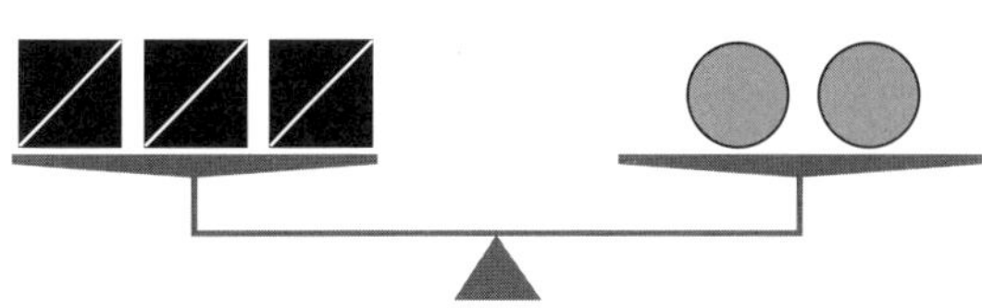

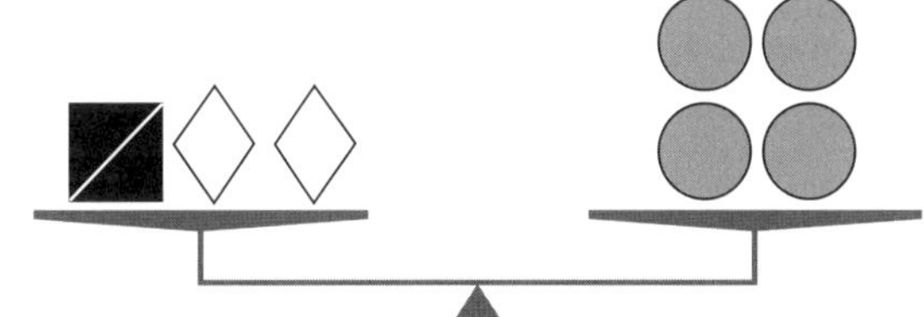

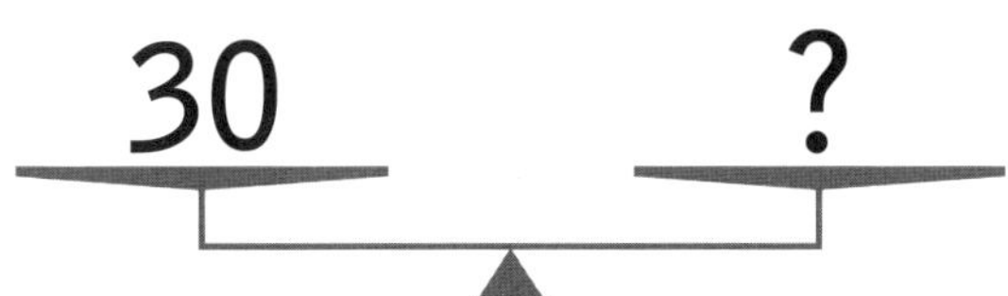

a. b.

c. d.

Hint: Divide 2nd balance in thirds.

2. What is the area of the shaded region? Round final answer to nearest whole number.

   a. The outer square has 12-inch sides. The half circles are identical in size.

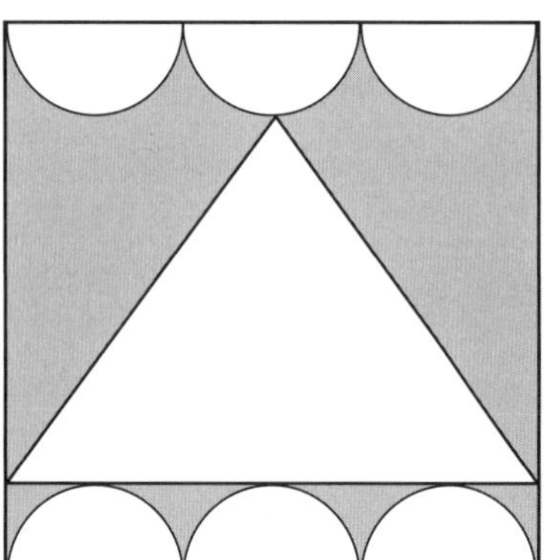

   b. The outer circle has a 20-inch diameter and the solid dots are the centers of their corresponding circles.

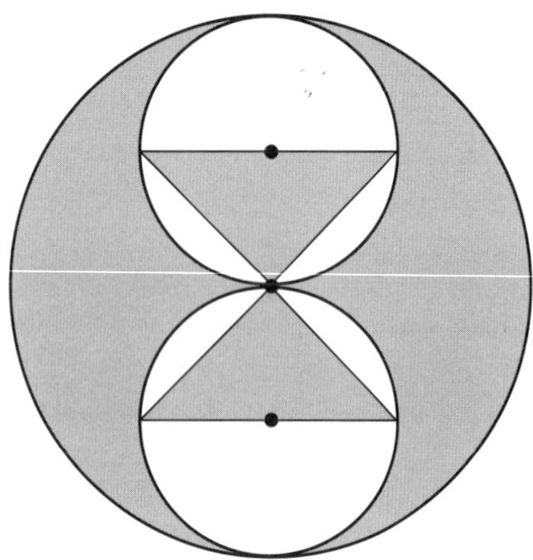

Math Facts

1. A triangle's area equals half the base times the height.
2. A circle's area equals π times the square of the radius.
3. The value of π is 3.14159....
4. A rectangle's area equals its length times its width.
5. A square's area equals the square of its length.

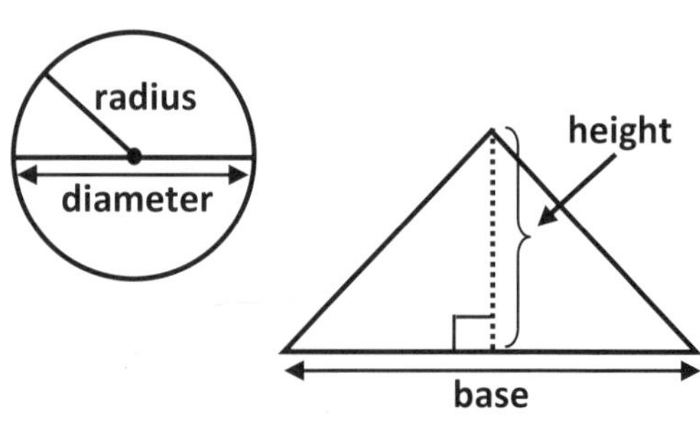

Glossary

acute angle .... An angle less than 90 degrees.

adjacent .... Two angles are adjacent if they are coplanar and they share a vertex and a side.

alternate exterior angles .... Angles created when two lines are cut by a transversal. In this picture, ∠1 and ∠2 are alternate exterior angles. ∠3 and ∠4 is another pair. They are on the exterior of the two lines and on alternate sides. Alternate exterior angles are congruent if and only if lines are parallel.

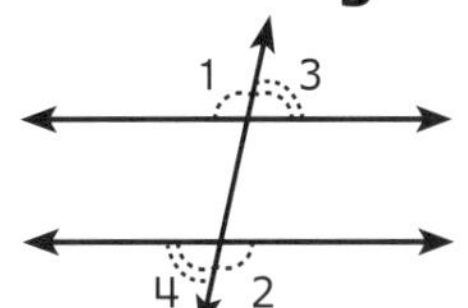

alternate interior angles .... Angles created when two lines are cut by a transversal. In this picture, ∠1 and ∠2 is a pair of alternate interior angles. So is ∠3 and ∠4. Alternate interior angles are congruent if and only if lines are parallel.

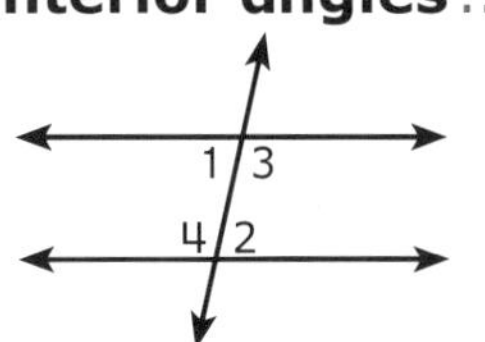

altitude .... Another word for height.

apex .... The point where the sides of a pyramid or cone converge.

area .... The number of square units taken up by a two-dimensional (coplanar) figure.

axiom .... Another word for postulate, or a statement that needs no proof. For example: If there is a line and a point not on the line, then there is exactly one line through that point parallel to the given line.

bases of a trapezoid .... The two sides of a trapezoid that are parallel.

bisect .... To cut in half.

centroid .... The point of concurrency where the three medians of a triangle intersect.

chord .... A segment that connects one point on a circle to another point on the same circle. The diameter is the largest chord of a circle.

circle .... The set of points (or locus) on a plane equidistant from one point called the center.

circumference .... The perimeter of a circle.

circumscribed .... A figure that is outside another figure where the second figure's vertices all lie on the first figure.

collinear .... Points on the same line.

complementary angles .... Two angles whose measures add up to 90°.

concave .... A polygon where one or more vertices collapse into the shape. See drawing.

concurrent .... See point of concurrency.

conditional statement.........An if and then statement.

cone ....A solid with a circular base and sides that rise to a point.

congruent vs equal.............The term congruent (≅) is used to compare shapes whereas the term equal is used to compare quantities.

consecutive ....In order, one after another.

construction ....A drawing made with only a compass and a straightedge.

contrapositive ....If a statement is *if p then q*, then the contrapositive is *if ~q then ~p*. The contrapositive is always logically equivalent to the original statement.

converse..............................If a statement is *if p then q*, then the converse is *if q then p*.

convex.................................A polygon is called a convex polygon if all its vertices stem out from the center of the polygon.

coordinate plane..................Or Cartesian plane, a grid with a horizontal axis called *x* and a vertical axis called *y*.

coplanar ....Lying on the same plane.

corresponding angles ....Angles that are created when a transversal intersects two or more lines. $\angle 1$ and $\angle 2$ is one pair of corresponding angles. These are the other pairs: $\angle 3$ and $\angle 4$, $\angle 5$ and $\angle 6$, $\angle 7$ and $\angle 8$. Corresponding angles are congruent if and only if lines are parallel.

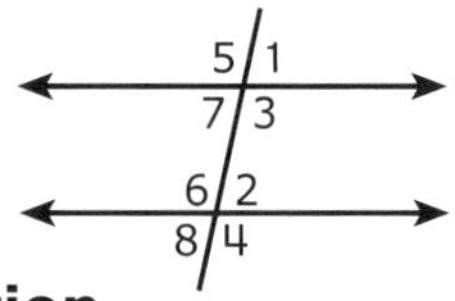

5 1
7 3
6 2
8 4

cross section ....A slice created by intersecting a plane through a solid.

cylinder ....A solid that has two circles for parallel bases. A food can is a good example of a cylinder.

decagon...............................A polygon with 10 sides.

degree..................................A unit of measure of an angle.

diagonal ....A segment connecting one vertex of a polygon to a non-adjacent vertex.

diameter...............................The biggest chord in a circle. It goes through its center.

difference.............................The answer to a subtraction problem.

dilation.................................A transformation where an object shrinks or enlarges in proportion. In a dilation, the corresponding angles remain congruent. A dilation is not an isometry.

dodecagon............................A polygon with twelve sides.

edge ....The segment part of a solid where two faces meet.

endpoint.............................. The point at each end of a segment or the point at the beginning of a ray.

equidistant ....Same distance apart.

equilateral...........................A triangle with three congruent angles and three congruent sides.

evaluate .... To substitute a value in a variable and then simplify to find the answer.

face of a polyhedra .... The polygon face of a three-dimensional solid.

glide reflection .... A transformation where a translation is followed by a reflection or a reflection is followed by a translation.

heptagon .... A polygon with seven sides.

hexagon .... A polygon with six sides.

hypotenuse .... The longest side of a right triangle.

hypothesis .... An assumption that can be followed by a conclusion.

image .... The figure after a transformation.

incenter .... The point where the three angle bisectors of a triangle intersect.

inscribed .... A figure is inscribed in another figure when the vertices of the first figure lie on the rim of the second figure. See circumscribe.

intersection .... Another word for where lines or segments meet.

inverse .... If the statement is *if p then q*, then the inverse is *if ~p then ~q*.

inverse operation .... Addition and subtraction are inverse operations. Multiplication and division are inverse operations.

isometry .... A transformation that preserves distance (the distance between vertices in the figure being transformed).

isosceles .... A triangle with two congruent sides and two congruent angles.

kite .... A quadrilateral with two sets of congruent sides. In order, the sides are short, short, long, long. The diagonals of a kite are perpendicular to each other.

lateral area .... The area of the sides (not the top or bottom bases) of a three dimensional solid.

legs of a right triangle .... The smaller two sides of a right triangle.

less vs less than .... *a less b* means $a - b$ and *a less than b* means $b - a$.

line .... A straight one dimensional figure, an infinite collection of points having no thickness.

line of symmetry .... An imaginary line where you could fold an image and have both sides match each other exactly.

line segment .... A piece of a line with two endpoints.

linear pair .... Two angles that are adjacent and supplementary.

locus .... A path or set of points.

median .... In geometry, a median is a line segment joining the vertex of a triangle to the midpoint of the opposing side. Each triangle has three medians that meet at a point called the centroid.

midpoint............................The half way point in a line segment.

midsegment........................In a trapezoid, the segment that connects the midpoints of the two non-parallel sides. The midsegment is always parallel to the bases and equal to half of the sum of the bases.

negation..............................The opposite of a statement. The negation of "It rains," would be "It does not rain." You can also say, "It is not true that it rains." The symbol for negation is ~.

non-adjacent........................Not next to each other, not adjacent.

non-collinear........................Points not all on the same line. Remember at least two points will always be on the same line.

obtuse angle........................An angle more than 90° but less than 180°.

octagon...............................A polygon with 8 sides.

ordered pair........................A pair of numbers that indicates a point on the coordinate plane. It's written as (x,y)

order of symmetry...............The number of times a figure can be rotated to where the image matches the preimage.

orthocenter..........................Point where the three altitudes of a triangle intersect.

parallel................................Lines, segments, or rays that are the same distance from each other. Parallel lines are always coplanar.

parallelogram......................A quadrilateral with opposite sides parallel.

pentagon.............................A polygon with five sides.

perfect square.....................The set {1, 4, 9, 16, 25, 36, 49, ...} is called the set of perfect squares. The square root of these numbers is *always* a whole number. If you multiply (1)(1), (2)(2), (3)(3), (4)(4), etc., you generate the set of perfect squares.

perimeter............................The total length around a closed figure.

perpendicular......................Two lines, segments, or rays are perpendicular if they intersect to make 90° angles.

plane...................................The idea of a flat surface with two dimensions.

point...................................A location in space. Points are always capitalized.

point of concurrency...........The point where several lines, segments, or rays intersect.

polygon...............................A many-sided closed coplanar figure.

polyhedron..........................A many sided 3-dimensional figure.

postulate.............................A statement that is assumed to be true and therefore needs no proof.

preimage.............................An image before it is transformed.

prism..................................A three-dimensional object where the top and the bottom bases are parallel and congruent.

product...............................The answer to a multiplication problem.

proof .... An organized list of statements and reasons to prove the truth of a statement.

pyramid .... A solid where the faces are triangular and come to point (apex). The base of a pyramid can be in the shape of any polygon.

pythagorean triple .... Any set of three numbers that satisfy the Pythagorean theorem.

quadrilateral .... A polygon with 4 sides.

quotient .... The answer to a division problem.

radical .... Another word for the square root symbol.

radius .... The distance from the center to the circle.

ratio .... Another word for fraction. The ratio of x to y is $\boldsymbol{x/y}$. The ratio of y to x is $\boldsymbol{y/x}$. You can write a ratio with a colon. For example: the ratio of x to y is also written $\boldsymbol{x:y}$.

ray .... A line with only one endpoint. Ray $\overrightarrow{\mathbf{AB}}$ means that the ray starts at **A** and passes through **B**.

rectangle .... A parallelogram with 4 right angles.

reflection .... A transformation where you flip the figure along a line of symmetry.

regular polygon .... A polygon with congruent angles and congruent sides.

rhombus .... A parallelogram with congruent sides.

right angle .... A 90° angle.

right cone .... A cone whose altitude is perpendicular to the base.

right cylinder .... A cylinder whose altitude is perpendicular to the base.

right prism .... A prism whose altitude is perpendicular to the base.

rotation .... A transformation where a figure is rotated about a fixed point.

satisfy .... When a value or values satisfy an equation it makes the equation true. The ordered pair (-2, 3) satisfies the equation $y = 2x + 7$.

scalene .... A triangle with no equal sides (and no equal angles).

semicircle .... Half of a circle.

similar .... Figures are similar if their corresponding angles are congruent and their corresponding sides are in proportion.

simplify .... To find the answer in simplest form, always reduce a fraction when you simplify.

skew lines .... Two lines that are on different planes. Skew lines do not intersect.

slope .... The number of vertical units divided by the number of horizontal units from one point to another point on a segment or line. Rise/Run.

solve .... To find the answer, usually in an equation or word problem.

sphere .... In three dimensions, the set of all points equidistant from the same point. That distance is called the radius of the sphere.

square .... A parallelogram with four right angles and four congruent sides. You can define a square as a rectangle with congruent sides or a rhombus with right angles.

straight angle .... A 180° angle.

sum .... The answer to an addition problem.

supplementary angles .... Two angles whose measures add up to 180°.

surface area .... The area of every face of a solid.

tessellation .... A tiling where one figure is repeated over and over such that it covers a plane without gaps or overlaps.

tetrahedron .... A pyramid where each of the four faces are equilateral triangles.

theorem .... A true statement that can be proven.

transformation .... A movement where a figure is changed by a translation, a rotation, or a dilation; or a combination of any of these in a plane.

translation .... A transformation where a figure slides in the plane without being rotated or dilated.

transversal .... A line that cuts through two or more lines.

trapezium .... American definition: A quadrilateral with no sides parallel. British definition: A quadrilateral with one set of parallel sides (which is the American definition of trapezoid).

trapezoid .... A quadrilateral with only two sides parallel.

triangle .... A polygon with three sides.

vertex .... In an angle, the point where the two rays intersect.

vertex angle .... In an isosceles triangle, the angle created by the two sides of equal length. It is always opposite the base of the triangle.

vertical angles .... The angles that are opposite each other when lines intersect. Vertical angles are always congruent.

volume .... The amount of cubic space taken up by a three dimensional shape.

Answers

A free, downloadable Detailed Solutions (PDF) is also available at www.criticalthinking.com.

Chapter 1: Notation Practice, p. 3

1. ≅
2. =
3. ≅
4. ≅
5. =
6. ||
7. ⊥
8. ⊥
9. Yes, if angles are congruent, then degree measures are equal.
10. Yes, in a plane if a line is perpendicular to one of two parallel lines it is perpendicular to the second line.
11. Because there is more than one angle with point A as the vertex.

Chapter 1: Build It!, p. 6

1. a. yes
2. a. yes
   b. Because when you have two intersecting lines you have three non-collinear points. See drawing:

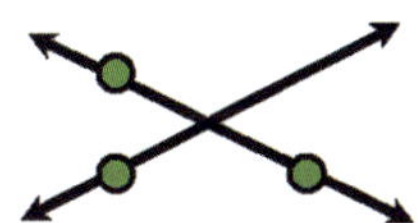

3. No, it's not possible for two planes to be skew since planes go on forever in all directions. Either planes are parallel or they intersect.
4. A line.
5. The wheel on a paddle boat is one of many examples.
6. Three planes in space can intersect in 0 points, 1 common line, 2 parallel lines, 1 common point, or they can coincide.

Chapter 2: Angles Activity, p. 9

Answers to the table:

	Right	Acute	Obtuse	Straight	Adjacent to ∠ECD
∠FCE		✓			✓
∠ECD		✓			
∠DCA				✓	
∠FCB			✓		
∠BCD	✓				✓
∠ACB	✓				

Triangle Activity, p. 10
You should discover that all three angles make a straight line (180°).

Triangle Practice, p. 11

1. 110°
2. 50°
3. 10°
4. No, because an obtuse angle is more than 90° so two obtuse angles would add up to more than 180°.
5. No, because 180° − 90° = 90°, so the other two angles of a right triangle must each be acute.
6. 45° and 45°.
7. An equilateral triangle has three 60° angles.
8. a. m∠C = 45°
   b. m∠B = 60°
   c. m∠C = 20.5°
   d. m∠B = 40°
   e. m∠A = 45°; m∠B = 45°
   f. m∠B = 5°; m∠C = 5°
   g. m∠A = 60°; m∠B = 30°

Quadrilateral Activity, p. 12
You should discover that the angles make a circle so they add up to 360°.

Complementary and Supplementary, pp. 13-14

1. 15°
2. 105°
3. 95°
4. 110°
5. 135°
6. The supplement of an acute angle is always bigger.
   For example: 90° − 1° = 89°
7. No, because the answer would be negative.
8. $(180 - x)°$
9. $(90 - y)°$

10.
11.

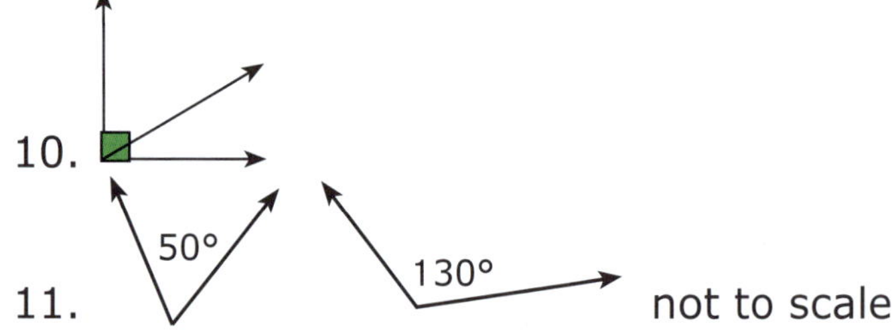

not to scale

12. They must be congruent.

Vertical Angles, p. 15

1. m∠x = 50°, m∠y = 130°, m∠z = 130°
2. Supplementary; They add up to 180°.
3. m∠x = 50°, m∠w = 90°, m∠z = 40°, m∠y = 40°
4. Complementary; They add up to 90°.
5. You would need to know at least 3 angles.
6. A circle is 360°.

Angles Puzzle 1, p. 16

a. 44°
b. 83°
c. 97°
d. 39°
e. 51°
f. 44°
g. 90°
h. 46°
i. 51°
j. 39°
k. 141°
l. 30°
m. 106°

Angles Puzzle 2, p. 17

a. 41°
b. 49°
c. 118°
d. 23°
e. 49°
f. 85°
g. 28°
h. 46°
i. 84°

Parallel Lines and Transversal I, p. 18

Top of the page: ∠5 and ∠6 are corresponding, ∠3 and ∠4 are corresponding.

1. 130°
2. No, because the corresponding angles are not congruent.
3. a. Because if a line is parallel to another line and this second line is parallel to a third line then the first line is parallel to the third line (transitive property).
   b. m∠1 = 80°
      m∠2 = 100°
      m∠3 = 80°
      m∠4 = 80°
      m∠5 = 100°
      m∠6 = 100°

m∠7 = 80°
m∠8 = 80°
m∠9 = 100°
m∠10 = 100°
m∠11 = 80°

Parallel Lines and Transversals I, p. 19

1. Because the alternate interior angles are congruent.
2. a. 50°; It is an alternate interior pair with the 50° angle.
   b. 130°; It is the supplement of 50°. Answer may vary.
   c. 130°;It is a corresponding angle with the supplement of 50°. Answer may vary.
   d. 130°; It is a corresponding angle with ∠3. Answer may vary.
   e. 130°; It is a vertical angle with ∠3. Answer may vary.

The 20- Angle Problem, p. 20

1. 60°
2. 60°
3. 120°
4. 60°
5. 120°
6. 120°
7. 60°
8. 120°
9. 60°
10. 50°
11. 70°
12. 70°
13. 70°
14. 50°
15. 50°
16. 68°
17. 42°
18. 42°
19. 68°
20. 70°

Chapter 3: Triangle Properties, p. 21

1. m∠x = 70°, m∠y = 110°
2. m∠x = 100°, m∠y = 80°
3. m∠x = 30°, m∠y = 150°
4. m∠x = 25°, m∠y = 155°
5. m∠x = 45°, m∠y = 65°
6. m∠x = 80°, m∠y = 100°
7. The exterior angle is always equal to the sum of the two remote interior angles.

Exterior Angle Exploration, p. 22

1. $x = g + e$ or $x = e + g$
2. $x = e + d$
3. $x = p + r$
4. $x = w - y$

Sum of Two Sides, p. 23

1. It is impossible to draw a triangle with those measurements.
2. Answers will vary. Any answer where the sum of any two sides is greater than the third side.

Triangle Property Practice, p. 24

1. C
2. B; Since any two sides must add up to more than the third side.
3. It would be impossible to draw a triangle with those measurements.
4. m∠E must be 85° and not 88° since the sum of the angle measures must be 180°. HT must be greater than 5.5' and less than 14.5'.

Triangle Opposite Property, p. 25

1. The 13.1 must be opposite the 19° angle. The 35 must be opposite the 59° angle. The 40 must be opposite angle the 103° angle.
2. The 90° must be opposite the largest 30 cm side. The 30° must be opposite the smaller 15 cm side and the 60° must be opposite the medium side of 25.98 cm. The largest side is always opposite the largest angle and the smallest side is always opposite the smallest angle.
3. It is facing the smaller angle.

Properties of Equilateral and Isosceles Triangles, pp. 26-27

1. m∠A = 45°, m∠B = 45°
2. m∠Q = 20°, m∠R = 80°
3. m∠N = 65°, m∠L = 65°
4. m∠A = 42.75, m∠R = 42.75°
5. The base angles must be opposite the congruent sides.

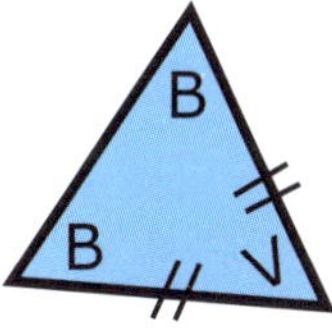

6. In an equilateral triangle the measure of each angle must be 60°.
7. No, because not all the sides would be equal. The side opposite the 90° would be the larger side.
8. a. T
   b. T
   c. F
   d. T
   e. F
   f. F
   g. T
   h. F

i. T
j. T

Algebra and Geometry, pp. 28-29

1. Equation: $5x + 4 = 3x + 6$, $x = 1$; AC = 9, BC = 9, AB = 4
2. $x = 9$, m∠E = 45°, m∠F = 45°
3. Equation: $x + x + 3x = 180$; $x = 36°$; m∠W = 108°; m∠Z = 36°; m∠U = 36°
4. m∠x = 76°; m∠ y= 48°
5. Equation: $5x - 40 = 3x + 10$, $x = 25$, m∠ADR = 85°; m∠RDT = 95°
6. Equation: $9x = 90$, $x = 10$, m∠AQE = 50°, m∠EQL = 40°
7. Equation: $4x = 60$ or $4x + 120 = 180$, $x = 15$
8. Equation: $3x + x + 116 = 180$; $x = 16$

Cumulative Review – Chapters 1-3, p. 30

1. The lines are perpendicular because they intersect at right angles. (Even though one right angle is shown, all angles are right angles because two adjacent angles on the same line are supplementary.)
2. a. 50°; b. 45°; c. 85°; d. 130°; e. 50°; f. 95°
3. a. complement: 60°, supplement: 150°
   b. angle: 65°, supplement: 115°
   c. complement: $90 - n$, supplement: $180 - n$
4. a. 120°; b. $(y + z)°$
5. a. The measures of the base angles of an isosceles triangle must be equal.
   b. In any triangle two sides must add to more than the third side.
   c. The largest angle must be opposite the largest side.
6. a. $x = 12$; b. $x = 10$; c. $x = 25$

Chapter 4: The Pythagorean Theorem, p. 31

1. The biggest angle is 90°.
2. 9 + 16 = 25; Yes!

Pythagorean Triples Practice, p. 33

1. $5^2 + 12^2 = 13^2$; 25 + 144 = 169
2. $9^2 + 12^2 = 15^2$; 81 + 144 = 225
3. b; $1^2 + 2^2 \neq 3^2$
4. b is not because $5^2 + 12^2 \neq 225$
5. a. $n^2 - m^2 = 9 - 4 = 5$; $2mn = (2)(3)(2) = 12$; $n^2 + m^2 = 9 + 4 = 13$
   Yes, it's a 5, 12, 13 Pythagorean Triple because 25 + 144 = 169.
   b. $n^2 - m^2 = 64 - 25 = 39$; $2mn = (2)(8)(5) = 80$; $n^2 + m^2 = 64 + 25 = 89$. Yes, it's a 39, 80, 89 Pythagorean Triple because 1,521 + 6,400 = 7,921.

	n	m	$n^2 - m^2$	$2mn$	$n^2 + m^2$	Is it a Pythagorean Triple?
	2	1	3	4	5	Yes
a	3	2	5	12	13	Yes
b	8	5	39	80	89	Yes

Using the Pythagorean Theorem, pp. 34-35

1. 13; $5^2 + 12^2 = x^2$; $25 + 144 = x^2$, $169 = x^2$, so $x = 13$.
2. 7'; $b^2 + 24^2 = 25^2$, $b^2 + 576 = 625$, $b^2 = 49$, so $b = 7'$.
3. 8'; $8^2 + 15^2 = 17^2$
4. 1.4 cm; $1^2 + 1^2 = x^2$, $2 = x^2$, $x = 1.4$ cm (rounded to the nearest tenth)
5. $a = 12'$; $9^2 + 12^2 = 15^2$
6. 26'; $10'^2 + 24'^2 = 26'^2$
7. 35m
8. 6.9 units

Pythagorean Applications, pp. 36-37

1. 22"; $16^2 + x^2 = 27^2$, $256 + x^2 = 729$, $x^2 = 473$, so $x = 22"$ (rounded to the nearest inch).
2. 127.3'; $90^2 + 90^2 = 8{,}100 + 8{,}100 = 16{,}200 = c^2$, so $c = 127.3'$
3. d; $60^2 + 100^2 = x^2$; $3{,}600 + 10{,}000 = x^2$; $13{,}600 = x^2$, so $x = 116.6$ yards which rounded to the nearest yard is 117.
4. 37 miles
5. 11.3' or about 11 feet 4 inches (rounded)

Solving Multi-Step Right Triangles Problems, p. 38

1. 36'; If AB = 10, then DB = 5. To find CB use the Pythagorean Theorem: $12^2 + 5^2 = CB^2$; $144 + 25 = CB^2$, $169 = CB^2$, so CB = 13. If CB = 13, then AC = 13. To find the perimeter add 13 + 13 + 10 which equals the answer of 36 ft.
2. 48 sq ft; The length of the mirror is 8′ so the area is (6)(8) = 48 ft.
3. c; let x equal each diagonal and use the Pythagorean Theorem, $100 + 25 = x^2$, so $125 = x^2$, so $x = 11.2$. The length of the two diagonals is 22.4. (You can also draw one larger triangle where $10^2 + 20^2 = x^2$.)
4. 14"; Find SZ first. $8^2 + 8^2 = (SZ)^2$, $64 + 64 = (SZ)^2$, so $SZ = \sqrt{128}$. Next $(\sqrt{128})^2 + 8^2 = (WZ)^2$, so $128 + 64 = (WZ)^2$, so $WZ = \sqrt{192}$ or 13.856... which rounds to 14.

Special Right Triangles, p. 40

1. AB = 8cm, BC = $8\sqrt{2}$ cm
2. DF = 4", DG = $4\sqrt{2}$ in.
3. $(.75)(\sqrt{2}) = 1.06$ ... which rounds to 1.1 cm.
4. QR = 13, QS = 13
5. $14\sqrt{2}$ "; The picture is 14" on each side (4 + 6 + 4) so the diagonals is $14\sqrt{2}$.

Special Right Triangles, p. 42

1. MN = 14', LN =$7\sqrt{3}$'
2. HG = 9.3 cm, GF = 16.0 cm
3. AJ = 20', JK = $20\sqrt{3}$′
4. $5\sqrt{3}$'; Since the altitude bisects the base, the triangle is a 30°-60° right triangle with a hypotenuse of 10 and 5 for the small side.
5. Yes, the hypotenuse of 100′ is twice the small side of 50' and the medium side is $50\sqrt{3}$'.

Review – Chapter 4, p. 43

1. a. 10"; b. 2.6' (not a 3-4-5 right triangle since the hypotenuse is not 5); c. 17.0"; d. 1.4 units; e. 6.9"
2. a. $8\sqrt{2}$; b. 5 units; c. $\sqrt{5}$ units
3. a. x = 40' and $y = 20\sqrt{3}$; b. x = 50" and $y = 50\sqrt{3}$; c. x = 8 units and y = 4 units

Chapter 5: Uncovering All Polygons, p. 44

1. equilateral
2. square
3. Only when a rhombus is a square can it be considered "regular." A rhombus has congruent sides. A square is "regular" because it has congruent sides and congruent angles.

Polygon Angle Exploration, p. 45

Polygon	Drawing	Number of Sides	Sum of All Interior Angles (Regular or Irregular)	Each Interior Angle (Regular Only)
Triangle		3	180°	60°
Quadrilateral		4	360°	90°
Pentagon		5	540°	108°
Hexagon		6	720°	120°
Heptagon		7	900°	128.57°
Octagon		8	1,080°	135°
Nonagon		9	1,260°	140°
Decagon		10	1,440°	144°

Polygon Angle Exploration, pp. 46-47

1. $(n - 2)180°$, where n is the number of sides in the polygon.
2. 2,340°
3. It's approaching a circle.
4. a. 180°, a straight line
   b. 135°
   c. 45°
5. 360°; (45°)(8)
6. Answers will vary. For example, in a regular nonagon an interior angle is 140°, 180° – 140° = 40°, and (40°)(9) = 360°.
7. Divide 360° by 72° to get 5 sides.
8. They are the same.
9. 179,640°
10. 179.64°; Yes, it's approaching a straight line because a straight line is 180°!

Summary of Polygon Properties, p. 48

Answers will vary, but the measurement should be 1,440°.

Diagonal Exploration, p. 49

Hexagon 6 3 9

Diagonals Exploration, p. 50

Polygon	Vertices	Diagonals Drawn From First Vertex	Total Diagonals
	7	4	14
	8	5	20
	9	6	27
	10	7	35

Diagonal Exploration, p. 51

1.

Polygon of *n*-sides	Number of Vertices	Diagonals Drawn From the First Vertex	Total Diagonals Formula
n-gon	n	$n-3$	$\frac{n(n-3)}{2}$

2. 54; $\frac{(12)(9)}{2}$
3. 560; $\frac{(35)(35-3)}{2}$
4. 498,500; $\frac{1,000(1,000-3)}{2}$

5. a. It represents that you cannot draw a diagonal to two consecutive vertices or to itself, so that is why you subtract 3 vertices.
   b. You have to do the process "*n*" times, where n represents the number of vertices.
   c. Dividing by 2 represents that once you go from one vertex to a non-consecutive vertex, for example from A to B, you do not need to retrace from B to A.

The Handshake Problem, pp. 52-53

1.

Number of People	Number of Handshakes
1	0
2	1
3	3
4	6
5	10
6	15

2. $\frac{n(n-1)}{2}$
3. 4,950; $\frac{(100)(99)}{2}$
4. Same: Both formulas multiply by "*n*" and divide by 2. Different: The diagonals formula has "$n - 3$" and the handshake formula has "$n - 1$".
5. In the handshake problem, you can go from one vertex to either of the consecutive vertices, but not to itself (cannot shake hands with oneself), so that explains why it's "$n - 1$" and not "$n - 3$".

Chapter 6: The Quadrilateral Family, pp. 55-56

1. a. rhombus
   b. rectangle
2. a. F
   b. T
   c. F
   d. F
   e. T
   f. T
   g. T
   h. F
   i. T
   j. T
   k. T
3. a. A
   b. N
   c. A
   d. S
   e. A
   f. S
   g. A
   h. A
   i. S
   j. A

Venn Diagram Activity, p. 57

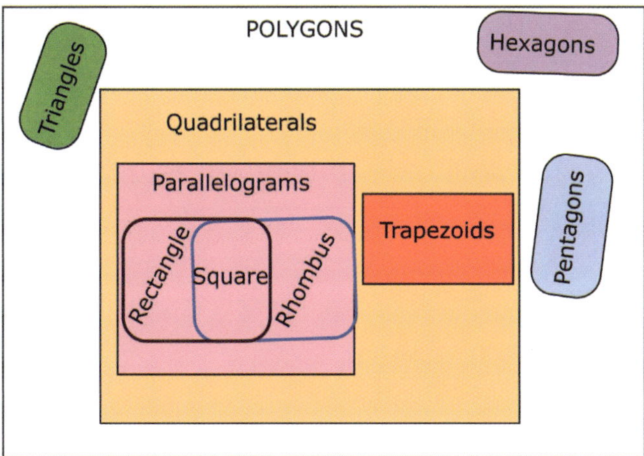

Parallelogram Discovery, pp. 58-59

1. The opposite angles are congruent. Exact measurements may vary.
2. The sum of the measures of the consecutive angles is 180°.
3. The opposite sides are congruent.
4. The diagonals bisect each other, so AF = CF and BF = DF.
5. The diagonals of a rectangle are congruent.
6. The diagonals of a rhombus are not always congruent. In a square (which is a rhombus) the diagonals are always congruent.
7. ∠APH and ∠APD are each 90°, so in a rhombus the diagonals are perpendicular. Yes, this would be true in a square because a square is a rhombus.

Working With Parallelograms, pp. 62-65

1. If a quadrilateral has opposite angles congruent then it is a parallelogram.
2. If a quadrilateral has diagonals that bisect each other, then the quadrilateral is a parallelogram.
3. Answers may vary. For example, since m∠DAB = 140° then m∠ABF = 140° since alternate interior angles are congruent when lines are parallel. Then m∠ABC = 40° since it's supplementary with ∠ABF which makes ∠DAB and ∠ABC also supplementary.
4. a. m∠*y* = 130°. In a parallelogram opposite angles are congruent.
   b. m∠*z* = 50°. It's supplementary with 130° and also with ∠*y*.
   c. m∠*x*= 50°. It's congruent to ∠*z* and supplementary with ∠*y* and with 130°
5. The first letter can start in any vertex but it has to go clockwise or counterclockwise around the outside of the shape. BE = 10 units. Diagonals of a rectangle are congruent.
6. a. m∠BWA = 90° because in a rhombus diagonals are perpendicular.
   b. If m∠BAW = 20°, then m∠ABW = 70°. Since m∠BWA = 90° and m∠BAW = 20°, then m∠ABW = 70° since the sum of the measures of all the angles in a triangle is 180°.

7. a. AU = 20"
   b. LU = 15"
   c. PQ = 12.5"
   d. QU = 12.5"
   e. A rectangle $15^2 + 20^2 = 25^2$
8. NK = 8, since BK = 6 (half of BM),(Pythagorean triple 6, 8, 10)
9. a. 145°
   b. 35°
   c. 35°
   d. 145°
10. a. T
    b. F
    c. F
    d. T
    e. F
    f. F; a regular hexagon has congruent opposite sides.
    g. T
    h. T
    i. T
    j. T
    k. T
    l. T
    m. T

Experimenting With Parallelograms, pp. 66-68

1. The center of gravity is the point where both diagonals intersect.
2. Sue is correct. The figure formed is always a parallelogram and not always a rhombus.
3. Hasani is correct. The parallel lines makes it possible for the sum of consecutive angles to equal 180°.
4. In each parallelogram the diagonal creates two congruent triangles.

A Look at Trapezoids, pp. 70-72

1. No, it's not possible since two sides must be parallel. The opposite side from the right angle must also be 90°. Alternate interior angles and corresponding angles are congruent when lines are parallel.
2. a. Two pairs of consecutive angles are congruent, but each set has different measures.
   b. Diagonals are congruent.
   c. One set of triangles created by the diagonals are congruent. (The other pair of triangles are *similar).*
3. No, if the bases (the parallel sides) are congruent then the quadrilateral is a parallelogram and not a trapezoid.

A Look at Trapezoids, pp. 73-74

1. 45°
2. ABCD is an isosceles trapezoid since it has congruent diagonals.
3. a. Trapezoid DEFG is isosceles since its base angles are congruent.
   b. m∠D = 130°, m∠E = 130°
4. a. 6"
   b. 12"
   c. 20"; $\frac{8 + 32}{2}$
5. 10 units; (4 + MA) ÷ 2 = 7, 4 + MA = 14, so MA = 10
6. 11 cm; Both diagonals are congruent (RY = 4 and RY + YT = 15)
7. 3′

Kite! Kite! p. 75

1. Diagonals are perpendicular and the large diagonal bisects the small diagonal.
2. The short diagonal in Kite 1 creates two isosceles triangles. The long diagonal in Kite 2 creates two scalene triangles.

Critical Thinking About Quadrilaterials, p. 76

1. F
2. T (remember a square is a rhombus)
3. F (the rectangle and the square have congruent diagonals)
4. T
5. T
6. T
7. F (the longer diagonal bisects the shorter diagonal)
8. T
9. F
10. F
11. T
12. F

Median Investigation, p. 77

Yes, it holds true. If you consider two of the parallel sides as the bases ($\overline{AR}$ and $\overline{CQ}$ for example), then XY = $\left(\frac{40 + 40}{2}\right)$ = 40.

Using Algebra to Solve Quadrilateral Problems, pp. 78-79

1. Equation: 5x + 10 = 3*x* + 18; *x* = 4; AC = 30. Property: In a rectangle the diagonals are congruent.
2. Equation: 2*x* + 3*x* + 120 = 180; *x* = 12; m∠T = 24° (same as m∠M). Property: In a parallelogram the consecutive angles are supplementary.
3. Equation: 5*x* + 20 = 90; *x* = 14. Property: In a rhombus the diagonals are perpendicular.
4. Equation: 10*y* + 30 = 2*y* + 70; JG = 80 units (since *y* = 5) Property: In an isosceles trapezoid the diagonals are congruent.
5. Equation: 2*x* + 25 = *x* + 95; TR = 330 units (since *x* = 70). Property: In a parallelogram the diagonals bisect each other.

6. Equation: $x + (x - 10) + 2(5x - 55) = 360$; $x = 40$, m∠A = 40°, m∠Y = 30°, m∠R = 145° and m∠L = 145°. Properties: In a kite, one pair of opposite angles are congruent. In a kite (and in all quadrilaterals) the sum of the angle measures 360°.

Quadrilateral Matching, p. 80

1. a, b, c, d, g, h
2. b, c, d, e, f, h
3. b, c, d, h ("f" only when it's a rhombus, "g" when it's a rectangle)
4. e, h
5. h ("a" is true only when it's isosceles)
6. a, h
7. a, b, c, d, e, f, g, h

Cumulative Review – Chapters 5-6, pp. 81-82

1. Use the formula $(n-2) \cdot 180°$ divided by n where n is the number of sides. So the answer is $6 \cdot 180/8$ or 135°.
2. Use the formula $n(n-3)$ divided by 2, so the answer is $9 \cdot 6 \div 2$ or 27 diagonals.
3. Nonagon. The sum of all the exterior angles in any polygon is 360°, so $360 \div 40 = 9$.
4. Answers a, c, e, f, and g should be checked. For b and d there could be a right trapezoid (trapezoid with two right angles).
5. You should have drawn a rectangle, a square, and an isosceles trapezoid.
6. You should have drawn a square, a rhombus, and a kite.
7. a. $x = 50°$, $y = 130°$; b. $x = 30°$; c. $x = 90°$, $y = 75°$
8. a. $x = 8$, $\overline{\mathbf{AB}} = 30$ units; b. $x = 5$, $\overline{\mathbf{AB}} = 10$ units;
   c. $x = 22$, $\overline{\mathbf{AB}} = 126$ units

Chapter 7: Metric Geometry, p. 84

Answers will vary. Student should see that the circumference divided by the diameter is a little over 3.

Perimeter and Circumference, p. 85

1. 70"
2. 49 meters
3. The perimeter of the square is larger since the perimeter of the square is 16" and the circumference is 15.7".
4. 3 cm; $\frac{8.84}{3.14} = 6$. Since the diameter is 6 cm then the radius is half.
5. 35"; A nonagon is a 9-sided polygon, so divide 315/9.

Archimedes' Idea for Approximating Pi, pp. 86-87

1. The word "inscribed" means that the shape is inside the circle so that each of its vertices touches the circle at one point.
2. The word "circumscribed" means that the outside shape surrounds the circle in such a way that the circle touches each side of the shape at one point.
3. The circumference of the circle must be between those two perimeters.
4. The more sides the closer the perimeter approaches the circumference of the circle.
5. No, as the inscribed polygon gets closer to the circumscribed polygon we get a closer approximation of π .

Area of Parallelograms, pp. 88-89

1. $60\frac{3}{8}$ sq in. or 60.375 sq in.
2. 625 sq ft
3. 60 sq mi
4. 10,000 sq in. ($400 \div 4 = 100$; $100^2 = 10{,}000$)
5. The width = 4'; the perimeter = 38' (15 + 15 + 4 + 4)
6. 88 sq in. (168 − 80)
7. Because the height of the parallelogram is 6' (Pythagorean triple, 6-8-10), so both the parallelogram and the rectangle have the same base and height. The area for each is 42 sq ft.

Parallelogram Area Activity, p. 90

The parallelogram is congruent to the rectangle which is why the area formula is the same for both shapes.

Area of Triangles and Trapezoids, pp. 92-93

1. No, if you rotate an equilateral triangle the base and height remain the same.
2. Yes, if you draw an obtuse isosceles triangle as shown, one altitude will be outside the triangle.

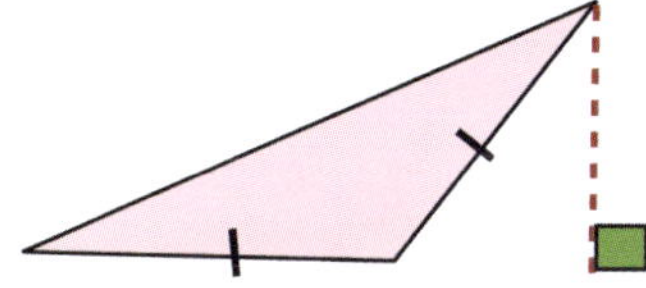

3. Both have the same area since both have the same base and height.
4. 3"; $(20)(x) \div 2 = 30$; $20x = 60$ so the altitude is 3".
5. 50 sq cm (Subtract the area of the triangle which is 25 from the area of the rectangle which is 75).
6.

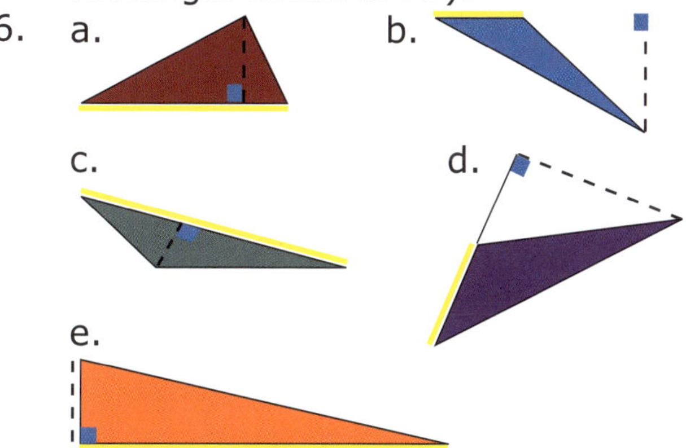

Discovering the Area of a Trapezoid, p. 94

Formula: $A = \frac{1}{2}h(b_1 + b_2)$

Area of a Trapezoid, pp. 95-96

1. Perimeter: 115 cm; Area: 750 sq cm
2. 4" ($30 = \frac{1}{2}h(10 + 5)$)
3. 3'; ($45 = \frac{1}{2}(6)(b + 12)$)
4. Break the trapezoid into a rectangle of area 40 sq in. (8 by 5) and a triangle of area 15 sq in. (base 6 by height 5). Add 40 + 15 to get a trapezoid area of 55 sq in. Notice that you get the same result if you use the area of a trapezoid formula: $A = \frac{1}{2}(5)(14 + 8)$.
5. 50 sq units (the height of the trapezoid is 4 not 5)
6. Perimeter: 34.7 cm; Area: 51.5 sq cm
7. Each missing side is 13 meters since it's isosceles $(76 - (20 + 30)) \div 2$; The height is 12 meters (the triangle containing the height is a 5-12-13; Pythagorean triple) Area: 300 sq m

Area of Circles, pp. 97-99

1. $C = 6\pi$ meters; $A = 9\pi$ square meters
2. r = 7", d = 14"
3. 16π sq ft.; ($\frac{1}{4}(8)^2 \pi$)
4. Area: 127.17 sq cm; ($\frac{1}{2}(9^2)(3.14)$) Perimeter: 46.26 cm (half of circumference + diameter) or ($\frac{1}{2}(18)(3.14) + 18$)
5. Yes, the base is 8" which is the diameter of the circle and the height is 4" which is the radius of the circle, so the area is $\frac{1}{2}(4)(8)$ which is 16 sq in.
6. 19 sq yds; $(2.5)^2(3.14) - (.5)^2(3.14) = 18.84$
7. The circle is larger by .31 sq cm. The circle is 12.56 sq cm; $(2^2)(3.14)$ The square is 12.25 sq cm; $(3.5)^2$
8. 18π sq units; The larger circle is 36π and the 2 small circles both total 18π (each circle is 9π) $36\pi - 18\pi = 18\pi$.
9. 128π sq ft; (each circle has an area of 64π)

The Arbeles Problem, p. 100

1. 4 units
2. 8π sq units; The area of large semicircle is $\frac{36\pi}{2}$. The area of the pink semicircle is $\frac{16\pi}{2}$ and the area of the blue circle is $\frac{4\pi}{2}$, so $18\pi - (8\pi + 2\pi) =$ 8π sq units.

Chapter 8: Geometric Constructions, p. 101-107

Student is following directions to several constructions. There are no answers that can be checked. Student will self-check based on the results.

Finding the Median in a Triangle, pp. 108-109

1. Constructing a perpendicular bisector will give you the midpoints of the triangle.
2. Three medians that all intersect at a point of concurrency called the "centroid."
3. 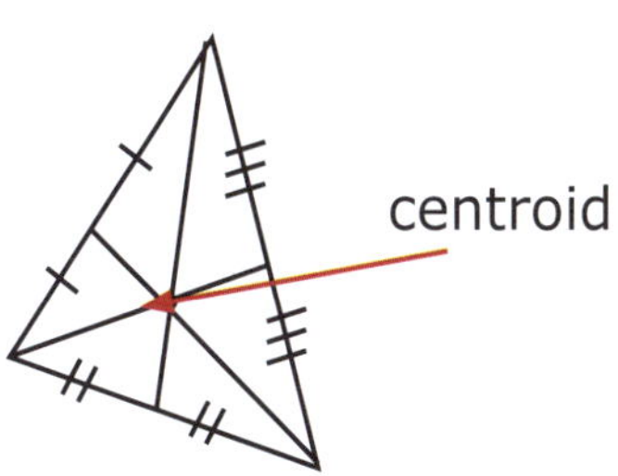

4. Student construction
5. The centroid is $\frac{2}{3}$ of the way along the median from each vertex of each angle in the triangle.

Geometric Construction Review, p. 111

1. Infinite number of lines can be parallel to another line.
2. Through one point only one line can be parallel to another line.
3. Those two congruent angles constructed are corresponding angles. If corresponding angles are congruent then the lines are parallel.
4. A protractor, like a ruler, would not give accurate measurements.
5. Only one. In three dimensions more than one line can be perpendicular to a line through the same point.

Problem Solving With Geometric Constructions, pp. 112-121

1. Construct a perpendicular bisector.

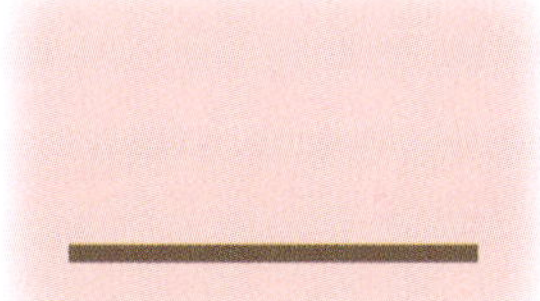

2. Bisect the angle.

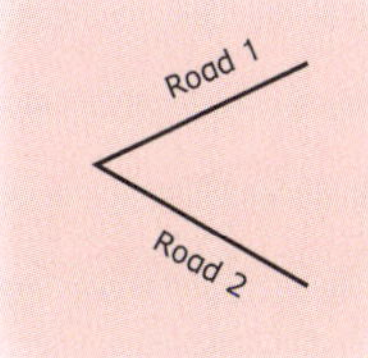

4. a. Six equilateral triangles.
   b. Bisect one of the angles in any of the equilateral triangles since each equilateral triangle has 3-60° angles.
   c. To construct a 15° angle you need to bisect the 30° angle.
   d. Answers may vary. One way is to construct a regular hexagon and copy two of the 60° angles. Another way is to construct a perpendicular and copy next to it a 30° angle.

5. Construct the perpendicular bisectors to each side of the triangle. The *circumcenter,* the point of concurrency (where they intersect). is the place where Mr. Baker should build his house. The circumcenter allows you to draw a circle with all three towns in the circle, thus making each town the same distance from Mr. Baker's house.

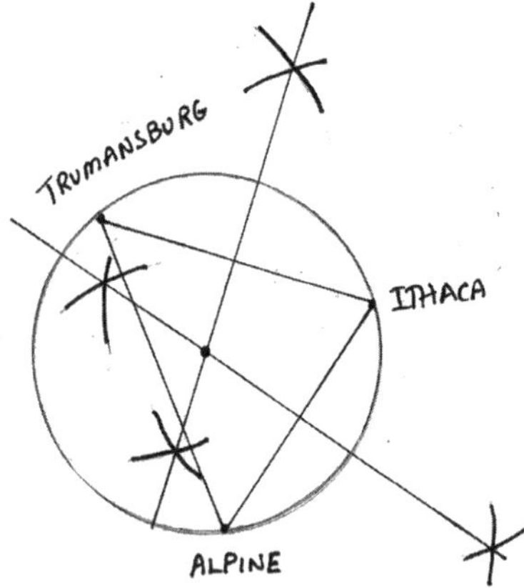

6. To find the *incenter*, find the point of concurrency where all the angle bisectors intersect. This point is equidistant from each side or road.

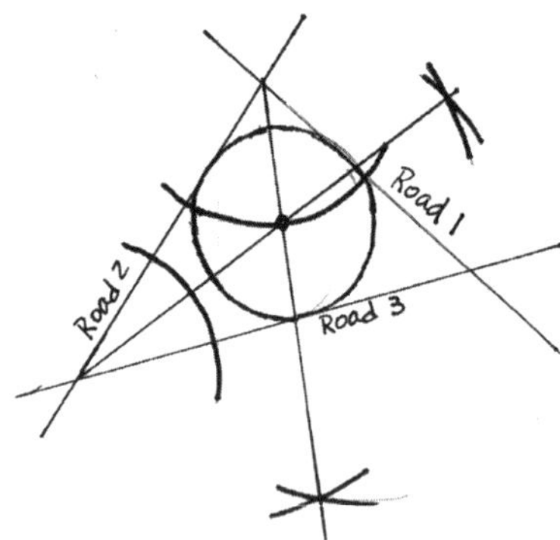

7. Measure AB with your compass and keep marking that length as many times as you are asked. You cannot use a straightedge, so you will only have the length from one point to the other.

8. The perpendicular bisectors to those chords are the perpendicular bisectors of isosceles triangles that you can draw using the chord and the two radii that go from the center of the circle to the endpoints of the chord. All radii meet in the center of the circle.

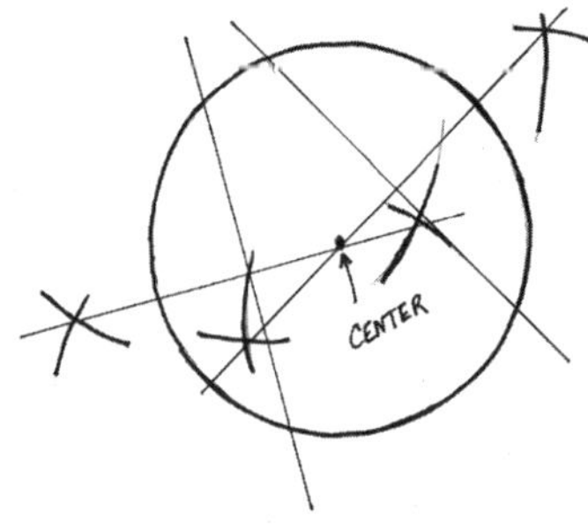

9. b. The orthocenter is outside the triangle in the obtuse triangle shown.
10. a. A right triangle.
    b. A right triangle.
    c. A triangle inscribed in a semicircle is always a right triangle.
11. You can construct a square inscribed in a circle and then bisect all four sides. Where the bisectors intersect the circle are new vertices that you can join with the existing vertices to construct an octagon.
12. a. 108°. The formula is ((*n* – 2)180°) ÷ 5 where *n* = 5)
    b. Bisect each side and where the bisectors intersect the circle are new vertices that can be joined with the existing vertices to construct a decagon.

Impossible Constructions?, pp. 122-132

1. The center angle will not be congruent to the two outside angles.
2. Draw a perpendicular bisector to create a right angle, then using your compass from the vertex of the 90° angle, draw an arc. Without closing or opening your compass, go to one side where the arc intersects the side of your 90° angle and make a marking on that arc to mark the same length. You have now created an equilateral triangle inside your right angle. Inside your right angle is a 60° angle, bisect it. You have now trisected the 90° angle since the remaining angle outside of the equilateral triangle and inside the right angle is 30°.

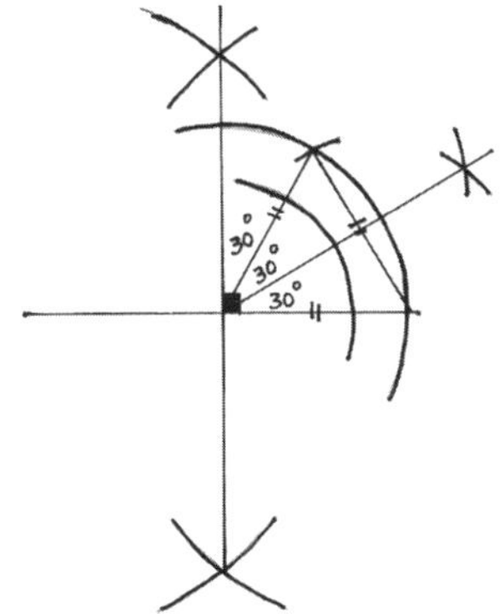

Chapter 9: The Geometry of Three Dimensional Shapes, p. 124
3D Shapes - Prisms, pp. 125-126

1. 6 cm
2. It looks like 512 to the 13th power! Correct way: 512 cubic ft or 513 ft^3
3. 1,008 cu cm $\left[\frac{4(6 + 12)}{2}\right](2)(14)$
4. 250 cu m; (50)(5)
5. 5,700 cu ft; Rectangular prism: 3,000 + Triangular prism: 2,700.
   [Triangular prism is 2,700 = $\frac{(18)(12)}{2}(25)$]
6. 19 cu in. Outside cube: 27 – inside cube: 8
7. Both have a volume of 200 cu in.

The Volume of Cylinders, pp. 127-128

1. 100π cu cm; The diameter is 10 cm so the radius is 5 cm. $(5^2)(4)\pi$
2. 3"
3. They have the same volume. $(2^2)12\pi = 4^2(3)\pi$
4. 942 cu in. $9\pi\ (60) - 4\pi\ (60)$
5. The student did not square the radius. The correct answer is $V = 16\pi\ (6) = 96\pi$ cu in.

Volumes of Pyramids and Cones, p. 130

1. It's three times greater.
2. pentagonal pyramid; 150 cu in.; $\frac{1}{3}(18)(25)$
3. 2π cu in.

Turn Up the Volume, pp. 131-132

1. Answers will vary. Possible answer: 10 by 5 by 2.
2. 40 cans; 808.3 cu in. Volume of the box: (16)(13(10) = 2,080 cu in.; Volume of each can $(1.5)^2\ (3.14)(4.5) = 31.7925$ cu in.; (40)(31.7925) = 1,271.7 cu in; Then 2,080 - 1,271.7 cu in. = 808.3 cu in.
3. 8 cm; $\frac{1}{3}(12)(H) = 32$
4. 43.96 in.; $\frac{1,846.32}{12} = 153.86$;

   $\frac{153.86}{14} = 49$, so the radius is 7 and the diameter is 14.
5. Maria is right. For example, if you let the smaller cube have a side of 6, then if the cube is increased by 20%, the new cube has a side of 7.2. The volume of the smaller cube is 216 cubic units and the volume of the bigger cube is $(7.2)^3$ or 373.248 cubic units. To find the percent of increase: $\frac{(373.248-216)}{216} = .728$ or 72.8%.
6. The cone is larger in volume. The cone has a volume of 1,339.733 cu in. The volume of the rectangular prism is 1,000 cu in.

Volume of a Sphere, p. 133

1. a. 11,488 cu cm; $\frac{4}{3}(3.14)(14)^3$

   b. 195 cu cm; $\frac{4}{3}(3.14)(3.6)^3$
2. 3′; $36\pi = \frac{4}{3}\pi\ r^3$, so $\frac{3(36)}{4} = r^3$, $27 = r^3$. The cube root of 27 is 3.

Volume of a Sphere, p. 134

1. 6"
2. 12"
3. 288π cubic units; $\frac{4}{3}(6)^3\pi$
4. 432π cubic units; $6^2\ (12)\pi$
5. Yes, it's true! $\frac{2}{3}$ of $432\pi = 288\pi$.

Surface Area of Prisms, p. 135

1. 226 sq cm; 2(5)(18) + 2(18)(1) + 2(5)(1) = 226
2. 96 sq ft; 24 +24 + 20 + 12 + 16 = 96.
3. 24 sq in.
4. The missing side is 2'; SA = 112 sq ft 2(30) + 2(6) + 2(20)= 112
   LA (Lateral Area) = 52 sq ft 112 – 30 – 30 = 52

Surface Area of a Cylinder Activity, p. 136

1. The surface area is $2\pi r^2 + 2\pi rh$
2. $2\pi (9) + 2\pi (3)(4.5) = 18\pi + 27\pi = 45\pi$ sq in.

Finding Surface Area, p. 137

1. f (2)(1) + (2)(3) + (2)(3) = 14
2. b (2)(6) + 2(10) + (2)(15) = 62
3. a (2)(3.14)(25) + (2)(3.14)(5)(4) = 282.6
4. e (2)(3.14)(9) + (6)(3.14)(9) = 226.08
5. d (2)(1)(1) + (2)(1)(2) + (2)(1)(2) + (2)(2)(3) + (2)(1)(3) + (2)(1) = 30
6. c (16 + (4)(18) = 88

Euler's Formula, p. 138

Euler's formula : F + V – E = 2

	Faces	Vertices	Edges
	6	8	12
	7	10	15
	8	12	18
	14	24	36

1. 6, 8, 12; (6 + 8 – 12 = 2)
2. 7, 10, 15 (7 + 10 – 15 = 2)
3. 8, 12, 18 (8 + 12 – 18= 2)
4. 14, 24, 36 (14 + 24 – 36 = 2)

Cumulative Review – Chapters 7-9, pp. 139-140

1. 44 inches
2. 800 sq ft
3. 25 units
4. 24 units
5. Here's one example: A triangle can have a base of 10 and a height of 2 with an area of 10 square units and another triangle can have a base of 5 with a height of 4 with an area of 10 square units and these triangles are not congruent.
6. 5 feet

7. see p. 102. Example:

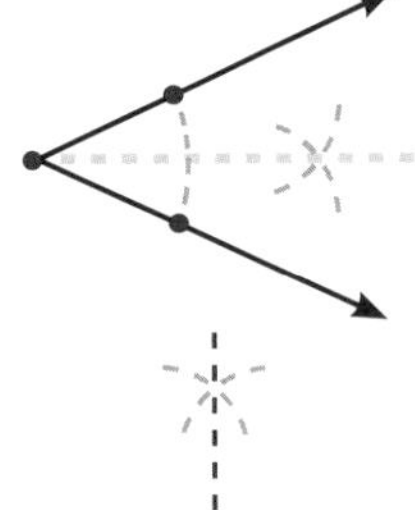

8. see p. 105. Example:

9. Follow the steps for p. 113, and then find the equilateral triangle.
10. a. 4 units; b. 5 units
11. 66 cubic units
12. The difference is 10.8 units. The trapezoidal prism has a volume of 576 cubic units and the cylinder has a volume of 565.2 cubic units.
13. The sphere is larger. The sphere has a volume of 113.04 cubic units and the cone has a volume of 84.78 cubic units.
14. Volume: 108 cubic units; Surface Area: 180 sq units

Chapter 10: Symmetry and Transformations, p. 141
What is Vertical, Horizontal, and Point Symmetry? pp. 141-143

1. The letter "O" has infinite lines of symmetry. The letter O also has point symmetry.
2. N, I, H, O, Z, X
3. It has point symmetry because every point is the same distance from a central point as another point in the opposite direction. Notice also that when you turn the card upside down it looks the same.
4. a. Isosceles triangle – vertical symmetry
   b. Regular hexagon – horizontal and vertical symmetry. It also has diagonal symmetry, and point symmetry
   c. rhombus – point symmetry
5. Yes, it is true. The equilateral triangle has 3 lines of symmetry. The square has 4 lines of symmetry, etc.
6. No, the star does not look the same upside down.
7. The snowflake is hexagonal. It has 6 lines of symmetry and it has point symmetry.

Transformations - Reflections, pp. 144-146

1. The *y* value changed. Reflecting about the *x*-axis keeps the *x* value and changes the *y* value.
2. C′ (0, 2); D′ (-1, 4); E′ (-5, 4); F′ (-4,2) The *y* value remained the same. The *x* value changed.
3. A′ (-5, -4); A″ (-5, 4). When A (5, -4) is reflected across the *y*-axis the *y* is fixed and the *x* changes sign. So the image A′ becomes (-5, -4) Then reflecting it across the *x*-axis results in *x* being fixed and the *y* changes, so A″ is (-5, 4). Fixed means it stays the same.
4. A′ (-4, 1); B′ (0, 4) and C′ (-2, 6).
5. The *x* becomes the *y* value and the *y* becomes the *x* value.

Transformations - Reflections, pp. 147-149

1. (*a*, *b*) becomes (−*a*, −*b*) W= (1,3), W′ = (-1, -3); Z= (4, 6); Z′ = (-4, -6); R = (5, 2), R′ = (-5, -2)
2. P′ (3, -5)
3. (*a*,*b*) becomes (*a*, -*b*) across *x*-axis, then (-*a*, -*b*) across *y*-axis. If you take (*a*,*b*) and reflected in the *x*-axis, you get (*a*, -*b*). Then if you reflect (*a*, -*b*) in the *y*-axis, you get (-*a*, -*b*) which is the same as a reflection in the origin.
4. a. Trapezoid; It has 4 sides and only two sides are parallel. It can also be called a right trapezoid because it has a right angle at vertex A.
   b. II to IV
   c. M′ (5, −4), A′ (5, −7), T′ (1, −7), H' (1, −1)

Transformations - Translations, pp. 150-153

1. A (−5, 3); A′(0, 0) B (−3, 6); B′ (2, 3)
2. Yes, because each vertex moved the same distance so congruency is preserved. The image is identical to the pre-image.
3. b. A → W
   c. T → L
   d. H → N
   e. G → D
   f. E → R
   g. O → C
4. (*x*,*y*) becomes (*x* + 0, *y* − 10) or (*x*, *y* − 10)
5. Yes, both images are the same. $T_{9,-2}$ (1, 5) = (10, 3); $T_{1,5}$ (9, −2) = (10, 3) The end result is the same.
6. a. isosceles; It has two congruent sides.
   b. III
   c. F′ (3, −6); G′ (4, 0); H′ (5, −6)
   d. F″ (3, 6); G″ (4, 0); H″ (5, 6)
7. The original point P is (-2, 4); -2 + 3 = 1 and 4 + -5 = -1; You can do the inverse operations. Take P′ (1, -1) and instead of adding 3, subtract 3 (1 − 3 = -2) and instead of subtracting 5, add 5 (-1 + 5 = 4)
8. a. The figure is an isosceles right triangle. It has two congruent sides and a right angle.
   b. $T_{0,3}$

Transformations - Rotations, p. 155-157

1. A′ (–2, 0) A″ (0, –2); A‴ (2, 0)
   B′ (–2, 4); B″ (–4, –2); B‴ (2, –4)
   C′ (0, 4); C″ (–4, 0); C‴ (0, –4)
   D′ (0, 0); D″ (0, 0); D‴(0, 0)
2. A reflection in the origin gives the same image as $R_{180°}$. So (*a*, *b*) results in the image (-*a*, -*b*).

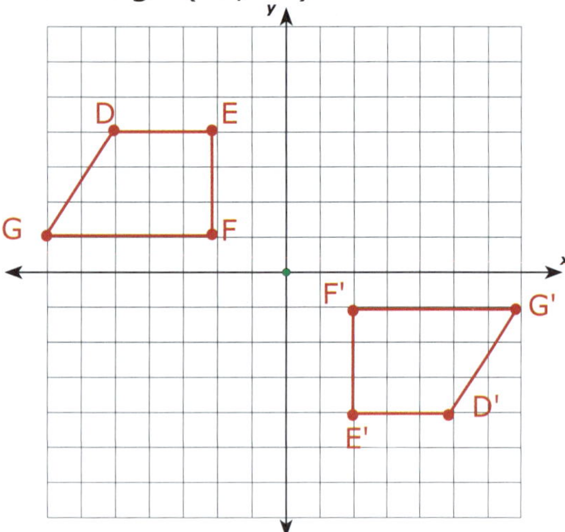

3. a. Right trapezoid.
   b. The new coordinates are D′ (5, -4); E′ (2, -4); F′ (2, -1); and G′ (7, -1).
   c. (*a*, *b*) results in (-*a*, -*b*)
4. $R_{90°}$ = (-5, -2); $R_{180°}$ = (2, -5); $R_{270°}$ = (5, 2)
5. Student should see figure ending in quadrant IV.
6. In $R_{360°}$ the image would fall in the same location as the preimage.
7. Answers may vary. A rotation is one answer. The triangles without color were reflected.

Transformations - Rotations, pp. 158-160

1. 360/5 = 72°
2. 360/4 = 90°
3. 360/6 = 60°
4. 360/10 = 36°
5. a. 5
   b. 2
   c. 8
   d. 3
   e. 2
6. Any figure with point symmetry has rotational symmetry of order 2.
7. Answers may vary. The one given has symmetry order 5.

Transformations - Dilations, pp. 161-163

1. A′ (−1/2, −1/2); B′ (1/2, 1); C′ (3/2, −1)
2. You need to multiply each ordered pair by 3 which is the multiplicative inverse of 1/3. D (-3, -3); E (0, 3); F (6, -3); G (3, -6)
3. 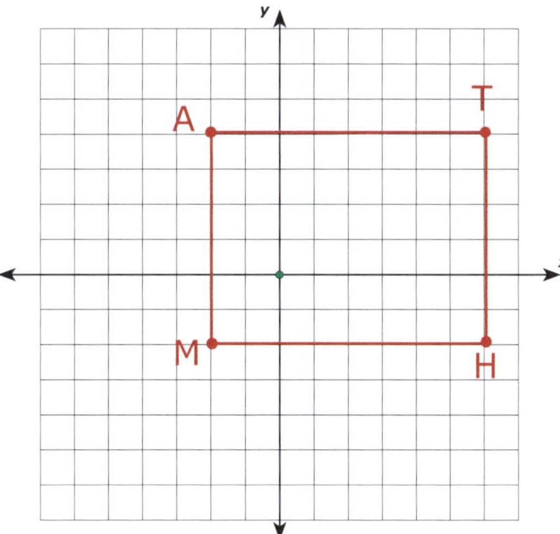

   a. P = 6 + 6 + 8 + 8 = 28 units
   b. M′ (-1, -1); A′ (-1, 2); T′ (3, 2); H′ (3, -1)
   c. 3 + 3 + 4 + 4 = 14 units
   d. $\frac{1}{2}$ The perimeter of the image is half that of the preimage. It's the same as the dilation factor.
   e. 12/48 = $\frac{1}{4}$
   f. The ratio of the areas is the square of the ratio of the perimeter. $\frac{1}{4} = (1/2)^2$
4. 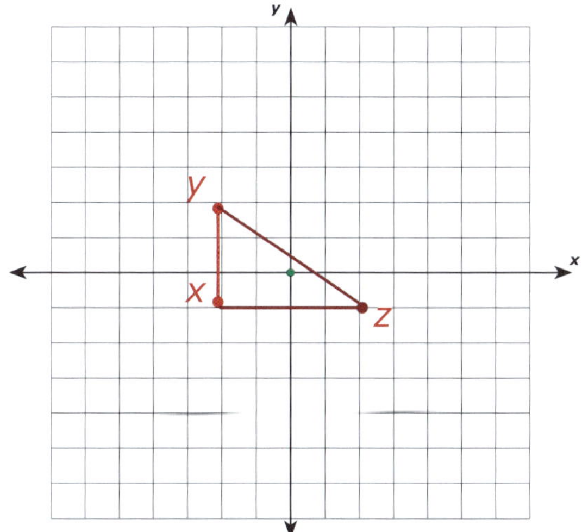

   a. Triangle XYZ is a right triangle.
   b. X′ (−4, −2); Y′ (−4, 4); Z′ (4, −2)
   c. The ratio of the perimeter of the image X′Y′Z′ to the perimeter of the preimage XYZ is 2:1. The perimeter of triangle X′Y′Z′ is 6 + 8 + 10 = 24. The perimeter of triangle XYZ is 3 + 4 + 5 = 12.
   d. The ratio of the area of X′Y′Z′ to the area of XYZ is 4:1. Area of triangle X′Y′Z′ is $\frac{1}{2}(6)(8) = 24$. Area of triangle XYZ is $\frac{1}{2}(3)(4) = 6$.
   e. The ratio of the perimeters equals the scale factor. The ratio of the areas equals the square of the scale factor.

Glide Reflections and Compositions, pp. 165-166

1. No, it's not a glide reflection because no reflection took place.
2. No, two reflections took place.
3.

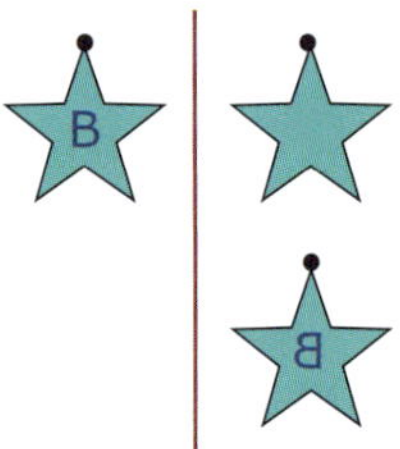

The final image should show a star that looks like the original but with a backwards B inside.

4.

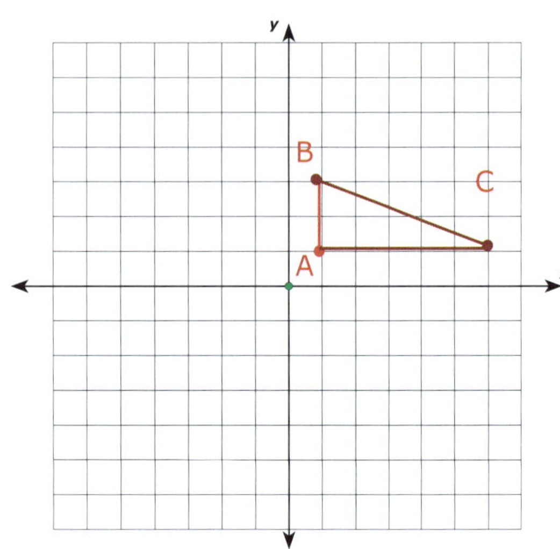

A′B′C′ is at A′ (1, -1); B′ (1, -3); C′ (6, -1) A″B″C″ is at A″ (-7, -1); B″ (-7, -3), C″ (-2, -1)

a. It's a reflection followed by a translation.
b. Yes, the end result is the same. Glide reflections are commutative.

Glide Reflections and Compositions, pp. 168-170

1. $T_{2,-3} \circ D_3(x, y)$
2. $T_{-2,0} \circ r_{y\text{-axis}}(a, b)$
3. P′ (-1, -5); P″ (1, -2), P‴ (-1, -2)
4. The correct choice is "c." The notation must have D_4 on the right and $T_{0,3}$ on the left. For example, if (x, y) was (6, 5) then a dilation of 4 would result in (24, 20) and then a translation of 3 units up would result in (24, 23) so $(4x, 4y + 3)$ is the correct choice.
5. A (3, 2); B (1, 3); C (1, 5); D (3, 6); $T_{-3,1}$ results in A′ (0, 3); B′ (-2, 4); C′ (-2, 6); D′ (0, 7) $R_{90°}$ results A″ (-3, 0); B″ (-4, -2); C″ (-6, -2); D″ (-7, 0)
6. There are several two step compositions that could result in A″B″C″. $r_{y\text{-axis}} \circ R_{90°}$ is one correct answer.
7. $r_{x\text{-axis}}$ first followed by $R_{90°}$ is another answer.
8. Yes, $r_{y=x}$ would result in triangle ABC becoming triangle A″B″C″ in one step.

Tesselations, p. 171

1. No, a regular pentagon does not tessellate.
2. A square.
3. Answers will vary.

Review – Chapter 10, pp. 174-175

1. H and S
2. a. A′ = (-2, -4), B′ = (1, -4), C′ = (1, -2), D′ = (-2, -2)
   b. A′ = (2, -4), B′ = (-1, -4), C′ = (-1, -2), D′ = (2, -2)
   c. A′ = (-4, 8), B′ = (2, 8), C′ = (2, 4), D′ = (-4, 4)
   d. A′ = (1, 3), B′ = (4, 3), C′ = (4, 1), D′ = (1, 1)
3. (7, 1); Rotating (-3, 5) 90° gives you the point (-5, -3). Then translating $(x-2, y+4)$ gives you the point (-7, 1) and then reflecting this point about the y-axis gives you the final answer of (7, 1).

Chapter 11: Proving Triangles Congruent, p. 176
Introduction to Proofs - Congruency, p. 177

1. c. $\angle W \cong \angle Q$; d. $\angle R \cong \angle J$; e. $\overline{WJ} \cong \overline{QR}$; f. $\overline{FR} \cong \overline{GJ}$
2. 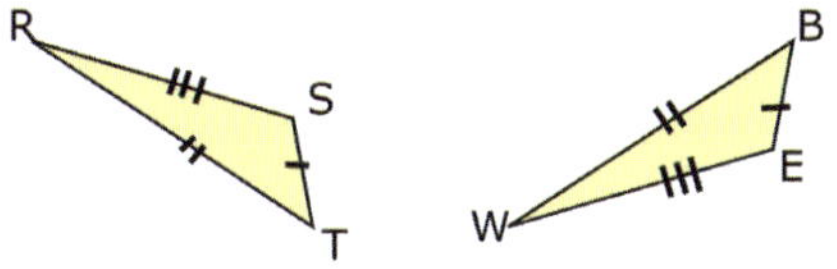 R S T B E W
3. $\Delta DMS \cong \Delta ABT$, $\angle M \cong \angle B$; $\angle D \cong \angle A$; $\angle S \cong \angle T$; $\overline{DM} \cong \overline{AB}$, $\overline{MS} \cong \overline{BT}$; $\overline{DS} \cong \overline{AT}$

SSS Activity, p. 178

1. Yes, if three sides of one triangle are congruent to three sides of another triangle then the triangles are congruent.
2. Yes, if three sides of one triangle are congruent to three sides of another triangle, then the triangles are congruent.

SAS Activity, p. 179

1. If two sides and the included angle of one triangle are congruent to two sides and the included angle of another triangle then the triangles are congruent.
2. Yes, the triangles are congruent.

ASA and AAS Activities, p. 180

Yes, because if two angles of one triangle are congruent to two angles of another triangle then the third angles must be congruent.

SSA Activity, p. 181

The figures are dilated so even though the angles remain congruent the figures are not congruent (they are in proportion).

The Essence of a Good Geometric Proof, pp. 182-183

	Description	Drawing
1	Vertical angles are congruent (≅).	3, 1, 2, 4
2	If lines are parallel (ll), then alternate interior angles are congruent (≅). Converse: If alternate interior angles are congruent (≅), then lines are parallel (ll).	2, 1
3	If lines are parallel (ll), then corresponding angles are congruent (≅). Converse: If corresponding angles are congruent (≅), then lines are parallel (ll).	1, 2
4	If two sides of a triangle are congruent (≅), then the angles opposite those sides are congruent (≅). Converse: If two angles of a triangle are congruent (≅), then the sides opposite those angles are congruent (≅).	1, 2
5	If two lines are perpendicular (⊥), then they intersect to form right angles	

Picture, Statement, and Reason, pp. 185-186

	Statement	Reason
1	a. $\overline{TV} \cong \overline{TV} \cong \overline{CB}$ b. $\angle A \cong \angle C$	a. Given (The fact is stated in the picture or in the information.) b. Angles opposite congruent sides are congruent.
2	a. $\overline{TV} \cong \overline{TV}$	a. Reflexive property
3	a. $\angle 1 \cong \angle 2$	a. Vertical angles are congruent.
4	a. $\angle GFA \cong \angle CEA$ b. $\overline{CE} \parallel \overline{GF}$	a. Given b. If alternate interior angles are congruent then the lines are parallel.
5	a. $\overline{BQ} \perp \overline{AC}$ b. $\angle BQA$ and $\angle BQC$ are right angles c. $\angle BQA \cong \angle BQC$	a. Given b. Perpendicular lines make right angles. c. All right angles are congruent to each other.
6	a. $\angle 1 \cong \angle 2$ b. $\angle 3 \cong \angle 4$ c. $\overline{DE} \cong \overline{FE}$ d. $\angle 1 \cong \angle 2$	a. Given b. Supplements of congruent angles are congruent. c. Sides opposite congruent angles are congruent. d. Definition of an isosceles triangle.

Finding Congruent Triangles, p. 187

1. Yes, SSS
2. Yes, SAS
3. No, SS
4. Yes, AAS
5. Yes, ASA
6. No, SSA
7. Yes, SAS
8. No, S
9. No, AAA

Two Column Proofs, pp. 188-191

Proof #	Statement	Reason
Proof 1	1. $\overline{ER} \cong \overline{ET}$ 2. $\overline{RF} \cong \overline{TF}$ 3. $\overline{EF} \cong \overline{EF}$ 4. $\triangle ERF \cong \triangle ETF$	1. Given 2. Given 3. Reflexive Property 4. SSS
Proof 2	1. $\overline{BA} \cong \overline{DA}$ 2. $\overline{CA} \cong \overline{EA}$ 3. $\angle CAB \cong \angle EAD$ 4. $\triangle CAB \cong \triangle EAD$ 5. $\angle E \cong \angle C$	1. Given 2. Given 3. Vertical angles are congruent 4. SAS 5. cpctc (corresponding parts of congruent triangles are congruent.)
Proof 3	1. $\overline{RC} \perp \overline{AB}$ 2. $\overline{AC} \cong \overline{BC}$ 3. $\angle ACR$ and $\angle BCR$ are right angles 4. $\angle ACR \cong \angle RCB$ 5. $\overline{RC} \cong \overline{RC}$ 6. $\triangle ACR \cong \triangle BCR$ 7. $\angle 3 \cong \angle 4$ 8. $\angle 1 \cong \angle 2$	1. Given 2. Given 3. Perpendicular lines make right angles. 4. All right angles are congruent 5. Reflexive Property 6. SAS 7. cpctc (corresponding parts of congruent triangles are congruent.) 8. Supplements of congruent angles are congruent.
Proof 4	1. $\overline{WR} \cong \overline{HL}$ 2. $\angle W \cong \angle H$ 3. $\angle ALW \cong \angle BRH$ 4. $\overline{RL} \cong \overline{RL}$ 5. $\overline{WL} \cong \overline{HR}$ 6. $\triangle AWL \cong \triangle BHR$ 7. $\angle A \cong \angle B$	1. Given 2. Given 3. Given 4. Reflexive Property 5. Addition Postulate 6. ASA 7. cpctc
Proof 5	1. $\angle A \cong \angle D$ 2. $\angle C \cong \angle F$ 3. $\overline{AB} \cong \overline{DE}$ 4. $\triangle ABC \cong \triangle DEF$	1. Given 2. Given 3. Given 4. AAS

Proof #	Statement	Reason
Proof 6	1. E is the midpoint of DC	1. Given
	2. ∠1 ≅ ∠2	2. Given
	3. ∠3 ≅ ∠4	3. Given
	4. $\overline{DE} \cong \overline{CE}$	4. A midpoint divides a segment into two congruent parts.
	5. $\overline{AE} \cong \overline{BE}$	5. In a triangle, sides opposite congruent angles are congruent.
	6. △ADE ≅ △BCE	6. SAS
	7. $\overline{DA} \cong \overline{CB}$	7. cpctc
Proof 7	1. $\overline{BC} \parallel \overline{DA}$	1. Given
	2. ∠B ≅ ∠D	2. Given
	3. ∠1 ≅ ∠2	3. If lines are parallel, then alternate interior angles are congruent.
	4. $\overline{CA} \cong \overline{CA}$	4. Reflexive property
	5. △ABC ≅ △ADC	5. AAS
	6. $\overline{BA} \cong \overline{DC}$	6. cpctc

Thinking Ahead: Investigate the Hypotenuse-Leg Theorem, p. 191

In the triangle on the left, $a^2 + x^2 = c^2$. In the triangle on the right $y^2 + a^2 = c^2$. Therefore, $a^2 + x^2 = y^2 + a^2$, since both expressions are equal to c^2. Subtracting a^2 from each side results in $x^2 = y^2$. Since sides are positive, x and y can only represent positive numbers, then $x = y$. By SSS, both right triangles are congruent.

Investigate Hypotenuse-Leg Theorem, p. 192

1. Yes
2. Yes
3. Yes
4. No, not a right triangle.
5. No, no information given about the hypotenuse
6. Yes, in a rectangle opposite sides are congruent. The hypotenuse is being shared by both triangles (reflexive property).

Similar Figures and Introduction to Similarity Proofs, p. 193

1. a. 14'
   b. 5.5'
   c. 50°
   d. 88°
   e. 144°
   f. 144°
   g. 78°
2. a. 20.5'
   b. 41'
   c. The perimeters are in the same ratio as the sides.

Similar Figures and Introduction to Similarity Proofs, pp. 194-195

1. y = 20"; (3 is to 7.5 as 8 is to y)
2. No, $\frac{33}{22}$ does not equal $\frac{24}{12}$.
3. 16'; (33 is to 22 as 24 is to x)
4. If $\overline{DE} \parallel \overline{BC}$, then ∠ADE ≅ ∠ABC and ∠AED ≅ ∠ACB since corresponding angles are congruent when lines are parallel. You may also notice that ∠A ≅ ∠A so ΔADE and ΔABC have corresponding angles congruent and will be similar (AA).
5. Yes, they have three 60° angles.
6. No, it's possible to have many right triangles with different angles for their other two angles (ex: 30–60–90 and 45–45–90, etc.) Drawings may vary.
7. Yes, the third set of angles will automatically be congruent (Third Angle Theorem).
8. Yes. The corresponding angles of congruent triangles would have congruent angles.

Proving Triangles Similar, p. 196

1. Yes, SSS similarity
2. Yes, AA
3. No, not enough information
4. Yes, AA
5. Yes, SSS similarity
6. No, not enough information

Proving Triangles Similar, p. 197

Yes, the new triangle would be similar. Corresponding sides are in proportion. This is called SAS similarity.

Test Your Reasoning Skills, p. 198

1. T
2. F
3. T
4. T
5. T
6. F
7. T
8. T
9. T
10. F
11. T
12. F

Review – Chapter 11, pp. 199-200

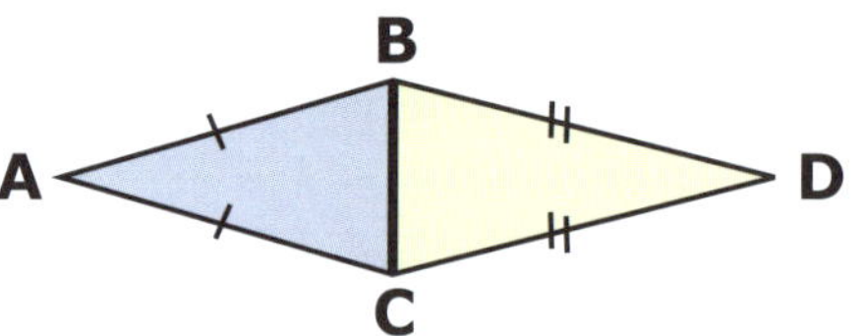

1. No, it's possible to have this situation where both triangles are isosceles and share $\overline{\mathbf{BC}}$ but $\overline{\mathbf{AB}}$ is not congruent to $\overline{\mathbf{BD}}$.

2.

Statements	Reasons
❶ $\angle\mathbf{1} \cong \angle\mathbf{2}$	❶ Given
❷ Both triangles are isosceles.	❷ Given
❸ $\angle\mathbf{1} \cong \angle\mathbf{3}$	❸ In every isosceles triangle, base angles are congruent.
❹ $\angle\mathbf{2} \cong \angle\mathbf{4}$	❹ Same as reason #3
❺ $\angle\mathbf{3} \cong \angle\mathbf{4}$	❺ Substitution
❻ $\overline{\mathbf{AC}} \cong \overline{\mathbf{AC}}$	❻ Reflexive property
❼ $\Delta\mathbf{ABC} \cong \Delta\mathbf{ADC}$	❼ ASA

3.

Statements	Reasons
❶ $\angle\mathbf{E} \cong \angle\mathbf{H}$	❶ Given
❷ **F** is the midpoint of $\overline{\mathbf{EH}}$.	❷ Given
❸ $\overline{\mathbf{EF}} \cong \overline{\mathbf{HF}}$	❸ Definition of a midpoint
❹ $\angle\mathbf{EFG} \cong \angle\mathbf{HFQ}$	❹ Vertical angles are congruent.
❺ $\Delta\mathbf{GEF} \cong \Delta\mathbf{QHF}$	❺ ASA
❻ $\angle\mathbf{G} \cong \angle\mathbf{Q}$	❻ cpctc

4.

Statements	Reasons
❶ $\overline{\mathbf{PR}}$ is the perpendicular bisector of $\overline{\mathbf{AB}}$	❶ Given
❷ $\angle\mathbf{ARP}$ and $\angle\mathbf{BRP}$ are right angles.	❷ Perpendicular lines make right angles.
❸ $\angle\mathbf{ARP} \cong \angle\mathbf{BRP}$	❸ All right angles are congruent.
❹ $\overline{\mathbf{PR}} \cong \overline{\mathbf{PR}}$	❹ Reflexive property
❺ $\overline{\mathbf{AR}} \cong \overline{\mathbf{BR}}$	❺ Definition of a bisector
❻ $\Delta\mathbf{APR} \cong \Delta\mathbf{BPR}$	❻ SAS

5. Yes, the triangles are similar since all equilateral triangles have 60° angles.

6. Yes, these triangles are similar since their corresponding sides are in proportion. The scale factor is 2.5.

Chapter 12: Coordinate Geometry, p. 201

Slope Formula, p. 202

The slope is $\frac{(3) - (-1)}{(-5) - (2)} = -\frac{4}{7}$

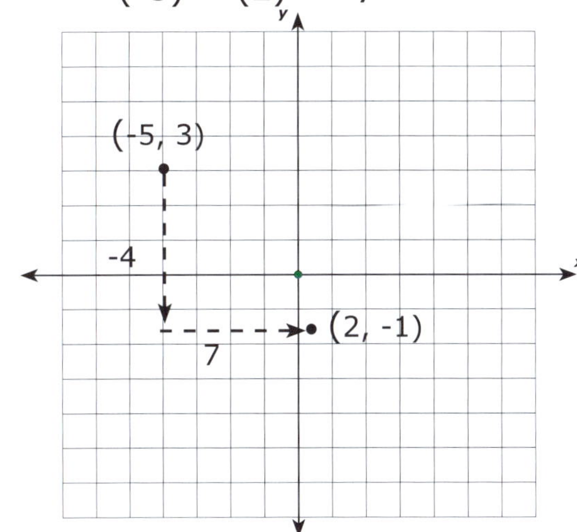

Slope Formula, pp. 203-206

1. 0; $\Delta y = 0$ (the change in y is 0)
2. Empty set or undefined. $\Delta x = 0$. Division by 0 is undefined.
3. m = −2; $\frac{(5) - (-1)}{(-1) - (2)} = \frac{6}{-3} = -2$
4. m = 1; The points (0,0) and (1, 1) are on the line $y = x$. The slope is $\frac{(0) - (1)}{(0) - (1)} = \frac{-1}{-1} = 1$

   Other points on the line $y = x$ may be shown.
5. a. $\frac{1}{2}$

   b. $\frac{1}{2}$

   c. The segments are parallel.
6. $y = 4$; If $\frac{y - 1}{5 - 1} = \frac{3}{4}$, then $y - 1 = 3$ and $y = 4$

7. a. 1
   b. 1
   c. $\frac{1}{6}$
   d. $\frac{1}{6}$
   e. Yes, opposite segments have the same slope so this means the opposite segments are parallel and the quadrilateral is a parallelogram.
8. a. $\frac{1}{2}$
   b. $\frac{-2}{1}$ or -2
9. Perpendicular lines have "negative reciprocal slopes." This means find the reciprocal and then change its sign.

How to Write and Equation of a Line, p. 208

1. a. m = 2; $\frac{(4)-(8)}{(-2)-(0)} = \frac{-4}{-2} = 2$
   b. $y = 2x + 8$
2. a. $y - 8 = 2(x - 0)$
   b. $y - 4 = 2(x + 2)$
3. Solving $y - 4 = 2(x + 2)$ gives you $y - 4 = 2x + 4$ which is $y = 2x + 8$. Solving $y - 8 = 2(x - 0)$ gives you $y - 8 = 2x$ which is $y = 2x + 8$.

How to Write an Equation of a Line, pp. 209-211

1. a. $m = -3$
   b. $y - 5 = -3(x + 6)$
   c. $y = -3x - 13$
2. Yes, if you plug in (-2, -4) it satisfies (or makes the equation true) -4 = 5(-2) + 6.
3. The lines are perpendicular because their slopes are negative reciprocals of each other.
4. They are opposite reciprocals of each other since n would be perpendicular to m.
5.

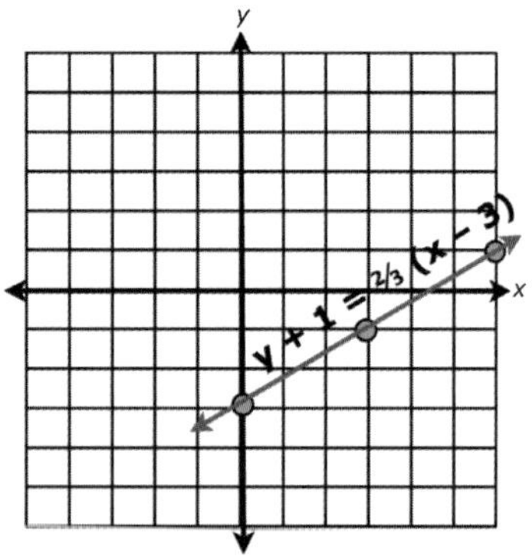

6. b = -3; Answers will vary.
7. Yes; You can plug in (6, 1) in the equation. The slope/intercept equation is $y = \frac{2}{3}x - 3$, so $1 = \frac{2}{3}(6) - 3$.

8. Not necessarily. It could be a trapezoid.
9. Not necessarily. It could be a trapezoid with a right angle.
10. a. Proved
    b. You would need to prove at least one angle is 90°. Answers may vary.
    c. You would need to prove two consecutive sides are equal. Answers may vary.
    d. You would need to prove it's a rhombus with one right angle. Answers may vary.

The Midpoint Formula, pp. 213-215

1. $\frac{1}{2}, \frac{7}{2}$
2. (-2, -2)
3. Yes, the line $y + x = -4$ or $y = -x - 4$ passes through the midpoint. You can plug in the point (-2, -2) into the equation. $-2 = -(-2) - 4$
4. (2, 4)
5. (4, -3)
6. (19, – 23) $\frac{(-13 + x)}{2} = 3$ means $-13 + x = 6$ and $x = 19$.
   $\frac{(15 + y)}{2} = -4$ means $15 + y = -8$ and $y = -23$.
7. a. (1, 2)
   b. (1, 2)
   c. (1, 2) The diagonals of a parallelogram have the same midpoint.

The Distance Formula, pp. 217-219

1. a. HS = 5.8
   b. HF = 3.6
   c. HI = 10
   d. HP = 1.4
2. a. AB = 5, BC = 5, DC = 5, DA = 5
   b. rhombus
   c. The slope formula can be used to prove that the adjacent sides are perpendicular which would prove that the figure has right angles and congruent sides which would make it a square.
3. a. 12
   b. 5
   c. It is the same as taking the square root of the sum of the squares of two sides of a right triangle.

Review Your Formulas, p. 221

1. 17
2. 3.2
3. 20
4. 4
5. $-\frac{1}{3}$
6. (0, 0)

7. a. (-5, 12)
   b. Not necessarily.

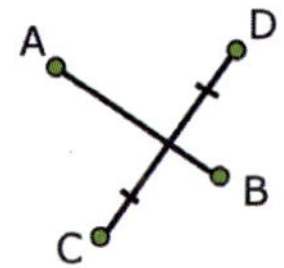

Review Your Formulas, p. 222

1. Distance formula
2. Midpoint formula
3. Slope formula
4. Distance formula
5. Midpoint formula
6. Slope formula
7. Distance formula
8. Distance formula
9. Distance formula
10. Slope formula and distance formula

Introduction to Coordinate Proofs, p. 223

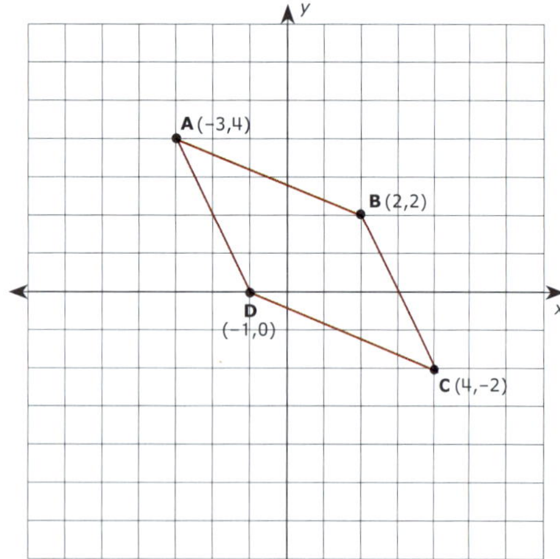

Slope of $\overline{AB} = -\frac{2}{5}$

Slope of $\overline{DC} = -\frac{2}{5}$

Slope of $\overline{AD} = -\frac{4}{2} = -2$

Slope of $\overline{BC} = -\frac{4}{2} = -2$

Introduction to Coordinate Proofs, pp. 225-228

1. The midpoint of diagonal $\overline{AC} = (\frac{1}{2}, 1)$ and the midpoint of diagonal $\overline{BD} = (\frac{1}{2}, 1)$. In any parallelogram the diagonals bisect each other.
2. You can use the distance formula to find the length of each side.
3. The figures should all be parallelograms.

4. 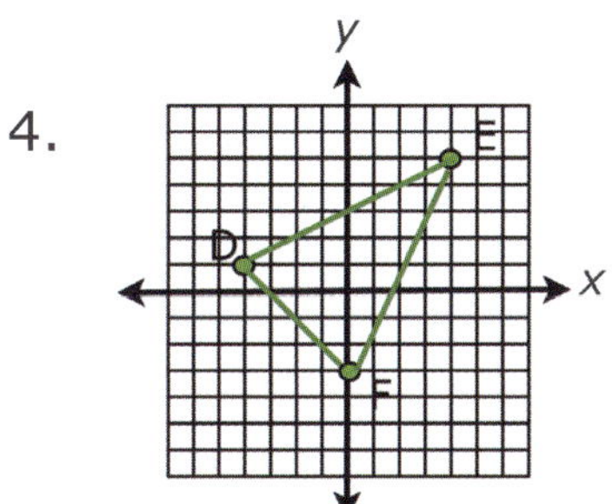

By using the distance formula, we find that DE = 8.9 and FE = 8.9 Therefore, since two sides are equal the triangle is isosceles.

5. 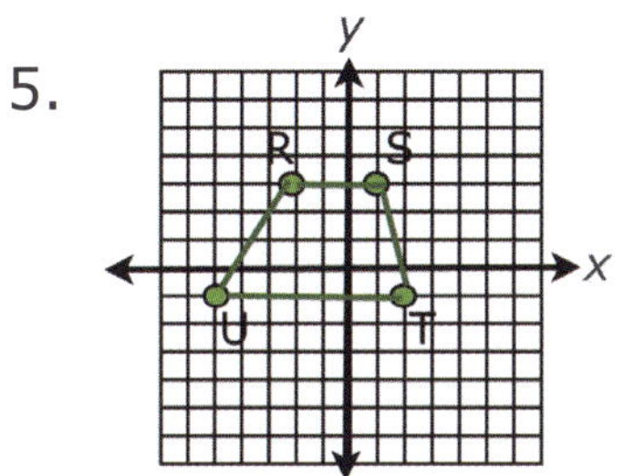

By using the slope formula, we find that the slope of RS = 0 and the slope of UT = 0. The slope of RU = $\frac{4}{3}$, and the slope of ST = -4. Since the quadrilaterals have two sides that are parallel (same slope. and two sides that are not parallel (slopes not equal), the quadrilateral is a trapezoid.

Introduction to Coordinate Proofs, pp. 230-231

1. Since in a parallelogram opposite angles are congruent and consecutive angles are supplementary, then if one angle of a rhombus is 90°, all the angles must also be 90°.
2. No, it's not possible. It will always be a square.
3. The figure could be a kite.

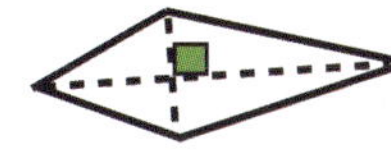

4. 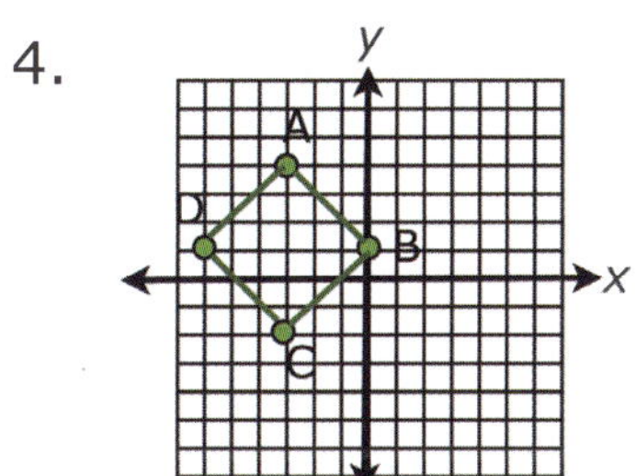

Answers may vary. One way to prove that a rhombus is a square is to prove that its diagonals are equal. By using the distance formula we find that AC = 6 and DB = 6. Since the figure is given as a rhombus and its diagonals are equal, therefore the figure is a square.

Review – Chapter 12, pp. 233-235

1. a. $m = \frac{3}{4}$, $b = -7$
   b. $m = \emptyset$, $b = \emptyset$
   c. $m = 3$, $b = -2$
   d. $m = -\frac{3}{4}$, $b = -\frac{5}{2}$
   e. $m = 0$, $b = -7$
   f. $m = 5$, $b = 2$
2. same, negative reciprocal
3. -7
4. $y = -7x + b$ (*b* can be any constant)
5. $y - 8 = 5(x + 3)$
6. (6, -1)
7. (10, 11)
8. 10 units
9. It is given that the figure is a parallelogram so if we prove its diagonals are perpendicular, then the parallelogram is a rhombus The slope of $\overline{\mathbf{EG}}$ is undefined and the slope of $\overline{\mathbf{DF}}$ is 0, so the diagonals are perpendicular.
10. To prove it's a trapezoid show that two sides are parallel and two sides are not. The slope of $\overline{\mathbf{AT}}$ = 1 and the slope of $\overline{\mathbf{MH}}$ = 1. The slope of $\overline{\mathbf{TH}} = -\frac{1}{2}$ and the slope of $\overline{\mathbf{AH}}$ = -2. This proves $\overline{\mathbf{AT}}$ and $\overline{\mathbf{MH}}$ are parallel and $\overline{\mathbf{TH}}$ and $\overline{\mathbf{AH}}$ are not parallel. To prove it's an isosceles trapezoid you can prove the diagonals are congruent or that $\overline{\mathbf{AM}}$ and $\overline{\mathbf{TH}}$ are congruent. Diagonals $\overline{\mathbf{TM}}$ and $\overline{\mathbf{AH}}$ each have a distance of 6 units. Also $\overline{\mathbf{TH}}$ and $\overline{\mathbf{AM}}$ each have a distance of $\sqrt{20} = 2\sqrt{5}$.
11. A parallelogram has opposite angles congruent and consecutive angles supplementary, so a parallelogram with one right angle has 4 right angles and is therefore a rectangle.
12. No, you can have a right trapezoid, a kite, or even a quadrilateral with only two congruent sides.

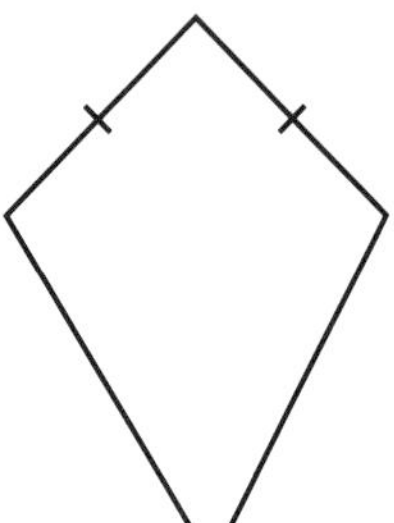

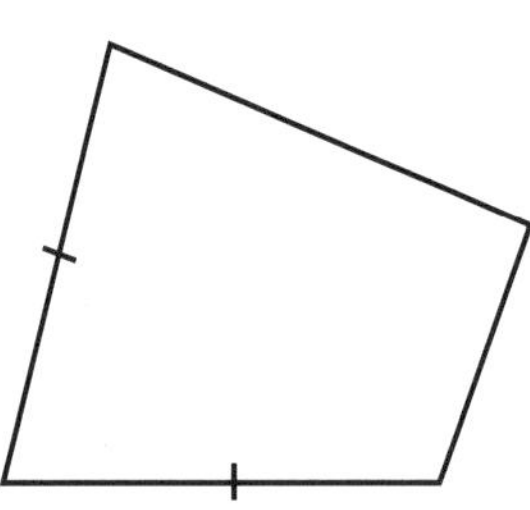

Final Review, pp. 236-241

1. $\overleftrightarrow{AC}$ (or $\overleftrightarrow{AB}$, or $\overleftrightarrow{BC}$, which are the same lines)
2. plane **ABD** (or **BCD** or **ACD** — any of the three non-collinear points)
3. 30°
4. 86°
5. 64°
6. Supplementary because their measures add up to 180°.
7. 4°; Complementary angles have measures that add up to 90°.
8. When lines are parallel then alternate interior angles are congruent.
9. 20 diagonals. The formula is $\frac{n(n-3)}{180°}$.
10. 1080°; The formula is $(n-2)\cdot 180°$.
11. 360°
12. T
13. F; To be a parallelogram a polygon must be a quadrilateral with opposite with both pairs of opposite sides parallel. A trapezoid only has one pair of opposite sides parallel.
14. F; A nonagon is a 9-sided polygon. A seven sided polygon is called a heptagon.
15. T
16. T
17. T
18. 36'
19. 25 sq ft
20. 55 sq ft
21. 37.7"
22. 36π
23. 51 cu cm
24. 100.5 cu ft
25. 261.7 cu in.
26. Example:

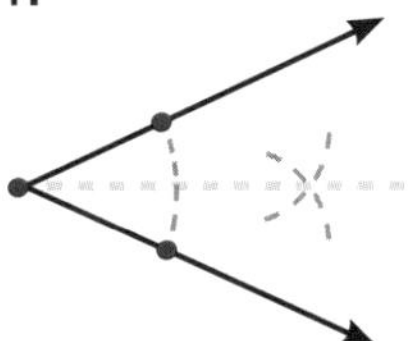

27. Example:

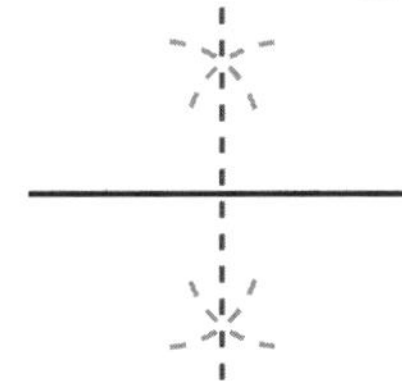

28. T′ = (-2, -2), A′ = (-1, -5), P′ = (3, -3)
29. T′ = (2, 2), A′ = (5, 1), P′ = (3, -3)
30. T′ = (-1, 1), A′ = (-.5, 2.5), P′ = (1.5, 1.5)
31. T′ = (-3, -2), A′ = (-2, 1), P′ = (2, -1)
32. $-\frac{1}{2}$
33. 3
34. They are not perpendicular. Perpendicular lines have negative reciprocal slopes.

35. $\overline{\textbf{AP}} = \sqrt{20}$ or $2\sqrt{5}$, $\overline{\textbf{TP}} = \sqrt{26}$ and $\overline{\textbf{AT}} = \sqrt{10}$. This triangle is scalene.
36. Equation A and Equation C represent lines that are parallel to each other. Each has a slope of 2. Parallel lines have the same slope. Equation B (slope $-\frac{1}{2}$) represents a line that is perpendicular to both lines represented by equations A and C because perpendicular lines have negative reciprocal slopes.
37. $x = -10$; The slope of this line is undefined.
38. (6, 1)
39. Supplements of congruent angles are congruent.
40. If two congruent angles are congruent to two angles of another triangle then the third angles must be congruent.
41. Vertical angles are congruent.
42. In similar triangles the corresponding angles are congruent.
43. $\overline{\textbf{BD}} = 10$; In similar triangles the corresponding sides are in proportion.
44. In a triangle if two angles are congruent to each other then the sides opposite those angles are congruent.
45. SSS
46. Given
47. Alternate interior angles are congruent when lines are parallel.
48. $\angle\textbf{PQR} \cong \angle\textbf{FQW}$
49. ASA
50. A median and a midsegment both bisects sides. However, a median originates from the vertex of an angle to bisect the opposite side of that angle. The midsegment as in the midsegment of this trapezoid connects the midpoints of the two non-parallel sides of the trapezoid and is parallel to its bases. The midsegment is half the sum of the bases.

Sample 1, pp. 242-243

1. Chenda 18; Sokhem 30

Sample 2, p. 244

13. 

14. $x = 45^\circ$
15. rate of descent is 30 feet per minute
16. $\frac{10}{x}$

Sample 3, p. 245

1. d
2. c

Sample 4, p. 246

2. a. 58 in.^{2}
   b. 207 in.^{2}